Social Justice in the U.S.-Mexico Border Region

Mark Lusk • Kathleen Staudt • Eva Moya
Editors

Social Justice in the U.S.-Mexico Border Region

Springer

Editors
Mark Lusk
College of Health Sciences
University of Texas
500 W. University Ave.
El Paso, TX
USA

Kathleen Staudt
Department of Political Science
University of Texas
500 W. University Ave.
El Paso, TX
USA

Eva Moya
Department of Social Work
University of Texas
500 W. University Ave.
El Paso, TX
USA

ISBN 978-94-007-4149-2 ISBN 978-94-007-4150-8 (eBook)
DOI 10.1007/978-94-007-4150-8
Springer Dordrecht Heidelberg New York London

Library of Congress Control Number: 2012940729

Printed on acid-free paper

Springer is part of Springer Science+Business Media (www.springer.com)

Contents

About the Contributors

Monsignor Arturo Bañuelas is a pastor at St. Pius X Church in El Paso, Texas. He obtained his master of divinity degree from Notre Dame Seminary in New Orleans and completed coursework for a master in sacred theology. He studied in Rome at the Gregorian University, where he earned his licentiate, STL, in 1986, and his doctorate, STD, in 1988. In 1988, he became the founding director of the Tepeyac Institute, a diocesan ministry information center. The Tepeyac Institute, one of the largest in the nation, has trained over 20,000 persons for parish ministry and has a visiting faculty of over 120 professors with doctorate and masters degrees who teach in the various programs. In 1989, he cofounded the Academy of Catholic Hispanic Theologians of the United States, now numbering 120 members, with a nationally recognized journal of Latino/a theology and over 300 books in theology from the unique Latino/a perspective. Bañuelas published *Mestizo* Christianity: Christian Theology from the Latino Perspective and articles in *Missiology, Apuntes, and Camino a Emaús*. Msgr. Bañuelas is active in the community and has served on numerous nonprofit boards, both nationally and regionally. He was past president of the Border Network for Human Rights Board of Directors.

Irasema Coronado has an M.A. in Latin American studies and a Ph.D. in political science from the University of Arizona. Her area of specialization is comparative politics. Her dissertation topic focused on the role of transboundary political elites on the US-Mexico Border. Dr. Coronado is a professor in the Department of Political Science and a contributing faculty member of the Environmental Science and Engineering Ph.D. program at the University of Texas at El Paso. She is coauthor of the book titled *Fronteras No Más: Toward Social Justice at the U.S.-Mexico Border* and several academic articles like "*Conflictos Ambientales Internacionales e Intranacionales*" and "Legal Solutions vs. Environmental Realities: The Case of the United States-Mexico Border Region." She has coedited *Dígame! Policy and Politics on the Texas Border* and the book *Juntos Pero No Revueltos: Estudios sobre la frontera Texas-Chihuahua*. She also coauthored *Latinas in Local Government* and *Políticas: Latina Public Officials in Texas*. She was the recipient of a Border

Fulbright in 2004 and continues to collaborate with the Universidad Autónoma de Ciudad Juárez. Presently, she serves as an associate provost at the University of Texas at El Paso.

Hector Antonio Padilla Delgado received Ph.D. in social sciences from the Latin American Faculty of Social Sciences, Mexico, 1997. He has served as a full-time professor at the Universidad Autónoma de Ciudad Juárez since 1993 in the Social Science Department. He is also a visiting professor at the University of Texas at El Paso. Presently, he is a coordinator of the doctorate of social sciences at the Universidad Autónoma de Ciudad Juárez (UACJ) and editor of the *Journal of Social Sciences and Humanities* – "Noesis" of UACJ. Dr. Padilla teaches political sociology, introduction to politics, social movements, and research seminars. Recently, he has coordinated research projects such as "Migration and Discrimination: The social status of migrants in Ciudad Juárez and Paso del Norte Region," with support from FOMIX-CONACYT. He also has led research projects on "Local Governments and border cooperation models. The cases of Ciudad Juárez, El Paso and Sunland Park," with support from CONACYT, and "Causes of absenteeism in Ciudad Juárez and electoral public policy alternatives," funded by the State Electoral Institute and the UACJ. He has published articles in several books and magazines and also coedited the books *Culture and Identity in the United States-Mexico Border* and *Together, But Not Scrambled: Studies of the Texas-Chihuahua Border.*

Pauline Dow, Ed.D. (The University of Texas at El Paso 2008), is an associate superintendent for academics at the Ysleta Independent School District, a 44,000-student system. She is active in community and nonprofit organizations, serving as former vice-chair of the City of El Paso's Tax Increment Reinvestment Zone Board and former president of Community Scholars, Inc. She has also provided leadership through her service on professional boards including the Texas Association for Bilingual Education, National Association for Bilingual Education, National Network for Educational Renewal, Girl Scouts of the USA, and the Kellogg Fellows Leadership Alliance. She is a founding member of the Institute for Language and Education Policy.

Sara E. Grineski is an associate professor of sociology at the University of Texas at El Paso. She received her Ph.D. in 2006 from Arizona State University. Her doctoral program was fully supported by a National Science Foundation (NSF) Integrative Graduate Education and Research Training (IGERT) fellowship in urban ecology. Her dissertation received a national award in the field of environmental hazards geography. Most recently, she was awarded a fellowship in the Enabling the Next Generation of Hazards Researchers program, also funded by the NSF. Her research interests center on environmental injustice and children's health inequalities in the Southwestern United States and US-Mexico border region. She uses qualitative, quantitative, and spatial methods and has approximately 30 peer-reviewed publications related to health and environmental inequalities in outlets including *Environmental Research*, *Social Forces*, and *Environment and Planning*.

Josiah McC. Heyman (Ph.D., CUNY, 1988) is a professor of anthropology and chair of the Department of Sociology and Anthropology at the University of Texas at El Paso. He has published three books and over 50 scholarly articles and book chapters, including *Life and Labor on the Border: Working People of Northeastern Sonora, Mexico, 1886–1986* (University of Arizona Press 1991); *Finding a Moral Heart for U.S. Immigration Policy: An Anthropological Perspective* (American Anthropological Association 1998); and *States and Illegal Practices* (edited; Berg 1999). In 1999, he received the Curl Essay Prize of the Royal Anthropological Institute of Great Britain and Ireland for a paper on immigration enforcement officers at the US-Mexico border and the morality of large-scale issues. His current work focuses on mobilities and enclosures in society, including a special edited issue (with Hilary Cunningham) of *Identities* (Vol. 11, No. 3) and (with Robert Pallitto) "Theorizing Cross-Border Mobility: Surveillance, Security and Identity," Surveillance & Society (Vol. 5).

Nuria Homedes is an associate professor of management, policy, and community health sciences at the El Paso Campus of the University of Texas Health Science Center, where she is responsible for the Global Health Program. During the 1990s, she was a public health specialist in the Latin American and Caribbean Regional Office of the World Bank and was responsible for major projects in Guyana, Bolivia, Honduras, and Colombia. She has worked in consulting assignments throughout Latin America and in several African countries. She holds degrees and credentials in general medicine, tropical medicine, preventive medicine, and public health from the University of Barcelona and other Spanish institutions, and a doctorate in public health from the University of Texas Health Science Center in Houston. Dr. Homedes has an extensive publication record in books, reports, and refereed journals. Her research interests include health sector reform, pharmaceuticals policies, and border health issues.

Arthur A. (Tony) Islas is an associate professor of medicine and director of sports medicine at the Department of Family and Community Medicine at the Texas Tech University Paul L. Foster School of Medicine. A native of El Paso, Dr. Islas received his bachelor's degree from Brown University and his medical degree from the Texas Tech University Health Science Center in Lubbock, Texas. He completed his residency in family medicine in El Paso, Texas, and received a master in public health from the University of Texas at Houston. He also has completed a fellowship in wilderness medicine from the Academy of Wilderness Medicine and a sports medicine fellowship at the Primary Care Sports Medicine Program in Lubbock. Dr. Islas was the director of community medicine for the Texas Tech Department of Family & Community Medicine from 2001 to 2007. He is one of the team physicians for the University of Texas at El Paso and is the team physician for the El Paso Diablos. He is also the current president of the Wilderness Medical Society.

Patricia M. Juárez-Carrillo, MPH, PhD (University of Texas at El Paso) is a native of the US-Mexico border region and was raised in Ciudad Juárez and now lives in El Paso, Texas. She worked as project coordinator at the Center for

Environmental Resource Management of the University of Texas at El Paso for 13 years for numerous community-based interventions related to environmental health issues along the border. She has experience in designing, implementing, and evaluating binational community interventions about topics such as drinking water, lead, asthma, pesticides, healthy homes, and waste management among others. She applies the Community Health Worker (CHW) model on community-based participatory research studies and is a strong supporter of community empowerment to prevent and reduce environmental risks of minority populations. Additionally, Dr. Juárez-Carrillo is coauthor of numerous educational materials and training and workshop curriculums related to environmental health intended for communities with limited access to information and media resources.

Oralia Loza (Ph.D., University of California at San Diego and San Diego State University, 2009) is an assistant professor of public health sciences at the University of Texas at El Paso College of Health Sciences. Dr. Loza has published three peer-reviewed articles in the past year pertaining to HIV and sexually transmitted infections among female sex workers on the US-Mexico border cities and coauthored several works about HIV risk among injection drug users. She is currently developing her research interests on HIV risks among transgender women in El Paso, Texas, men who have sex with men in Ciudad Juárez, Mixtec-Zapotec migrant farm workers from Oaxaca, and populations on the US-Mexico border.

Mark Lusk is a professor of social work at the University of Texas at El Paso. Dr. Lusk has worked in international development for over three decades on projects funded by the United States Agency for International Development, World Bank, Inter-American Development Bank, Asian Development Bank, Japan International Cooperation Agency, and the US Information Agency. He was a senior Fulbright Scholar at the Catholic University of Peru and a senior research Fulbright Scholar at the Catholic University of Rio de Janeiro. He was a visiting professor at the University of Costa Rica and the University of Guyana. Mark has managed international programs at three public universities. He is coauthor of *International Development* (Allyn & Bacon) and numerous journal articles on international social development.

Eva M. Moya (Ph.D., University of Texas at El Paso, 2010) is a native of the US-Mexico border. She is an assistant professor in the Department of Social Work at the University of Texas at El Paso and the Advocacy, Communication, and Social Mobilization coordinator for SOLUCION TB Project Concern International. A specialist in border health, she has more than 25 years of professional experience in the border region. Dr. Moya has published a number of papers on health disparities and infectious diseases in Mexico and the US-Mexico border region. Her expertise includes border health, tuberculosis and stigma, HIV/AIDS, and community health workers. Eva conducted studies throughout the world during her tenure as a Kellogg National Leadership fellow. In 2009, Secretary Kathleen Sebelius reappointed her to Health Promotion and Disease Prevention for Healthy People 2020 Committee.

Guillermina Gina Núñez-Mchiri (Ph.D., University of California, Riverside, 2006) is an assistant professor of anthropology at the University of Texas at El Paso. She teaches courses on urban anthropology/colonias on the US-Mexico border, cultural anthropology, ethnographic methods, applied anthropology, and the professionalization of sociology. She has published articles and book chapters on the political ecology of colonias, entrapment processes, and barriers to health care on the US-Mexico border. She is currently writing her book manuscript *Roots, Transplants, and Transformation on the U.S.-Mexico Border: Community Building in New Mexico's Colonias.* Núñez-Mchiri has been recognized as a Texas Compact Faculty fellow for excellence in service learning, a 2008–2009 UTEP Impact Leadership fellow, a 2009 Kauffman Faculty fellow for Entrepreneurship, and as a 2010 American Association of Hispanics in Higher Education Junior Faculty fellow. She is active in projects that apply anthropology toward addressing social concerns, immigrant rights efforts, and social justice issues affecting Mexican and Mexican American populations in the United States.

Tony Payan received his B.A. in philosophy and classical languages (1992) and his MBA (1994) at the University of Dallas and his Ph.D. in International Relations at Georgetown University (2001). He has taught on the US-Mexico border for the last 10 years. He is the author of two books: *Cops, Soldiers and Diplomats: Explaining Agency Behavior in the Drug War* and *The Three U.S.-Mexico Border Wars: Drugs, Immigration and Homeland Security*. He is also coeditor of two other volumes: *Gobernabilidad e Ingobernabilidad en la Región Paso del Norte* and *Human Rights along the U.S.-Mexico Border: Gendered Violence and Insecurity*. He is currently working on two books: *A War That Can't Be Won: A Journey Through the War on Drugs* (coedited) and *In the Eye of the Storm: Why Ciudad Juárez Is the Way It Is* (single-authored). He is also the author of numerous articles and book chapters on the US-Mexico border, US-Mexico relations, and the war on drugs.

Kathleen (Kathy) Staudt (Ph.D., University of Wisconsin, 1976) is a professor of political science at the University of Texas at El Paso. She teaches courses on democracy, public policy, borders, and women and politics. She has published many articles and 16 books, including *Violence and Activism at the Border* (UT Press 2008), and two collections for which she served as lead editor: *Human Rights Along the U.S.-Mexico Border* (University of Arizona Press, 2009) and *Cities and Citizenship at the U.S.-Mexico Border* (Palgrave USA, 2010), the latter with coeditors at El Colegio de la Frontera Norte, where she was a visiting researcher in 2008–2009. Staudt was the founding director of UTEP's Center for Civic Engagement, which she led for 10 years. She is active in community organizations and nonprofit organizations, serving as former cochair of Border Interfaith, affiliated with the Texas Industrial Areas Foundation.

Father John Stowe, OFM Conv., is the rector of the Basilica and National Shrine of Our Lady of Consolation in Carey, Ohio, and vicar provincial of the Conventual Franciscans in the Midwest and Southwest United States. For 15 years, he served in El Paso at Our Lady of Mount Carmel Church/Ysleta Mission and Our Lady of the Valley Church and for 7 years as moderator of the Curia and vicar general of the Diocese of El Paso. Fr. John has B.A. degrees in history and philosophy from St. Louis University and a master of divinity and a licentiate in church history from the Jesuit School of Theology at Berkeley. With his order, he has had opportunities for study in Italy, Germany, and Spain and has worked with friars of his province in Central America. During his time in El Paso, he was a leader with EPiSO (El Paso Interreligious Sponsoring Organization), chaired the Commission on Social Justice for his province, and lectured at the Tepeyac Institute.

Rosalía Solórzano Torres (ABD, Michigan State University) is a *Borderóloga* native of El Paso, Texas. She is a sociologist and Chicanologist who has held academic and research appointments at various academic institutions including the University of Colorado at Boulder, Colorado; the Center for US-Mexico Studies at the University of California, San Diego, and the Center for Inter-American and Border Studies; the Department of Sociology and Anthropology; and the Department of Chicana and Chicano Studies at the University of Texas at El Paso. She is a licensed marriage and family therapist in counseling and guidance. She is member of MALCS, *Mujeres Activas en Letras y Cambio Social*, a national Chicana Latina organization. She is coeditor of the books *Survey and Analysis of Chicana and Chicano Studies* and *La Chicana: An Introduction, Volume I.* She currently teaches Chicana and Chicano studies, sociology, history, and women's studies at Pima Community College in Tucson, Arizona.

Griselda Villalobos, Ph.D., LCSW, is an assistant professor of social work at the University of Texas at El Paso and received her MSW from New Mexico State University. She is a licensed clinical social worker in the state of Texas with expertise in mental health with an emphasis on cognitive behavioral therapy. Her practice experience is in the areas of mental health, child protection, gerontology, medical social work, and guardianship. Dr. Villalobos earned her Ph.D. in social work at the University of Texas at Austin. The research for her dissertation examined whether or not acculturation played a role in how Mexican Americans respond to a culturally adapted version of cognitive behavioral therapy. Dr. Villalobos has dedicated her health sciences career to the study of culture, acculturation, and social work practice with Hispanics. In March 2010, Dr. Villalobos was awarded a grant by *the Programa de Investigación en Migración y Salud* from the UC Berkeley Health Initiative of the Americas to conduct binational research with the University of Guadalajara in Guadalajara, Mexico. The title of the project is "Depression, Anxiety and Substance Consumption among Mexican Migrants." Dr. Villalobos holds an appointment as adjunct faculty at the Department of Family and Community Medicine at the Paul L. Foster School of Medicine in El Paso, Texas, where she lectures on behavioral and mental health to medical staff and residents.

Part I
Introduction and Conceptual Framework

Chapter 1
Social Justice in the US-Mexico Border Region

Mark Lusk, Kathleen Staudt, and Eva M. Moya

The US-Mexico border region is a distinct geographic, economic, cultural, and social area that is affected by systematic social and economic injustice. This is evidenced by social and economic problems that are apparent throughout the region, including poverty, health disparities, social inequities, and low-wage assembly, service, and agricultural employment. The endemic poverty coexists with institutional racism, gender violence, and structural violence. The area, while populated by resilient families and communities that have confronted governmental neglect and social isolation, is at the periphery of the American economy. In this chapter, we provide an overview of the challenges in the US-Mexico border region, drawing on conceptual frameworks that address relative power and powerlessness in center-periphery relations. During both historical and contemporary eras, the border zone relates to the capital cities of both Washington, D.C., and Mexico City as a colonized periphery. First, however, we examine social justice from various disciplinary perspectives, grounded at the border.

Like Appalachia, the "Four Corners," and the "Black Belt" regions, underdeveloped and exploited, distortions are present in the US-Mexico border region.

M. Lusk (✉)
Department of Social Work, College of Health Sciences, University of Texas at El Paso, 500 W. University Ave., 79968 El Paso, TX, USA
e-mail: mwlusk@utep.edu

K. Staudt
Department of Political Science, University of Texas at El Paso, 500 W. University Ave., 79968 El Paso, TX, USA
e-mail: kstaudt@utep.edu

E.M. Moya
Department of Social Work, University of Texas at El Paso, 500 W. University Ave., 79968 El Paso, TX, USA
e-mail: emmoya@utep.edu

M. Lusk et al. (eds.), *Social Justice in the U.S.-Mexico Border Region*,
DOI 10.1007/978-94-007-4150-8_1, © Springer Science+Business Media B.V. 2012

Yet the border is distinct in its Mexican origin and Mexican-American majority population and the significant cultural, economic, and familial ties which cross the international borderline, with historic and ubiquitous inequalities between both sides. The border zone is also a major international trade zone, a huge illicit drug use and trafficking region, overseen by an enormous law enforcement presence that further marginalizes residents on each side of the border. As a geographic space where the global meets the local, we offer theories of international development to make a case that the US-Mexico border region resembles the developing world far more than it represents the US mainstream.

Social Justice: The Concept

A consensus concept around which contributors to this volume cohere is that of social justice with both secular and philosophical or religious meanings. The phrase is commonly used in selective academic and professional disciplines, including social work, public health, sociology, and education. For over 30 years, an academic journal titled *Social Justice* has focused on "crime, conflict, and the world order" as its subtitle indicates, yet the phrase has become surprisingly marginalized for those who conduct specialized, narrowly focused "scientific" research. We seek to revive and apply research in and to social justice.

Social Justice in the Academic Disciplines

According to the National Association of Social Workers (NASW), social justice is a key value underlying the field. NASW defines social justice as ". . . the view that everyone deserves equal economic, political and social rights and opportunities. Social workers aim to open the doors of access and opportunity for everyone, particularly those in greatest need" (National Association of Social Workers [NASW] 2010).

In this definition, we can see attention to rights, opportunities, access, and by implication, equality and inequality. For all who research, teach, and practice in the social sciences, education, health, and humanities, concepts like equality and inequality are often studied in race, ethnic, class, and gender terms. With the global and border lenses used in this volume, we include more terms, such as nationality and geographic space. Center-periphery perspectives, once a common way to study global centers and marginal peripheries, are applicable at borders, where the potentially exploitative relations between capital city and economic centers run parallel to those in the global economy. Rather than limiting our work to define social justice, we seek to further the conversation and social action. This volume contributes ideas and concrete examples of experiences to spur new, innovative andragogy toward instilling the readers with passion for social justice.

Border Perspectives

The border region is an international space, where the global meets the local in culturally and linguistically creative and stunning ways, but also in shockingly unequal ways. A decade ago, border scholars used Spanish in the book title *Fronteras no más* with multiple meanings for the phrase: "no more borders," but also "only borders." In their subtitle, *Toward Social Justice at the U.S.-Mexico Border*, they develop the avowedly normative meanings of what a socially just border would look like: "Equality in rights, wages, and responsibilities from one side of the border to the other" (Staudt and Coronado 2002, 9; also see Chap. 7 in this book).

The normative orientation in *Fronteras no más* promoted, in historian Oscar Martínez's terms (1994), an "integrated" border, not simply an "interdependent" border. In hindsight, the border a decade later moved (again in Martinez's terms) toward an "alienated" one, with a garrison state on one side and, on the other, a shrunken state with a feeble commitment to the rule of law and where global corporations displaced state policies in hard-fought economic and social rights (see selections in Staudt et al. 2010). In this volume, our contributors are not of one mind about integrated borders or even analytic attention to both sides of the border. Recent aggravated levels of violence since 2008, given the role of Ciudad Juárez as the militarized drug trafficking gateway to the profitable US drug consumption market, have turned the city into the world's murder capital, with over 3,000 killed in 2010 alone (Associated Press 2011).

Globalization: An International Look at Human Development

In the disciplines of political science and economics, which include attention to nations, regions including border regions, and international development, including their philosophic foundations, we find the philosopher John Rawls who wrote *A Theory of Justice* in 1971. In his conception of justice, "All social values – liberty and opportunity, income and wealth and the bases of self-respect – are to be distributed equally unless an unequal distribution of any, or all, of these values is to everyone's advantage. Injustice, then, is simply inequalities that are not to the benefit of all" (cited in Pearce 2005, p. 65).

In international studies, much analytic attention focuses on inequalities among nations, codified in the annual *Human Development Report* from the United Nations Development Program (UNDP). Key founders of the human development orientation within the UNDP include scholars from South Asia, among them the economist Amartya Sen who helped give birth to the focus on "human capabilities" (Sen 2005).

Sen, a Nobel Laureate economist who has studied poverty, famine, and inequality, has argued that freedom is the ultimate goal of social development. He contends that societal development should aim for the fullest manifestation of human potential largely because free people will act in their individual and collective best interests and will keep governments and corporations accountable in the process (Sen 1999). Sen has observed that human rights are a comparatively recent philosophical construct and that human rights and social justice have been criticized since the time of Jeremy Bentham. Bentham argued that rights could only derive from law and in the absence of legal sanction are without foundation. But, in response, Sen has countered that rights are ethical assertions that are the foundation of law. The American Declaration of Independence, the French Declaration of the Rights of Man, and the United Nations Universal Declaration of Human Rights were articulated as the basis of American, French, and international law, respectively. And, so it has happened, the laws of nations born in the Enlightenment reflect such ethical assertions based on the belief that they are "self-evident." In other words, rights are not derived from the law; rights are the "parents of law" (Sen 2010, p. 363). The European Court of Human Rights, born in 1950, evidences the application of the UN Declaration in a global legal institution. At a practical level, Sen places human rights in the context of "capabilities," or the "opportunity to achieve valuable combinations of human functioning – what a person is able to do or be" (Sen 2005, p. 157). Such capabilities can be described as entitlements, opportunities, and freedoms – such as the right to vote, own property, pursue and education, or obtain health care. In addition, human rights are the freedom *from* certain conditions, such as chattel slavery, false imprisonment, and torture (Sen 2010). Human capabilities are connected with human rights, the latter a phrase with little traction in US politics and policies. Despite Rawls and his ideals, in the international sphere, the value of equality has been questioned, particularly in the 1980s, when much policy "thinking moved away from government regulation and intervention in markets for any purpose, including social justice" (Pearce 2005, p. 68). The existence of democracies, however flawed their structures, sustains social justice activism, particularly with resilient civil society nongovernment organizations (NGOs).

While some chapters in this volume evoke the phrase of human rights, authors also recognize the challenges of a rights-based approach to social justice. Activists often evoke universal human rights, but time-consuming, high-cost litigation strategies are pursued to achieve them. Moreover, the ability of international or inter-American courts to enforce court decisions remains limited to nonexistent. A case in point involved mothers from Ciudad Juárez seeking justice for their murdered daughters, winning an Inter-American Court of Human Rights decision against the Mexican state in 2009, but still awaiting justice in 2010. The US Government, with policies that may help rather than hinder Mexico, does not recognize or respect the Inter-American Court of Human Rights or any bodies that would undermine its sovereignty.

Another approach from international development is that of human security. Staudt (2009) contrasts the approaches and policy implications of human security with national security and its bordered version, border security. The national security approach focuses on control, militarization, and fences (or walls). Since the tragedy of September 11, 2001, much rhetoric and money have been spent over militarizing the border with the rhetorical wars on drugs and terror and the conflation of immigration policy with those "wars."

Social Justice: An Operational Base in Community Development and Organizing

Whatever the academic discipline, the world of community development and organizing frequently evokes social justice, as in various organizations that train leaders to change power relations. National organizations like the late Saul Alinsky-inspired Industrial Areas Foundation (IAF), People Improving Communities Organization (PICO, n.d.), Direct Action and Training Network (DART, n.d.), and Gamaliel (Gamaliel 2010) have established grassroots and congregational or faith-based organizing for social justice. The word "faith" is used because many religious traditions contain common principles addressed to distributive and redistributive justice, in efforts to challenge systemic poverty and indebtedness. Many border nongovernment organizations (NGOs) also focus on human rights and security concerns, such as No More Deaths, Humane Borders, Casa Amiga, and the Border Network for Human Rights. The regional or community focus of many of these organizations limits their ability to challenge national laws (see selections in Orr 2007).

Historical Perspectives: The Border Context

The US-Mexico border region has been at the peripheral margins of the American society since the area was conquered by the United States during the US-Mexico War of 1846–1848. President James Polk, an advocate of the expansionist concept of America's Manifest Destiny, proposed the annexation of the Republic of Texas upon his election in 1844. The Texas Legislature agreed to the annexation, and the state became part of the United States in December 1845. The annexation was done without the consent of Mexico and without the negotiation of either an international treaty or a clearly defined border. The United States claimed the Rio Grande as the southern border of Texas, while Mexico claimed sovereignty up to the Nueces River. The dispute eventually led to an all-out war that resulted in the US acquisition of the northwestern half of Mexico (Bauer 1974).

Manifest Destiny, a widely held belief of Americans during the mid-1800s, was (and to a large degree still is) a belief that the United States is a chosen nation with a divine right to control the land between the Atlantic and Pacific Oceans and beyond (Cherry 1998). Such a destiny would be achieved either through purchase, such as the Oregon Territory, or through war. Manifest Destiny is a rationale for colonization and imperialism – the incorporation and subjugation of new lands and peoples. In Manifest Destiny, it is enshrouded in pseudo-religious confabulations about the United States and its special place in history (Cherry 1998).

Because it provided access to the Pacific and coincided with the Gold Rush, the real prize under the doctrine of Manifest Destiny was the Pacific Southwest and California, won by conquest at the conclusion of the US-Mexico War. While

US troops occupied Mexico City, the Treaty of Guadalupe Hidalgo was signed under duress on February 2, 1848. The treaty ceded half of Mexico to the United States for $15 million – America's cheapest land grab ever (Del Castillo 1992). The accord conferred US citizenship upon the approximate 80,000 Spanish-speaking residents and provided for the protection of the civil rights of Mexicans who lived on what had become US soil. However, these civil rights provisions were ignored and a second class of citizens emerged. Moreover, when the US Senate ratified the treaty, Article 10, which guaranteed Mexican land grants, was nullified and Article 9, which governed citizenship rights, was severely weakened (Rosales 1992).

Subsequent disagreements between the two countries over the border west of the Rio Grande led to military tensions. President Pierce, wanting access to the lower Rio Grande Valley for a southern railway route to the west, acquired an area of northern Mexico the size of Pennsylvania under the Gadsden Purchase – a region that presently comprises the southern borders of New Mexico and Arizona (Rosales 1992). This treaty, known in Mexico as "*La Venta de La Mesilla*" (The Sale of La Mesilla), was so repugnant to Mexican citizens that it led to the overthrow of Dictator Santa Anna. It is no coincidence that the US ambassador who negotiated the "purchase," and for whom it is named, was a baron of the railway industry (Rosales 1992).

Critical Perspectives on the Border Region

A central premise of this analysis is that the US-Mexico border region is an underdeveloped region within an advanced economy. The region has been at the periphery of the American mainstream, geographically, culturally, and economically since its incorporation into the United States (Martínez 1989). This volume is informed by critical theories including the center-periphery model and neocolonialism. More recent contributions, such as the concepts of "moral panic" and "counterdevelopment," are also included (Filler 2003; Lusk 2010).

The Border as Peripheral and Colonial

The center-periphery model explicates the skewed relationship between the empowered "center" and the less developed "periphery." The center is understood as the core of power from which decisions are made that affect or control the peoples, economies, and cultures which can be found at the margins of capitalist societies. The model has been most commonly used to explore the relationship of advanced nations of the industrialized "North" with the developing societies of the "South." It has also been applied to internal regions of advanced societies using "internal colonialism" perspectives. Among many analysts of the southwestern United States, we note historian Rodolfo Acuña, who wrote *Occupied America: A History* (1972), and Mario Barrera, who wrote *Race and Class in the Southwest: A Theory of Racial Inequality* (1979).

In the history of international development theory, the center-periphery model stands in juxtaposition and as a counterpoint to the more prosaic modernization theory, which advocates on behalf of development that facilitates the transition from premodern to advanced societies. Implicit in this approach is the view that developing societies are held back by traditional culture, resistance to innovation, and the absence of entrepreneurship (Lipset 1959). Underdevelopment is also associated with low levels of industrial production due to the absence of centrally accumulated capital, a "modern" educated work force, and a lack of emphasis on value-added exports. Moreover, it is argued that the path to development is both through and toward democracy (Gilman 2003).

To be precise, in the case of the US-Mexico border region, policies and programs that affect the territory have historically been designed and funded by elites in Washington, D.C., and Mexico City (Mora-Torres 2001). As de Cosio and Boadella (1999) argue:

> Although borders are interdependent, they are at the same time independent. This means that the policies, norms and regulations of one side are not applicable to the other. For some people, borders are peripheral communities, leading to inequitable access to resources and services. This is the case of the U.S. Mexico Border in which the developed and developing regions merge. They mix to combine some of the best and worst of both worlds. (p. 1).

The view of the border is paradoxical. On the one hand, border control, protection, and immigration are federal responsibilities. However, the border is both distant from and peripheral to Washington, D.C. Border states have made claims to enforcing border policies on their own, passing ostensibly unconstitutional laws such as Arizona Senate Bill SB 1070, which gives increased local police control over immigration detention and which deploys, with federal approval, National Guard troops to the border. Local elites and grassroots activists at the periphery are increasingly making their voices heard. Largely lost in this policy making and program implementation are the voices of those most affected – the Mexican origin and the Mexican-American majority that live there. Apart from border coalitions, human rights demonstrations, and voter registration drives, they are able to contribute little to the national debate because of (1) the isolation of the region and (2) the control of the message by nationalistic and xenophobic entities. That being said, the money and power that dictate US border policy come from Washington.

Moreover, local conservative activists on the border have successfully created the illusion that the federal government has failed to control the border and left a vacuum of law enforcement in the region. This is widely accepted by local elites and flies in the face of evidence to the contrary, including Operation Hold the Line, begun in El Paso in 1993 (Dunn 2009), and Operation Gatekeeper, begun in 1994 in San Diego – two blockades that effectively brought border crossings and commerce to a snail's pace. This same fabrication flies in the face of a decade of increasing levels of federal investment in personnel, surveillance, and military equipment after 9/11. It was after a major terrorist strike on US soil when the border region began to be militarized due to growing American fearfulness of terrorists, outsiders, and immigrants. Borders became the intense focus of the national security apparatus.

The perpetuation of this illusion by anti-immigrant special interest groups such as the Center for Immigration Studies and "media hysteria" results in a climate that is conducive to vigilantism, racial profiling, immigrant dragnets, assembly plant raids, and citizenship checkpoints on roads leading away from the border. This pushes the region further into the periphery of American society.

Summarizing Gloria Anzaldúa, Luis D. Leon summarizes the peripheral nature of the border:

> It is a place, in the words of Anzaldúa, "where the third world grates against the first and bleeds." Indeed, it has given rise to a distinctive consciousness – a borderlands consciousness. At the basis of this formulation lies a "tolerance for ambiguity, a tolerance for contradiction." (cited in Leon 1999, p. 544).

The Border: Premodern?

Though seemingly discredited after its half-century-ago origins, Modernization Theory was developed during the Cold War as part of the Western strategy of bringing nations under the umbrella of the West where they could achieve greater levels of wealth and democratization and thereby be less susceptible to the growing power of the Soviet Union and its allied and associated states throughout the developing world (Gilman 2003). Yet, during the recent decades in which globalization has come to be a driving force in international development, modernization has enjoyed significant resurgence as advanced nation states compete with traditional societies against a backdrop of what the late Samuel Huntington called the "clash of civilizations" (Gilman 2003; Huntington 1996). The modernization model of understanding social and economic development has reemerged with considerable strength within the dominant contemporary development strategy of neoliberalism and its sequela, neoconservatism. The traditional societies critiqued by Lipset and the first modernization thinkers have morphed into fundamentalist Muslim societies that are socially constructed by elites and media into "terrorists" and "threats to Western civilization."

The neoconservative view of foreign policy, while holding fast to principles of modernization and democratization, has evolved away from the plowshare to the sword. As one of its advocates duly notes:

> Today, three years after September 11 brought the United States face-to-face with a new totalitarian threat, liberalism has still not "been fundamentally reshaped" by the experience. On the right, a "historical re-education" has indeed occurred – replacing the isolationism of the Gingrich Congress with George W. Bush and Dick Cheney's near-theological faith in the transformative capacity of U.S. military might (Beinart 2004).

Thus emerged the Bush Doctrine of preemptive war, one that is not based on the Cold War doctrine of deterrence, but is instead based on the prerogative of striking first, thereby justifying the use of "armed might to secure American preeminence across the region, especially in the oil rich Persian Gulf" (Bacevich 2005, p. 201). It is in this manner that the United States has returned to the ideology of the nineteenth-century Manifest Destiny, not just by controlling the American Hemisphere through the modern expressions of the Monroe Doctrine but also by projecting hegemonic militarism into every time zone on the globe (Cypher 2007). This militarization is also quite evident in the US-Mexico border regions as thousands of new federal agents have been located in the region, accompanied in four US border states by National Guard soldiers.

Much as modernization theory and neoconservatism have viewed the Middle East and Afghanistan through the lens of a clash of civilizations that merits "preventive" warfare and occupation, they also have seen Latin America as a similarly backward region that is held back by tradition and tyranny. In *The Clash of Civilizations*, Huntington (1996) divides the world's cultures into eight distinct civilizations – Sinic, Islamic, Western, Hindu, Orthodox, Latin American, and so on. Huntington has argued that the state sovereignty has been weakened in an increasingly globalized economy and that failed states, such as Somalia, are proliferating. Nation-state power has diminished with the rise of non-state actors such as international bureaucracies and global corporations whose loyalty is to no state. Moreover, as globalization has led to greater international interdependence and integration, "counter forces of cultural assertion and civilization consciousness" (Huntington 1996, p. 36) have been generated in response to these global forces. To go even further, he states that, "The world, in short, is divided between a Western one and a non-Western many" (p. 36). Finally, he claims that the world is "increasingly anarchical, rife with tribal and nationality conflicts" (p. 36). One can see very quickly that Huntington's logic readily facilitates a Western "us against them" with "them" being the non-Western world.

It is striking that in Huntington's view, the Western and Latin-American civilizations represent distinct and substantially different classifications in his paradigm. Latin-American civilization is described as corporatist, authoritarian, culturally Catholic (as opposed to Protestant), and incorporating indigenous cultures. Twentieth-century Mexican intellectual Octavio Paz used similar dichotomies (1997). In contrast, the West, comprised of North America, Europe, Australia, and New Zealand, is characterized by Protestant values, cultural pluralism, a multiplicity of languages, separation of church and state, rule of law, representative government, political equality, and individualism – all of which are less manifest in non-Western civilizations, including Latin America.

The fear that has been used to drive the policies of the Cold War and, more recently, the policies behind US warfare in the Islamic world has been at the source of a new sense of threat: immigrants, migrants, and Hispanics – in particular Mexicans. In the preface to his paper on immigration, entitled "The Hispanic Challenge," Samuel Huntington makes no attempt at subtlety:

> The persistent inflow of Hispanic immigrants threatens to divide the United States into two peoples, two cultures, and two languages. Unlike past immigrant groups, Mexicans and other Latinos have not assimilated into mainstream U.S. culture, forming instead their own

> political and linguistic enclaves – from Los Angeles to Miami – and rejecting the Anglo-Protestant values that built the American dream. The United States ignores this challenge at its peril (Huntington 2004a, p. 1).

Detailed in the journal *Foreign Policy* as "The Hispanic Challenge" (2004a) and more fully developed in *Who Are We: The Challenges to America's National Identity* (2004b), Huntington describes with alarm the decline of the distinctive American creed and its rich history of individual rights, the work ethic, and "the belief that humans have the ability and the duty to try to create a heaven on Earth, 'a city on a hill'" (Huntington 2004b, p. 2). In his view, the two most important threats to the "bedrock of U.S. identity" (p. 2) are:

- Doctrines of multiculturalism and diversity; the rise of group identities based on race, ethnicity, and gender over national identity
- The immense and continuing immigration from Latin America, especially from Mexico, and the fertility rates of these immigrants compared to black and white natives (2004b, p. 2)

It is not hard to go from this point of view, elaborated by one of Harvard's most famous scholars, to the politics of Arizona Governor Jan Brewer, who signed SB 1070 – a bill that effectively requires Arizona law enforcement to check for documentation of citizenship. Her government also seeks to ban ethnic studies programs at schools and universities. The governor's efforts enjoy the strong support of the "Tea Party baggers," the Sarah Palin's, and other modern versions of the "Know-Nothings"[1] who are the tails that happen to be wagging the dog in the United States at the moment. The tradition of exclusion is as old as the country, and this more contemporary and unsettling mixture of xenophobia and nativism comingled with cultural and military imperialism has led to the militarization of the US-Mexico border. The national security perspective that now dominates the federal government's perspective is reflected through one agency that has amassed enormous resources to control the border – the Department of Homeland Security (DHS). DHS is tasked with five mission areas – "preventing terrorism and enhancing security; securing and managing the nation's borders; smart and effective enforcement of immigration laws, safeguarding and securing cyberspace; and ensuring resiliency in disasters" (Department of Homeland Security [DHS] 2005). The DHS annual budget is over $55 billion per year (DHS 2010). Among its border initiatives is

- The enactment of the Secure Border Initiative, which raises the budget of Border and Customs Enforcement to $7 billion (DHS 2010)
- Raising detention capacity in immigration prisons to 20,000 inmates (DHS 2010)

[1]The Know Nothing Party, or American Party, was founded in 1849 to oppose immigration on the grounds that it took jobs away from Americans, was strongly opposed to the Catholic Church, and tried to keep immigrants and Roman Catholics from being elected to public office (Anbinder 1992).

- Expenditure of 2.4 billion dollars on the development of a physical fence supplemented by a virtual fence of remote-sensing devices (DHS 2010)

It is important in order to comprehend the US-Mexico border region from a conflict perspective, that one place, the border in the context of an American legacy throughout Latin America and Mexico as our "backyard," where we have been free to interfere with sovereign states, exploit natural resources, while attending to more "important" global matters on even more distant shores. The contemporary border with Mexico can be understood through the lens of a renewed Manifest Destiny and the latest iteration of regional hegemonic militarism. Continuing a two-century-old tradition, during the past three decades, US military power has been projected into El Salvador, Nicaragua, Grenada, Haiti, Panama, and Colombia. Because of its growing instability and because of the "War on Drugs," Mexico is once again being seen through the national security perspective that led to the nation's conquest a century and a half ago.

The current conception of the US-Mexico border is greatly affected by the explosion of drug-related violence in Mexico, including homicide, kidnapping, and gang warfare. And, even though America's power has been overextended by a war on two fronts, Mexico has increasingly been seen not just as a neighbor with an emigration problem but also as a potentially "failed state." With foreign and defense policy vastly overstretched to extend a decade-long war in Afghanistan and Iraq, America's attention has been turned to Mexico.

Since 9/11, the once relatively porous border has been hardened and militarized across its length. With the efforts of Arizona to criminalize a large segment of its population with Draconian search and detention laws, as our colleague and contributor Tony Payan (personal communication, April 14, 2011) says "I am increasingly convinced that it is not about immigration, it is not about illegal immigration, but I am beginning to think that it's about Mexicans."

Counterdevelopment

Finally, one additional concept from development theory can be brought to bear on the US-Mexico border region. "Counterdevelopment is the manner by which political, cultural, criminal, and social factors diminish positive human welfare outcomes, inhibit human potential, destabilize societies, erode social capital, and jeopardize quality of life" (Lusk 2010, p. 165). Traditionally, development theories have emphasized the inputs (wealth, human capital, and development projects) that are designed to achieve desirable social and economic outcomes, such as increased GDP per capita, longer lifespan, increased years of schooling, decreased mortality and morbidity, high employment, democracy, and other positive measures of development. Too little emphasis has been given to those forces which work against social development such as corruption, wars and conflict, entrenched elites, conservatism, aversion to risk, brain drain, environmental externalities, fundamentalism, rent-seeking, terrorism, and drug trafficking.

The counterdevelopment model does make reference to culture as an impediment to development, but gives far greater emphasis to other social problems that obstruct advancement. Three of these are crucial: corruption, terrorism, and drug trafficking (Lusk 2010). *Corruption* is the abuse of power, both public (governmental power) and private (cartels, monopolies, banks, corporations for personal and group gain through the accumulation of money and power, thereby impeding human development and democracy (Lusk 2010; Ackay 2006)). *Terrorism* is the calculated use of violence or the threat of violence against the public and its elected and appointed officials to undermine the rule of law, create fear, and to promote a political, religious, or social cause or economic outcome, which undermines political freedom and creates poverty (Lusk 2010; Abadie 2006). While not a new phenomenon, terrorism is increasingly sophisticated and deadly. In addition, its use is not limited to political and religious extremists – it has now become a weapon of organized crime and governments. Large-scale international *drug trafficking* has profound adverse effects on social development. It engenders public corruption of officials, erodes the rule of law, distorts markets, and can lead to a culture of impunity. It is linked not only to organized crime, but is also practiced by narco states such as Afghanistan. Global drug capitalism is a barrier to social development because it increases violence, erodes trust in public institutions, and skews economic development by money laundering and gun running (Lusk 2010).

These three counterdevelopment forces are at the heart of the current crisis on the Mexican side of the US-Mexico border, and the fear, chaos, and panic they engender have led to the hardening and militarization of the border and the widespread public perception, rightly or wrongly, that the United States is at risk. The border is thus further marginalized as it is defined by the counterdevelopment forces that reign on the Mexican side.

Moral Panic and the US-Mexico Border

What is happening at the moment on the border can also be understood as a *moral panic*. When confronted with the appearance of a crisis, as defined by *moral entrepreneurs* in the media and government, public social anxiety can escalate to the point at which a group is demonized or used as scapegoats to explain away social problems (Filler 2003). Moral panics are collective belief systems that are founded on incidents or group actions that appear to threaten the status quo, seem to be dangerous to the majority, and which tend to be based on an embellished belief that some group, particularly a minority group, is responsible. The implication is that such a group is a menace to society and must be responded to harshly and immediately (Filler 2003; Goode and Ben-Yehuda 1994). Examples of moral panics include the "preventive" incarceration of Muslims after 9/11 and the nationwide adoption of Megan's Law on tracking sex offenders after a 7-year-old was abducted (Filler 2003). In each case, a popularly defined "morally deviant" group is singled out on exaggerated terms for harsh retaliation.

Moral panics have been associated with other ethnic groups in the United States, including the Anti-Chinese Riots of 1886, the lynching of African-American men on trumped-up rape charges during the period 1880–1930, the trial of Sacco and Vanzetti during the Red Scare in 1920, the McCarthy Hearings on suspected communists and sympathizers, the Mariel Boatlift from Cuba in 1980, and many others. As Jordan Camp observes in his analysis of the way in which the events in New Orleans after the Katrina Hurricane were socially constructed via stereotypes about Black people, the event of Katrina "reveals the ways in which anti-Black racism, racist violence and neoliberal security narratives permeate the cultural and political landscape of the United States" (Camp 2009, p. 696).

One of the worst examples of a moral/legal panic was the incarceration of Japanese-Americans. In 1942, President Roosevelt issued Executive Order 9066 authorizing the US military to relocate and imprison Americans of Japanese descent. The commander of Western Command of the US Army issued Civilian Exclusion Order No. 34 to exclude Japanese-Americans from the West Coast to prevent collaboration and espionage. It was the *Korematsu vs. the United States* ruling in 1944 that upheld the constitutionality of the relocation. The *Ex parte Endo* decision, written by William O. Douglas, lessened the effect of Korematsu by concluding that the military could not exclude a person the government deemed to be loyal to the United States, eventually thereby leading to the closure of the camps (Gudridge 2003). Nonetheless, a terrible precedent was set that the government could exclude and relocate its own citizens on the basis of national origin.

The parallels between previous immigrant and ethnic group panics and the present legal harassment of "suspect" foreigners are clear. One example was the campaign of Attorney General John Ashcroft to use immigration laws to "preventively detain" foreign nationals who were deemed to possibly having some link to terrorist organizations. Over 5,000 individuals from Arab countries were detained. Of them, three persons were charged with an offense and only one conviction was obtained (Cole 2004). The suspension of civil liberties and First Amendment Rights are "always rationalized by a crisis" (Gellman 2002).

Another example is the imprisonment of asylum seekers from Central American and Mexico. In both cases, the persons are innocent of seeking illegal entry or of constituting a threat to the state. Refugees from Mexico and Latin America are fleeing murder, extortion, kidnapping threats, paramilitary organizations, state terrorism, and drug cartels and gangs.

Most flagrantly, of late, moral panic is seen in the demonization of so-called illegals who are purportedly flooding our nation, talking away our jobs, smuggling drugs, using public welfare, having babies in US hospitals to gain citizenship, refusing to speak English, diluting and endangering American culture, and threatening the nation's core values. A look at practically any blog on immigration evidences the vilification of immigrants. This serves as a convenient way to avoid looking at much more pressing issues in the United States, such as a the conduct of a foreign policy of military expansionism and conquest of distant nations under the guise of "democratization" at a time at which the country is for all practical purposes bankrupt.

The trajectory of moral panics is to provoke public alarm over a perceived threat to national values, to invoke "national security," and to incarcerate or deport and otherwise "criminalize" and intimidate the "undesirable" parties. Fears are trumped up to generate hysteria. In a moral panic, there is a tendency to create facts and fictions to serve the tide of resentment toward the group that has been associated with the manufactured social problem – be it HIV/AIDS as the "gay disease" panic of the mid-1980s or now the immigrants "who are taking away our jobs and coming to the U.S. to get on welfare." It matters not that undocumented immigrants are ineligible for welfare, Medicaid, Food Stamps, CHIP, or other governmental benefits restricted to citizens; one just needs to say it out loud for it to be true. And in stark contrast to the myth that immigrants take "our" jobs, evidence reveals that:

> Data show that, on net, immigrants expand the U.S. economy's productive capacity, stimulate investment, and promote specialization that in the long run boosts productivity. Consistent to previous research, there is no evidence that these effects take place at the expense of jobs for workers born in the United States (Peri 2010, p. 4).

Since 9/11, immigrants have also been conflated with terrorism (Shamir 2005). The fact that immigrants seek entry into the United States for economic reasons is lost in a national discussion that sees them as criminals. Mobility and migration are natural by-products of globalization as labor seeks to find the best market and as corporations search for the lowest cost worker. Yet in the post-9/11 environment, a paradigm of suspicion now permeates the question of immigration (Shamir 2005). In effect, US immigration law can best be understood as the social and legal construction of nonpersons (Johnson 1996).

Of course, the place for nonpersons is in a *total institution* – prisons or asylums where every aspect of their lives is controlled by the state (Goffman 1961; Foucault 1995). Currently, according to US Immigration and Customs Enforcement (ICE) documents, "ICE operates the largest detention and supervised release program in the country. A total of 378,582 aliens from 221 countries were in custody or supervised by ICE in FY 2008" (Schriro 2009, p. 2). Most of them will eventually be deported. In the meantime, they are housed for the most part in 1 of 22 detention centers (which for the most part are owned by private, for-profit corporations) where they are subject to prolonged detention, inhumane conditions, inadequate health care, and cases of illegal beatings (Dow 2004). The moral panic associated with Mexican migration has led to what has been called the "Border Security Industrial Complex" in recognition of its peculiar admixture of military interdiction, corporate capitalism, and hegemonic masculinity (Staudt et al. 2009).

Tides of antipathy toward immigrants, documented or otherwise, rise and fall with the economy. The United States has lost much of its high wage manufacturing jobs as multinational corporations have shipped those jobs offshore in search of the cheapest labor, so working class antipathy toward the latest immigrant groups is thriving (Staudt 2009). Among its more vile forms are the nativism and vigilantism of paramilitary groups such as the "Minutemen" who, while they hold no badge and are sworn to no law enforcement code of conduct, believe that they are taking back their country from foreign invaders by use of illegal military force (Doty 2009).

The ideology of groups such as the Minutemen has been tied to white supremacy and the Christian Right; their xenophobia is masked under the doctrine of national sovereignty, but is more closely allied to racism, wherein "illegals" are the *enemy* (Doty 2009).

Vigilante groups conflate immigration with criminality, not just by claiming that crossing borders without documents is illegal, but that the immigrants are themselves a criminal element that are responsible for high rates of crime on the US side of the border. Claims are also made that, as Doty quotes, "the U.S. is engaged in a silent war conducted by illegal aliens that is causing a higher toll than the war in Iraq" (Doty 2009, p. 27). Such delusions lead to the militarization of the border, either by the steady rise of the US Border Patrol or the June 2010 decision of President Obama to send US National Guard troops to the border to assist in border enforcement primarily in Arizona, where antagonism toward Mexican immigration is the strongest. It is also the rationale behind the emergence of self-appointed paramilitary forces bent on protecting US soil from foreign invaders. These exaggerations contain all of the elements of a classic moral panic.

The Social Construction of the US-Mexico Border

In any event, the border has come to symbolize two themes that distract from the underdevelopment of the region. The moral panic that has led to the demonization of immigrants is the leading story in the stereotypical view of the region as a source of "illegals." We have summarized this phenomenon. The second social construction or "story" that typifies public perception about the border is comprised of the drug wars. By focusing on these two social constructions, public and private institutions are crippled in any effort to get to the root of the problems caused by the marginalization of the US-Mexico border and its asymmetry with the economic development of the interior of the nation.

The drug wars refer to two distinct battles. The first is America's "War on Drugs," which began as a moral panic in the Nixon administration and which subsequently became a four-decade-long multibillion-dollar venture that by all accounts has had no measurable effect on drug consumption and importation in the United States (Campbell 2009). The latter battle is the "Drug War in Mexico," being fought among and between cartels, gangs, federal police, municipal police, and the Mexican Army to gain preeminence and greater control and profits in the enormous drug smuggling operations aimed at the North American market. From the time Mexican President Felipe Calderón began his crackdown on cartels in 2006 to the present, there have been more than 80,000 homicides in Mexico (Washington Valdez 2012). It is partly through the lens of this drug "war" that foreigners increasingly see Mexico and its border with the United States as a region of chaos, ungovernability, crime, and a failed state. It is hardly an environment conducive to a serious examination of the underlying injustices that have led to the region's lagging development, of which, the enormous drug trade is partly symptomatic.

Heyman and Campbell aptly summarize the current social construction of the border, observing that, "The long history of sensationalist journalistic treatments of the border region reflects American uneasiness about the edges of the nation state and its ambiguous relationship with the Midwest and East Coast centers of power and mainstream culture" (Heyman and Campbell 2004, p. 206). Indeed, the narratives of the border often have little connection to reality. Note for example that common themes are widely utilized by journalists and politicians to describe the region, that it is a dangerous place, ridden with crimes and drugs, and overflowing with "illegal aliens." Yet, as Archibold observes, "Truth pales compared to ideas" (Archibold 2010, p. 1). In fact, as he and others have documented, the four safest large cities in the United States are located on or are close to the US-Mexico border: San Diego, Phoenix, El Paso, and Austin. Moreover, as Finnegan has documented, the apprehension of undocumented migrants has declined over 60% since 2000 "... the lowest figure in thirty five years" (Finnegan 2010, p. 19). As a result of these ways of understanding the border, what was once a highly permeable border has become relatively impermeable and in many sections is a "Wall" – both literally and metaphorically.

In an environment of anti-immigrant hysteria, policies shift and become more Draconian. Take for example the treatment of people who flee violence, death threats, extortion, and kidnapping in Mexico and migrate to the United States; they are, for all practical purposes, treated the same way as economic migrants. The *Observatorio de Seguridad y Convivencia Ciudadana*, a think tank at the Autonomous University of Ciudad Juárez, has estimated that over the past 2 years, 230,000 Mexicans have fled the violence in the city. They estimate that about half of the refugees have fled to the United States, a majority of them residing in or around El Paso. These refugees are effectively afforded no legal asylum in the United States and must blend in with relatives or go underground. Because so few Mexicans are granted asylum (2% according to US Department of Justice figures), last year only 200 applied for political asylum (Becker and McDonnell 2009). The reason is because when they apply for asylum, they go straight to jail. One notable example is newspaper reporter Emilio Gutiérrez, who against the will of the Mexican Army reported for the *Diario del Noroeste* that Mexican troops regularly robbed innocent citizens. After a series of death threats, Gutiérrez fled to the US border crossing at Antelope Wells New Mexico and after asking for asylum was swiftly taken to an immigration detention where he spent a year. Even today, his case has not been resolved and he awaits a residency hearing while living in poverty (Aguilar 2010).

Gustavo de la Rosa Hickerson, head of the Chihuahua State Human Rights Commission, crossed into the United States in October 2009 on a legitimate tourist visa. A leading civil rights activist in Mexico, he had worked for decades on the protection of worker's rights, women's safety, and related social justice causes. More recently, he had been doing research on abuses by the Mexican Army and had also been threatened with death. Although he was not seeking political asylum, Hickerson was swept into federal custody and detained in an immigration prison (Ortiz Uribe 2009). Although he was eventually released, Hickerson has continued to be an outspoken critic of Mexican President Felipe Calderón's war on the drug cartels and the United States for its billion-dollar-plus support of the war with funding for weapons and technology under Plan Mérida. He claims that Calderón invented the war for his own ends, just as Vice President Cheney had "invented" the War in Iraq – dangerous words during a time of hysteria (Borunda 2009). In essence, the drug war and violence in Mexico have created a new class of refugees (Becker and McDonnell 2009).

Since 9/11, which has also generated a national moral panic, the American social construction of borders has changed immensely, and several entirely new agencies have been created to patrol, monitor, control, regulate, and manage the US borders, not only at the borders themselves but inside other countries (i.e., watch lists, espionage, surveillance) and within the United States itself such as US Immigration and Customs Enforcement (ICE). The US Border Patrol jurisdiction encompasses the entire territory of the United States, not just its border regions. The plethora of new agencies and redesigned former agencies, as is well known, is under the eerily named Department of Homeland Security created in 2003.

More to the point and in contrast with the stereotypes, people on the US side of the border are largely dependent upon the extraction industries, along with agriculture and the near-slave migrant labor that sustains it, coupled with military bases, a huge law enforcement sector and for-profit prisons. That is, as they say, how we make a living down here.

The Border in the Context of National Security

Since 9/11, the border has been seen primarily through the prism of national security. A vibrant trade zone that is situated in a uniquely interactive binational and bicultural setting has, in the public imagination, been turned into a region scourged by narco-wars, rampant crime, and instability.

At the heart of US foreign policy toward Mexico are combating terrorism, drug trafficking, and organized crime. While there is no question that these are critical issues within Mexico, this reality should not overshadow the fact that on the US side of the border, there are very low rates of crime – in particular, a lack of violent crime. To direct federal, state, and local efforts to "stem the tide of illegal immigrants and drugs" is not a path to the sustainable development of the region. While this strategy may create thousands of regional jobs in federal, state, and local law enforcement, not to mention "gainful" employment at dozens of regional immigration prisons, these expenditures do not create the kind of growth that could be had through the development of a healthy manufacturing and high technology sector. Links to business incubators, universities, and high technology firms would create more lasting investments in the border region's growth than the huge expenditures associated with the militarization of the border.

An example of the nation's posture toward the south is Plan Mérida. As recently as 2007, US expenditures on drug control within Mexico and Central America were comparatively modest. After Plan Mérida was launched in 2007, the United States has allocated $1.3 billion to Mérida initiatives in Mexico, $248 million for the Central American region, and $42 million for Caribbean countries (Seelke 2010). These expenditures are designed to disrupt organized crime, institutionalize rule of law, build a twenty-first-century border, and "build resilient communities" (Seelke 2010). Yet despite the mention of resilient communities, at heart Plan Mérida is about combating drug cartels and securing the US-Mexico border.

These substantial international expenditures of Plan Mérida have been directed to the purchase of weapons, high technology surveillance equipment, helicopters, airplanes, police training, communication equipment, and counterterrorism training for the Mexican Army (Seelke 2010).

In contrast, the US Agency for International Development's budget for Mexico has been declining and hovers around $30 million a year, most of which is aimed at "(1) promoting environmental protection, alternative energy and ecotourism; (2) improving public administration, transparency and accountability; (3) broadening microfinance and remittance utilization; (4) preventing infectious diseases, and (5) furthering higher education and competitiveness" (United States Agency for International Development [USAID] 2010, p. 1). Clearly, US foreign policy in Mexico is not directed toward creating the social development conditions and standards of living that would make it possible for Mexicans to find gainful employment and a decent standard of living within their own country. It should be no surprise, given the economic conditions within its borders that in a nation of 109 million residents, over a tenth have migrated to the United States, with or without immigration documentation. Despite the fact that American agriculture, construction, and industries depend heavily on such migration for a cheap source of labor, the rhetoric identifies such migrants as a threat to national security.

Missing from the national security perspective by which the US-Mexico border region is viewed is an understanding of the question of human security. As Staudt (2009) observes, "Border security should encompass life with dignity, living wages and basic human security" (p. 3).

Plan Mérida is not a strategy that gets to the heart of the problems associated with life on the border. It does not address the reduction of demand for drugs in the United States, which is the root cause of drug violence throughout the Andes and Mesoamerica. It does not provide a strategy for economic development of the region that produces jobs, raises incomes, and provides alternatives to the organized crime lifestyle. Moreover, the government of Mexico, bound as it is to the interests of global capitalism by the North American Free Trade Agreement (NAFTA) and the World Trade Organization (WTO), has done little for its own people's development. Lost in between the war between the government, the gangs, and the cartels are millions of "ni-ni's" (*ni estudian, ni trabajan*) – the countless Mexican youth, who due to dangerous neighborhoods and the absence of jobs "neither study nor work" (Rodríguez 2010).

Plan Mérida is much like its predecessor Plan Colombia. Ostensibly, Plan Colombia was developed in the late 1990s by President Pastrana to eradicate illegal drugs, end armed conflict, and promote economic development. Funded by the US Foreign

Military Financing Program, the Department of Defense and the Andean Counter Drug Initiative to the tune of over $4.5 billion from just 2000 to 2005, its primary goal was claimed to be to restrict the flow of narcotics into the United States (Villette 2005). Yet, it can just as easily be seen as an effort by the United States to extend and strengthen US intervention and control of the Andean Region, particularly in light of challenges to US hegemony by several Latin American countries during the past two decades (Petras 2000). It can also be argued that Plan Colombia is merely the latest iteration of the American effort to control trade, keep down wages, and maintain its neoliberal posture in the northern regions of South America. Colombia is a country of continuous and entrenched conflicts between government and various guerilla and revolutionary elements that date to the 1950s. It is a country that evolved from being a "problem country" to a "destabilizing force in the region," and US policy there reflects that larger reality (Pizarro and Gaitan 2006). While the role of destabilizing force in the region now may be displaced by the more "troublesome" Venezuelan regime, the US foreign policy legacy in Colombia has notwithstanding been one based on a neo-Monrovian perspective of the need for ongoing US interventions into the domestic arena of Latin American republics.

In that respect, Plan Mérida mirrors Plan Colombia. The United States senses a threat from Mexico, to its border, to its exports, and to its manufacturing sector as outsourced to Mexican *maquiladoras*. In response, the US counters this perceived threat, not by helping to develop the economy and living conditions of Mexicans but to further militarize and centralize the state of Mexico's control over its people. Plan Colombia cost thousands of innocent lives in that country as a protracted war between the military, paramilitaries, guerillas, and cartels. The war displaced over a million Colombians, and countless others lost their land and lives in the cross fire (Molano 2005). In a parallel fashion, Mexicans are being displaced from their homes and farms by intractable violence. Civil society in Mexico has all but collapsed. In border cities, the night is owned by the soldiers and criminals. Thousands of businesses have closed in the face of extortion and death threats. Families are growingly house bound and children are staying home from school. Tourism is nonexistent. The drug war in Mexico has brought that country to its knees.

Underdevelopment in the US-Mexico Border Region

Context

A fundamental question about the border region is one of definition. Attempts to define the border region by units of governments or ecological zones, market areas, historical demarcations, or geographical boundaries tend to create conflicting data and analysis resulting in confusion and uncertainty. For reasons of consistency and convenience, we define the border region as the corridor extending 100 km (62.5 miles) north and south of the US-Mexico border. This definition is derived from Public Law 103–400 (22 US Code, 290 n-5) and the La Paz Agreement of 1983 on environmental cooperation (U.S.-Mexico Border Health Commission [USMBHC] 2002).

The US-Mexico border is a binational, transborder region of great diversity in environment, economic, social conditions, and governance. However, it is an area that also exhibits many commonalities. There are several significant characteristics of the border region that make the region different from other areas within the United States and Mexico. The border is defined by high rates of population growth, rapid urbanization, spillover effects from Mexico, asymmetrical economies, international commerce, high rates of poverty, and a distinct ethnic identity and culture. These characteristics present challenges that localities within the interior of the United States and Mexico often do not understand or have to overcome, particularly when they happen simultaneously and in the same region (Good Neighbor Environmental Board [GNEB] 2010).

The border climate is generally semiarid to arid, with very limited water resources. Ecosystems that lie partially within the border region contain important natural resources, like vegetation and birds in the deserts and fish and other marine wildlife in the coastal areas.

The border region consists of 80 *municipios* (municipalities) in six Mexican states (Baja California, Sonora, Chihuahua, Nuevo León, Coahuila, and Tamaulipas) and 48 counties in four US states (California, Arizona, New Mexico, and Texas). On the US side of the border, the border counties comprise a distinct social and economic region – analogous to a 51st state (U.S.-Mexico Border Counties Coalition 2010). The stark contrast between the distinct economies and levels of socioeconomic development and the magnitude of cross-border exchanges between the US-Mexico border communities demand the attention of policy and decision makers from outside of the region.

It has been said that the border region does not completely identify with one particular country but instead possesses a border identity and culture of its own. Border counties and municipalities are not homogeneous, yet there is a distinct blending of economic, social, and cultural factors, as well as single set of development challenges. The existing obstacles to achieving social and economic justice in the region will require border binational solutions, yet the impediments to development are far more profound on the Mexican side. Our emphasis in this book is primarily given to the development of social justice on the American side of the border, but several chapters focus on Mexico.

Population

The border between the United States and Mexico is 1,993 miles in length, ranging from the seawall barrier between southern San Diego, California, and Tijuana to Brownsville, Texas, and Matamoros, Tamaulipas, and the river and barrier system that separates them (Congressional Research Service 2006). By 2000 (Migration

Information Source 2010), 12.4 million lived in the US-Mexico border counties and municipalities, and by 2010, the figure reached 14 million. By 2020, the border population is projected to reach 20 million. Over one-fourth of residents of the 48 counties on the border live below the official US poverty line – a figure which is twice the US average of 13.2% (Migration Information Source 2010; U.S. Census Bureau 2005).

The *2010 Human Development Report* (HDR) identifies Mexico as a "High Human Development Country" ranking 56th overall among the 169 nations included in its ranking. Yet the report points to several challenges. Labor force participation by males is 85%, while only 46% for females. The Gini coefficient measure of income inequality at 51.6 is very high, ranking at a higher level of income inequality than other most high, medium, and low human development countries. Mexico also ranks poorly on HDR measures of political freedom, civil liberties, and corruption (United Nations Development Programme [UNDP] 2010).

There are 14 twin city complexes on both sides of the international boundary, such as Ciudad Juárez, Chihuahua, paired with El Paso, Texas, Tijuana, Baja California, next to San Ysidro, California, and Nogales, Sonora, linked with Nogales Arizona. These 14 urban areas represent 79% of the border's population. Mexico's three largest border *municipios* are Ciudad Juárez, Tijuana, and Mexicali, account for slightly more than half of the total Mexican border population (Instituto Nacional de Estadística y Geografía [INEGI] 2000). The counties of San Diego, California; Pima, Arizona; and El Paso, Texas, are home to two-thirds of the US border population (U.S. Census Bureau 2005).

US-Mexico border crossings are among the busiest in the world. Daily crossings have risen with rapid population growth and economic development on both sides of the border. Information on border crossings is incomplete. According to the USMBHC (2002), current estimates by the Immigration and Customs Enforcement approximate a range from 300 to 400 million legal crossings in each direction per year, or between 800,000 and 1.1 million legal crossings daily in both directions each day to pursue jobs, housing, education, commerce, and health care and to visit family and friends.

Population Growth

Border communities have experienced extraordinary population growth over the past three decades, particularly in urban areas. Mexico border states population grew by 26% in the decade of the 1990s, with an annual growth rate of 2.4%. Population growth in the border states was substantially lower than in the border municipalities, which grew by 4.2% or at the annual growth rate of 3.5%. Driven by migration, particularly of young people, the northern municipalities of Mexico have grown in population at a faster rate than their US counterparts. The population growth trends make the border region the most demographically dynamic region of Mexico and the United States.

The *maquiladora* (twin plants) industry contributed significantly to population growth by creating more than a million jobs in the border region, primarily in the 1980s and 1990s. This growth was for the most part unplanned and was accompanied by widespread social problems such as inadequate housing, schools, and law enforcement. The growth has overwhelmed the capacity of the municipal infrastructure and caused severe deterioration on the social and physical environment. Urban growth has outpaced the ability of governments to provide adequate infrastructure in the border cities, particularly on the Mexican side, where most if the urbanization has been unplanned. On both sides of the border, a large number of residents do not have access to safe water piped into their residences; residents also lack proper sewage and sanitation services. By 2000, the deficit in environmental infrastructure in the US-Mexico border ranged from $5.8 to $10.4 billion, and by 2010, the deficit was more than $1 billion for water and wastewater projects in border communities (Good Neighbor Environmental Board [GNEB] 2010).

Social and Economic Determinants of Border Inequities

The US-Mexico border is the most traveled border in the world (Pan American Health Organization [PAHO] 2007). In 2004, 60% of the 500 million visitors admitted into the United States entered across the US-Mexico border, as did 90 million cars and 4.3 million trucks. This vehicular and human traffic is a major contributor to the US economy, with more than $638 million in trade conducted along the border each day (PAHO 2007). Mexico is the United States' third leading business and trade partner, and the United States is Mexico's primary trading partner. Many border residents had optimistic expectations that the North American Free Trade Agreement (NAFTA) would address environmental and poverty problems and bring greater economic development including well-paying jobs. NAFTA produced an increase in trade and investment across the border, but it did not create prosperity in US border communities, and NAFTA stimulated migration to the United States as small-scale farm families could no longer support themselves. The jobs created by NAFTA tended to be low-skill and low-paying. Border communities lost higher-paying manufacturing and assembly jobs that transferred offshore without the risk of trade sanctions. Residents of the border lost thousands of jobs to Asia. Ironically, cowboy boots sold in El Paso are now mostly manufactured in China.

The increase of cross-border trade and the associated vehicular crossings overwhelmed the border infrastructure and increased air pollution, resulting in health and safety risks and concerns. In addition, border communities absorbed a disproportionate share of health and environmental risks and costs.

Despite the degree of cross-border interdependence, economic development along the border is uneven. Mexico's border states have lower unemployment rates than the interior, higher wages, lower poverty rates and higher literacy rates when compared to other regions of the country.[2] In the United States, the conditions are reversed. Four of the seven poorest cities and five of the poorest counties in the United States are located in Texas along the Mexico border. In addition to growing trade between Mexico and the United States, there are cross-border networks of informal and illegal trade. There is a huge level drug trafficking along the border; El Paso, in particular, is one of the main corridors for drug smuggling into the United States. According to the US Drug Enforcement Agency, 65% of the cocaine consumed in the United States enters through the Mexican border, and 99% of the heroin produced in Mexico and South America targets US consumers (GNEB 2010).

US border counties have experienced an increase in unemployment and decrease in per capital income over the past 30 years. The poverty rate in El Paso is twice the national average, and average income is one-third of the national figure (PAHO 2007; DeNavas-Walt et al. 2009). Lack of adequate educational facilities on both sides of the border has produced a growth effect in US border school districts. Border populations are comparatively young, female, undereducated, and vulnerable.

Border per capita income is a core measure of community success. A low per capita income indicates that families are struggling to earn more money and break the cycle of poverty. Forty of the US border counties have capita income lower than the state averages. The border region's per capita is among the lowest in the nation, ranging from 35% of the US per capita income in Starr County to 97% in Kerr County. The entire border, with the exception of the more affluent county of San Diego, has suffered from an increase in income inequality. The gaps between the rich and the poor are also increasing. The rich have been getting wealthier, while the middle and lower class continue to struggle (Shapleigh 2008).

The educational attainment level of the US border residents is lower than the national average. The national percentage of persons without middle school education of is 0.5%, compared to 22.1% in Luna County, New Mexico, and 21% in Presidio County, Texas. The opposite is true for the Mexican border residents (Annie E. Casey Foundation 2005). In the Texas-Mexico border region, 20% of residents age 25 or older had fewer than 9 years of education, as compared to 11.5% of the state as a whole. Educational attainment is improving in Mexican border communities. As residents of the Mexican border communities become more educated and highly skilled, residents on the US border counties will face greater difficulties in remaining competitive for a shared workforce (Regional Stakeholders Committee 2009).

Low levels of educational attainment and high poverty rates indicate a pervasive cycle of poverty that becomes overwhelmingly difficult to break. Increased educational attainment delivers clear economic benefits (U.S. Census Bureau 2005). But without an educational system on the US-Mexico border region that delivers

[2] Although unemployment rates in border states are lower, it must be noted that Mexican official statistics inflate employment by including all part time and informal labor.

higher graduation rates and better education to meet the needs of the employers, lower wages will persist, and the entire border region will continue to suffer the consequences.

The US-Mexico Border Counties Coalition 2006 report, *At the Cross Roads: U.S.-Mexico Border Counties in Transition,* presents an analysis of several key features of the US-Mexico border region. The report points out that if the 24 US counties along the border were aggregated as the 51st state, they would rank 40th in per capita income, fifth in unemployment, second in tuberculosis, seventh in adult diabetes, 50th in insurance coverage for children and adults, 50th in high school completion, and first in poverty (U.S.-Mexico Border Counties Coalition 2006).

Hispanics (primarily of Mexican, Mexican-American origin) constitute the largest ethnic group in the border region, comprise the largest minority in the United States, and make up the majority of the population in 18 of the 24 counties along the US-Mexico border. In addition, the percentage of Hispanics in the US border population is increasing due to ongoing migration from Mexico and the high birth rate of border Hispanic populations (Ennis et al. 2011). Border income disparities are also influenced by the region's large Hispanic population. Hispanics, on an average, earn a lower income than non-Hispanic whites. In 2005, the median income of Hispanics was $37,867, a $4,774 increase over 1972 earnings. Over the same time period, non-Hispanic whites' income increased $15,864 (U.S. Census Bureau 2005). As the Hispanic population continues to grow, the border will rely on a Hispanic workforce to generate revenue for state services. Increased educational attainment rates are necessary, or serious consequences will confront the border future workforce. There are significant wage earning differences between male and female workers in the Hispanic population. In 2007, women working full-time earned 78% of what their male counterparts earned, a disparity that exists in almost all professions according to the Census. However, when broken down further, by gender and ethnicity, Hispanic women's earnings are 37% of non-Hispanic white men (Romero and Yellen 2004, p. 16). One important contributor to the high poverty rates in the US-Mexico border region is the rates of unemployment and underemployment. The border counties have unemployment rates that are higher than that for their respective state as a whole in 2006. The unemployment rate along the US side of the Texas-Mexico border is 250–300% higher than in the rest of the country (Texas Secretary of State 2010).

Within the border region are some 1,300 *colonias* (Migration Information Source 2010).[3] The majority of the *colonias* are in located in Texas where approximately 400,000 individuals live in 2,294 such communities (Texas Secretary of State 2010). It is estimated that 98% of *colonia* residents are individuals of Latino descent, mostly of Mexican ancestry (Giusti 2010). These communities are characterized by substandard housing, inadequate infrastructure, poor roads and drainage,

[3] A *colonia* is an economically distressed, unincorporated community along the US-Mexico border, which does not have adequate potable water, electricity, sanitary sewage systems, and/or other basic needs.

substandard water and sewer facilities, and no garbage disposal services. Poverty is dangerously high in *colonias*.

There are also 26 US federally recognized Native American communities in the border region that range from 9 to 28,000 members. Several of these tribes share family and cultural ties to indigenous peoples in the border region on Mexico. Health and economic inequalities in the border region affect indigenous populations, who are particularly vulnerable as a consequence of poverty and lack of health insurance.

Environmental Issues

The combination of rising population densities and rapid urban growth has aggravated environmental problems in a region characterized by a fragile and limited natural resource base. Growth has outstripped the capacity of Mexican border communities to plan and invest in housing, health and social services, sanitation, and other infrastructure. Pollution of the regional watercourses is found on both sides of the border due primarily to the trans-boundary nature of the watershed. Poor air quality, water scarcity and contamination, lead and arsenic soil contamination, and inadequate sewage processing are just a few of the most pressing environmental issues in the border area. Air pollution ranks among the worst environmental problems as particulate matter levels continue to exceed national standards. Even though a relaxation in the ozone standards was established (from a 1-h average to an 8-h average), ozone pollution continues to threaten some communities, particularly in El Paso.

It is evident that the border will face a severe water crisis in the near future. Current water supplies are very limited on the Mexican side, and supplies from rivers will not increase, due to the treaty with the Unites States that allocates the Rio Grande and Colorado River waters. Water scarcity and the growing vulnerabilities are likely to increase, considering the low ratio between population and existing water supply, the high ratio between water use and water availability, and the border region elevated dependency on external resources. The region's water supply is drawn down by irrigated agriculture, and heavy industrial and municipal demands that outstrip surface water supply (Paine 2000). Consequently, the aquifer in the Lower Rio Grande Valley is depleting rapidly with a resulting inflow of contaminants (Schulmeister 2006).

Air quality is particularly poor during the thermal inversions of the winter months. Many families in the Mexican border region live in substandard housing and use scrap wood, pallets, and sawdust (often chemically treated) as fuel to heat their homes. Vehicular pollution is aggravated by the fact that in Mexico, vehicle fleets tend to have poor maintenance, and legal environmental requirements for vehicles are not enforced. High levels of solid particulate matter, a factor associated in asthma and other respiratory conditions, are also associated with unpaved streets and roads in many border communities (Michel and Lara 2003).

Among the environmental hazards are agricultural activities that injure field workers who are contaminated by industrial pesticides. Local efforts and programs to reduce pesticide-related injury and to monitor human exposure are scattered and not well coordinated – particularly for migrant farm workers (Das et al. 2001).

The US-Mexico Border Region in a Changing America

The United States is undergoing rapid demographic change. Fueled by high fertility rates, mobility, and immigration, the American demographic is increasingly comprised of minority groups. According to the US Census Bureau, "Minorities, now roughly one-third of the U.S. population, are expected to become the majority in 2042." (U.S. Census Bureau 2008, August 14). Nonwhite minority groups account for 48.6% of all births nationwide; over 50% of all births in the United States will be to nonwhite minorities by the end of 2011 (Dougherty 2010). In 2005, Texas became the fourth state in the union to become a minority majority state, preceded by Hawaii, New Mexico, and California (U.S. Census Bureau 2005). Ironically, given the politics in that state, Arizona is among the group that will soon be joining the minority majority club. Demographically, the United States will increasingly resemble the US-Mexico border. The future face of America can be seen here. But, while the face of America will increasingly look like the border, unless the country begins to make investments in the border region, the border region will continue to lag behind the rest of the country in all other aspects of development.

There are several similar pockets of poverty and oppression that can be found around the country – places that look more like the developing nations of the postcolonial nations of "South," from Latin America and Africa to South Asia. Appalachia is one such distinctive cultural and economic space. It has been characterized by centuries of exploitation, isolation, and underdevelopment. "King Coal" has dominated the region's economy and people since the area was settled by white people of "Scotch-Irish descent." Within its cultural, geographic, and economic isolation at the margins of American society, Appalachia has developed unique dialects and musical traditions. Yet accompanying its regional uniqueness has been a legacy of union-busting mines backed by governors and state troopers intent on keeping wages down and productivity up; it can best be described as an "internal colony" (Billings and Blee 2000). The legacy has been incalculable mining deaths and injuries, an epidemic of black lung disease, economic exploitation through "company stores," miserable school systems, and an unrivaled set of social pathologies that result from exploitation – including alcoholism, joblessness, family violence, methamphetamine use, homicide, and family disintegration (Schwaner and Keil 2003). The environmental externalities of strip mining, mountaintop removal, and deep mining will be felt for centuries (Lillis 2010).

Similarly, the Four Corners Region of the American southwest typifies environmental and racial injustice in a way few places in the country can equal. Apart from the initial injustices of conquest, forced relocation, and near genocidal policies toward the indigenous peoples of the New Mexico, Arizona, Utah, and Colorado crossroads, the region has been successively exploited for its reserves of uranium and coal. Like other resource extractive economic regions, the money and wealth are removed by absentee landlords, and the poverty and environmental externalities are left behind by the "Polluter Industrial Complex" where "not all people are polluted equally" (Faber 2008, p. 7). Like Appalachia and the US-Mexico border region, the "Four Corners Region" is culturally distinct with its majority First Nations population. In addition, like Appalachia, the border region is culturally unique, at the periphery of American society, absent any political power, and without a shift in national priorities will remain poor, distant, exploited, and forgotten.

Finally, comparison can be drawn between the US-Mexico border region and what has come to be known as the "Black Belt." The region's name has its origin in two elements that characterize the 623 counties that range from rural Virginia through the American South to east Texas. The first and most important derives from the fact that these counties are rural, very poor, and have an exceptionally large proportion of African-Americans residing there. The second element of the region's name derives from the fact that the soils there tend to be dark, fertile loam (Calhoun et al. 2000).

The region was recognized as an intensely underdeveloped place in the American landscape at least as early as the mid-1800s when Booker T. Washington wrote about the wretched social and economic conditions that were found there in counties that were predominantly black (Wimberley and Morris 1997). Although large numbers of African-Americans have migrated out of the region since Washington wrote about the Black Belt, the region remains one of the least developed parts of the country. Like other parts of America's periphery, the area is ethnically distinct, rural, chronically poor, and its residents are more likely to be unemployed (Allen-Smith et al. 2000). Like the extractive economies of Appalachia and the Four Corners, the economy of the territory is not diverse – it is almost solely reliant on agriculture. Unlike Appalachia, which has long been understood as an underdeveloped region of an advanced economy, the Black Belt has received comparatively little attention from the public, the government, or the scientific community (Allen-Smith et al. 2000). While the New South has experienced extraordinary growth in prosperity, especially in urban areas, the Black Belt is home to some of the worst quality-of-life conditions in the country. Out of the public eye and distant from centers of power, this region, like the US-Mexico border region, the people of the Black Belt languish at the social and economic margins of America.

Chapter Organization

In this book, the contributors cover all major aspects of the border region's inequitable treatment of people at the margins of American society. This book is divided into four parts. In Part I, the editors present an overview of the challenges of achieving social justice in the US-Mexico border region. They describe the region –

both past and present – and present it in the context of international development theory. The region is placed at the periphery of an advanced capitalist state. Its underdevelopment is described in relation to its history and its economy. Chapter 1 sets the stage by drawing attention to the importance of understanding the border from a critical perspective, emphasizing the structural nature of the region's development and by arguing that much of the social pathology seen in the border region is a byproduct of its social and economic marginalization, set against a nativist and xenophobic background, which is currently being driven along by a moral panic.

The second part, "Critical Perspectives on the Border Region," addresses the region from various theoretical perspectives. The approaches are derived from political economy, the law, feminism, and theology. Each shares a critical perspective in assessing the region's deferred development and its structural inequality which characterize the border environment. In Chap. 2, "Political Economy and Social Justice in the US-Mexico Border Region," Josiah Heyman develops this theme in detail and argues that two political economic forces are profoundly shaping the border world. The first is the territorialized nation-state with large police and military apparatuses, as well as socially regulatory and redistributive functions. The latter is the transnational movement of capital investments, relocating in pursuit of reduced labor costs. This is evident in the dramatic growth of the *maquiladora* (export manufacturing) sector in Mexico's northern border cities, as well as other shifts in capital and labor to and from the region. His perspective illustrates that the situation in the border region is in large part due to the forces of globalization.

In Chap. 3, "How Citizenship Produces Inclusion and Exclusion on the US-Mexico Border," Tony Payan explicates how citizenship is used as a tool of structural violence to divide, type, include, exclude, and differentially treat people on the basis of their immigrant and citizenship status. He notes that citizenship is now layered and at the lowest rung of citizenship "undocumented," people are disposable. He observes that it is a kind of quiet violence that strips all dignity from human beings.

Kathleen Staudt addresses women, gender, and violence in the US-Mexico border region in Chap. 4. She has long studied the border region and has developed a unique and novel way of characterizing the violence that pervades the region. Integrating the structural violence of poverty with hegemonic masculinism, she addresses violence against women with an emphasis on misogynistic-driven femicide and partner violence and murder.

John Stowe brings a fresh perspective to the border. His chapter "A Theological Perspective on Social Justice in the US-Mexico Border Region" delineates the importance of faith-based traditions in understanding social justice. He details the evolution of Catholic thought in Latin America and how it has evolved from conservative "Establishment Perspectives" that enabled statist oligarchies toward a people-based theology that seeks to liberate citizens from oppression and violence. The theology of liberation has provided the people of the border region with a perspective that has helped them mobilize grassroots organizations and promote social justice.

Part III, "Problems and Opportunities on the US-Mexico Border," identifies and discusses specific social problems that affect the region, from housing to health to the environment. This part provides evidence of the region's underdevelopment and the pervasive social injustices that pervade the border.

In Chap. 6, Guillermina Gina Núñez-Mchiri describes the growth of the population that has led to a housing shortage for low-income people, the effects of NAFTA, and the displacement of workers as factors that have led to the emergence of *colonias* and substandard housing and homelessness throughout the region. Her chapter on "Housing, *Colonias*, and Social Justice in the US-Mexico Border Region," reviews strategies that have been successful in. Before 9/11, the US-Mexico border was highly permeable, and people in the region navigated in both directions to receive optimal and affordable health care, including the purchasing of prescription medications at low cost in Mexico. Now, as the border has been hardened and as residents of the United States have reduced their travel to Mexico, achieving equitable health has become more difficult. Nuria Homedes has long studied border health, and in Chap. 7, "Achieving Health Equity and Social Justice in the US-Mexico Border Region," she notes that several obstacles now confront borderlanders who seek health services. These factors include a shortage of primary care physicians and other health-care providers, very low rates of health insurance coverage, large expanses of the border which are far from health-care facilities, and other factors that produce health disparities and inequities.

Similarly, mental health services in the border region lag behind the nation. The situation is aggravated by a difference in the type of treatment individuals from different ethnic groups receive. Although the border is a minority majority region, minorities have less access to mental health services. In Chap. 8, "Mental Health Disparities and Social Justice in the US-Mexico Border Region," Griselda Villalobos and Arthur Islas detail the state of mental health disparities on the border, noting that minorities experience limited availability of mental health services and receive lower quality mental health services. They also document that minorities are underrepresented in mental health research. Coupled with underfunding and recent targeted funding cuts in mental health services, they frame the situation in relation to social injustice in readily visible ways, but also focus their analysis on social disparities which contribute to differential rates of infection.

As is the case with most developing nations and underdeveloped regions of advanced economies, the border region is disproportionately affected by infectious disease – in particular, human immune deficiency disorder, tuberculosis, and acquired immune deficiency syndrome. In Chap. 9, "Border Health: Inequities, Social Determinants, and the Cases of Tuberculosis and HIV," Eva Moya, Oralia Loza, and Mark Lusk detail the situation on the border with respect to infectious diseases that are heavily stigmatized and which further push those border residents who are affected by these diseases to the margins of an already marginalized population. They relate the disorders to the unique border environment where intravenous drug use is not uncommon and in which prostitution thrives.

As was previously stated in this chapter, the border region has been adversely affected by environmental practices that treat the region as a toxic waste dump. In Chap. 10, "Environmental Injustice in the US-Mexico Border Region," environmental scientists Sara Grineski and Patricia Juárez-Carrillo document the numerous environmental risks that are found in the region and their contribution to health disparities. The authors catalog and explain environmental injustices in the region as a whole, with a focus on the largest cross-border pair: El Paso, Texas, and Ciudad Juárez, Chihuahua. They emphasize hazards of particular interest including *maquiladoras*, factories, brick kilns, smelters, and poor housing conditions.

With the rise of the "Border Security Industrial Complex," Mexican migrants to the United States are increasingly subject to detention, incarceration, and forced deportation (Staudt 2009). They are wrongly blamed for many of the problems of the region and experience enormous discrimination. In Chap. 11, "Migration and Discrimination: Contradictory Discourses Regarding Repatriations in Ciudad Juárez, Chihuahua, Mexico," Irasema Coronado and Héctor Padilla document the treatment Mexican migrants experience on the US side but also hone in on the unjust situation they find themselves in when deported back to Mexico. US immigration enforcement agencies generally deport migrants to the closest international bridge, regardless of the migrant's state of residence, and Mexico has had a limited response to repatriation – a situation of great social injustice.

In Part IV, "Moving Forward: Steps in Achieving Border Justice," the book turns toward policy and action plans for redressing the social injustices of the region and the barriers that retard the region's development. In Chap. 12, Kathleen Staudt and Pauline Dow describe the challenges to border residents through the lens of the region's schools. They make the case that standardized testing has important negative implications for students in the region – most of whom have Spanish as their primary language. As education is central to development, they propose new strategies for educational advancement.

In the penultimate chapter, Rosalía Solórzano Torres addresses "Border Challenges and Ethnic Struggles for Social Justice in Arizona: Hispanic Communities Under Siege." She draws particular attention to growing national and international awareness that has resulted in confronting the racism and xenophobia which underlines the recently enacted Arizona Senate Bill 1070. She observes that hate crimes have been increasing nationally and anti-immigrant sentiments and intimidation have been crystallizing into human rights violations and attacks against Latina/o communities in Arizona and beyond. Chapter 13 describes the effects of SB 1070 on the lives of Latina/o ethnic groups, and their sociopolitical and economic situated lives on the US-Mexico border. The chapter concludes with Latina/o collective actions, struggles, resistance, and their community responses for social justice.

In the concluding chapter, "Social Justice at the Border and in the Bordered United States: Implications for Policy and Practice," editors Mark Lusk, Kathleen Staudt, and Eva Moya distill the findings and recommendations from the preceding 16 chapters. They begin by noting that "the *new* border is everywhere." Immigration and border policy is now framed through the lens of national security and the perceived threat of terrorism. Federal and state agencies, emboldened by new nativist laws and policies, enforce an internal border throughout the 50 states and at every level from municipal to county and state law enforcement.

They note that structural problems, like environmental racism, misogynistic violence, chronic poverty and underemployment, structural violence, and health disparities, are remedied with structural solutions. Piecemeal programs of remediation will ultimately serve to reinforce the status quo. It will take more than a few cookie crumbs from Washington to get the border region out of its economic doldrums, and it will require bold national level solutions to begin to turn around the oppression that has affected this region since it was incorporated into the United States. The editors call for a Border Investment Initiative and Free Trade Zone for the US side of the border. The incentive structure that would result from low tax and tax-free investments in the border, coupled with a program of national investment in the region's degraded infrastructure and schools, could lead the region into the American mainstream for the first time in its history. The manufacturing jobs that were shipped offshore by corporations that worship profit at any human or social cost will only invest in this region if it serves their bottom line. Such an investment zone would do just that.

In addition, they call for a fundamentally different way of looking at immigration. Presently, immigration is viewed as a social and economic "problem" that threatens American workers and erodes American social institutions, when exactly the opposite is the case. Immigrants enter the workforce at the bottom and rapidly rise up the income ladder, contributing to taxes and Social Security in a rapidly aging country that will soon have an unsustainable dependency ratio of younger workers to retirees. As we have seen for decades, immigrants move out of low-wage employment to start small businesses and within a short time span have children who enter higher/professional education and take positions as leaders in the relatively monochromic upper echelons of government and business. As important, immigration reform will reignite the idea that made the United States so successful – people from anywhere can come to America and be successful and make the country a better place in the process.

Also among their proposals is a redirection of border policy from a national security perspective to a human security viewpoint. They call for a demilitarization of the border, the end of Arizona-style right-wing demonization of Hispanics, and call for a renewed investment in children and the future.

Finally, they argue that the current situation on the border as thousands of Mexican citizens have fled the country to escape widespread violence, homicide, kidnappings, and opportunistic crime requires a multinational response. They call for a shift away from the failed Mérida Plan that spends over a billion on combating narcotics by building a Mexican police state and instead investing those dollars in economic development by building programs through the auspices of the US Agency for International Development. On the American side of the border, ill-equipped to help refugees and hostile to their presence in the first place, the United States should invite the United Nations High Commission on Refugees to set up refugee camps along the border to assist migrants in health care, housing nutrition, education, and obtaining fast-track refugee visa status.

References

Abadie, A. (2006). Poverty, political freedom, and the roots of terrorism. *The American Economic Review, 96*(2), 50–56.

Ackay, S. (2006). Corruption and human development. *Cato Journal, 26*(1), 29–48.

Acuna, R. (1972). *Occupied America: The Chicano's struggle toward liberation.* San Francisco: Canfield Press.

Aguilar, J. (2010, September 2). *Mexican reporter seeks asylum after doing his job.* Retrieved from *The Texas Tribune*: http://www.texastribune.org/texas-mexico-border-news/texas-mexico-border/mexican-reporter-seeks-asylum-after-doing-his-job/

Allen-Smith, J., Wimberley, R., & Morris, L. (2000, August). America's forgotten people and places: Ending the legacy of poverty in the rural south. *Journal of Agricultural and Applied Economics, 32*(2), 310–329.

Anbinder, T. (1992). *Nativism and slavery: The northern know nothings and the politics of the 1850s.* New York: Oxford University Press.

Annie E. Casey Foundation. (2005). *Kids count data book.* Baltimore: Annie E. Casey Foundation.

Archibold, R. (2010, June 19). *On border violence, truth pales compared to ideas.* Retrieved from *New York Times*: http://www.nytimes.com/2010/06/20/us/20crime.html?emc=eta1

Associated Press. (2011, January 1). *Mexico border city has record drug killings in '10.* Retrieved June 16, 2011, from http://www.signonsandiego.com/news/2011/jan/01/mexico-border-city-has-record-drug-killings-in-10/

Bacevich, A. (2005). *The new American militarism: How Americans are seduced by war.* Oxford: Oxford University Press.

Barrera, M. (1979). *Race & class in the southwest: A theory of racial inequality.* Notre Dame: University of Notre Dame Press.

Bauer, K. (1974). *The Mexican war, 1846–1848.* New York: Macmillan.

Becker, A., & McDonnell, P. (2009, March 4). *Drug war creates a new class of refugees.* Retrieved from *Los Angeles Times*: http://articles.latimes.com/2009/mar/04/nation/na-asylum4

Beinart, P. (2004, December 2). *An argument for a new liberalism: A fighting faith.* Retrieved from *The New Republic*: http://209.157.64.200/focus/f-news/1292836/posts

Billings, D., & Blee, K. (2000). *The road to poverty: The making of wealth and hardship in Appalachia.* Cambridge: The Cambridge University Press.

Borunda, D. (2009, February 29). *Rights activist cites Mexican army abuses.* Retrieved from *El Paso Times*: http://www.elpasotimes.com/ci_11796634

Calhoun, S., Reeder, R., & Bagi, F. (2000). Federal funds in the black belt. *Rural America, 15*(1), 20–27.

Campbell, H. (2009). *Drug war zone: Frontline dispatches from the streets of El Paso and Juárez.* Austin: University of Texas Press.

Camp, J. (2009) We know this place: Neoliberal racial regimes and the Katrina circumstance. *American Quarterly, 61*(3), 693–717.

Cherry, C. (1998). Introduction. In C. Cherry (Ed.), *God's new Israel: Religious interpretations of American destiny* (pp. 2–20). Chapel Hill: University of North Carolina Press.

Cole, D. (2004). The priority of morality: The emergency constitution's blind spot. *The Yale Law Journal, 113*(8), 1753–1800.

Congressional Research Service. (2006). *U.S. international borders: Brief facts.* Retrieved from http://www.fas.org/sgp/crs/misc/RS21729.pdf

Cypher, J. (2007, June). From military keynesianism to global-neoliberal militarism. *Monthly Review, 59*(2), 37–55.

Das, R., Steege, A., Baron, S., Beckman, J., & Harrison, R. (2001). Pesticide-related illness among migrant farm workers in the United States. *International Journal of Occupational and Environmental Health, 7*, 303–312.

de Cosio, F., & Boadella, A. (1999). Demographic factors affecting U.S.-Mexico border health status. In M. Loustaunau & M. Sanchez-Bane (Eds.), *Life, death, and in-between on the U.S. Mexico Border: Asi es la vida* (pp. 1–22). London: Bergin and Garvey.

Del Castillo, R. (1992). *The Treaty of Guadalupe Hidalgo: A legacy of conflict*. Norman: The University of Oklahoma Press.

DeNavas-Walt, C., Proctor, B., & Smith, J. (2009, September). *Income, poverty, and health insurance coverage in the United States: 2008*. Washington, DC: U.S. Census Bureau. P60–236(RV).

Department of Homeland Security [DHS]. (2005, November 2). *Fact sheet: Secure border initiative*. Retrieved June 15, 2011, from http://www.dhs.gov/xnews/releases/press_release_0794.shtm

Department of Homeland Security [DHS]. (2010, February 1). *Secretary Napolitano announces fiscal year 2011 budget request*. Retrieved June 16, 2011, from Press Release: http://www.dhs.gov/ynews/releases/pr_1265049379725.shtm

Direct Action and Training Network [DART]. (n.d.). Retrieved from www.thedartcenter.org

Doty, R. (2009). *The law into their own hands: Immigration and the politics of exceptionalism*. Tucson: The University of Arizona Press.

Dougherty, C. (2010, June 11). *U.S. reaches racial milestone*. Retrieved from *The Wall Street Journal*: http://online.wsj.com/article/NA_WSJ_PUB:SB10001424052748704312104575298512006681060.html

Dow, M. (2004). *American gulag: Inside US immigration prisons*. Berkeley: University of California Press.

Dunn, T. (2009). *Blockading the border and human rights: The El Paso operation that remade U.S. border enforcement*. Austin: University of Texas Press.

Ennis, S., Ríos-Vargas, M., & Albert, N. (2011, May). *The Hispanic population: 2010*. Washington, DC: U.S. Census Bureau. 2010 Census Briefs. C2010BR-04.

Faber, D. (2008). *Capitalizing on environmental injustice: The polluter industrial complex in the age of globalization*. Lanhan: Rowman and Littlefield.

Filler, D. (2003). Terrorism, panic and pedophilia. *Virginia Journal of Social Policy and the Law, 10*, 345–382.

Finnegan, W. (2010, July 26). Borderlines. *The New Yorker*, pp. 19–20.

Foucault, M. (1995). *Discipline & punish: The birth of the prison*. New York: Vintage.

Gamaliel. (2010). Retrieved from www.gamaliel.org

Gellman, S. (2002). The First Amendment in a time that tries men's souls. *Law and Contemporary Problems, 65*(2), 87–101.

Gilman, N. (2003). *Mandarins of the future: Modernization theory in cold war America*. Baltimore: Johns Hopkins University.

Giusti, C. (2010, April 19). *Border communities: The case of colonias in Texas*. Retrieved from International Institute of Social Studies of Erasmus University Rotterdam: http://www.iss.nl/DevISSues/Articles/Border-Communities-The-Case-of-Colonias-in-Texas

Goffman, E. (1961). *Asylums: Essays on the social situation of mental patients and other inmates*. New York: Anchor.

Good Neighbor Environmental Board [GNEB]. (2010). *A blueprint for action on the U.S.-Mexico border. Thirteenth report of the Good Neighbor Environmental Board to the President and Congress of the United States*. Washington, DC: GNEB.

Goode, E., & Ben-Yehuda, N. (1994). *Moral panics: The social construction of deviance*. Oxford: Blackwell.

Gudridge, P. (2003). Remember "Endo"? *Harvard Law Review, 116*(7), 1933–1970.

Heyman, J., & Campbell, H. (2004). Recent research on the U.S. Mexico border. *Latin American Research Review, 39*(3), 205–220.

Huntington, S. (1996). *The clash of civilizations and the remaking of world order*. New York: Simon & Schuster.

Huntington, S. (2004a, March/April). The Hispanic challenge. *Foreign Policy*, pp. 1–13.

Huntington, S. (2004b). *Who are we? The challenges to America's national identity. The clash of civilizations and the remaking of world order*. New York: Simon & Schuster.

Instituto Nacional de Estadística y Geografía. (2000). *Censo de población y vivienda: Tasas especificas de participación económica por municipio* [Population and housing census: Specific rates of economic participation by municipality]. Retrieved from http://www.inegi.org.mx/est/libreras/tabulados.asp@tabulado=tab_em04a&c=10279&e

Instituto Nacional de Estadística y Geografía. (2010). *Conteo de población y vivienda 2005: Micro datos de muestra CPVII* [Population and housing counting 2005: Microdata of sample CPVII]. Retrieved from http://www.inegi.org.mx/inegi/default.aspx?c=10202&s=es

Johnson, K. (1996). Aliens and the US immigration laws: The social and legal construction of nonpersons. *University of Miami Inter-American Law Reviews, 28*(2), 263–292.

Leon, L. (1999). Metaphor and place: The U.S.-Mexico border as center and periphery in the interpretation of religion. *Journal of the American Academy of Religion, 76*(3), 541–571.

Lillis, M. (2010, February 10). *The story of coal's deadly, dirty legacy*. Retrieved from *The Washington Independent*: http://washingtonindependent.com/76219/now-on-stage-the-story-of-coal%E2%80%99s-dirty-deadly-legacy

Lipset, S. (1959). Some social requisites of democracy. *American Political Science Review, 53*(1), 69–105.

Lusk, M. (2010). International social development and counterdevelopment. *Journal of Comparative Social Welfare, 26*(2), 165–176.

Martínez, O. (1989). *Troublesome border*. Tucson: The University of Arizona Press.

Martínez, O. (1994). *Border people: Life and society in the U.S.-Mexico borderlands*. Tucson: University of Arizona Press.

Michel, J., & Lara, F. (2003). *Responding to development challenges and opportunities in the U.S.-Mexico border region. A report to the Director of the USAID in Mexico*. Washington, DC: Caribbean Resources International.

Mier, N., Ory, M., Zhan, D., Conkling, M., Sharkery, J., & Burdine, J. (2008). Health-related quality of life among Mexican-Americans living in colonias at the Texas-Mexico border. *Social Science & Medicine, 66*(8), 1760–1771.

Migration Information Source. (2010). *The US Mexico border*. Retrieved from http://www.migrationinformation.org/feature/display.cfm?ID=407

Molano, A. (2005). *The dispossessed: Chronicles of the desterrados of Colombia*. Chicago: Haymarket Books.

Mora-Torres, J. (2001). *The making of the U.S.-Mexico border: The state, capitalism and society in Nuevo León, 1948–1919*. Austin: The University of Texas Press.

National Association of Social Workers [NASW]. (2010). *Social justice*. Retrieved from http://www.naswdc.org/pressroom/features/issue/peace.asp

Orr, M. (Ed.). (2007). *Transforming the city: Community organizing and the challenges of political change*. Lawrence: University Press of Kansas.

Ortiz Uribe, M. (2009, October 17). *Human rights worker flees Mexico*. Retrieved from National Public Radio: http://www.npr.org/templates/story/story.php?storyId=113899756

Paine, J. (2000). *Assessing and identifying groundwater in the lower Rio Grande Valley Texas using airborne electromagnetic induction*. Austin: Texas Water Development Board.

Pan American Health Organization. (2007). *Health of the Américas: United States-Mexico border area* (Vol. II). Washington, DC: Pan American Health Organization.

Paz, O. (1997). *El laberinto de la soledad [The labyrinth of solitude]*. New York: Penguin.

Pearce, J. (2005). Inequality: Politics in the developing world. In P. Burnell & V. Randall (Eds.), *Politics in the developing world* (pp. 59–73). New York: Oxford University Press.

People Improving Communities Organization [PICO]. (n.d.). Retrieved from http://www.piconetwork.org/

Peri, G. (2010, August 30). The effects of immigrants on the U.S. employment and productivity. *Federal Reserve Bank of San Francisco Economic Newsletter*, pp. 1–4.

Petras, J. (2000). Geopolitics of plan Colombia. *Economic and Political Weekly, 35*(52/53), 4617–4623.

Pizarro, E., & Gaitan, P. (2006). Plan Colombia and the Andean regional initiative: Lights and shadows. In B. Loveman (Ed.), *Addicted to failure: U.S. security policy in the Andean region* (pp. 53–79). Lanhan: Rowan and Littlefield.

Regional Stakeholders Committee. (2009). *The Paso del Norte region, US-Mexico: Self-evaluation report.* Retrieved from OECD Reviews of Higher Education in Regional and City Development, IMHE: http://www.oecd.org/edu/imhe/regionaldevelopment

Rodríguez, O. (2010, December 7). Intervencion de ejercito norteamericano traeria guerrillas a Mexico. *El Diario de El Paso*, p. 4A.

Romero, M., & Yellen, T. (2004). *El Paso portraits: Women's lives, potential & opportunities. A report on the state of women in El Paso, Texas.* El Paso: YWCA and UTEP Center for Civic Engagement.

Rosales, F. (1992). *Chicano: The history of the Mexican American civil rights movement.* Houston: University of Houston Press.

Schriro, D. (2009). *Immigration detention overview and recommendations.* Washington, DC: Department of Homeland Security.

Schulmeister, M. (2006). *Rio Grande aquifer system.* Retrieved from http://academic.emporia.edu/schulmem/hydro/TERM%20PROJECTS/Corley/geowat.html#groundwaterquality

Schwaner, S., & Keil, T. (2003). Internal colonization, folk justice, and murder in Appalachia: The case of Kentucky. *Journal of Criminal Justice, 32*(3), 279–286.

Seelke, C. (2010). *Mérida initiative for Mexico and Central América: Funding and policy issues.* Washington, DC: Congressional Research Service.

Sen, A. (1999). *Development as freedom.* New York: Knopf.

Sen, A. (2005). Human rights and human capabilities. *Journal of Human Development, 6*(2), 151–166.

Sen, A. (2010). *The idea of justice.* Cambridge: Harvard Belknap.

Shamir, R. (2005). Without border? Notes on globalization as a mobility regime. *Sociological Theory, 23*(2), 197–217.

Shapleigh, E. (2008, September). Demographics of the frontier of the future. *Texas borderlands 2009.* El Paso: Texas Senator Eliot Shapleigh. District 29.

Staudt, K. (2009). Violence at the border: Broadening the discourse to include feminism, human security, and deeper democracy. In *Human rights along the U.S.-Mexico border: Gendered violence and insecurity* (pp. 1–27). Tucson: University of Arizona Press.

Staudt, K., & Coronado, I. (2002). *Fronteras no más: Toward social justice at the U.S.-Mexico border.* New York: Palgrave.

Staudt, K., Payan, T., & Dunn, T. (2009). Bordering human rights, social democratic feminism, and broad-based security. In *Human rights along the U.S.-Mexico border: Gendered violence and insecurity* (pp. 185–202). Tucson: University of Arizona Press.

Staudt, K., Fuentes, C., & Monárrez Fragoso, J. (Eds.). (2010). *Cities and citizenship at the U.S.-Mexico border: The Paso del Norte metropolitan region.* New York: Palgrave.

Texas Secretary of State. (2010). *Texas colonias: A thumbnail sketch of conditions, issues, challenges and opportunities.* Retrieved from http://www.sos.state.tx.us/border/colonias/faqs.shtml

U.S. Census Bureau. (2005). *Texas becomes nation's newest majority-minority state.* Retrieved from Census Bureau Announces: http://www.census.gov/newsroom/releases/archives/population/cb05118.html

U.S. Census Bureau. (2008, August 14). *An older and more diverse nation by midcentury.* Retrieved June 15, 2011, from *Newsroom*: http://www.census.gov/newsroom/releases/archives/population/cb08123.html

U.S.-Mexico Border Counties Coalition. (2006). *At the cross roads: U.S.-Mexico border counties in transition.* El Paso: University of Texas at El Paso/U.S.-Mexico Border Counties Coalition Institute for Policy Economic Development.

U.S.-Mexico Border Counties Coalition. (2010). *Coalition fact sheet.* Retrieved from http://www.bordercounties.org/

U.S.-Mexico Border Health Commission [USMBHC]. (2002). *Annual Report, October 2002.* El Paso: U.S.-Mexico Border Health Commission.

U.S.-Mexico Border Health Commission [USMBHC]. (2009). *Situación de la tuberculosis en la frontera Mexico-Estados Unidos* [the situation of tuberculosis in the border Mexico-United States]. El Paso: U.S.-Mexico Border Health Commission.

United Nations Development Programme. (2010). *Human Development Report 2010. The real wealth of nations: Pathways to human development. 20th Anniversary Edition.* New York: Palgrave Macmillan.

United States Agency for International Development [USAID]. (2010). *USAID budget: Mexico.* Retrieved from USAID: http://www.usaid.gov/policy/budget/cbj2006/lac/mx.html

Villette, C. (2005). *Plan Colombia: A progress report*. Washington, DC: Congressional Research Service.

Wimberley, R., & Morris, L. (1997). *The southern black belt*. Lexington: TVA Rural Studies.

Washington Valdez, D. (2012, January 26). Special report: Calderón years trail other for Mexico homicides. El Paso Times, Retrieved from http://www.elpasotimes.com/ci_19824147.

Part II
Critical Perspectives on the Border Region

Chapter 2
Political Economy and Social Justice in the US-Mexico Border Region

Josiah McC. Heyman

Introduction

Political economy is study and action emphasizing unequal power relations in social affairs (useful introductions are Wolf 1982, 1999). Its definition of power is relational, not just a quantity or possession (i.e., having more units of power); a basic but helpful way to convey the idea of a power relation is that domination is necessarily linked to subordination. It includes politics, obviously, but not just party politics, or even governmental activity, but all forms of organized efforts to influence collective action (following the classic definition of Weber 1946, pp. 194–195). All social life is thus shot through with politics. Likewise, political economy attends to economics, including the actual processes of pricing, buying, and selling, but also the wider (and more interesting) dimensions of how we value things, how we organize ourselves to buy, sell, work, consume, and produce the material bases of our daily lives. A third element is ideology, equally essential, though not found in the phrase political economy. Ideologies are patterned sets of ideas (and the feelings and meanings associated with them), especially with reference to economic and political topics. Each of these topics is associated with a separate field of study, but the political economy perspective emphasizes the connections: the political power consequences of economic arrangements, or the idea systems that shape the politics of border control, and so forth.

Political economy matters. Its perspective enables us to penetrate apparently dense and irrational social questions such as why people denigrate the immigrant labor from which they benefit. Such penetrating understandings, in turn, help us act in practical ways; rather than banging our heads against the wall, asking why

J.M. Heyman (✉)
Department of Sociology and Anthropology, University of Texas at El Paso, El Paso, TX, USA
e-mail: jmheyman@utep.edu

M. Lusk et al. (eds.), *Social Justice in the U.S.-Mexico Border Region*,
DOI 10.1007/978-94-007-4150-8_2, © Springer Science+Business Media B.V. 2012

some issue seems so intractable and irrational, we can step back and ask what ideological, political, and economic relationships must be addressed for meaningful social change to happen. Unfortunately, political economy is often discouraging. It exposes strong, dense, and enduring patterns of unequal power. Such patterns mean that personal change, empowerment strategies, localized or limited reforms, and so forth may do little or nothing to change human suffering and social injustice. Of course, even a little change is good, and more importantly, the perspective that power is a relationship means that there are always two sides, two potential sources of change. Since there is no exploitation without exploitability, high power without low power, even the people on the weaker side of a relationship are necessary, and thus have some ability to make their ideas and actions matter.

The political-economic perspective is inherently historical. It involves elements that are dynamic drivers of change, such as the accumulation and movement of investment capital (e.g., into manufacturing in Mexican border industries). Such dynamics set off further ricocheting changes, such as the dramatic growth of Mexican and some US border cities. The historical view also suggests that people operate with powerful inheritances—ways we view the world, ways we interact with each other. We do not survey the world each day anew, in a rational fashion, as a clean slate. We are tied up in geographies, habits, and relations we do not want to and indeed cannot break. Unfortunately, we cannot do justice to the historical perspective on the US-Mexico borderlands here, due to limitations of length. Useful overviews include (Ganster and Lorey 2008) the works of the dean of border history (Martínez 1988, 1994) and a strictly political-economic interpretation (Fernández 1977). One thing that history does teach us, which matters enormously, is that the border is not inherent, an unquestioned division between two uniform and eternal nation-states, without causes and without alternative possibilities. It was made historically and is today a complex and dynamic work, always under construction.

The Construction of the Border

Construction, in the social sciences, is a term of art. It means that specific social arrangements are not inherent, natural, or permanent. Anything that is constructed can be (conceivably) done differently. In this view, then, power is needed to build, to hold in place, to tear down, to transform. And so it is with the border. The territorial location of the border, obviously, was constructed by political acts—war, treaties, and forced cession of land. But today, the actual boundary is a given. It is the similarities and differences between Mexico and the United States that are constructed and reconstructed every day. We cannot assume that something is inherently Mexican, inherently North American, solely because of their spatial location.[1] Some social

[1] Properly said, American covers both countries, so I use North American as an adjective pertaining to US citizens.

and cultural patterns span both sides of the border, some are distinctly national, and others relate differences across borders in more complex fashions.

This seems endlessly complex and fluid. We can specify this analytically, however, by listing three categories of phenomena to look for. There are processes that reinforce the border itself, as a separating line or even barrier, and also those that make the two national territories more and more different, socially, culturally, and so forth. There are processes that meld the two sides of the border, or just ignore the border, flowing back and forth (on debordering and rebordering, see Spener and Staudt 1998). And there are processes that combine the two sides without mixing them, in which the relation of one side to the other maintains or even reinforces their difference. The jargon term for this paradoxical relation/difference set is "combined and uneven development." It is fundamental to the political economy of the border (Heyman 1994, 2010a).

All three of these processes, in turn, involve political, economic, and ideological elements. They form a grid of tools for understanding, as follows:

	Border reinforcing	Border erasing	Combined and uneven development
Economic	Laws restricting commodities	Everyday trade and gifts	Border industries; local labor commuting
Political	Border enforcement; national institutions	Cooperative arrangements (e.g., emergency response)	No evident example
Ideological	Nationalist imagery and discourses	Shared/mixed cultural and linguistic phenomena	Mexican modernist image of US and US exotic other image of Mexico

Not every cell in this concept chart has some actual world example corresponding to it. But the open spaces in these cells usefully encourage creative questions about the realities of the borderlands.

Several examples illustrate processes of border reinforcement.[2] US border enforcement against contraband drugs and unauthorized migration has grown, in fits and starts, since the 1970s. There is a long-term trend toward tighter government surveillance of and controls over the border. This trend escalated from late 1993 onward (Heyman 1999a). Border Patrol officers and equipment were placed on the very front lines of the boundary. The first crude border walls were built. From this turning point to the time of writing (late 2010), the Border Patrol quintupled from 4,000 to 21,000 officers. Seven hundred miles of border wall has been installed. Thousands of National Guard soldiers are periodically stationed at a border that

[2] I do not use an example of Mexican political, legal, and administrative border reinforcement here. In fact, such examples exist in abundance, though less well funded than those of the wealthy US federal government. Mexican customs inspections and barriers are representative. But the extreme drug war in Mexico's northern border region has led to considerable weakening in the Mexican state in this region (see Olson et al. 2010).

has not seen war for 90 years. The public policy debates over migration and drugs matter, of course, but setting them aside for the moment, the striking fact is that the border is being reinforced and reinforced again (Andreas 2009; Nevins 2010).

But border reinforcement is not just political, legal, and military in nature. The sense of difference and separation across the border is constantly produced by nationalist ideologies—not just obvious, chauvinist ones, but also taken-for-granted forms of patriotism and identification. Child training in schools in both countries is documented in Rippberger and Staudt's (2002) aptly named study, *Pledging Allegiance*. Children who often come from binational or bicultural families and communities are provided a clear sense of distinctive national identity by various normal patriotic lessons and activities. These occur throughout both nation-states, but are strikingly important in the border setting, where boundaries are easily questioned otherwise (on border polarization, see Grimson and Vila 2002; Vila 2000).

Both the border regulation, surveillance, and enforcement examples and the school nationalism are examples of the presence of the two nation-states in the border region. Just because it is a border region does not mean the state is less present; if anything, it is more present both in the form of huge bureaucracies (police, military, regulatory bodies) and ideological communication. The persistent, pervasive, and powerful growth of the territorial nation-state is fundamental to understanding the intensity of border reinforcement even in a period ostensibly characterized by globalization (Nevins 2010).

Combined and uneven processes both rely on flows back and forth across the boundary, and they maintain—or even produce—the clear differences between the United States and Mexico (see Heyman 2004, 2010a for systematic expositions). Often, they build on inequalities between direct producers on or migrating from one side and recipients of value on the other side. The maquiladoras are an illustrative example. These are processing and assembly factories in Mexico (examples being auto parts, medical supplies, and consumer electronics) that are key parts of transnational corporate manufacturers. Their markets are global, but predominantly United States and Canada for the Mexican plants. The key point is that such plants only occur because of an unequal exchange. Labor value (purchasing power of workers and their households) is low in Mexico. A typical factory wage is the equivalent of $60 a week, including bonuses. But purchasing power of prosperous households in the United States and Canada is high—many hundreds of dollars, even thousands, per week. Low labor value goods are exchanged to high labor value consumers. Mediating this exchange and taking considerable profits from it are large transnational corporations and their subcontractors (Fernández-Kelly 1983; Kopinak 1996; Peña 1997).

Many other processes at borders take advantage of the various ways that inequality between the United States and Mexico can be combined without leveling that inequality. Many such transactions are profitable, but it is not purely economic. Cross-border tourism and shopping may make profits, but to the actors themselves, it is the difference in cultural-ideological values between the two sides that matters. A useful source is Vila (2000). The United States offers the dream of perfect modernity to Mexicans (no matter the reality of US corruption, inefficiency, and speculation); Mexico offers exotic pleasure and release to North Americans (again, no matter the drab modern reality of much of Mexico).

Emerging from the border-reinforcing and maintaining processes are ironic by-products, processes of crossing, exchanging, blending that weaken border distinctions (Garcia Canclini 1995; Heyman and Campbell 2010). There are a few collaborative political (administrative, legal, etc.) networks, though this arena is dominated by nation-state organizations and ideologies that impede cross-border cooperation (Staudt and Coronado 2002). More often, there are parallel and collaborative economic arrangements that undermine borders, especially in the economics of the common people, rather than corporate economics, as described in Staudt's (1998) outstanding study, *Free Trade?* Perhaps most important are the hybrid forms of cultural ideas and practices, as exemplified by Spanglish, the mixing of Spanish and English linguistic codes as an effective form of borderite communication (Martínez 2006, pp. 94–108). English words are given Spanish endings, or vice versa; whole phrases are moved from one language to the other; and people alternate between full sentences. This works efficiently when both parties are in command of the two languages and are comfortable with ignoring rigid linguistic boundaries. It is often devalued, however, because of border-reinforcing ideologies of linguistic purity, despite millennia of evidence that languages are creative, dynamic, and interrelational phenomena.

All three processes operate and interact at the same time. Border reinforcement effects occur side by side with processes that blur and erase the border. Admittedly, the balance of processes differs at various times, sites, and for diverse populations and issues. In recent years, it seems that border-reinforcing forces have become predominant, with the Mexican drug war and the US political panic over immigration that translates to escalating border enforcement. But combined and uneven relations remain central to the border—in ways we will explore below—and border-blending processes continue to operate below the ideological and political official surface. The simultaneity of all three elements is important. To understand the region, we need to recognize how these process cut across each other, creating paradoxical but important realities—Border Patrol officers who speak Spanglish and employ unauthorized migrant domestics being a representative example. No one depiction of the border, neither pure barrier nor idealized hybrid, not even subtle analyses of relations of inequality, is adequate to capture the full dynamism and complexity of the border region (Heyman 2001a; Heyman and Campbell 2010).

The Border as a Subordinate Region

The border is a subordinate region in two nation-states and in the continental economy as a whole. Many policies that affect it are set by political and bureaucratic decisions in Washington, D.C., and Mexico City, and those politics in turn determined by publics in Iowa and Georgia who have little or no contact with or knowledge of the realities of the borderlands (Ganster and Lorey 2008). Its economic drivers are transnational manufacturers, transnational drug cartels (producers, shippers, retailers, and consumers), and transnational migratory paths between Mexican and Central American villages and North American restaurant owners and eaters and so forth (e.g., Chavez 1998; Gomberg-Muñoz 2011). Least noticed, but perhaps most importantly, the border is conceived of as an outer margin of the center, the places that really matter, rather than an important place of its own (Ortíz-González 2004).

In political economy, these sorts of geographic-power hierarchies are discussed in dependency theory (see Cardoso and Faletto 1979; Frank 1970). The basic notion of dependency is that value—be it economic, political, or ideological—is produced in apparently poor and marginal locales, but transferred to and accumulated in wealthy and powerful ones. Places are thus not poor because of lack of development, lack of connections, but precisely because they *are* connected in ways that deny autonomous development and self-determination. It also implies that prosperity and power are less a matter of self-merit than of being on top of pyramids of extraction from the middle tiers and then the poor.

Dependency theory has limitations—in particular, critics have emphasized the ways that some regions can escape its chains, while others do not—but it does describe some of the key dilemmas of the US-Mexico borderland, as seen in the following chart:

Economic dependency	Political dependency	Ideological dependency
Maquiladoras	Dominance by national policies and federal government agencies	Shaped by media images and interior public opinion more than local perspectives
Drug trade	Focus on national security not local security	
Long-distance migration		
Tourism		
Profits go elsewhere		

Of course, about 12 million people live in this dependent region.[3] They have an entire set of needs, resources, activities, homes, communities, families, ideas, hopes, and dreams that should be considered when decisions are made and policies are implemented. Dependency means that such considerations often are secondary, even just flatly ignored.

[3]Properly phrased, the borderlands are not at the absolute bottom of the dependency pyramid—though millions of workers dwelling in marginal neighborhoods do indeed fit that description (see Fernández-Kelly 1983; Núñez 2009 for examples). Rather, the border mediates between places like migrant-sending communities in Oaxaca, Mexico, that are further down the pyramid and suburban California that are further up the pyramid, as migrants pass through the boundary region on their sad path of self-surrender to exploitative labor (Nagengast et al. 1992; Stuart and Kearney 1981; Velasco Ortíz 2005).

It is worth particularly emphasizing the way the border is viewed from a distance and then diagnosing the effects of that gaze. Borders and boundaries of all kinds are unquestionably vital conceptual markers. We use them to distinguish between important entities—self and others, home and outside, work and play, and so forth. The orderliness may well be arbitrary; one culture places it in this order, another in that. But once the order is set, it provides a sense of existential security. Safety is inside, risk is outside (or better said, outside penetrating in). As symbolic anthropologist Mary Douglas (1966) points out, things that cross boundaries (physically and conceptually) are both unusually powerful and unusually dangerous. They are, in the ways that people think about things, matter out of place, on the wrong side of a boundary, and thus polluting.

In the case of the US-Mexico border, the conceptual distinction is between one territorialized nation-state, and the people it claims as its subjects, and opposed—but also parallels—others (Nevins 2010). As such, it might seem like borders are natural places to "defend" the national community. We cannot dismiss that line of analysis—the nation-state and its various subfederal entities indeed do important things for people's lives—but we also cannot buy it unquestioningly. Businesses operate across the border, and common products are assembled from parts in both countries. Labor arrangements are increasingly unified across the continent, as seen in international migratory movements in search of work, in spite of laws that poorly reflect such realities. People have friends and family in both Mexico and the United States, long a reality that is only becoming more and more important. Thus, the boundary between home and outside, self and other, cannot and should not be reduced to the borders between the nation-states United States and Mexico.

Often, however, domestic politics in the United States treats the border as an absolute and ultimate boundary. For example, mass media depictions of the border unvaryingly focus on short-term, frightening events (e.g., killings in Mexico) and obscure the important, enduring realities (e.g., that the US side has very low rates of violent crime and that communities there report feeling safe and secure) (Border Network for Human Rights 2010). Just as Douglas would have predicted, "scary invasions from outside" are characteristic of mass media and then political views of migration through the borderlands (Chavez 2001). Border communities are ignored, and flows through the border are handled in a simplistic manner. This is clearly indicated by a careful, systematic, and objective review of US border security policy in the era of al-Qaeda (Heyman and Ackleson 2009; Leiken and Brooke 2006).

The 9/11 bombers entered on legal visas, through airports, mostly undetected because of international and domestic failures in intelligence and law enforcement (and thus unrelated to borders, especially not the US-Mexico land border). Despite this, the US-Mexico land border has received the overwhelming majority of congressional effort (e.g., the border wall law) and Department of Homeland Security resources. Mexican family and labor migration have remained the focus of security policy—without any reason to see them in security terms (whatever one's public policy assessment of such migration). This border is treated from the outside as a dangerous, fearful place—and undoubtedly, violence in Mexico is indeed dangerous to Mexicans—expressing unthinking domestic US stereotypes and ideologies rather than national, regional, and local realities. It is a thoroughly misconstrued icon of threat in the collective American imagination. But such distant thinking often determines the border's fate.

The Operational Border: Openings and Barriers to Flows

The border itself—not the borderlands, but the literal border—consists of a diplomatically drawn line. Much of this line consists of barriers from massive walls to remote sections of barbed wire fence, but all actively monitored and patrolled, places where crossing is not officially allowed. It occurs, of course, which will be discussed shortly. At main transportation points (roads, railroads, and, indirectly, border region airports), there are legitimate points of entry. These are called ports of entry. They are of central importance. If the total attempts at border crossing outside the ports (entry without inspection, in government jargon) are roughly in the range of 500,000 to one million annually, the total crossings at legitimate ports are 400–500 million—500–1,000 times more. Yet we rarely think about ports in the public imagination, which is dominated by images of unauthorized border crossers. Ports are crucial to the North American economy. They are the mainstay of border communities, which largely have grown up around them. The border—in a literal sense—is the totality of these barriers, openings, laws, and government agencies (Heyman 1999b). It is far more complex and subtle, then, than a line on a map.

We may think of the border as a giant filter, if we realize that such a metaphor is far too simple and also too automatic. It is in fact a complicated web of action and counteraction among many different people. It "sorts" (Adey 2004)—that is, distinguishes among, categorizes, and treats differently (from prison sentences to 10 seconds of smiles and greetings), the various people, conveyances, and goods that cross the border. Even the attempted interdiction outside the ports of entry (the wall, the patrols, the sensors, the planes and helicopters, and so forth) may be considered the most extreme, most negative form of sorting. The Mexicans and Central Americans who try to enter illegally, for example, do not do that in most cases, because they positively want to break the law, but because they have no chance of obtaining legal visas to work, to be with their families, and to reside in the United States. They are the least well connected, poorer, unable to travel to the United States openly, etc.—the most vulnerable, the most marginalized—sorted out to struggle through deserts, to pay smugglers, perhaps to die.

At the ports of entry, more complex sorting takes place (Heyman 2004). Ports broadly are places where entry and exit is legitimate, is allowed. But there are various potentially illegal goods and entries mixed into this legitimate flow. So port inspectors need to sort through entries, but in extremely rapid time, so traffic does not build up. Thirty seconds is the standard for initial ("primary") inspection and the go/further examination decision—30 seconds to decide who or what enters the national territory. There are two fundamental political-economic considerations here. One is what people and goods are sorted for/against by each government, and the politics, economics, and ideology behind those emphases. The United States inspects every person, but only 3–7% of each item of cargo. People, in the United States, are more suspect than commodities, though each brings benefits (visitors, legitimate travelers, legal trade goods) and risks (unauthorized workers, possible terrorists, possible drugs, possible terrorist materials in cargo).

This is an extension of the general pattern by which the United States favors capital and commodities ("free trade"), but does not liberate the movement of labor (Heyman 1999b). Even among commodities, there are important differences in sorting—between, say, legal psychotropic drugs imported from Mexico (alcohol) and illegalized ones (from Mexico, some marijuana, some heroin, and most cocaine supplies). Mexico too shows its political economy in what it sorts out—guns from the United States, because US guns are easily available and are used often to kill in Mexico, the deadly inverse of the destructive drug trade. Many consumer retail items are subtly protected in Mexico. In both countries, it is not just what is sorted out but also, importantly, who and what is privileged to enter.

Besides the differentiation among people and goods, there are complicated decisions made by port inspectors. In 30 seconds of primary decision, and a few minutes of secondary decision (and rare, longer inspections), inspectors apply an amazing set of social and psychological judgments—documentary evidence, legal categories, apparent nationality, apparent race (conflating Mexicans with people of Mexican ancestry), apparent class (assuming that would-be workers look poorer than would-be businessmen and rich shoppers), language (linked sometimes to nationality), gender, age, sometimes sexuality, stories, interactional cues, and nonverbal and paraverbal behavior. Each of these, obviously, bears detailed social analysis that tells us much about who is privileged and who is at risk (of inspection, delay, arrest) in border crossing. The totality, too, tells us about power and privilege, powerlessness, and marginality—the social figures who move about the world at ease, the ones who travel with fear or with smugglers (Heyman 2009a, b).

To make sense of it all—and it is indeed complex but important—we can envision three ways the border filters flows or creates responses to them:

- *Favored flows* —Flows that are legal and in some cases facilitated in crossing the border (though still delayed and hassled by traffic and inspections at the border)
- *Interdiction of flows* —Efforts to define specific flows as forbidden (especially not allowed entry into the national territory)
- *Defiant flows*—Responses to interdiction, defiant flows attempt to avoid, indeed defy government authority (Spener 2009), though in the process, they accept other forms of domination (employers of migrant labor, purchasers of guns and drugs, and so forth; Campbell and Heyman 2007, pp. 23–24)

To these, we must add another distinction between long-distance flows that go from places deep in a national interior, pass through the border, and end deep in the other national interior, and local flows between communities each just on the other side of the boundary. The combination of these elements can be seen in this table:

	Favored flows	Interdiction of flows	Defiant flows
Long distance	Continental trade in auto parts	Border patrolling of migration and guns, drugs, and money	Unauthorized migrants; smuggling of guns, drugs, and money
Short distance	Local shopping; family visiting	Port of entry inspections	"Ant" smuggling (Gauthier 2010): fruits, medicines, used clothing, and other goods

The border system, then, is a dynamic interaction of boundary filters with all these various flows. The border system, its flows and filters, in turn tie together a large part of the continental society and economy.

The filtering system of the border, especially the sorting of long-distance flows, is central to the system of capital, power, and privilege in North America. (Short-distance flows matter, of course, more to border communities.) By making workers coming northward more desperate, more in debt (to smugglers and kin), and more vulnerable, the defiant flows produce a superexploited working class (Heyman 1998a, 2001b; Kearney 2004). By favoring comfortable executive travelers, shoppers, and tourists, it facilitates their higher-ranking roles in the political economy, as well as their social status. By freeing most business investment and commodities (but not all) to move, unlike labor, the border creates a unified continent for capitalism but divided for workers and community dwellers. By dividing Mexico and the United States as governments, it perpetuates the ideology of nation-states, making them seem very separate and distinct, while allowing extensive integration in reality, as in the manufacture of "American" cars. It is a subtle but profound filter (Heyman 1999b; Kearney 2004).

Major Border Phenomena

The political-economic perspective emphasizes the power of clear, abstract analytical reasoning to penetrate and explain the hurly-burly surface of everyday life. This has been the goal so far in this chapter. It is useful, next, to summarize the major empirical phenomena that shape the borderlands, which have emerged from these political-economic dynamics (also see Ruiz 2000). First, for example, are the maquiladoras, the Mexican-side (mainly) export manufacturing plants, in which transnational corporations take advantage of the huge profits in controlling combined and uneven exchange across the border (mediating inexpensive Mexican labor and prosperous North American consumers). Even with strains from competition from China and Central America, and violence in urban border Mexico, the maquiladoras are a world-scale manufacturing complex with over a million employees in Mexico, mostly still at the northern border. They remain the mainstay of Mexico's border cities and are indirectly important to the economies of US border cities. Maquiladora products can be found in all corners of North American life (see citations earlier in this chapter).

Besides the maquiladora-based exchange of parts and products, the border is vital to the continental trade system. Mexico is the third largest US trade partner, and the United States is Mexico's first, and almost all this trade flows through the land border ports. Numerous roles exist in this trade, required great cross-cultural dexterity, as documented in Robert Alvarez's (2005) outstanding ethnography of the North American fruit and vegetable trade. Local trade of goods and services is also vital in the region. Besides its economic impact, border trade encourages the pervasive binationalism and biculturalism of many border people (Martínez 1994).

Guns, money, and drugs are important part of border trade, although to various extents illegalized and defiant trades (Campbell 2009); they are closely interconnected. Guns and ammunition are easily available in the United States, but heavily restricted in Mexico; there is thus an active smuggling trade bringing these harmful commodities across the border. Some drugs (marijuana, heroin, cocaine, methamphetamine components) are not only illegal but heavily interdicted in the United States, and more weakly so in Mexico. There is also an active smuggling trade bringing these harmful commodities across the border. Money, power, and status are the goals. Unaccountable liquid cash specifically drives the system, moving from prosperous consumers in North America to the pyramidal transnational drug cartels of Mexico, the United States, and South America. Northern Mexican border cities, termed "plazas," are valuable locations to assemble drugs in smuggleable form to defy US law enforcement in border crossing. As a result, extreme violence is exerted to control these plazas. On the US side, the guns-money-drug economy is also important (it is plausibly speculated that most drugs move through US ports of entry alongside legal goods), but conducted in a very quiet and peaceful way.

Migratory movement through the border includes nonimmigrant visitors, going in each direction, US citizens to reside in Mexico (e.g., retirees), legal immigrants to the United States, and unauthorized migrants from Mexico, Central America, and in smaller numbers other countries to the United States. Parts of this migratory system, though not all, are systematically presented and analyzed in Massey et al. (2002). It is worth emphasizing that there are both long-distance migratory flows through border communities that impact local economy and society and constant day-to-day movement that substantially shape border life. Hundreds of thousands (but we do not know how many) of US citizens live in Mexico, but travel often to the United States, or Mexican citizens in the reciprocal pattern (anecdotally, see Martínez 1994). The term mobility is increasingly being used to describe the wider patterns of complex movement within and across boundaries (Cunningham and Heyman 2004), something that the more substantial moves of migration does not seem to capture. Mobility actions, rights, regulations, enforcement, and defiance are mainstays of border communities.

Both central states are hypertrophied at the border, for reasons discussed above (flow inspection and interdiction), but the US state at the border is much more massive, expensive, and powerful—one of the largest assemblages of coercive force in a peaceful location in the world (Andreas 2009).[4] Tony Payan (2006) has usefully characterized US border policy as mixing up three separate initiatives, three separate policy domains, or as he critically terms them, "the three border wars." These are migration inspection and interdiction, illegal drug-money-arms interdiction, and prevention of terrorists and materials entering the homeland. As Payan points out, these are three very different issues, involving very different tactics and organizations of enforcement, yet they are allocated to the same agency, the Department of Homeland Security, and are merged as border fears/threats at the ideological level. In particular, Heyman and Ackleson (2009) have shown that border enforcement matches poorly its national security task and remains overwhelmingly focused on low-level undocumented migrants.

National security is more important as an ideological justification of border enforcement than its real agenda, the fear of the Mexicanization of the United States. As Timothy Dunn (1996, 2009) has demonstrated, this focus on controlling little people (poor migrants, rather than genuine security threats) is a bit like a low-level war or, in the military jargon, low-intensity conflict. It has resulted in the US military being assigned to the border periodically, but equally important, the civilian border enforcement apparatus becoming more and more military in its technology, tactics, surveillance, and ideological persuasion tools. "Securitization" is another way of analyzing this (Heyman 2009a and references therein). It is the practical, rhetorical, ideological, and political process of turning standard civilian policy issues into matters of alleged national security and turning existential threats to the state equivalent of mass warfare. Payan's point about the merging of the three very different border "wars" reflects securitization. In any case, these trends profoundly affect border life, both exacerbating the delays and barriers at the border and sustaining a large number of employees and contractors in well-paid federal law enforcement jobs who substantially affect US-side border society.

Border Communities in Political-Economic Perspective

The main reason that there are millions of people living in large urban clusters along the US-Mexico border are the flows, channeled into bottlenecks (ports and barriers), passing through the boundary (Alegría Olazábal 2009; Herzog 1999; Staudt et al. 2010). Although there are some natural settlement areas (passes, river valleys) on the border, most border settlements are products of the boundary line itself. In particular, the border has grown around the many sources of values and profits to be had by mediating the combined but uneven exchanges back and forth between the United States and Mexico. For a systematic survey of this statement, see Heyman (2007).

[4]Violence is extensive and horrific in northern border Mexico, but not at all on the US side, where the US government presence is assembled. The Mexican coercive state presence has grown in this region, due to military intervention. Most US government operations at the border do not seek violence reduction in Mexico, as discussed in the text.

Twin cities, one Mexican and one American, each centered on a crossing point, characterize the border. Usually, the Mexican city is larger than the US city (the exception is that metropolitan San Diego is larger than metropolitan Tijuana). The Mexican border cities have been dynamic sources of employment, attracting extensive internal migration. US border cities perform more unevenly, and many have chronic patterns of unemployment and underemployment. At the same time, US border cities are still more prosperous on average than Mexican border cities. We need to realize, however, that both countries are highly unequal, and there are absolutely wealthy and absolutely poor people on both sides. The border has an apparent paradox: it is one of the most prosperous parts of Mexico and one of the poorest parts of the United States, but still, the US side is better off than the Mexican side. This applies not only to strictly economic views but also quality of life measures (health, education, etc.), as seen in the informative statistical survey of conditions in all border municipalities by Anderson and Gerber (2008).

A major stressor in the border region is its rapid urban growth. The border region's infrastructure badly lags its population expansion. Big political-economic interests (maquiladoras, government enforcement bureaucracies, smugglers) profit from the region while paying few of the social expenses, such as paving streets, installing clean water and sewage systems, providing public transportation, and so forth (Kopinak 2004). Planning systems at the border are absent or poorly implemented, exacerbated by the difficulty of binational coordination (Peña 2006, 2007). In addition, a number of small settlements remain desperately poor, isolated, and underserved, including home places of many Native Americans and working class Mexicanos.

We can think of the border region's challenges as combining the *social costs of prosperity* (a poorly prepared and supported boom) and the *social costs of poverty* (large numbers of low-wage workers or workers in sporadic, informal employment sectors). This paradoxical mix is manifested clearly in growing informal settlements, colonias (United States) or *colonias populares* (Mexico), which fundamentally stem from the need of low-income workers to find housing near their employment (see Chap. 6 in this book and Núñez 2009; Núñez and Klamminger 2010; Ward 1999). Colonias are not simply a manifestation of failure, poverty, and misery; they are often actually an accomplishment in the struggle for survival in the face of multiple marginalities, within a region of dynamic growth and in-migration but little investment in housing and services. Still, they deserve more political power and infrastructural support.

Ordinary Life Amid Political, Economic, and Ideological Behemoths

Border people experience the triumphs and tragedies, successes, and struggles of everyday life amid these massive complexes of power, profit, barrier, and exchange. "Lifeworlds" is a term of art that links intimate domains, such as relations between children and parents, with wider patterns and forces. A number of sensitive studies explore these connections (Fernández-Kelly 1983; Heyman 1991; Martínez 1994; Núñez and Heyman 2007; Richardson 1999; Richardson and Resendiz 2006; Talavera 2008; Velasco Ortíz 2005; Vélez-Ibañez 1996, 2010; Vila 2000, 2005; Wright 2006). Of course, individuals and small social groups have a degree of autonomy, variability, and initiative, but they are never-absent social-cultural contexts and influences. Personal, social, and cultural domains, in turn, are situated within large-scale political, economic, and ideological dynamics.

One of the more perceptive and empirically rich efforts to explore these issue is Pablo Vila's (2000, 2005) ethnography of narratives of self and others at the border. In this work, he shows the mutual construction of intimate ideas about self and wider ideologies of nation-state, class, race, modernity, and so forth. For example, Mexican Americans face a dominant society narrative that all poverty is Mexican and that all Mexicans are "aliens," both stereotypes being demonstrably false or misleading. Their counternarrative is to identify themselves as US citizens, though proud of Mexican culture, and to portray poverty as applying to the Mexican side but not themselves. Vila provides such analysis across a range of narrative positions, in both Mexico and the United States, in what amounts to a whole network of mutual comparisons and reflections in the socially charged environment of the borderlands.

I have taken a related, but not identical, tack, in which I suggest that the pattern of combined and uneven development is not just economic but also one that shapes intimate feelings and thoughts (Heyman 1994). It particularly implies that no one idea or cultural practice can ever be sufficient, since that sort of relation requires the juncture of radically different, even opposite elements—rich and poor, capital and labor, state and migrant. I suggested that the apparent mixed-up, hybridized style of many people and practices at the border (Garcia Canclini 1995) is in fact a reflection of the contradictory unity of combined and uneven relationships (Heyman 2001a, 2010a).

Still, there is much more to be learned about the connection of wider forces and lifeworlds on both sides of the border. It is useful simply to list some of the key variables—gender, sexual orientation, age, generation, kin relation, and so forth—and ask how they interact with the border reinforcement, border erasure, and combined and uneven relations, with the various flows and barriers and with the major political, economic, and ideological complexes listed earlier in this chapter. It is also important to emphasize that individuals do not occupy lifeworlds alone, but rather as members of cooperative households, friendships, and peer groups. Such intimate groups both have internal dynamics of equality and power and also interact with ideas, resources, and power relations at larger scales (the political economy). Finally, it is important to emphasize that people occupy their lifeworlds in mental ways (as seen in Vila's narrative identities) and corporeal ways (as seen dramatically in the deaths of migrants in mountains, deserts, and canals, discussed in Payan's chapter, and also Cornelius 2001; Eshbach et al. 1999, 2001; Rubio-Goldsmith et al. 2007). Far too little is known about how this lifeworld-dominant political economy plays out in the highly charged and dynamic binational environment of the borderlands.

Bordering the Future

The political-economic perspective often is critical, pointing out social injustices, but it also tends to be pessimistic. Focusing on unequal power, and emphasizing the workings of deep and profound forces, makes it hard to see how to escape such workings. This is undoubtedly true, but should not hold us back from such efforts as we are able to make, either in shorter-term/more intimate amelioration of suffering or longer-term/more collective struggles for social justice. While collective action at the border faces considerable challenges, it does occur with regularity (Staudt and Coronado 2002).

Staudt (2009) and Staudt et al. (2009) explore feminist theory as a basis for rethinking the concept of security and particularly border security to include what really matters to the life and well-being of people. Heyman (1998b) uses deep explorations in human nature from anthropology to argue for mutual moral obligations that emerge between migrants and hosts and in turn takes this moral argument to the stage of proposing a practical alternative immigration policy architecture for the United States. Hing (2010) takes a different tack, examining the European Union, with limitations, as a model for using development to reduce migration pressures, in the process reducing the use of borders as barriers. He points out that the European Union provided an alternative vision to NAFTA, which regulates the US-Mexico border, which frees capital to move investments, property rights, and goods around the continent, but not for people themselves to cross boundaries. Dunn (2009) provides an important vision of nonnationalistic human rights, building on borderlander efforts to curb abuses of border enforcement. And several engaged social scientists and activists have examined the lessons of the El Paso-based Border Network for Human Rights and the Border and Immigration Task Force as a community-based, policy-oriented, social movement and related civil society coalition (García 2008; Heyman et al. 2009; Heyman 2010b).

The US-Mexico border is a vision into the future. It is youthful, growing, and dynamic. It is transnational, combined and uneven, culturally mixed, and creative. It is also poorly supplied with infrastructure and community services, and far too many people suffer from material poverty. It is a testing place for the North American continental synthesis. Which politics, which economics, and which ideology we embrace matters, not just to the borderlands but to the future of all of us.

References

Adey, P. (2004). Secured and sorted mobilities: Examples from the airport. *Surveillance and Society, 1*, 500–519.

Alegría Olazábal, T. (2009). *Metrópolis transfronteriza: Revisión de la hipótesis y evidencias de Tijuana, Mexico y San Diego, Estados Unidos* [Transborder metropolis: Revision of the hypothesis and evidence of Tijuana, Mexico and San Diego, United States] Mexico City: Miguel Angel Porrúa.

Alvarez, R., Jr. (2005). *Mangos, chiles, and truckers: The business of transnationalism*. Minneapolis: University of Minnesota Press.

Anderson, J., & Gerber, J. (2008). *Fifty years of change on the U.S.-Mexico border: Growth, development, and quality of life*. Austin: University of Texas Press.

Andreas, P. (2009). *Border games: Policing the U.S.-Mexico divide* (2nd ed.). Ithaca: Cornell University Press.

Border Network for Human Rights. (2010, August 10). *Border community security poll: Border residents say they feel safe living on the U.S. border.* Retrieved January 5, 2010, from http://bnhr.org/wp-content/uploads/2010/08/BorderPollREPORT.pdf

Campbell, H. (2009). *Drug war zone: Frontline dispatches from the streets of El Paso and Juárez.* Austin: University of Texas Press.

Campbell, H., & Heyman, J. (2007). Slantwise: Beyond domination and resistance on the border. *Journal of Contemporary Ethnography, 36*, 3–30.

Cardoso, F., & Faletto, E. (1979). *Dependency and development in Latin America*. Berkley: University of California Press.

Chavez, L. (1998). *Shadowed lives: Undocumented immigrants in American society* (Rev. edn). Forth Worth: Harcourt Brace College Publishers.

Chavez, L. (2001). *Covering immigration: Popular images and the politics of the nation*. Berkeley: University of California Press.

Cornelius, W. (2001). Death at the border: Efficacy and unintended consequences of US immigration control policy. *Population and Development Review, 27*, 661–685.

Cunningham, H., & Heyman, J. M. (2004). Introduction: Mobilities and enclosures at borders. *Identities: Global Studies in Culture and Power, 11*, 289–302.

Douglas, M. (1966). *Purity and danger: An analysis of pollution and taboo*. London: Routledge & Kegan Paul.

Dunn, T. (1996). *The militarization of the U.S.-Mexico border, 1978–1992: Low-intensity conflict doctrine comes home*. Austin: CMAS Books/University of Texas at Austin.

Dunn, T. (2009). *Blockading the border and human rights: The El Paso operation that remade immigration enforcement*. Austin: University of Texas Press.

Eshbach, K., Hagen, J., Rodríguez, N., Hernández-León, R., & Bailey, S. (1999). Death at the border. *International Migration Review, 33*, 430–440.

Eshbach, K., Hagen, J., & Rodríguez, N. (2001). Deaths during undocumented migration: Trends and policy implications in the new era of homeland security. *In Defense of the Alien, 26*, 37–52.

Fernández, R. (1977). *The United States-Mexico border: A politico-economic profile*. Notre Dame: University of Notre Dame Press.

Fernández-Kelly, M. (1983). *For we are sold, I and my people: Women and industry in Mexico's frontier*. Albany: State University of New York Press.

Frank, A. (1970). *Latin America: Underdevelopment or revolution*. New York: Monthly Review Press.

Ganster, P., & Lorey, D. (2008). *The U.S.-Mexican border into the twenty-first century* (2nd ed.). Lanham: Rowman & Littlefield.

García, F. (2008). Human rights and immigrants in the U.S.: An experience of border communities. *Georgetown Immigration Law Journal, 22*, 405–414.

Garcia Canclini, N. (1995). *Hybrid cultures: Strategies for entering and leaving modernity*. Minneapolis: University of Minnesota Press.

Gauthier, M. (2010). Researching the border's economic underworld: The 'fayuca hormiga' in the U.S.-Mexico borderlands. In H. Donnan & T. Wilson (Eds.), *Borderlands: Ethnographic approaches to security, power, and identity* (pp. 21–34). Lanham: University Press of America.

Gomberg-Muñoz, R. (2011). *Labor and legality: An ethnography of a Mexican immigrant network*. New York: Oxford University Press.

Grimson, A., & Vila, P. (2002). Forgotten border actors: The border reinforcers. A comparison between the U.S.-Mexico border and South American borders. *Journal of Political Ecology, 9*, 69–88.

Herzog, L. (1999). *From Aztec to high tech: Architecture and landscape across the Mexico-United States border*. Baltimore: The Johns Hopkins University Press.
Heyman, J. (1991). *Life and labor on the border: Working people of northeastern Sonora, Mexico 1886–1986*. Tucson: University of Arizona Press.
Heyman, J. (1994). The Mexico-United States border in anthropology: A critique and reformulation. *Journal of Political Ecology,1,* 43–65. Retrieved January 6, 2011, from http://jpe.library.arizona.edu/volume_1/HEYMAN.PDF
Heyman, J. (1998a). State effects on labor exploitation: The INS and undocumented immigrants at the Mexico-United States border. *Critique of Anthropology, 18*, 157–180.
Heyman, J. M. (1998b). *Finding a moral heart for the U.S. immigration policy: An anthropological perspective*. Washington, DC: American Anthropological Association.
Heyman, J. (1999a). Why interdiction? Immigration law enforcement at the United States-Mexico border. *Regional Studies, 33*, 619–630.
Heyman, J. M. (1999b). State escalation of force: A Vietnam/US-Mexico border analogy. In J. M. Heyman (Ed.), *States and illegal practices* (pp. 285–314). Oxford: Berg Publishers.
Heyman, J. (2001a). On U.S.-Mexico border culture. *Journal of the West, 40*(2), 50–59.
Heyman, J. (2001b). Class and classification on the U.S.-Mexico border. *Human Organization, 60*, 128–140.
Heyman, J. (2004). Ports of entry as nodes in the world system. *Identities: Global studies in culture and power, 11*, 303–327.
Heyman, J. (2007). Environmental issues at the U.S.-Mexico border and the unequal territorialization of value. In A. Hornborg, J. McNeill, & J. Martinez-Alier (Eds.), *Rethinking environmental history: World-system history and global environmental change* (pp. 327–344). Walnut Creek: AltaMira Press.
Heyman, J. (2009a). Ports of entry in the 'homeland security' era: Inequality of mobility and the securitization of transnational flows. In S. Martinez (Ed.), *International migration and human rights: The global repercussions of U.S. policy* (pp. 44–59). Berkeley: University of California Press.
Heyman, J. (2009b). Trust, privilege, and discretion in the governance of the US borderlands with Mexico. *Canadian Journal of Law and Society/Revue Canadienne Droit et Societe, 24*, 367–390.
Heyman, J. (2010a). US-Mexico border cultures and the challenge of asymmetrical interpenetration. In H. Donnan & T. M. Wilson (Eds.), *Borderlands: Ethnographic approaches to security, power, and identity* (pp. 21–34). Lanham: University Press of America.
Heyman, J. (2010b, May 10). The border network for human rights: Building an immigrant movement in the besieged borderlands. *Blog entry, Race Talk*. http://www.race-talk.org/?p=4210, Kirwan Institute, Ohio State University.
Heyman, J., & Ackleson, J. (2009). United States border security after September 11. In J. Winterdyck & K. Sundberg (Eds.), *Border security in the Al-Qaeda era* (pp. 37–74). Boca Raton: CRC Press.
Heyman, J., & Campbell, H. (2010). Bordering culture: The U.S.-Mexico case. In E. P. Durrenberger & S. Erem (Eds.), *Paradigms for anthropology: An ethnographic reader* (pp. 189–201). Boulder: Paradigm Publishers.
Heyman, J., Morales, M., & Núñez, G. (2009). Engaging with the immigrant human rights movement in a besieged border region: What do applied social scientists bring to the policy process? *NAPA Bulletin, 31*, 13–29.
Hing, B. (2010). *Ethical borders: NAFTA, globalization, and Mexican migration*. Philadelphia: Temple University Press.
Kearney, M. (2004). The classifying and value-filtering missions of borders. *Anthropological Theory, 4*, 131–156.
Kopinak, K. (1996). *Desert capitalism: Maquiladoras in North America's western industrial corridor*. Tucson: University of Arizona Press.
Kopinak, K. (Ed.). (2004). *The social costs of industrial growth in northern Mexico*. La Jolla, San Diego: Center for U.S.-Mexican Studies, University of California.

Leiken, R., & Brooke, S. (2006). The quantitative analysis of terrorism and immigration: An initial exploration. *Terrorism and Political Violence, 18*, 503–521.

Martínez, O. (1988). *Troublesome border*. Tucson: University of Arizona Press.

Martínez, O. (1994). *Border people: Life and society in the U.S.-Mexico borderlands*. Tucson: University of Arizona Press.

Martínez, G. (2006). *Mexican Americans and language: Del dicho al hecho*. Tucson: University of Arizona Press.

Massey, D., Durand, J., & Malone, N. (2002). *Beyond smoke and mirrors: Mexican immigration in an era of economic integration*. New York: Russell Sage.

Nagengast, C., Stavenhagen, R., & Kearney, M. (1992). *Human rights and indigenous workers: The Mixtecs in Mexico and the United States*. La Jolla, San Diego: Center for U.S.-Mexican Studies, University of California.

Nevins, J. (2010). *Operation gatekeeper and beyond: The war on "illegals" and the remaking of the U.S.-Mexico boundary*. New York: Routledge.

Núñez, G. (2009). The political ecology of the colonias on the U.S.-Mexico border: Human-environmental challenges and community responses in southern New Mexico. *Southern Rural Sociology, 24*, 67–91.

Núñez, G., & Heyman, J. (2007). Entrapment processes and immigrant communities in a time of heightened border vigilance. *Human Organization, 66*, 354–365.

Núñez, G., & Klamminger, G. (2010). Centering the margins: The transformation of community on the U.S.-Mexico border. In K. Staudt, C. Fuentes, & J. E. Monárrez Fregoso (Eds.), *Cities and citizenship at the U.S.-Mexico border: The Paso del Norte metropolitan region* (pp. 147–172). New York: Palgrave Macmillan.

Olson, E., Shirk, D., & Selee, A. (Eds.). (2010). *Shared responsibility: U.S.-Mexico policy options for confronting organized crime*. Washington, DC/San Diego: The Woodrow International Center for Scholars and the Trans-Border Institute, University of San Diego.

Ortíz-González, V. (2004). *El Paso: Local frontiers at a global crossroads*. Minneapolis: University of Minnesota Press.

Payan, T. (2006). *The three US-Mexico border wars: Drugs, immigration, and homeland security*. Westport: Praeger Security International.

Peña, D. (1997). *The terror of the machine: Technology, work, gender, and ecology on the U.S.-Mexico border*. Austin: Center for Mexican American Studies, University of Texas at Austin.

Peña, S. (2006). Contingency planning + the border space. *Projections, 6*, 14–35.

Peña, S. (2007). Cross-border planning at the U.S.-Mexico border: An institutional approach. *Journal of Borderlands Studies, 22*, 1–18.

Richardson, C. (1999). *Batos, bolillos, pochos, and pelados: Class and culture on the south Texas border*. Austin: University of Texas Press.

Richardson, C., & Resendiz, R. (2006). *On the edge of the law: Culture, labor, and deviance on the south Texas border*. Austin: University of Texas Press.

Rippberger, S., & Staudt, K. (2002). *Pledging allegiance: Learning nationalism at the El Paso-Juárez border*. New York: Routledge/Falmer.

Rubio-Goldsmith, R., McCormick, M., Martinez, D., & Duarte, I. (2007). *A humanitarian crisis at the border: New estimates of deaths among unauthorized immigrants*. Washington, DC: Immigration Policy Center.

Ruiz, R. (2000). *On the rim of Mexico: Encounters of the rich and poor*. Boulder: Westview Press.

Spener, D. (2009). *Clandestine crossings: Migrants and coyotes on the Texas-Mexico border*. Ithaca: Cornell University Press.

Spener, D., & Staudt, K. (1998). *Transcending divisions, contesting identities*. Boulder: Lynne Rienner.

Staudt, K. (1998). *Free trade? Informal economies at the U.S.-Mexican border*. Philadelphia: Temple University Press.

Staudt, K. (2009). Violence at the border: Broadening the discourse to include feminism, human security, and deeper democracy. In K. A. Staudt, T. Payan, & Z. A. Kruszewski (Eds.), *Human rights along the U.S.-Mexico border: Gendered violence and insecurity* (pp. 1–28). Tucson: University of Arizona Press.

Staudt, K., & Coronado, I. (2002). *Fronteras no más: Toward social justice at the U.S.-Mexico border*. New York: Palgrave Macmillan.
Staudt, K., Payan, T., & Dunn, T. (2009). Closing reflections: Border human rights, social democratic feminism, and broad-based security. In K. A. Staudt, T. Payan, & Z. A. Kruszewski (Eds.), *Human rights along the U.S.-Mexico border: Gendered violence and insecurity* (pp. 185–202). Tucson: University of Arizona Press.
Staudt, K., Fuentes, C., & Monárrez Fragoso, J. (Eds.). (2010). *Cities and citizenship at the U.S.-Mexico border: The Paso del Norte metropolitan region*. New York: Palgrave Macmillan.
Stuart, J., & Kearney, M. (1981). *Causes and effects of agricultural labor migration from the Mixteca of Oaxaca to California*. La Jolla: Program in U.S.-Mexican Studies, University of California, San Diego.
Talavera, V. (2008). *Factors affecting health behaviors in Mexican immigrant households: A case study approach conducted in the rural U.S.-Mexican border community of Tornillo, Texas*. Saarbrücken: VDM Verlag.
Velasco Ortíz, L. (2005). *Mixtec transnational identity*. Tucson: University of Arizona Press.
Vélez-Ibañez, C. (1996). *Border visions: Mexican cultures of the southwest United States*. Tucson: University of Arizona Press.
Vélez-Ibáñez, C. (2010). *An impossible living in a transborder world: Culture, confianza, and economy of Mexican-origin populations*. Tucson: University of Arizona Press.
Vila, P. (2000). *Crossing borders, reinforcing borders: Social categories, metaphors, and narrative identities on the U.S.-Mexico frontier*. Austin: University of Texas Press.
Vila, P. (2005). *Border identifications: Narratives of religion, gender, and class on the U.S.-Mexico border*. Austin: University of Texas Press.
Ward, P. M. (1999). *Colonias and public policy in Texas and Mexico: Urbanization by stealth*. Austin: University of Texas Press.
Weber, M. (1946). *From Max Weber: Essays in sociology* (H. Gerth & C. W. Mills, Eds. & Trans.). New York: Oxford University Press.
Wolf, E. (1982). *Europe and the people without history*. Berkeley: University of California Press.
Wolf, E. (1999). *Envisioning power: Ideologies of dominance and crisis*. Berkeley: University of California Press.
Wright, M. (2006). *Disposable women and other myths of global capitalism*. New York: Routledge.

Chapter 3
How Citizenship Produces Inclusion and Exclusion on the US-Mexico Border

Tony Payan

Introduction

The American immigration system as it stands today has become a patchwork of laws, rules, and regulations that contain an increasing number of contradictions from legal, economic, racial, and political standpoints.[1] In effect, the system embodies concepts that are highly controversial among critical scholars. Many of these scholars criticize the immigration system because it has created, like tectonic plates, contradictory layers of law and justice, and in the process it has exacerbated the divisions and inequalities created by global capitalism. Legally and constitutionally, the immigration system has created separate tiers of justice for citizens, pitting them against residents with papers and against residents without papers. Economically, the system pits the poor against the rich, punishing the "have-nots" and increasingly privileging the "haves" in everything from employment to access to the welfare state. Politically, the immigration system has created privileged spaces (in participation, protest, voting, etc.) against oppressive or exclusionary spaces for those considered "outsiders." It reinforces the political disenfranchisement of the outsiders up against those considered insiders. In addition, racially, the system has raised tensions between white and nonwhite populations. The contradictions and tensions inherent today in the American immigration system do not flow from the mélange of laws and regulations as it has evolved since the 1980s alone or even from them in combination with the exclusionary processes of globalization but have to do with the culture of security that prevails since September 11, 2001, as well.

[1]For the reasons why the Immigration and Naturalization Service was dismantled and how it was recreated, see Donovan (2005).

T. Payan (✉)
Department of Political Science, University of Texas at El Paso
e-mail: lapayan@utep.edu

M. Lusk et al. (eds.), *Social Justice in the U.S.-Mexico Border Region*,
DOI 10.1007/978-94-007-4150-8_3, © Springer Science+Business Media B.V. 2012

This new layer of security added to it creates even more contradictions in the system because it places individuals not as the subjects of security but as the objects of security and puts even more emphasis on the idea that anyone, anytime, anywhere can be a threat to the integrity of the nation-state itself. Security has been injected into the immigration system like a plague of nanorobots, invading every individual process within the already convoluted immigration system. The result, I argue, is that the system has created even more vulnerability and disenfranchisement than ever before and divided territory from population, geographical boundaries from legal boundaries, and wealth generation from economic citizenship and has given shape to a generalized system of castes among various social groups. This system of disenfranchisement and vulnerability pivots around the possession or lack of documents.

Nowhere are the contradictions and tensions of the immigration system, with the tiers of privilege that it creates, more evident than on the US-Mexico border. To show this, this chapter takes a few cases: Alonso, Adrián, Efraín, Gabriel, Gastón, and Raúl. These are real people living on the US-Mexico border. Each of them has been caught by the grinding power of the American immigration system. Their lives, alone and in contrast to each other, are clear examples of the dislocations that the system has created. In order to eke from their cases the contradictions that are found in the American immigration system, this chapter briefly explains the case of each of them. It highlights some of their individual situations and draws from them evidence to make the argument that the current immigration system is legally, economically, politically, and racially unjust and probably unsustainable in the long run. This is not to mention that over time, it has created tensions that rub against the American constitution, American capitalism, and American values. This, I argue, makes the system indefensible. In the end, the need for a more just immigration reform is reaffirmed.

The Cases[2]

Alonso is a young man who was born in Mexico. His parents brought him to the United States early on and made him a US citizen. Alonso attended school on both sides of the border and is perfectly bilingual and bicultural. Alonso has enjoyed all the opportunities of a dual citizen and has finally moved away from the border to pursue an academic degree. Alonso has been in trouble with the law twice because of drunk driving. Alonso has been able to settle those issues through the various legal venues available to US citizens. While in the county jail, however, the first time

[2]These are real persons, living today on the US-Mexico border, on one side or the other, and with whom I have had continued contact over several years, witnessing their personal drama, which pivots considerably around their American citizenship or lack thereof. The names of these individuals have been changed.

he was arrested, he was quickly visited by Immigration and Customs Enforcement (ICE) agents and asked if he was a US citizen. After showing proof that he was a US citizen, he was left alone to continue with his legal process.

Adrián is a young man who was born in El Paso, Texas, to Mexican parents. His parents did what many Mexican parents along the US-Mexico border do. They crossed the borderline and made sure that Adrián was born in the United States. Adrián's parents understood that *ex soli* American citizenship is an advantage that they were leaving to their child. They also knew that it has little to do with civic duty or national loyalty and everything to do with opportunity, access, and mobility. Adrian grew up mostly in Ciudad Juárez but attended school on both sides of the border and is bilingual and binational but clearly prefers Spanish and identifies with the community of Mexican students on the University of Texas at El Paso's campus. Two years ago, Adrián was caught by US inspectors smuggling weapons into Ciudad Juárez in the middle of an already difficult security situation that the city is going through and, eventually, with good legal help, he pled guilty to a relatively minor charge (attempt to smuggle a weapon) and was given a 6-month probation because it was his first offense. Adrián lives in El Paso and continues his studies.

Efraín is a man in his 30s. He was brought to El Paso, Texas, from Mexico when he was a very small child. He was a legal resident of the United States since he was practically a baby. Efraín grew up in El Paso. He went through school in the city and feels more comfortable speaking English and is well versed in the American culture and way of life. He seldom traveled to Mexico and was not well acquainted with the Mexican social, political, or economic system. Efraín was caught driving drunk in El Paso and he was arrested. While he was able to avoid the consequences of that first-time offense, he was caught driving drunk a second time. While in the county jail for that second offense, he was visited by ICE agents. His record was reviewed and eventually he was deported into Ciudad Juárez, across the border from El Paso, Texas. During that review of his case, he came to be considered a "removable alien." Efraín now lives in Ciudad Juárez. He has had considerable trouble adjusting to his new environment. His Spanish is not up to par, and he is often seen as inferior for it. He has not been able to get a good job even though he has a B.A. from the University of Texas at El Paso, and he remains highly dependent on his family's income subsidy from El Paso to make it in Ciudad Juárez. He does not know how to navigate the Mexican voting ID system, the driver's license system, or even the employment and benefits system. He does not know how to access the health-care system or even understands the education system either. His learning curve has been very steep and clearly very difficult. He is patently uncomfortable with the idea of never being able to return to the United States since he became a "removable alien" inside the United States and has become an "excludable alien" once outside the United States. Efraín is clearly suffering and having to make enormous psychological, social, and economic adjustments to his life in Mexico.

Gabriel is a man in his early 40s. He traveled back and forth between Mexico and the United States, sometimes legally (with a B1-B2 visa) and sometimes illegally (across the river in Texas). He was never caught by the Border Patrol, but he was questioned many times by US Customs (now Customs and Border Protection) as he crossed the border. He eventually married an American citizen, and they had two daughters, both born in the United States. Gabriel spent time with them in the United States, but he never bothered to become a legal permanent resident. He started a job as an undocumented worker and was eventually apprehended during an immigration raid and deported to Mexico. He was separated from his daughters and his wife and has not seen them in years, as they do not travel to Mexico. Because he was in the country illegally and he was deported, he has become an "excludable alien" and not likely to qualify for a crossing card (B1-B2 visa), much less for permanent legal residency or citizenship. He is probably condemned to never see his daughters again unless they, as full adults, choose to travel to visit him in Mexico. In fact, the girls he left as children are approaching university age today and show no inclination of wanting to see him. The result of this family separation is not only a psychological price (in the form of resentment from his daughters toward him) but also in a lowered standard of living for the family as Gabriel is not able to send money for them in the United States, where things are considerably more expensive as wages in Mexico are considerably lower. The stories of family separation are becoming more common, as the US government continues to step up its efforts to deport undocumented workers at a faster pace than ever before.

Gastón is a young man whose mother, a Mexican citizen, decided to have him born in El Paso, Texas. She was a nurse in a hospital in Ciudad Juárez, across from El Paso, Texas. When she began to experience the pains of labor, she ran to her car in the middle of the night, crossed the border, and rushed to Thomason Hospital (now University Medical Center) in El Paso, where Gastón was born. Gastón spent his early years in Ciudad Juárez and then finished growing up in El Paso. He later moved to Phoenix, Albuquerque, and back to El Paso. Gastón has been caught with drugs, driving drunk, and has been arrested several times. For the last 10 years, Gastón has gone to school (B.A. and M.A.) and made full use of financial aid to finish his degree. In fact, Gastón has never been able to support himself but has instead made full use of the loans and even welfare benefits available to US citizens. To this day, Gastón continues to struggle to gain a footing, even as he displays a disdain for Mexico and everything Mexican and often expresses contempt for immigrants and wishes that they all be expelled.

Finally, there is Raúl. He came to the United States 20 years before he was detained and deported. He and his wife, who remained without documents in the United States for nearly two decades, were deported and separated from their children, who were born in the United States and are American citizens. Raúl made the decision to bring his daughters to Mexico with him and his wife, where they are growing up. His daughters, however, will likely return to the United States when they grow up, but even though they are American citizens, they will find themselves at a disadvantage because their proficiency in the economic, social, cultural, and political systems of the United States is likely to be low. They will have to make the adjustment that Efraín had to make, but the other way, to the United States.

Behind these brief case descriptions, we find harrowing stories of pain, resentment, separation, disenfranchisement, and vulnerability. Each of them is a different case, and behind each of these men is sometimes an entire family—women and children, who are often left unprotected, without their father, like Gabriel's wife and two daughters who are still in the United States without him; or the case of Raúl's two daughters and son, who are US citizens and condemned to cultural and linguistic disenfranchisement when they decide to return to the United States as adults. Put together, these illustrations lead us to ask: What do these cases have to teach us about the US immigration system? What do these seemingly trivial cases show about the way we deal with people today? What do they reveal about the way we deal with human beings? What are the potential lessons for the current legal, economic, social, and political systems? Let us take each of these elements and, starting from our cases, show why the immigration system is increasingly indefensible.

Territory Versus Law

The most cited argument in favor of the prevailing attitude toward immigration is the rule of law. The rhetoric is largely based on the idea of the necessity to ensure a strict implementation of the law and to ensure that everyone obeys the law. This is a largely conservative argument, and it translates into the argument that undocumented workers broke the law when they entered the country illegally and therefore immigration reform would be tantamount to amnesty.[3] In other words, opponents of immigration reform maintain that an immigration reform that includes regularizing the situation of undocumented workers would be a kind of reward for breaking the law. The invocation of the rule of law goes well beyond the debate on immigration reform. It is now the symbolic foundation in the current immigration system. What is interesting about both the rhetoric and the practices surrounding immigration to the United States is that they reveal the deep tensions between the geographical-territorial understanding of the nation-state and the constitutional-legal system that underlies and sustains it. These tensions amount, in fact, to a dislocation between geography and law. Let us analyze why this is so.

Immigration law enforcement has become a kind of legal no man's land, where US constitutional rights, particularly those rights referring to due process, do not apply. In a general understanding of the law and law enforcement within a democratic context, it is accepted that the geographical territory of a nation and its legal system are coterminous. In fact, the geographical territory of a nation-state and the application of its legal system must be coincident, if a country is to be said truly sovereign over itself and given to the rule of law, let alone democratic. The acceptance of lacunae, where its constitution and the rights of those within its geographical boundaries do not apply, is in and of itself problematic. Unfortunately,

[3]See, for example, the press release by the office of Congressman Roscoe G. Bartlett titled "Kill the Bad Bargain Senate Immigration Bill before It Kills Our Country" found in the Congress member's official website http://bartlett.house.gov/UploadedFiles/IimmigrationBartlettColumn604007.pdf

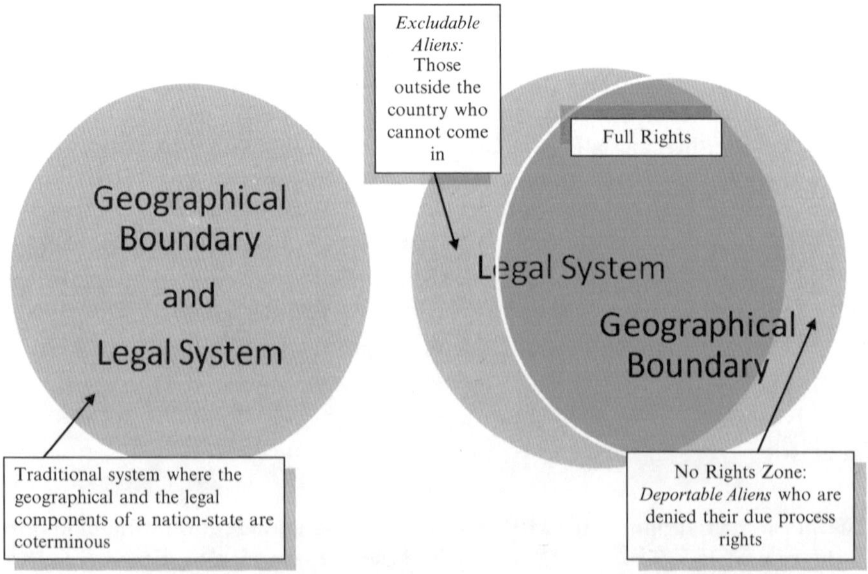

Fig. 3.1 Contrast between the classical view of geopolitical-territorial and legal coincidence and current American immigration enforcement view. Immigrants are increasingly excluded from the "Rights Zone" even if they are physically present in the geographical territory of the United States. Similarly, others are a priori excludable, even if they are not present in US territory

in the United States, the immigration law enforcement system has been moving sideways and has created spaces with no due process rights based on a territorial presence without documentation. In effect, those spaces can be said to amount to a constitution-free zone. Citizens can enjoy the due process given to them by the Constitution, such as the case of Alonso, Adrian, and Gastón, but denied certain rights under due process if they do not hold citizenship but have documents to be in the country, such as Efraín, and denied nearly every right when they do not have any documents, such Gabriel and Raúl. In other words, the immigration enforcement system has created a delegalized space, where bureaucratic discretion prevails and where law enforcement agencies are allowed to deny the applicability of constitutional and even human rights. Figure 3.1 helps us understand this problem of territorial and legal-constitutional dislocation.

In addition to the constitution-free or no-rights zone, where immigrants present within US territory and labeled "deportable" or "removable aliens" and are denied all due process rights, a new zone has also been created, a zone where certain aliens are denied entry a priori, the "excludable aliens." While it is understandable in a traditional system that certain noncitizens may be denied entry before they are present in the territory of a nation-state, it is less understandable that those with a demonstrated physical presence in the territory of the nation-state be denied their rights under the laws of that nation-state. This denial, in fact, rubs right up not only the traditional understanding of territorial and legal boundaries but against the international law.[4] In this new system of immigration law enforcement, which has prevailed in the United States over the last 25 years or so, American courts have increasingly deferred to the executive and its agencies, effectively abdicating their responsibility to adjudicate immigration issues and the very applicability of the US Constitution. It can effectively be said that the United States has a two-tier (and perhaps even a three-tier) justice system, one that applies to individuals that are full citizens and have a physical presence within the area where the geographical boundary and the legal system coincide and those that fall in that geographical area where absolute discretion as to applicability of constitutional and human rights is granted to the executive agencies in charge of immigration issues (BCIS, ICE, etc). In those areas are the excludable aliens (those outside denied entry) and the deportable aliens (those inside being "removed"). Congress, the judicial system, the executive branch, and the public all seem to be at ease with this system where the geographical boundary and the legal boundaries are not coincidental. There seems to be, in fact, a high degree of tolerance for the inapplicability of the constitution to certain individuals, even when these individuals are physically present within US territory. In the end, this marks an explicit denial that the US Constitution applies to all those physically present within US territory and that American constitutional rights are inherently universal and inalienable.

It cannot be denied that some of the characters in our narrative broke the law, either by crossing the border without documents or by driving drunk or engaging in other crimes such as drug possession or even gun smuggling. No one has sympathy for drunk drivers or gun smugglers. Many readers may even say that they deserved what they got. I would reply that some of these individuals are driven to criminal activity precisely because they are denied a decent livelihood in cities with high unemployment or where they are already considered criminals a priori.[5] However, this debate would miss the main point of this chapter, which is not to justify or condemn individuals who break the law or to evoke sympathy toward them but to show how the law itself is unevenly applied, that is, that individuals are dealt with not on an even application of the law but by the papers they possess and that this creates odd boundaries and dislocations that we should be concerned about in a democratic society, particularly one that boasts of its dedication to the rule of law.

There is yet another piece to this puzzle. The concept of expeditious or summary removal is more liberally applied to a band of territory of 100 miles inside of the border of the United States. Within this band, established by the Department of Homeland Security in 2005, foreign nationals with criminal histories or repeated attempts to enter the United States without documents would be removed from the country without even the hint of due process. This goes beyond the dislocation between the geographical and the legal boundaries in practice and effectively creates an actual territorial section of the country where the application of the

[4]See Articles 9, 14, and 15 of the *International Covenant for Civil and Political Rights*. Document can be found at the following site: http://www2.ohchr.org/english/law/ccpr.htm

[5]This argument is lucidly presented in Campbell (2009).

US Constitution is further reduced, this time by a boundary that is no longer fixed or stable but movable and wavering, given to discretionary perspectives on territoriality.[6] When it comes to undocumented workers and some permanent residents, within this territorial belt, constitutional or due process rights or any other rights for that matter do not even enter the consideration of the courts and are processed purely administratively at the discretion of the officer in charge at the moment.[7]

There is at least some intuitive understanding among US immigration enforcement bureaucrats that there might be a problem with the current system and its dislocated borders. This is evident first by the fact that the removal of an alien can be adjudicated by a federal judge but also interchangeably by the Department of Homeland Security as a purely administrative matter. The authority of the federal judge is not discarded entirely, but it is often substituted for an administrative adjudication. Moreover, once US immigration officers engage a removal process, they do not always act on a removal action unilaterally but seem to prefer to ask each detainee who is a noncitizen, documented or undocumented, to sign a voluntary departure form. This form also skirts the possibility that the removable alien may ask for relief and hire an attorney, essentially involving the bureaucracy in a process that they can no longer adjudicate administratively but may have to go to federal court. Through this form, immigrants sign away "voluntarily" any rights to due process or to any legal relief. Often, detainees are not told what they are signing. Efraín, for example, was made to sign such form upon his departure, although he did know what he was signing. This evidence might in the end be an attempt at diminishing the impact of the dislocation between the geographical and the legal boundaries, but it remains a convoluted way of attempting to keep these boundaries together at best. Some bureaucrats argue, of course, that the problem of undocumented migration is so big that processing each detained migrant through the federal court system would overwhelm the resources of the state. Few would acknowledge, however, that the economic system itself contributes to the problem by attracting migrants. In any event, the current immigration enforcement system creates inclusion and exclusion, depending on the possession or lack of papers, and directly bears on the rights of individuals by creating spaces of privilege (inclusion) and spaces of oppression (exclusion). In this system, those who are citizens can be reassured that their constitutional and due process rights are guaranteed against the discretionality of law enforcement agents, bureaucrats, and even judges, whereas those that are

[6]"DHS Expands Expedited Removal Authority along Southwest Border" (September 14, 2005). DHS Press Release at http://www.cbp.gov/xp/cgov/newsroom/news_releases/archives/2005_press_releases/092005/09142005.xml (Accessed on January 2, 2011).

[7]See *Are You Living in a Constitution-Free Zone?* by the American Civil Liberties Union. Article found at http://www.aclu.org/national-security_technology-and-liberty/are-you-living-constitution-free-zone

noncitizens can no longer aspire to have their day in court. This is equivalent to legal disenfranchisement.[8]

Now, let us turn to how the current immigration system creates spaces of economic privilege (inclusion) for those with papers and generates systems of oppression (exclusion) for those without papers.

Rich Versus Poor

The nonsynchronous shape of the geographical-territorial and the legal boundaries, with its conferral of rights (citizen or legal resident) or its denial of them (undocumented, excludable, or deportable), is not the only way in which the current American caste-like immigration system of enfranchisement and disenfranchisement produces oppressive conditions. Beyond the "geographical-legal" dimension, there is also an economic dimension to this border dislocation. On the US-Mexico border, the system through the possession of *papers* separates the "wanted from the unwanted, the imagined barbarians from the civilized, and [most importantly] the global rich from [the] global poor" (Agamben 1998). Much of this separation process hinges precisely on the documentation an individual possesses but often has little to do with an individual's actual contribution to the economic chain.

At a first level, citizenship, permanent legal residence, or the condition of being undocumented grants or denies access to economic opportunity. The nexus between geopolitical citizenship and economic citizenship has become stronger. Citizenship confers the right to be employed, to access the welfare state, to borrow, and other forms of economic enfranchisement. Excludable and deportable aliens are denied any such privileges, even if they possess economic value by virtue of the fact that they are productive human beings and are perfectly capable of generating wealth. The irony of all this strikes any observer because there is an obviously awkward relationship between economic access and economic contribution. In other words, economic benefits are denied to undocumented workers no matter how long they have been working or how much their contribution, past or potential, to the economic system and national wealth may be. In the case of both Gabriel and Raúl, we have two individuals who contributed to the creation of wealth in the American economy for many years, but who, upon their detection and deportation by the system, lost every single right to claim any benefits accrued and will forever be denied access to any of that wealth. And economic benefits are granted to individuals who are likely to have contributed very little to the system, as is the case of Gastón, who has never in his 30 years of life been able to be self-supporting but has made ends meet by borrowing from the school loans system for years. Thus, citizenship (or "papers") confers the ability to become employed and create wealth and thus

[8]The issue of aliens and the constitution is not new. It has been widely discussed elsewhere. See, for example, the work of Neuman (1993).

contribute to economic growth, but on the reverse side, it confers also access to certain economic rights, even if it is only welfare or school loans and the citizen has not necessarily contributed to it. Although all are recognized, at a deeper level as a *homo oeconomicus* not everyone enjoys the benefits of being such. Worse yet, the very economic nature of the worker is turned on its head and "working" is criminalized. Undocumented workers are thus no longer "workers" but criminals by virtue of their wealth production activities.

The irony of this is that many noncitizens contribute just as much, if not sometimes more, than many citizens to the economic prosperity of a community, but are denied access to the social welfare benefits that membership in a community can bring. In the United States, the *Personal Responsibility and Work Opportunity Reconciliation Act* (PRWORA), passed in 1996, reduced the ability to draw welfare benefits even by legal permanent residents and closed all opportunity for undocumented workers. PRWORA provided that legal permanent residents could not draw SSI, TANF, Food Stamps,[9] or Medicaid until after 5 years of being in the country legally (for refugees that minimum is 7 years). Indeed, by 1999, legal immigrants' and refugees' use of welfare benefits had decreased considerably.[10] Undocumented residents are even worse off. Being an undocumented worker implies that although the employee without papers may have the ability to obtain a job and contribute to the national wealth creation, that person's right to access the very benefits of the wealth that he/she produced before or after immigration enforcement catches them is practically zero.

In the United States, this dislocation between a worker's ability to contribute to wealth and his/her ability to access the fruits of that wealth when times are tough is further reinforced by the creation of these economic tiers: Citizens can access any welfare benefits at any time, regardless of their contribution; legal permanent residents have stringent limitations as to when they can begin to draw these benefits, also regardless of their contribution; and undocumented workers are completely denied any social and economic benefits, even when they contribute to national wealth. Undocumented workers, often poor by any standard, do not even claim their tax reimbursement and leave their entire contributions to the tax system in the government's coffers. Undocumented workers are also increasingly denied loans or even basic banking services. The following chart enables us also to understand how the current legal and economic system creates a dislocation in economic boundaries (Fig. 3.2).

The increasing dissociation among the concepts of identity, citizenship, and economic opportunity is well understood by borderlanders on the US-Mexico divide. The choices that Adrián and Gastón's parents made to cross the border and have their children born in United States territory was a choice carefully chosen

[9]Access to Food Stamps for legal permanent residents was restored in the *Farm Security and Rural Investment Act* of 2002.

[10]For a lengthier explanation of this, see http://www.migrationinformation.org/usfocus/display.cfm?ID=45

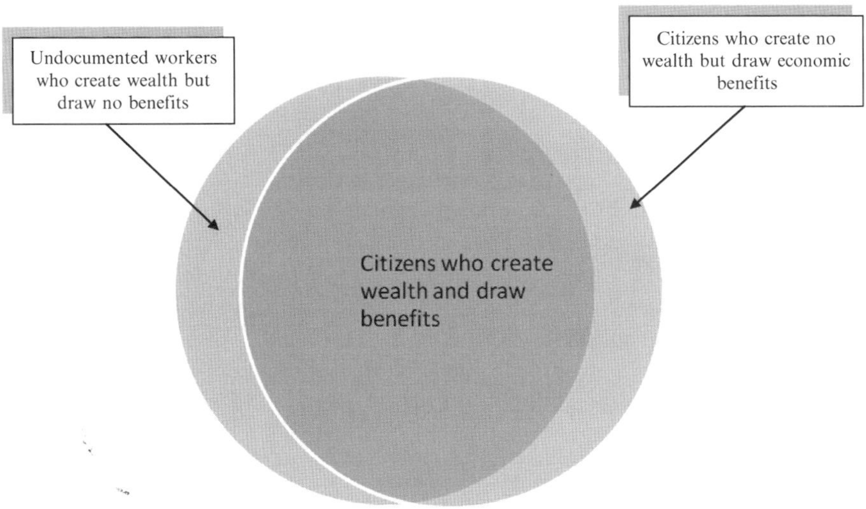

Fig. 3.2 The dislocation of the immigration legal system extends to the boundaries of economic rights and privileges, both of which are equally distorted by the current system of inclusion and exclusion and the manipulation of work, the right to work, and the right to draw benefits from the economic system. Currently, in the United States, there are 12 million undocumented workers who create wealth and draw no benefits, and there are millions of unemployed and over 40 million citizens who collect Food Stamps, for example, making the absurdity of the who system even more severe

because they knew that their birth on this side of the border would automatically grant these young men certain privileges, specifically economic enfranchisement, something which would be denied to those "outside." They knew well that they were opening for their children the possibility of participation in American economic citizenship, clearly a far superior membership than, say, membership in the Mexican economic system. Their choice to cross the border and have their children born in the United States was a rational choice as much as one might consider it irrational for a parent who chooses not to cross the border to birth their child on American soil. One's status within the American legal system bestows on those who belong economic rights (Adrián and Gastón's cases) much as they are denied to non-US citizens (Gabriel and Raúl's cases) or continually made vulnerable among those legal residents who might commit a crime (such as Efraín's case).

There is another link between wealth, citizenship, and inclusion on the one hand and poverty, lack of papers, and exclusion on the other. In addition to the privileged economic spaces created by citizenship and presence within the United States, those not present in US territory and who are not citizens can easily access those spaces of privilege by demonstrating that they have the resources and are therefore labeled "admissible" or "eligible" and perhaps even "desirable" aliens and can cross the border easily to have their children born on the US side, to petition for and obtain a visa to move themselves and their families to the United States, or to migrate entirely. The case of the US-Mexico border is illustrative again.

With the wave of violence recently experienced along the US-Mexico border, it has become clear that many Mexicans with abundant economic resources can easily obtain visas and travel to or to study and live in the United States. Traveling to the United States enables parents to have their children born in the space of privilege that lies just on the other side of the border (like Gastón's case). That helps explain why so many of those who recently fled the US-Mexico border violence are already US citizens and have no trouble crossing the border to safer ground and make the transition to their new home in the American border environment quite easily. In the group *La Red*, which is an El Paso group comprised of hundreds of Mexican exiles of the recent violence in Ciudad Juárez, around 80% are already US citizens by virtue of having been born in the United States.[11] Many of their children were already living in the United States, enjoying full legal protection and the economic enfranchisement refused to many non-US citizens. Such is not the case with those who do not enjoy citizenship and cannot demonstrate the resources to apply for a visa or residency, something which would enable them to flee the violence of the border. Many of those who try the asylum route are denied at rates that reach 99%. This is the case even though most of those who seek asylum are real victims of violence or the threat of it and subject themselves to a cumbersome and often humiliating asylum process. Still, the denial rates reach enormous proportions because most are denied entry since American law requires that they demonstrate with a high degree of certainty that either the government of Mexico itself is the persecutor or cannot protect them in any way. Both of these standards are hard to meet.

This link is even more evident when we consider the links between wealth, citizenship, and inclusion on the one hand and poverty, lack of papers, and exclusion on the other in the context of the so-called E-visas or investment visas. Those who are not American citizens but who have the economic and financial resources can obtain an E-visa by investing in a small business on the US side and bringing their families to the safety of US border cities. Such option is, of course, not open to poorer Mexicans, whose lives are no less threatened by the violence but who must endure the brutal exclusion occasioned by their lack of resources to obtain such visas. An immigration lawyer in town reported that the applications for E-visas are "way up" since the violence began in Ciudad Juárez in 2008. An E-2 visa, which is the most commonly requested document, enables an investor to bring his/her family across with as little as $40,000, although there seems to be a de facto $100,000 limit imposed by bureaucratic discretion. These E-2 visas enable an investor to move himself/herself and family into the United States to "develop and direct"

[11] Information about this group can be found at http://www.laredmexicoelpaso.org/. The percentage of citizens varies, depending on the membership and who reports it. The lowest percentage cited, however, is about 70%, but it can possibly be as high as 90%. There are certain requirements to be a member of La Red. An implicit requirement seems to be a person of certain means, particularly because there is an initial fee of several hundreds of dollars and a minimum membership fee of 20 dollars a month.

his/her investment in the country. Contrary to popular belief, there is no number of jobs required, although a business that employs many US citizens is viewed quite favorably.

This type of opportunities are completely closed to poor Mexicans, of course, who must venture across the border without papers and may not have access to expensive lawyers who can help them out with the best legal strategy to follow when pursuing an E-visa. Poor people must stand in long lines at cost-free legal advice centers for migrants, like Las Americas or the Catholic Migrant and Refugee Centers in El Paso, Texas, and others along the border. When they gather resources to pay, they may even fall victim to lawyers who make promises they cannot deliver on until the poor migrants run out of money.

The creation of these spaces of privilege would be less shocking if this did not come couched in the context of the type of globalization that is creating greater inequality, much of it wrapped around the concept of citizenship, and a kind of cross-border interaction which has created a number of refugees.[12] Much of this cross-border interaction, for example, has to do with the issue of drug trafficking (the main cause of border violence on the Mexican side) or is directly related to the North American Free Trade Agreement, which has had devastating effects on Mexican farmers and low-income wage earners.

Political Disenfranchisement

The caste-like classification of citizens and noncitizens that the current US immigration system has created is also evident in the political landscape. Politically, rights and privileges are distributed not according to territorial presence or time, energy, or activist investment in the community of residence or even legal compliance or economic productivity, but on the basis of citizenship. In other words, the reality of citizenship trumps the reality of physical or territorial presence or involvement or the willingness to care for the community. Citizens, even when they are not physically present within the United States, do not lose their right to participate in the political process and recover these rights as soon as they step back into US territory. Green card holders or permanent legal residents, however, no matter how long they have been physically present and no matter how invested they have been in the American way of life or active in their communities, are considered to be always in the process of seeking entry. Whether they have been in US territory only a short time or their entire life, such as Efraín's case, they are always considered deportable.

[12]This growing gap between the rich and the poor, not only among individuals but among nations, and the relationship it keeps with citizenship and immigration is not new. It has been drawn attention to by authors such as Bruce R. Scott, who wrote that "As the poor have become more aware of inequality, rich nations have raised immigration barriers—making the world economy more like a gated community than a global village." See Scott (2001).

In fact, their political disenfranchisement is evident when it comes not only to voting and being voted but also to participating in numerous political activities such as campaign donations, political proselytism, and other political activities. This political disenfranchisement exists even in spite of the fact that noncitizens generate national wealth, pay taxes—from sales to income—and are often full-fledged members of the communities where they reside. The deportability of these permanent legal residents is increasing, and today they are actively sought out by immigration authorities for deportation under various pretexts and even for smaller offenses.[13] The number of cases such as Efraín's is on the rise.

Moreover, when a documented migrant breaks the law, chances are that he/she will find himself/herself increasingly in a process known as "removal." Removal is a process established by the Secure Borders Initiative (SBI) in 2006. Often, it does not matter that the immigrant's physical presence in the country extends to nearly their entire lives, as in the case of Efraín. If they break the law, they are considered criminals, and the government seeks their summary removal. Sometimes even relatively minor infractions may result in expulsion because the word "felony" is more broadly defined for noncitizens than for citizens. Individuals like Adrián and Gastón, however, whose parents had the sense of crossing the border to have them born on the US side of the border, often break the law (Gastón was fond of drunk driving and drugs, and Adrián was smuggling weapons into Mexico) but will never be subject to deportation. Their citizenship constitutes their immunity from removal.

Still, there are nuances. Legal residents are subjected to a process known as "removal" proceedings and, if they are knowledgeable enough, may request a lawyer and thus postpone their deportation for at least the length of time the process may last. At the same time, nonlegal residents are subjected to a process known as "expedited removal," and their request for a lawyer is often ignored, a further denial of any due process rights. About 100,000 cases of summary (as it is also known) or expedited removal are practiced in the United States every year. The numbers have only increased under the Obama administration (Fig. 3.3).[14]

White Versus Nonwhite

Unfortunately, the general self-understanding of the United States is tied up with a national identity where "whiteness" is central. Every other ethnic group is seen as a "minority." Many of the national debates are in fact often framed as white (European) versus minority.[15] Yet, today's immigrants to the United States tend

---

[13]See Bernstein (2010). Article found at http://www.nytimes.com/2010/03/31/nyregion/31drug.html

[14]"Deportation of Illegal Immigrants Increases Under Obama" in *The Washington Post* (July 26, 2010). Article found at http://www.washingtonpost.com/wp-dyn/content/article/2010/07/25/AR2010072501790.html (Accessed on January 5, 2011).

[15]For an interesting debate on the relationship between culture, politics, and law, see Barzilai (2003).

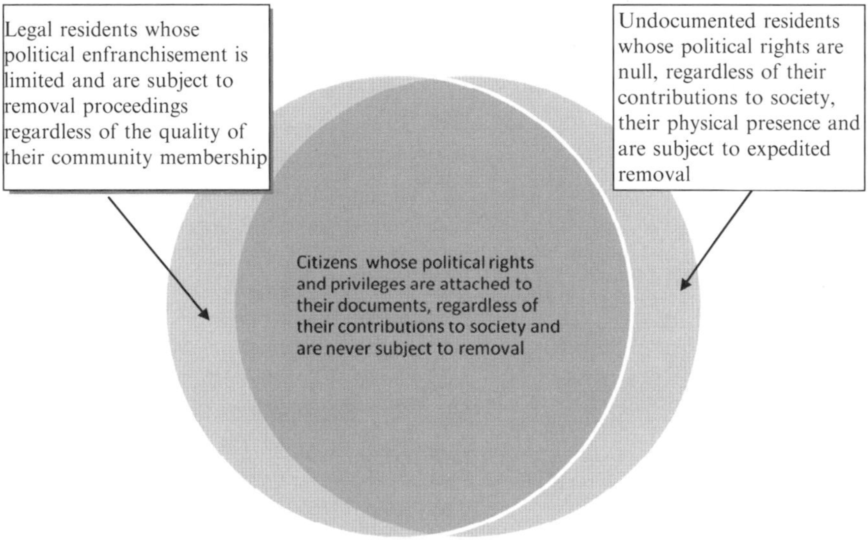

Fig. 3.3 Figure further shows the caste-like system of rights and privileges in the US political system

to be non-European[16] and therefore generally understood as nonwhite. This is the equation that tends to put white Americans against immigrants, who are often perceived as coming to the country to "exploit" the system.[17] The huge debates surrounding the use of welfare benefits by minorities, for example, are clearly framed in the myth that immigrants come to the United States to siphon resources off the public coffers or to live off welfare.[18] Consequently, it is hard to understand the current law enforcement system and its dislocations without this underlying juxtaposition of racial or ethnic issues. Still the *racialization* of the problem of immigration is probably not the cause of the dislocation of borders (legal, political, and economic) but rather a contextual variable that fuels discontent, particularly in times of economic hardship. The feedback loop between the problems outlined

[16]According to the US Census Bureau, the top ten source countries for the US foreign-born population are Mexico, China, the Philippines, India, Vietnam, Cuba, El Salvador, the Dominican Republic, Canada, and Korea. Clearly, most new Americans are non-European. The same Bureau predicts that by 2050, one-quarter of the population will be of Hispanic origin. See www.census.gov

[17]See "Why Americans Think (Wrongly) That Illegal Immigrants Hurt the Economy" in *Newsweek* (May 14, 2010). Article: http://www.newsweek.com/2010/05/14/why-americans-think-wrongly-that-illegal-immigrants-hurt-the-economy.html

[18]In the website http://www.factcheck.org/2009/04/cost-of-illegal-immigrants/, a number of researchers set out to debunk a series of myths regarding immigration and welfare use. The piece is titled "Coast of Illegal Immigrants," posted on April 6, 2009.

above and the racial dimension of this dislocation is self-reinforcing and is likely to get worse as the country has to begin to reconceive itself as multicultural and multiracial rather than white with scattered minorities.

Conclusion

The dislocation between the geographical-territorial and the legal boundaries, the odd political enfranchisement we observe, and the tensions between economic citizenship and inclusion and exclusion expose the increasingly odd construction of citizenship, residency, physical presence, legal rights, and law enforcement in the United States. The ideological debates that take place within country have driven the system to the contradictions that now lie at the heart of it. It separates the individual self from the territory and sets aside the significance of physical presence, even against the Constitution and the rights it outlines. This rebordering of national life alienates the individual's activities and its contributions from his/her legal status. In effect, it diminishes the value of physical presence and creates a caste-like system, where some enjoy full legal, political, economic, and social enfranchisement, while others are denied it, regardless of their actual links to the community in which they resided sometimes for a very long time and where their roots lie. Thus, the very idea of citizenship is a construct that creates not only caste-like divisions among human beings at a legal and at a practical level but actual mindscapes among those who are superior (legal) and those who are subordinated (illegal).

Finally, manipulating the "internal" borders of the United States as a way of coping with immigration ignores several important facts. Not the least of these is the American active promotion of globalization. Even though there is sometimes resistance to inserting the American economy into the world's economy, most Americans understand that the path of prosperity is precisely through the globalization of America's economy. The voices of disagreement regarding the globalization of the national economy, for example, are often very isolated and have little political weight. Globalizing the American economy means that labor too has to be denationalized, and yet the immigration system does not account for that odd "special relationship" between legal, economic, political, and social enfranchisement and the possession of documents. The immigration system has in fact been closing, while the economy has become more globalized. The dislocations outlined in this chapter, for example, have only become worse since NAFTA and other broad free trade agreements came into line. As Douglas Massey[19] argues quite eloquently, most immigration enforcement efforts ignore the "facts on the ground," that we are actively pursuing an economic integration with Mexico but refuse to accept that such integration may have to include a new legal, political, and labor relationship with the people of Mexico. The stepped-up efforts to close the border

[19]See his book with Durand and Malone (2002).

have only exacerbated its exact location (see our charts) and have instead ground the lives of many immigrants who are only pursuing the logic of future prosperity for them and their family.

There is a need for a national debate about the meaning of borders, the meaning of the laws that regulate immigration and enfranchisement, and about the future of the global economy. We have not fully engaged in that debate, and time is running out before we end up with a patchwork of law and regulations that will balkanize our society and create caste-like systems among its population—something that rubs against the fundamental ideas upon which the country was founded.

References

Agamben, G. (1998). *Homo sacer, sovereign power and bare life* (D. Heller-Roazen, Trans. into English). Stanford: Stanford University Press.

American Society of News Editors. (2010, December 5–6). *Summit on violence against journalists along Mexican border* (Staudt in attendance).

Amnesty International. (2003). *Intolerable killings: Ten years of abductions and murders of women in Ciudad Juárez*. New York: Amnesty International.

Amnesty International. (2008). *Women's struggle for justice and safety: Violence in the family in Mexico*. New York: Amnesty International.

Bachratz, P., & Baratz, M. (1970). *Power and poverty: Theory and practice*. New York: Oxford University Press.

Barzilai, G. (2003). *Communities and law: Politics and culture of legal identities*. Ann Arbor: University of Michigan Press.

Bernstein, N. (2010, March 30). How one marijuana cigarette may lead to deportation. *The New York Times*.

Campbell, H. (2009). *Drug war zones: Frontline dispatches from the streets of El Paso and Juárez*. Austin: University of Texas Press.

Cornelius, W., & Shirk, D. (Eds.). (2007). *Reforming the administration of justice in Mexico*. Notre Dame: Notre Dame University Press.

Donovan, T. W. (2005). The American Immigration System: A structural change with a difference emphasis. *International Journal of Refugee Law*, *17*(3), 574–559.

Durand, G., & Malone, N. J. (2002). *Beyond smoke and mirrors: Mexican immigration in an era of economic integration*. New York: Russell Sage.

Lipsky, M. (1980). *Street-level bureaucracy: Dilemmas of the individual in public services*. New York: Russell Sage.

Martínez, O. (1996). *Border people*. Tucson: University of Arizona Press.

Monarrez Fragoso, J. E., & Bejarano, C. (2010). The disarticulation of justice: Precarious life and cross-border feminicides in the Paso del Norte region. In K. Staudt, C. M. Fuentes, & J. E. Monárrez (Eds.), *Cities and citizenship at the U.S.- Mexico border* (pp. 43–70). New York: Palgrave Macmillan.

Neuman, G. L. (1993). *Strangers to the constitution: Immigrants, borders, and fundamental law*. Princeton: Princeton University Press.

Paterson, K. (2010, December 18). International court holds Mexico accountable for Ciudad Juárez femicides. *Frontera News Service*.

Ruiz Marrujo, O. (2009). Women, migration, and sexual violence: Lessons from Mexico's borders. In K. Staudt, T. Payan, & Z. A. Kruszewski (Eds.), *Human rights along the U.S.-Mexico border: Gendered violence and insecurity* (pp. 31–47). Tucson: University of Arizona Press.

Scott, J. (1998). *Seeing like a state: How certain schemes to improve the human condition have failed*. New Haven: Yale University Press.

Scott, B. R. (2001, January/February). The great divide in the global village. *Foreign Affairs, 801*, 160–177.

Staudt, K. (2008). Bordering the other in the U.S. southwest: El Pasoans confront the local sheriff on immigration enforcement. In D. Brotherton & P. Kretsedemas (Eds.), *Keeping out the other: A critical introduction to immigration enforcement today* (pp. 291–313). New York: Columbia University Press.

Staudt, K. (2010). Strengthening law enforcement, democratic, and economic institutions to Confront the Crisis in Ciudad Juárez. *Americas Program*. Text found at http://www.cipamericas.org/archives/3403.

Staudt, K., & Montoya, G. (2009). Violence and activism at the U.S.-Mexico border: Women, migration, and obstacles to justice. In J. S. Jaquette (Ed.), *Feminist agendas and the challenges of democracy in Latin America* (pp. 186–207). Durham: Duke University Press.

Staudt, K., & Ortega, R. R. (2010). Surviving domestic violence in the Paso del Norte border region. In K. Staudt, C. M. Fuentes, & J. E. Monárrez (Eds.), *Cities and citizenship at the U.S.-Mexico border* (pp. 71–90). New York: Palgrave Macmillan.

Staudt, K., Payan, T., & Kruszewski, Z. A. (Eds.). (2009). *Human rights along the U.S.-Mexico border: Gendered violence and insecurity*. Tucson: University of Arizona Press.

Chapter 4
Violence Against Women at the Border: Binational Problems and Multilayered Solutions

Kathleen Staudt

For almost 10 years, I have been engaged in research on violence against women, but for three decades, this seemingly intractable perpetual problem also formed part of my teaching in the course women, power, and politics. In this chapter, I first offer lenses through which to examine violence against women at the US-Mexico border, focusing especially on Ciudad Juárez. Then I highlight empirical findings from research in two stages, femicide and post-femicide stages of violence, and finally offer solutions to reduce or eliminate violence from top-down policy and grassroots society levels to individual everyday actions.

State and Civil Society Through a Gender Lens

My training as a political scientist posits two key lenses through which to examine problems and their solutions: *government*, also known as the state, and *civil society*, particularly nongovernment organizations (NGOs). Whether state or civil society, one must engage with a gender lens, namely, the social constructions of men's and women's behaviors. Attention to violence against women must take into account the construction of notions about masculinity, or masculinities, in given societies, and the way masculine privilege and control over women are performed in everyday life. One must also take into account the way in which women internalize, resist, and/or struggle against such constructions.

The first political science lens examines government action (or inaction), including public policies, practices, and their flaws, frequently found in the budget and policy implementation processes. Like James Scott, in his book entitled *Seeing Like*

K. Staudt (✉)
Department of Political Science, University of Texas at El Paso, 500 W. University Ave., 79968 El Paso, TX, USA
e-mail: kstaudt@utep.edu

M. Lusk et al. (eds.), *Social Justice in the U.S.-Mexico Border Region*,
DOI 10.1007/978-94-007-4150-8_4, © Springer Science+Business Media B.V. 2012

a State (1998), I am wary of whether top-down perspectives and solutions implanted upon complex societies can be totally effective, yet government is responsible for securing public health and safety under the "rule of law" in representative democracies.

Beyond top-down perspectives, another focus is the interaction of state and society in encounters between people and officials, such as police and social workers, analyzed insightfully in *Street-Level Bureaucracy* (Lipsky 1980). Even with public policies and laws that outlaw assault and murder, officials in law enforcement agencies frequently assign low priority, provide limited response, and, ultimately, demonstrate inadequate accountability to eliminate or reduce violence against women. In Mexico, where the descriptor impunity/*impunidad* best characterizes law enforcement, we have a recipe for disaster in everyday insecurity and poor health, especially for women—at least a quarter of whom are victims of intimate partner violence and sexual assault. Among government institutions, law enforcement and the military are among the most masculinized of institutions, valuing control, aggression, dominance, and force. Women generally represent a small percentage of staff, especially frontline staff, in those institutions, but as those numbers grow, masculine ideology and values may still pervade organizational culture.

The second lens through which political science examines society is that of civil society activism, namely, NGOs (nongovernment organizations) and social movements wherein people network and organize around their commonalities to advance and defend their interests in democratic societies. The process works as follows. Those outside of government exert *power*—with large numbers of people, expertise, and money—to press elected officials, political appointees, and civil servants (also known as bureaucrats) at local, state, and national levels to respond to flaws in laws and policies and to advocate reforms. In many countries, women have been relatively powerless, given delays in the right to vote along with other civil rights; however, some women have risen to the challenge of seeking response and accountability from government through NGOs and social movements. Moreover, the rise of transnational movements has made it possible for local NGOs, unable to influence their own nonresponsive governments, to connect with international NGOs who provide leverage and in turn influence other governments, UN organizations, and/or the media to influence their governments. However, even media institutions focus, frame, distort, or ignore issues in selective manners.

Not only is power unevenly distributed equally among people in society but also some problems have only recently entered the *public* realm, once normalized as "private" problems. Violence against women is a good case in point. With the rise of the transnational women's movements in the late 1960s and 1970s, violence against women finally surfaced as a public issue. In power terms, Bachrach and Baratz referred to "two faces of power," both overt and indirect (1970). Abusers' ability to keep problems outside of public debate, hidden in a private sphere until the latter part of the twentieth century, long represented enormous indirect power.

Once violence against women entered public debate, evoking some change in law and public policy, gender power relations shifted slightly. Victim-survivors acquired some leverage against abusers, now labeled "criminal," to make justice claims and seek relief. However, civil society antiviolence activism has fallen primarily on women to exert power to maintain visibility on the problem and thereby seek redress and justice. Although men's relationships with mothers and perhaps sisters, daughters, aunts, friends, and partners would seem to rouse their interest in safety and health, women continue to be more active than men in NGOs and social movements relating to violence reduction. Community-based organizations, even those committed to social justice, avoid addressing complex issues like family violence. Indeed, in mainstream society, violence against women forms the stuff of jokes and bullying, both in private conversation and the media.

While the notion of "women's interests" has an elusive quality, potential violence against women is the clear and common experience that women share worldwide, regardless of ethnicity, race, class, and nationality. In transnational border regions, the existence of two or more sovereign governments and variations in law enforcement policies and practices make violence a compelling issue for examination and action. Border zones are magnets for violence, as Ruiz (2009) has analyzed at Mexico's northern and southern borders.

In this chapter, I analyze data on violence toward women at the border, the incidence of these underreported crimes of violence, and the movements against violence which continue to be marginalized and gain little traction along with other human rights issues in the wider political process. One can analyze two key stages of violence against women in contemporary Mexico. During the infamous femicide stage—the 1990s and early 2000s—the region *previewed* the chaos of 2008 and beyond. Had government heeded and addressed law enforcement impunity during the femicide stage, the near breakdown of security and the murders of approximately 7,000 men and women might have been avoided in Ciudad Juárez. The second, post-femicide stage of violence reflects the total breakdown of security and peace in everyday life. This chapter, then, contends that femicide and violence against women remain a priority, but that it has yet to be addressed in policy implementation, street-level police-resident interactions, and everyday life in Juárez (and much of Mexico). In El Paso, professional law enforcement contains violence against women enough to keep women's murder rates low. Yet women on both sides of the border experience some fear, threat, and dread, given the ease with which dead bodies can be disposed of in the large desert surroundings of a transnational urban region (see also Monárrez and Bejarano 2010).

Violence Against Women in the Paso del Norte Region

As other chapters documented, El Paso and Ciudad Juárez constitute one large metropolitan region in two sovereign countries with numerous north-to-south and south-to-north crossings, whether by relatives, friends, workers, and shoppers (see selections in Staudt et al. 2009). In this transnational space, which historian Oscar Martínez calls an asymmetrical "interdependent" border region (1996), law enforcement institutions operate quite differently. For 15 years, CQ Press has named El Paso (population ~700,000) the first or second safest big city in the United States, based on FBI serious crime reports, while Ciudad Juárez (Mexico's fifth largest city with a population ~1.3 million) has been called the world's murder capital in an undeclared war zone comparable to Iraq and Afghanistan (ASNE 2010).

Stage I: Femicide: Women Killing Amid Total State Impunity

My entrée into studying broad-based violence against women was the growing visibility of sexualized killings called femicide/*feminicidio*. From the mid-1990s onward, girls' and women's bodies were found in the desert periphery of Ciudad Juárez, with evidence of torture, mutilation, and gang rape. Many victims were teens. While some mothers mourned in silence and despair, other mothers pressed the police to find the killers, only to learn about the limited police investigations and general disregard for responding to these crimes. Human rights and feminist activists began counting the bodies and naming the victims, holding marches and rallies with testimonials from the mothers.

When eight girls' bodies were found in a cotton field inside the city, 2001, the horrors galvanized people on both sides of the borders to press for justice. Two cross-border organizations were born, one of them Amigos de las Mujeres de Juárez and other, the Coalition Against Violence Toward Women and Families at the Border (the latter, in which I participated).

Besides committed activists, the cultural community of artists, filmmakers, and musicians spread awareness about the murders and violence against women generally. A documentary by Lourdes Portillo, *Señorita Extraviada* (2001), roused people to activism. Eve Ensler, creator of *Vagina Monologues*, wrote a monologue about the murders in Ciudad Juárez. Cross-border solidarity marches on International Women's Day (March 8), V-Day (February 14), and the United Nations International Day for the Elimination of Violence Against Women (November 25) attracted attention from the national media in both the United States and Mexico and eventually around the world, with protests at Mexican embassies in Tokyo, London, Paris, and Belgrade. Furthermore, thousands of performances of *Vagina Monologues* occurred annually, worldwide (see Staudt 2008b: Ch 4).

In 2003, the international human rights NGO pressure peaked when Amnesty International issued its monograph, *Intolerable Killings: Ten Years of Abductions and Murders of Women in Ciudad Juárez, Chihuahua.* A US Congressional delegation visited the border, and, subsequently, Representative Hilda Solís introduced a resolution in the House, voted by consensus there and in the Senate (no doubt, even with votes from abusers who engage in unreported family violence). High-visibility antiviolence activism soared in 2003–2004, with the largest-ever border solidarity march of 5,000–8,000 people crossing the international border from El Paso to Ciudad Juárez on V-Day, 2004. At the federal level, the Mexican government sent high-profile "Special Investigators" and "Special Prosecutors" legitimizing Mexico

City-level concern over the crimes, but producing few results in this federal system of government where state laws, like those in the State of Chihuahua, define and enforce law. I referred to special investigators and prosecutors as "bureaucratic decorations" (Staudt 2008b). The Mexican Congress later passed laws condemning the murders of women nationwide, as little to no investigation and prosecution exists throughout the country. The business and government elite of Juárez criticized the activists who, they said, sullied the image of the city (Staudt 2008b: Ch 4). For me, the larger problem beyond femicide has been the violence against women, including domestic violence, attempted murder, sexual assault, and sexualized killings.

De-normalizing the 1 in 4 Pattern

Historically, violence against women has been normalized among significant portions of men and women. Such violence is exhibited in peculiar forms of masculinity: performing manhood through controlling women in physically violent ways. In the United States, both government and academic researchers report dismally similar findings—that one in four women have experienced violence at the hand of a partner in their lifetime (see Staudt 2008b: Chapter 2, including discussions of national-level studies in Mexico and the United States).

My methods for learning and acting on violence against women at the border involved participant observation in the Coalition Against Violence Toward Women at the Border since 2002 and quasi-experimental survey research in collaboration with a health NGO in Ciudad Juárez. About the reported murders of women (370 from 1993 to 2003, according to AI (2003)), approximately one-third displayed the femicide profile, while the others, the more "ordinary" less dramatic killings, were likely domestic violence murders (see Staudt 2008b). With a large health NGO, we surveyed a representative sample of 404 women aged 15–39 to document the incidence of domestic violence to determine which women were at greatest risk and to learn about women's strategies to deal with the violence. Thanks to Graciela de la Rosa, a community organizer and workshop facilitator with the NGO, half the sample of women participated in three 2 hour workshops. We conducted before-and-after surveys to assess the effects of the workshops on women's attitudes and behaviors compared with women who did not participate in the workshops.

Drawing on the Mexican Census for the city, we found that the sample contained women with typical characteristics for women aged 15–39: approximately two-thirds achieved sixth grade education (*primaria*) or less and lived in households with earnings of 1,000 *pesos* weekly (US $100 with exchange rates at the time); the majority of them moved to the city from elsewhere. In analyzing results, we found that half of women lived in fear in their neighborhoods, but their only "security" consisted of patrols from police—distrusted by over 70% of the sample.

In the workshops, women discussed the problem of violence against them and possible solutions. The most prominent cause women expressed was men's lack of respect for women, followed by economic problems, drinking and drugs, and police corruption among other factors. Slightly over a quarter, or 27%, of women reported physically violent experiences with partners in their lifetimes. These findings are remarkably similar to those in the United States. A big difference with the United States is that in Mexico, few women trust the police, domestic violence is a low priority for law enforcement, and the city had no battered women's shelter at the time.

Women with low incomes and limited education face certain obstacles in leaving dangerous relationships. Migrants from other parts of Mexico, especially recent migrants, lack social and familial support networks in which to confide or retreat for shelter. We identified one key factor in the research connected to physical violence: emotional and psychological abuse, such as threats, intimidation, and humiliation. Abusers seem to psychologically prepare their victims for the gross "normality" of violence through nonphysical abuse.

Given the massive mistrust in the police, the criminalization of abusers alone appears to be unable to address, reduce, and eliminate the violence. Moreover, untrained police officers, operating under policies which assign low priority to domestic violence, offer little security or assistance. Another Amnesty International monograph that came out 5 years later on domestic violence in Mexico, focused on legal cases in three non-border states, provided horrifying examples of police inaction and neglect. "Come to us with one foot in the grave," said police officers to a woman with repeatedly escalated violence from her partner (Amnesty International 2008: 31). Rosalba Robles' in-depth research with a dozen victim-survivors contains graphic details about a more accurate label for the crime: attempted murder rather than the phrase domestic violence, seemingly trivializing the violence (Staudt and Robles 2010). Studies like these raise questions about the limits of criminalization approaches under the conditions of police impunity, neglect, inaction, and complicity with criminals. Multiple, multilayered strategies are necessary to save lives and prevent trauma and injury. Government alone cannot solve the problem, especially the government in Mexico which thus far has emphasized rhetorical commitments alone with national laws that evoke "lives free of violence" for women in a federal system where criminal law is determined and enforced at the state level.

Cultures of Non-reporting

Not surprisingly, few women in Juárez report domestic violence. For those who do, a 15-day rule applies: if injuries and bruises remain for 15 days and more, the fine the abuser will likely pay is larger. The Amnesty International report (2008) documents similar practices in other states. Rosalba Robles and I analyzed police report data in 2007 and 2008 for both Cd. Juárez and El Paso. Although twice the size of El Paso, only 6,000 reports were made in Juárez. In El Paso, where data indicators include both actual incidents and calls, the number of domestic violence *incidents* was 11,000, with triple the number of *calls* (32,000) over fear or threats (2010).

According to El Paso's Center Against Family Violence staff, those who seek shelter or counseling from them wait an average of seven incidences (in Staudt 2008b). Thus, one can only speculate about the real and absolutely high number of cases in both cities, especially in Cd. Juárez with its size double that of El Paso and its deep distrust of police and consequent underreporting of crimes. Domestic violence can and does escalate to attempted or real murder; thus, shelter space saves lives. El Paso has over 30 shelters, three of them "specializing" in domestic violence for short, 3-month, and 2-year stays, while Cd. Juárez opened its first shelter in 2005 with spaces for ten families and guidelines for a maximum 3-day stay.

Law Enforcement: Keeping Women Alive (or Not)?

On the Mexico side of the border, little trust exists in the municipal and state police, given their long traditions of complicity with criminals, extortion, overall impunity, and the limited attention to the investigation and prosecution of crimes. This characterization is not unique to Juárez, but exists in different degrees all over Mexico (Cornelius and Shirk 2007). Consequently, crime victims rarely "denounce" crime, sustaining a culture of non-reporting.

On the US side of the border, residents exhibit greater trust in the local police and sheriff deputies. For approximately 30 years, state laws and local law enforcement increased their attention to violent crimes against women, after pressure from the women's movement of the 1970s (Staudt 2008b: Ch 5). However, abusers who commit crimes like domestic violence and sexual assault may be intimate partners and fathers with victim-survivors' children. Such circumstances also perpetuate a "culture of non-reporting" as well.

The Special Case of Migrants

Domestic violence, an underreported crime, is even less likely to be reported among undocumented immigrants or people living in households with people who have yet to arrange their citizenship. They are reluctant to engage with law enforcement and other government agencies, given fears about deportation, interagency information sharing, and constant changes in legal requirements to become naturalized citizens. Dependency burdens and criminal histories could undermine their prospects for citizenship should they decide to become naturalized citizens.

Undocumented people have good reason to be fearful. In 2008, given the need to generate nonlocal revenue for his department, former Sheriff Leo Samaniego authorized deputies to conduct checkpoints in the outlying *colonias* of El Paso County. Deputies sought not only licenses and insurance but also social security cards and citizenship documents, resulting in the deportation of 800 people in a 3-month period (and likely family separation for nearly as many households) (see full analysis in Staudt 2008a). Several community-based organizations (NGOs)—among them, the Border Network for Human Rights and two faith-based social justice organizations affiliated with the Industrial Areas Foundation (IAF), using tactics of the late Saul Alinsky, EPISO, and Border Interfaith—negotiated with the sheriff and subsequently sponsored campaign forums with hundreds in their audiences and media coverage. At forums with community-based organizations, one citizen-grandpa told his story with testimony that he had been stopped 7 times in 3 months as he was taking his grandchildren to school. Sheriff candidates publicly and uniformly promised to penalize deputies who engaged in these practices at forums with these NGOs (Staudt 2008a). While these community organizations challenge human rights abuses, they have not focused on violence against women in order to avoid potential internal conflict. Also, a focus on violence against women might demonize Mexican men in the xenophobic, anti-immigrant climate of early twenty-first century US public life.

Some victim-survivors qualify to apply for special visas under the Violence Against Women Act (VAWA), renewed three times in the US Congress. However, the provisions are quite narrow: only women who report violence against them by a US citizen or legal permanent resident legally married husband can qualify to apply. The daunting forms that need to be completed further discourage victims to report (Staudt and Montoya 2009). As one staff person at a faith-based VAWA clinic said, "We have a basement full of file cabinets with incomplete applications" (communication to Staudt 2008a, b).

Stage II: Post-femicide 2008 and Beyond in the World's Murder Capital

Murder rates in Ciudad Juárez escalated sharply in 2008 and beyond, initially over cartel competition and subsequently with the Mexican military and federal police, sent by President Felipe Calderón. Femicide experts claim that sexualized killings have decreased, even as the absolute number of women murdered increased dramatically (Monárrez Fragoso and Bejarano 2010). Men's murders (homicide) have increased by tenfold to approximately 3,000 annually.

El Paso is home to birthright and naturalized citizens, legal permanent residents, and undocumented people, including at least 30,000 who fled the military-drug war violence in Ciudad Juárez in 2009 and 2010 up to as many as 100,000, according to local asylum attorneys (Carlos Spector personal communication to Staudt 2010). Many people live in the shadows, traumatized by the deaths of relatives, friends, and neighbors in the drug war zone from which they fled.

While courageous mothers of three murdered daughters whose bodies were dumped in the cotton field took their case to the Inter-American Court of Human Rights (IACHR), they achieved a judgment that mandated numerous changes in Mexican law enforcement practices, especially those in the realm of bureaucratic and court procedures. Few hold their breath awaiting action from government. As Kent Paterson of Frontera Sur stated:

> In addition to conducting a serious murder investigation and investigating law enforcement officials responsible for obstructing the cotton field case, which included the fabrication of scapegoats under torture, within one year the Mexican government must hold a public ceremony in Ciudad Juárez to apologize for the crimes; build a monument to the three murdered women in the border city; publish the sentence in the official government record and in newspapers; expand gender sensitivity and human rights training for police; step-up and coordinate efforts to find missing women; permanently publicize the cases of disappeared women on the Internet; and investigate reported death threats and harassment against members of the families .... (2010)

Meanwhile, elites in the State of Chihuahua and Municipality of Ciudad Juárez continue to marginalize and/or deny the problems. As late as 2010, the publisher and editor of the largest newspaper in the city, publicly called the killings a "myth" that "dirtied our city's image" at the American Society of News Editors/Inter-American Press Association (ASNE 2010: 2–3). While he acknowledged the hundreds of girls and women killed over the decade, 1993–2003, which his newspaper *El Diario* reported and from which the names and numbers were counted, he also referred to the media reports as "exaggerations and fantasies," culminating in the phrase: a "great lie."

Stage I femicide killings previewed the devastating violence that followed in 2008 through the current time period. Had the government and law enforcement institutions taken the killings seriously, perhaps the lives of 7,000 (80–90% men) could have been saved from 2008 to 2010. During Stage I, and even now, the victims were "just" women, and some politicians blamed the victims for their deaths (their clothing, their presence on streets at night). Few politicians use that discourse in Stage II; however, the crimes are nearly invisible, even though the average annual deaths of women (once 30) have more than quadrupled. Government and society have much work to do before the impunity ends, crimes are prevented or investigated when they occur, and people no longer tolerate violence against women.

What Is to Be Done? The State, Individuals, and Civil Society

In Mexico, outside of several cosmetic changes, police continue to avoid investigations and prosecutions. Residents continue to distrust the police, along with the military and federal police who, under the militarized drug war, seem to have aggravated crime rather than prevented it or actually committed some of the murders, according to hundreds of complaints filed with the State and National Commissions for Human Rights that investigate and report, but lack authority to change or penalize impunity by institutions and their personnel.

The US approach to national security is to militarize the US side of the border, extend fences or walls, and conduct surveillance of security threats in the form of drugs and unauthorized immigrants. This approach to border security does not attend to everyday insecurity and violence against women. See analysis in Staudt (2009).

Let us go back to the lenses of state and society. Clearly, the states can do more, both the United States and Mexico, separately and binationally. Mexico can respond to the IACHR. It can implement rhetorical, but still unfunded, mandates to professionalize law enforcement and make it accountable to address violence against women. It can create a police force worthy of people's trust and respect.

The United States can broaden the provisions of VAWA. It can grant asylum to those fleeing Mexico and its violence; currently, only 2% of Mexicans seeking asylum are granted asylum, according to Department of Justice figures. From 30,000 to 100,000 refugees live in El Paso, according to El Paso's Police Chief and asylum lawyers, yet no special attention or resources are provided for this humanitarian crisis. According to Mark Lusk, this crisis warrants attention from the United Nations High Commissioner for Refugees (see him quoted in Staudt 2010).

While violence is pervasive, people should by no means assume it will never end. We all can act in ways to reduce and end the scourge. I begin with the actions of people in Ciudad Juárez, people who have inspired others on both sides of the border and in the rest of the world to struggle against the violence and in so doing struggle for democracy and accountability from their governments.

Mothers of murdered daughters stood up, asked questions, and persistently pressed authorities for response on disappeared and murdered daughters. They organized themselves and allied themselves with other human rights and feminist groups that demanded justice. Some mothers retreated in mourning and silence; we must respect those decisions.

Many people joined the mothers in solidarity, marching, protesting, and asking questions of both the Mexican government and their own governments about laws and enforcement practices relating to violence against women. As I analyze in the book (Staudt 2008b: Ch 4), the antifemicide movement rejuvenated activism in El Paso, Texas, as US activism of the 1960s and 1970s had waned after the passage of laws and the professionalization of nonprofit organizations that offer counseling and shelter to victim-survivors and 26-week batterer resocialization programs to abusers. For an example of this rejuvenation, the Coalition Against Violence went to City Council, with documentation about a City Council Representative who had severely beaten a woman 30 years before. As was typical in the 1970s, the police offered limited interest or response to the victim-survivor (somewhat like the police in twenty-first century Juárez), but she was able to get a civil court judgment of $50,000 against him for the hospital, dental, and medical bills for her broken ribs, hair tufts pulled out by the roots, and knocked-out teeth. He had never paid these bills and never acquired property or accepted wages in order to avoid garnishment. When his actions were publicized, El Pasoans were embarrassed and roused, although some wondered "did she deserve it." This was read out loud on a local TV station and cited in Staudt 2008b: Ch 4. The public seemed more outraged, or perhaps finally convinced, when the media uncovered a police report documenting that he gutted his fiancé's dog. He was not reelected to City Council.

People used their talents and skills to spread awareness and analyze the problem of and solutions for violence against women. Courageous journalists like Diana Washington Valdez and Kent Paterson wrote many articles and followed up so that the media generated more than single-day attention to the problem.

Researchers also generated data and analyzed findings, publishing findings for the broader community. It is important to remember that governments often do not act unless the problem is identified, counted, and communicated—over and over—to political decision makers for action. My book will likely be read both at the border and far from the border: in the mainstream United States and Mexico. Parts of the analysis have been translated into Spanish, available in Mexico in written and narrative communication. For people without the patience to read, the pictures themselves in the book and on websites communicate a 1,000 words.

Professors and teachers also incorporate the themes of violence against women in their classrooms. The *Violence and Activism* book was adopted for classroom use at various universities, perhaps grooming the next generation of researcher-activists with knowledge, skills, and action ideas as they locate violence against women in their own communities.

Some professors and teachers incorporate community-based teaching and learning—which some call "service-learning"—in their classes. At the University of Texas at El Paso, the Center for Civic Engagement once offered a program called Ni Una Más (Not One More). University students were trained by community partners to participate in 20 hours of one of two activities: (1) presentations in high schools to identify the warning signs of controlling behavior in dating or intimate relationships that may lead to physical violence, and (2) court observations in protective order hearings (a civil remedy, ordering abusers to maintain a distance) and criminal trials to determine whether "fair" processes have been evident. Experiential learning deepens knowledge and practice beyond reading and discussing that occurs in traditional classrooms.

Men and women alike can join organizations, donate funds to antiviolence groups and service centers, and participate in high-visibility marches. They can attend plays like *Vagina Monologues*, such as the thousands performed annually worldwide, that raise funds for antiviolence work. In El Paso, mother-activist Linda King's daughter Lisa was brutally killed by her son-in-law even though a Protective Order had been issued for him to stay hundreds of feet away from Lisa. However, a jury sentenced him to only 10 years in prison, possibly free after 5 years of "good behavior." In the United States, some juries treat the murder of a woman less seriously than the use of drugs or theft. King wrote a play, *Domestic Violence: The Musical*, an odd title, but an arts-oriented experience with a devastating awareness message that will reach many people and raise funds for antiviolence work (www.helpfixthehurt.org).

Besides all the activist roles above, EVERYONE, including men and women, can pause and question conversational remarks that joke about and normalize rape, control over women, the sexualization of violence, verbal abuse, and interpersonal violence to partners, children, and strangers. EVERYONE can listen to and believe what victim-survivors have to say about their experiences, offering support and suggesting options to them. EVERYONE can donate money in tiny to larger amounts for antiviolence work: to shelters, counseling centers, and political organizations that press governments for stronger policies and enforcement practices. EVERYONE can volunteer time at shelters. Mothers, fathers, and teachers should raise girls and boys to reject violence and bullying. EVERY adult can vote for candidates who support antiviolence policies and funding, peaceful practices in domestic and foreign affairs, and gun-control legislation.

I emphasize EVERYONE: men and women, boys and girls. All too often, antiviolence work is perceived as a "women's issue" that women organize around. Rather, antiviolence is a people's issue: a human rights concern for public safety and health. How many men have no mothers, sisters, daughters, partners, women friends, or aunts—all of whom could have been or will be victims or survivors of violence? And when men speak out against violence and rape, their voices carry weight. I believe that women will continue to shoulder much of the antiviolence work, but their voices and actions will be strengthened with those of men. EVERYONE must develop the quality of empathy, asking themselves: suppose violent acts were against me, my mother, sister, daughter, friend, grandmother, or aunt?

I hope EVERYONE will also conceptualize the many "violences" in our world beyond the scourge of violence against women, including economic violence and war. Deeply entrenched poverty is a violence that renders many hungry and destitute. And wars—whether between/within countries or among family members—leave legacies of lasting pain. Together, we can heal that pain and act daily to reduce and eliminate violence against women.

References

American Society of News Editors. (2010, December 5–6). *Summit on violence against journalists along Mexican border* (Staudt in attendance).

Amnesty International. (2003). *Intolerable killings: Ten years of abductions and murders of women in Ciudad Juárez*. New York: Amnesty International.

Amnesty International. (2008). *Women's struggle for justice and safety: Violence in the family in Mexico*. New York: Amnesty International.

Bachratz, P., & Baratz, M. (1970). *Power and poverty: Theory and practice*. New York: Oxford University Press.

Cornelius, W., & Shirk, D. (co-editors). (2007). *Reforming the administration of justice in Mexico*. Notre Dame: Notre Dame University Press.

Lipsky, M. (1980). *Street-level bureaucracy: Dilemmas of the individual in public services*. New York: Russell Sage.

Martínez, O. (1996). *Border people*. Tucson: University of Arizona Press.

Monárrez Fragoso, J. E., & Bejarano, C. (2010). The disarticulation of justice: Precarious life and cross-border feminicides in the Paso del Norte region. In K. Staudt, C. M. Fuentes, J. E. Monárrez, et al. (Eds.), *Cities and citizenship at the U.S.-Mexico border: The Paso del Norte metropolitan region* (pp. 43–70). New York: Palgrave Macmillan.

Paterson, K. (2010, December 18). International court holds Mexico accountable for Ciudad Juárez Femicides. *Frontera News Service*.

Ruiz Marrujo, O. (2009). Women, migration, and sexual violence: Lessons from Mexico's borders. In K. Staudt, T. Payan, Z. A. Kruszewski, et al. (Eds.), *Human rights along the U.S.-Mexico border: Gendered violence and insecurity* (pp. 31–47). Tucson: University of Arizona Press.
Scott, J. (1998). *Seeing like a state: How certain schemes to improve the human condition have failed.* New Haven: Yale University Press.
Staudt, K. (2008a). Bordering the other in the U.S. Southwest: El Pasoans confront the local sheriff on immigration enforcement. In D. Brotherton & P. Kretsedemas (Eds.), *Keeping out the other: A critical introduction to immigration enforcement today* (pp. 291–313). New York: Columbia University Press.
Staudt, K. (2008b). *Violence and activism at the border: Gender, fear, and everyday life in Ciudad Juárez.* Austin: University of Texas Press.
Staudt, K. (2009). Violence at the border: Broadening the discourse to include feminism, human security, and deeper democracy. In K. Staudt, T. Payan, & Z. A. Kruszewski (Eds.), *Human rights along the U.S.-Mexico border: Gendered violence and insecurity* (pp. 1–27). Tucson: University of Arizona Press.
Staudt, K. (2010). *Strengthening law enforcement, democratic, and economic institutions to confront the crisis in Ciudad Juárez.* Americas Program, Center for International Programs. http://www.cipamericas.org/archives/3403
Staudt, K., & Montoya, G. (2009). Violence and activism at the U.S.-Mexico border: Women, migration, and obstacles to justice. In J. S. Jaquette (Ed.), *Feminist agendas and the challenges of democracy in Latin America* (pp. 186–207). Durham: Duke University Press.
Staudt, K., & Robles Ortega, R. (2010). Surviving domestic violence in the Paso del Norte border region. In K. Staudt, C. M. Fuentes, J. E. Monárrez, et al. (Eds.), *Cities and citizenship at the U.S.-Mexico border: The Paso del Norte metropolitan region* (pp. 71–90). New York: Palgrave Macmillan.
Staudt, K., Payan, T., Kruszewski, Z. A., et al. (Eds.). (2009). *Human rights along the U.S.-Mexico border: Gendered violence and insecurity.* Tucson: University of Arizona Press.

Chapter 5
A Theological Perspective on Social Justice in the US-Mexico Border Region

Rev. John Stowe

Every November 2 over the last decade, the faithful from Ciudad Juárez led by their bishop join with their counterparts from El Paso and Las Cruces, New Mexico, and their bishops, to celebrate the Eucharist on the "Day of the Dead." The site of the celebration is divided right at the altar by the fence that separates the United States of America from the United States of Mexico, but that dividing line does not prevent the participants from gathering around common symbols at a common table. Prayers, songs, and fraternal bonds are shared across this porous border. The liturgical feast officially known as the Commemoration of the Faithful Departed but more popularly called "All Souls Day" or "*El Día de los Muertos*" takes on an enhanced meaning because the prayers for the dead are offered especially for those who have perished in the New Mexican desert after crossing this international boundary into the imagined promised land without documents. Their deaths are a direct result of compounded injustice, both the lack of opportunity for survival in their homeland and immigration laws that force their quest for survival far into the hostile and unforgiving desert. The shoes and backpacks left behind in the desert are poignantly brought to the altar, which is surrounded by crosses bearing the names of the known deceased.

This privileged moment of celebrating the hope of resurrection for the deceased and the hope of a more just and humane immigration policy for the living offers a colorful snapshot of the border reality. The border is both porous and deadly; culture, language, tradition, family, faith, friendships, joys, sorrows, and many other intangibles exist without distinction on either side without reference to the border; yet human passage is largely possible only for those who do not need to cross for survival, those who have economic means or who live on the wealthier side. Through the chain link fence or steel post wall, Mexicans can see a place where their usual daily wage can be earned in an hour or less. Expressions of fraternity as well as

Rev.J. Stowe (✉)
Basilica and National Shrine of Our Lady of Consolation, Carey, OH, USA
e-mail: jstowe317@hotmail.com

M. Lusk et al. (eds.), *Social Justice in the U.S.-Mexico Border Region*,
DOI 10.1007/978-94-007-4150-8_5, © Springer Science+Business Media B.V. 2012

a shared anger over failed immigration policies are expressed in a common voice through the wall. Yet no one is unaware of the huge discrepancies that distinguish one side of this artificial but well-enforced separator. For people of faith or in search of faith, liturgical gatherings give meaning to their existence as they mourn loss, celebrate hope, and create community in the midst of a common struggle; such community transcends national boundaries.

Christian faith is more than a collection of doctrines and laws; it is meant to be a perspective on life itself which is understood as a gift from a benevolent and omnipotent Creator who longs to be in solidarity with creation, a solidarity that culminates in the Creator becoming incarnate in the person of Jesus of Nazareth. Jesus who revealed God in his very person was rejected, died as a victim of capital punishment, and rose from the dead to new life. The testimony of the undying love and message of Jesus is celebrated in ritual and memorialized in the lives of countless women and men who have lived and died sharing Jesus' vision of the Reign of God, the new world order of justice, peace, and fraternal love at the very heart of Jesus' preaching. Christian doctrine arises out of deep reflection on the teachings of Jesus, which are rooted in the Jewish Scriptures, and the study of human experience and reality in the light of these teachings. Saint Anselm is the origin of an unsurpassed definition of theology, "faith seeking understanding." Theological reflection begins with this faith which is best understood in its practice, a practice rooted in the solidarity between Creator and creation as personified in Jesus. The Church, as the institution that emerged to preserve the memory and charism of Jesus however imperfectly, must announce the values of the Reign of God and must denounce injustice and sin which ruptures the solidarity among God's people and with God. The border fence dividing the eucharistic table represents the major barrier to justice in the region. Communion across the border embodies hope in the Reign of God as yet unrealized. Theology, as faith seeking understanding, arises from the praxis (reflective and deliberative practice) of faith seeking the justice that is constitutive of God's Reign.

The Christian Faith in Latin America and on the Border

The Christian faith was first established on the US-Mexico border by Spanish Franciscan friars and Pueblo Indians who had together migrated south during the Pueblo Revolts in New Mexico in 1680. The Pueblos had received the Christian Gospel a century earlier from missionary friars whose inspiration was the thirteenth-century saint Francis of Assisi. Francis rejected the material wealth of his successful merchant father and sparked an internal reform of the institutional church by serving lepers and the outcast and creating fraternal communities. But the human sinfulness of the missionary friars, their inherent worldview of Spanish superiority, and especially the exploitative and violent *conquistadores* who accompanied them distorted the essential Christian message. These Spaniards could not have understood that their Gospel and its implementation was as much Spanish as it was Christian.

Nonetheless, the faith was planted and grew deep roots within the native peoples and merged in creative ways with their religious worldview (Gutierrez 1991b) just as it had in Mexico and throughout Latin America in similarly painful and conflictive circumstances.

The story of the apparition of the Virgin of Guadalupe as a pregnant Aztec woman whose presence was surrounded with flowers and music, familiar indigenous signs of the divine presence, spread the hope-filled faith in a God incarnate and in solidarity with His/Her people better than any catechisms and doctrines of the missionaries. The perennial challenge for the Christian churches is to incarnate the unconditional love of God and to promote the justice of God's reign as Jesus did. The prologue of the Gospel of John refers to Jesus as the eternal word of God which became flesh. This incarnation happened in the cultural context of first-century Palestine; the Gospel message must also be incarnate in the local culture for it to be effective and liberating, as the brown-skinned Virgin of Guadalupe amply demonstrates.

A theological perspective must be conscious of its context and its content. Early Spanish missionaries were not capable of critiquing their own social and cultural context which enveloped the gospel they proclaimed. In the period of the reconquest of Spain by Christians after a considerable spread of Islamic rule on the Iberian Peninsula, the Spaniards who ventured to the New World had an evangelical fervor combined with a *conquistador* mentality (Rivera 1992). The institutional church was planted in America with the support of the Spanish crown and given considerable power and influence. The long alliance which grew up between the church and the politically and economically powerful throughout the Spanish realm was not accidental, but it was not the only vehicle by which the faith was transmitted. A hierarchical church structure dominated by Europeans and those trained in Europe has coexisted with the colorful expressions of grassroots popular religiosity for the half millennium of Latin American Christianity's existence (Dussel 1992). The emphasis on the humanity of Jesus in medieval piety, especially his birth and suffering, was an aspect of the faith easily adopted and interiorized by the native people. The importance of the Virgin Mary and the role of the saints as intercessors were meaningful in the feudal society of medieval Europe and easily applicable to the systems created by the Spanish in the new world. Mary and the saints made holiness and access to God seem possible to common people who had no access to power in their environment. The celebrations of Mary, the saints, and the humanity of Jesus went beyond the sacramental structure of the church and involved all the people in processions, festivals, and a variety of other expressions.

The societal influence and power of the Catholic Church, patronized from the earliest days by the Spanish crown, became a target of the Mexican revolution in 1910. The resulting government became increasingly hostile to manifestations of Catholic faith and practice; clergy, religious, and laity were objects of persecution. Just as the revolution itself impacted the US-Mexico border (Romo 2005), persecuted church personnel found a home on the US side of the border and created a network of institutions along the border which would impact the region religiously and through educational and social services. Ordinary Mexicans never forgot that it was a priest aligned with the *campesinos* in Central Mexico that led their initial cry for independence from Spain a century earlier, bearing the standard of the Virgin of Guadalupe into battle even as much of the higher clergy remained allied with crown of Spain.

Origins and Impact of Latin American Theology

Throughout Latin America, Roman Catholics were empowered by the ecumenical council in Rome known as Vatican II (1962–1965). The council convened by Pope John XXIII and concluded by Pope Paul VI recognized and celebrated the global nature of the church and was a strong impetus for moving beyond centuries of Eurocentrism. While most Catholics were affected by the change in the language of worship from Latin to the vernacular languages following the council, Latin American bishops and theologians realized that it was not only the mass that was being heard in Spanish and Portuguese but also that the experience of the church in this marginal region was beginning to have a voice heard at the center (Boff 1986). The council's emphasis on forging a relationship with the modern world, and the new attention paid to context and culture, stirred the theological imaginations of many Latin American theologians who could now read the Scriptures and tradition not in Latin but as Latinos. European-trained theologians began to read the "signs of the times"[1] with Latin American eyes in a society where the church's long-standing influence tolerated or supported the privilege and wealth of the elite classes while the vast majority of the population experienced poverty and suffering. They began to proclaim not merely the beatitude in Matthew's Gospel, "Blessed are the poor in spirit, for the kingdom of heaven is theirs" (Mt 5:3) with its future promise of reward but also the beatitudes of Luke, which address the materially poor without the qualification "in spirit" and in the same passage add, "but woe to you who are rich, for you have received your consolation" (Lk 6:24). The poverty of the people became the *locus* or the starting point of theology. Not only theologians at the margin but the full conference of Latin American bishops at a plenary session in Medellin, Colombia, in 1968 declared the church's "preferential option for the poor" as constitutive of the example and Gospel of Jesus. This phrase from Latin America would be echoed by future popes and find its way into the universal church's social doctrine (cf. John Paul 1986).

Aristotelian philosophical constructs, first adapted by Thomas Aquinas with great controversy in the thirteenth century and dominant in theology ever since, were deemed inadequate to convey the truths of the Christian faith meaningfully in a context of enormous social inequity. The materialistic philosophy of Karl Marx, whose own context was the sense of alienation among workers in an industrializing

[1]A phrase from the Gospel of Matthew newly interpreted in the council's pastoral constitution on the Church in the Modern World, *Gaudium et Spes,* which came to be a buzz word of the council.

society, seemed better suited for a theological enterprise among the poor. The class conflict that is part and parcel of Marxist thought could not be dismissed by wishful thinking among Christians but would have to be considered in light of the nonviolent stance of the Gospel (Antoncich 1987). Marx's famous critique of religion as the "opium of the people" was taken seriously by these theologians. Was the popular religiosity so strong in Latin America a means of distraction from suffering and addressing its causes? Was the Christian hope in an everlasting happiness in the afterlife an excuse not to work for justice in the world? These questions and their pursuit became known as "liberation theology," a phrase coined by the Peruvian priest Gustavo Gutierrez (1973). The Christian message was being reclaimed as essentially a message of liberation by Christ, not one of patient suffering of oppression because of a future reward. Such suffering may indeed be necessary as witnessed by Latin American martyrs like Archbishop Oscar Romero, the church women, and Jesuit martyrs of El Salvador, but it is not the goal of faith nor the reign of God that Jesus preached. The Scriptures, read from the perspective of the poor and theology read with a "hermeneutic of suspicion" that the thought of the dominant in society has a disproportionate claim on historical theology, led to new insights. Theologians working and living with the poor discovered that the God of history is on the side of the poor (Gutierrez 1991a, b).

The implications of this approach to theology reached far beyond Latin America and beyond the confines of Catholicism. African and Asian, feminist, gay, and many other forms of liberation theology have germinated and sprouted from the rich soil of this theological reflection. African Americans in the United States began to theologically reflect on their situation as a theological *locus*. Hispanic or Latino theologians, who share a language and cultural similarities with the Latin American theologians, have produced a rich harvest of theological reflection on their experience (cf. Fernandez 2000) as a minority in the United States.

Latino Theology North of the Border

Recognizing their cultural and linguistic roots in Latin America, Hispanic theologians in the United States assimilate the history of the conquest of Amerindia by the Spaniards as a starting point for their own theological reflection. Yet theological reflection north of the border is different because Hispanics in the United States also live as a minority population in what is arguably the most affluent and powerful nation in the world. Hispanics in the United States know that their cultural assumptions and worldview are different than that of the majority population. Very often, the loyalty of Hispanics to the United States is questioned when they wish to celebrate a Mexican holiday or prefer to speak or pray in Spanish, even though Hispanics have fought in the US wars, contribute to the US economy, and have integrated themselves in society in much the same way as earlier waves of immigrants. Their theologians give great emphasis to the concept of *mestizaje,* the fusion of races and cultures born of the conquest that is their origin, as a theological concept (Elizondo 1989; Bañuelas 1995). Virgilio Elizondo, a priest of the Archdiocese of San Antonio and the founder of the Mexican American Cultural Center (MACC), describes the violent context of *mestizaje,* and how the ranking of cultures as superior (*conquistadors*) and inferior (conquered) is "imposed and interiorized by all the media of communication: dress, food, manners, language, modes of thinking, art, music, bodily gestures, mannerisms, entertainment and all the institutions of society: economics, school, politics, and Church . . . " (Bañuelas 1995, p. 10). The culturally enforced notion of inferiority is easily applied to the Latino immigrants who find themselves overwhelmed by the language, values, and worldview of the dominant culture and must adopt a servile role to survive. Even the Hispanic who has decades or centuries of generational roots in the United States can be affected by this sense of inferiority as it is reinforced in cultural stereotypes in politics, entertainment, and other venues. Arturo Bañuelas, the El Paso priest who founded the Tepeyac Institute there and began the work of compiling and analyzing the works of US Hispanic theologians, focuses on the positive connotations of *mestizaje*. Spaniards, Amerindians, and Africans in the Americas created a new race, which Elizondo has referred to as the "cosmic race" (Elizondo, 9). Still, in the United States, members of this race are outsiders on the fringe of the dominant culture and strangers in their own land (Bañuelas 1995, p. 1).

US Hispanic/Latino theologians insist that their work is a collaborative effort, a *pastoral de conjunto*, which gives as much credibility to the voice of the unskilled worker and single mother as to the priest or professional theologian. Like their Latin American counterparts, the Latino(a)/theologians weigh heavily the importance of *praxis* and the need to hear from the voiceless. The border is a significant feature in this theology because it emphasizes and symbolizes the liminal character of the US Hispanic's existence: neither fully part of the culture of Latin America nor fully part of North American culture.

The Mexican American Cultural Center in San Antonio, which has evolved into the Mexican American Catholic College, was founded by Father Virgilio Elizondo, both to familiarize those who would be working pastorally with Hispanics with their language and culture and also to provide a center for reflection on the faith from the Mexican-American experience. With the seminal insights of Elizondo, MACC has trained generations of priests, religious, and lay pastoral ministers and has been the sight of important gatherings of Hispanic theologians. On the El Paso-Ciudad Juárez border, Monsignor Arturo Bañuelas founded the Tepeyac Institute in 1989 with the support of Bishop Raymundo J. Peña. Named for and rooted in the story of the apparitions of the Virgin of Guadalupe on the hill of Tepeyac, the institute for lay ministry found inspiration in the character of Juan Diego, the indigenous visionary to whom Guadalupe appeared. According to the oldest accounts, Juan Diego was a catechist, a lay person responsible for teaching the faith. He was charged by the Virgin to convert the Franciscan bishop of Mexico to believe that she really chose this Indian as her messenger and that she desired to have a temple built where she could demonstrate her motherly love for all. Barely noticing the Castillian roses that Juan Diego brought in December as proof of the Virgin's presence, the bishop saw the imprint of the Aztec maiden with hands folded in prayer on the *tilma* he was wearing and was convinced. Certain that the people of the border in El Paso also had something to teach the institutional church like Juan Diego, the Tepeyac Institute was created to train lay ministers for service in the church and to be a center for theological reflection in the most populous metroplex on the border. Theologians from across the United States and beyond share their insights with Tepeyac participants but also learn about the way theology is shaped by the border: the discrimination, the underemployment, and the exploitation experienced by so many of the border's residents.

The Border and Migration

Whether defined by the river called *Grande* from the north and *Bravo* from the south or by a line through the desert separating New Mexico and Arizona from Chihuahua and Sonora and Alta from Baja California, the US-Mexico border set by the Treaty of Guadalupe Hidalgo in 1848 is an artificial political creation that contradicts the geographical and sociocultural unity of these lands. More than just separating the United States of America from the United States of Mexico, the border is a line of demarcation between what were once referred to as the first and third worlds, between Latin and Northern or Anglo America. It is an economic border that creates unnecessary social and cultural difficulties. The river is obviously fluid and the wall of steel is porous, and so is the border. The culture of the Mexican people with all its richness has roots on the United States' side which pre-date the border itself. The migration of people from one side to the other is a story that is much older than the establishment of immigration law (Garcia 1981). The migration of ideas, of commerce, and of people has been the most significant factor in the border region's history and necessarily features prominently in any theological reflection on justice. The border is a privileged place for theological reflection, and the experience of migration throughout human history provides plenty of material for that reflection.

When Archbishop Wilton Gregory of Atlanta spoke to an interfaith gathering on the topic of immigration, he pointed to Abraham, who is recognized as the common father of the faith for Jews, Christians, and Muslims (2006). Abraham began his faith relationship with God by migrating from a land where he had everything to a land he did not know in the obedience of faith. The stories of these three major faith traditions begin with the story of an immigrant, although the trajectory is the opposite of today's immigrant who leaves a situation of desperate need with the faith that something better exists. The central story of the Hebrew Scriptures is the story of mass migration, once as the extended family of Joseph made its way to Egypt to find food in a time of famine, and then again as Moses led the children of Israel out of the Egypt, the land of plenty that became a place of racial discrimination, exploited labor, and enslavement. The period of the Babylonian Captivity is another story in the Hebrew Scriptures of the forced migration of the Israelites into exile and their return migration in joy to the homeland. Although the reality and hardship of migration was so integral to the experience of Israel, God's people had to be reminded again and again by the prophets of their obligation to the widow, the orphan, and the alien. Often, the divine admonition was paired with the poignant reminder, "you too were once strangers and aliens in a foreign land (Ex. 22:20)." In the annual ritualized remembrance of the Passover event, the storytelling begins with the foundational narrative, "my father was a wandering Aramean." The identity of each participant in the *seder* is connected to the story of being in a strange and foreign land. It was a particular celebration of the Passover that became the setting for the Christian Passover as Jesus passed over from death to life.

When the evangelist Matthew in the New Testament presents Jesus of Nazareth as the long awaited Messiah, the Jesus he depicts incarnates his people's own history, one who had to flee into the ancient land of his ancestors' captivity and who was called out of Egypt as a child (Matt 2:15). Theologically, we can say that the greatest example of migration is the Incarnation itself, God metaphorically journeying from eternity to share in our human history, crossing the chasm between Creator and creature.

The Asian-American theologian Peter Phan has pointed out the root of our word "parish" is *paroikos* which means a temporary resident, a guest, or a person on the move, a word used to describe the Christian believers in the New Testament (Kerwin 2006). The Second Vatican Council called the Church itself a "pilgrim people" (Flannery 1975). Saint Augustine called all Christians "resident aliens." Francis of Assisi told his brothers in his rule that they were to go about in the world as "pilgrims and strangers" with no place to call home (1223). Pilgrimages to holy places in Christianity have long served as a metaphor of the journey through life to the ultimate homeland in God. Indeed, it can be said that migration is written on each page of the Christian story.

The Pontifical Council on Migrants and Refugees (2004) argues that migration was gaining recognition as a natural right in the 1200s, long before the advent of the nation-state. Pope Pius XII in *Exul Familia Nazarethena*, a 1952 Apostolic Constitution, explicitly states that migration is a human right. He builds his argument on the right to a living space asserted by Pope Leo XIII in *Rerum Novarum* (1897) and again mentions this right to migrate in a 1948 Christmas letter to the American bishops. Pope Pius XII directly addressed the migration between Mexico and the United States, citing with approval the actions of American bishops who responded to Pope Benedict XV's plea that those fleeing religious persecution in Mexico find refuge in the American church. In a qualified way, Pope John XXIII restated the right to migration in his remarkable encyclical *Pacem in Terris*. Pope John asserted that there had to be just reasons for one to emigrate and called on nations to accommodate immigration flows according to their ability. (John XXIII, 1968)

The theme of migration and the rights of migrants was a theme that Pope John Paul II addressed repeatedly during the 27 years of his pontificate; to the basic right to migrate, John Paul added that refugees had other rights: the right to be reunited with their families and the right to dignified work and a just wage (1990 Lenten message). In his annual messages for World Migration Day, a tradition maintained by Pope Benedict XVI, John Paul II reiterates the pastoral concern for migrants set forth so well by his predecessor Pius XII and, in 1995, lamented that undocumented immigrants are often exploited by developed nations as a source of cheap labor (John Paul II 1995). As Pope John XXIII had noted decades earlier, as long as there is global underdevelopment and an enormous gap between the rich and the poor, the phenomenon of migration will continue. As the United States Conference of Catholic Bishops has argued repeatedly in recent years, the elimination of global poverty is the only lasting solution to the challenge of immigration.

In 1996, the US bishops realized the necessity of a two-pronged approach to the resolution of the migration crisis: (1) ameliorate the conditions that force people to migrate and (2) integrate immigrants to our nation's life (National Conference of Catholic Bishops Committee on Migration 1996). While the ultimate solution depends on the former, work must begin with the latter. The integration of immigrants would mean that they have a voice in society, access to common goods such as education and health care, earn fair wages, and enjoy freedom of movement. The detention of immigrants without just cause or due process and law enforcement practices which force immigrants to live in the shadows for fear of deportation are violations of the human dignity of the migrant. In his Apostolic Exhortation *Ecclesia in America*, flowing from the Synod of America in 1999,[2] Pope John Paul II was very cognizant of the differences between north and south, Hispanic and Anglo America, but he called the church of the whole continent, north and south, to an experience of solidarity (John Paul II 1999). In the midst of his very challenging message to all America, John Paul explicitly mentioned undocumented immigrants. "Attention must be called to the rights of migrants and their families and to respect for their human dignity, even in cases of non-legal immigration (p. 109, par. 65)."

By the time the bishops of both the US and Mexican conferences jointly issued a historic first pastoral letter on migration in 2003 called "Strangers No Longer: Together on the Journey of Hope," (United States Conference of Catholic Bishops (USCCB) and Conferencia del Episcopado Mexicano 2003) there was already a body of church teaching on the issue. This letter addressed the experience of migration and the pastoral care of migrants from the perspectives of both the emigrant and the immigrant, the places of sending and the places of receiving. Five guiding principles were established: (1) persons have the right to find opportunities in their homeland, (2) persons have the right to migrate to support themselves and their families, (3) sovereign nations have the right to control their borders, (4) refugees and asylum seekers should be afforded protection, and (5) the human dignity and human rights of undocumented migrants should be respected. Theological reflection on the border requires a direct application of the body of this official teaching to the lives of both the migrants and the people who receive or resist them, always asking about the requirements of the Christian faith in these situations.

When Cardinal Roger Mahony, archbishop of Los Angeles, stated that "immigrants are us" (2007), he was referring especially to Catholics but knew that his words were true for the vast majority of Americans. The history of earlier waves of immigrants to the United States is well known but frequently forgotten in recent

[2]One of a series of such synods organized by John Paul II for various continents; a synod is a consultative gathering of representative bishops.

discussions of an immigration crisis (Sandoval 1990). The waves of immigrants who largely arrived at Ellis Island and in many cases stayed in New York and the east coast eventually followed the dominant trajectory in United States' history, moving from east to west. The people on the border remind the rest of the United States that the movement from west to east is not the only way to read the development of American history. There has always been a movement from south to north, a movement well underway before today's borderlands were incorporated into the United States of America (Rodriguez 2002). At the time of the pilgrims' landing at Plymouth Rock, there had already been nearly a century's history of Catholicism among the Spaniards and Pueblo Indians in northern New Mexico. Many people with deep roots in the borderlands can say with historical accuracy that they did not cross the border, the border crossed them! It is ironic and with blatant historical ignorance when descendants of the eighteenth- and nineteenth-century European immigrants are the loudest voices in the anti-immigrant sentiment heard today. How often do we need to be reminded that we too were aliens and strangers in a foreign land? In 1920, 75% of the Catholics in the United States were immigrants (Kerwin 2006, p. 445), and the Church responded with a phenomenal network of parishes, schools, hospitals, charities, religious communities, mutual aid societies, and social groups. Some of those who are most vocal in voicing the ugly anti-immigrant rhetoric owe their integrated status in the United States to these institutions from their parents' and grandparents' era.

The negative attitudes of people in the United States toward immigrants present leaders of faith communities with a timely opportunity to be prophetic. The vast majority of attention in the immigration debate focuses on the enforcement of immigration policies. People of faith have been trying to emphasize the impracticality and the injustice of the current laws and policies which do not work and which actually create the situation whereby so many people enter the United States illegally because there is no practical manner of doing so legally.

The theological hope of building a new humanity must begin with a consciousness of human dignity rooted in the belief that human beings are created in the image and likeness of God. From the perspective of faith, it is more important for all people to see themselves as members of the human family than as citizens of a particular nation. For too many churchgoing people, the common elements of humanity or even a shared faith tradition is not as important as being defined as American. Americans tend to see themselves as unique and special while seeing everyone else as "other"; from this superiority complex, the inferior "other" is often viewed as threatening. Recognizing commonalities in the human family is the foundation of respect for human rights and can allow for the celebration of the differences among peoples as a richness and asset for society.

Arturo Bañuelas sees the work of the antireign strongly behind the anti-immigrant sentiment in the United States. He notes that the antireign is well organized around a political strategy and argues that the Hispanic theologians in the United States who have made such progress in reflecting on their identity need to pay more attention to the sociopolitical element. Latin American liberation theologians have been criticized for substituting a political agenda for the genuine reign of

God, but what is needed is a political agenda on behalf of the reign of God, as an instrument of the reign of God, and on the way to the reign of God. Reflection on *praxis* in light of the word of God and the tradition is meant to lead back to *praxis*, making theology incarnate and putting it into practice in order to continue the process.

Theology in Action on the Border

The existence of *colonias* is one of the very visible products of all the injustices described as the border reality in the first chapter of this book. *Colonias* are underdeveloped neighborhoods on the US side of the border which lack basic infrastructure and whose residents live in conditions worse than many people in the developing world. Safely out of the view of the majority of residents, the phenomena of *colonias* exist all along the US-Mexico border. The *colonias* of El Paso County, Texas, which exist on the western and eastern periphery of the city of El Paso, are typical examples. Undeveloped land was offered at an affordable price to recently arrived immigrants with the promise of being part of a new neighborhood that will soon have running water, drainage, electricity, paved streets and sidewalks, and playgrounds and parks for their children, a promise that never materializes. Although the land is relatively cheap, it still requires all the material resources of the purchasers, who discover that they must still pay for water and that transportation from these remote parts is very difficult. Infuriated by the injustice of expanding *colonias* and seeking a way to work for the common good following the principles of faith, some El Paso religious leaders looked to the organizing strategy of the Industrial Areas Foundation which had successfully empowered Hispanics and other low-income residents of San Antonio to better their circumstances through the organization of local churches and other institutions called Communities Organized for Public Service or COPS.

In 1980, the El Paso Interreligious Sponsoring Organization (EPiSO) was formed. Various denominations of churches were involved at the beginning, although as in the general population, Catholics were the most numerous. This network of organized church institutions taught its members how to read and reflect on their scriptures and tradition and apply what they learn to their actual circumstances. Such an application requires an analysis of the power structures within the larger community. The shared frustrations of individuals angered by their own experiences of injustice and feelings of helpfulness are transformed by a discovery of the power of an organized group that speaks with one voice. Through series of one-on-one conversations, individuals who have worshipped together and share the same neighborhoods and schools come to discover their common interests and hopes. The individual meetings fold into house meetings of several individuals who identify leaders and those with leadership potential among them. Critical needs surface in these meetings as well as the commitments of people who want to work for their resolution. One of the guiding principles of these meetings is that the price of criticism or complaint is a constructive alternative. When a community sees its dreams of constructive alternatives take shape and move toward realization, apathy and hopelessness diminish.

Participants in a community organizing strategy learn more about the nature of participatory democracy, one of the founding ideals of the United States. Organized parishes with networks of relationships create a visible constituency for the elected officials, who in return recognize the power in such organized groups and take them seriously. The participants commit to studying the issues they are addressing and discover additional power as the formerly disenfranchised begin to grasp the complex issues of local government and social problems as well as or better than their elected officials. Community organizing in El Paso began to produce responses from local and state government that led to potable water in more and more of the *colonias*, along with paved roads, sewers, playgrounds, and other things that most residents take for granted. It also produced extended-day programs in schools that were plagued with low test scores in poor districts. Immigrant parents went from timidly dropping off their children at school to being actively engaged as partners in their children's educations. In turn, these parents learned how to advocate for themselves and even face the state legislature with the confidence of knowing their issues and their rights. This application of theology in action also created Project ARRIBA, a high-skills living-wage job training program in which businesses partner with the organization to leverage funding for train workers from the local population rather than recruiting outsiders for the highest paying jobs. With hard work and persistence, people who earned minimum wages and received government assistance discovered they were capable of a career that produced a decent salary.

Conclusion

A theological perspective of social justice on the border is the product of a faith that is actively engaged in seeking and creating the justice, peace, and fraternal order constitutive of the reign of God. It must be born out of the experience of the people of the border, especially those who have been victimized by the systematic oppression of poverty and a minority status within the dominant culture. It is in dialogue with theologians of liberation in different locations and contexts and produces its own fruits as the hope for a better world becomes incarnate in the lives of the participants. This theology necessarily leads back to active engagement in the struggle for a more just order.

References

Antoncich, A. (1987). *Christians in the face of injustice*. Maryknoll: Orbis.
Bañuelas, A. (1995). *Mestizo Christianity*. Eugene: Wipf and Stock.

Boff, L. (1986). *Ecclesiogenesis*. Maryknoll: Orbis.
CELAM (1968) Documentos finales de Medellin: Segunda Conferencia General del Episcopado Latinoamericano. Medellin, Columbia: 1968.
Dussel, E. (Ed.). (1992). *The church in Latin America 1592–1992*. Maryknoll: Orbis.
Elizondo, V. (1995). *Mestizaje* as a locus of theological reflection. In A. Bañuelas (Ed.), *Mestizo Christianity* (pp. 5–27). Eugene: Wipf and Stock.
Fernandez, E. (2000). *La Cosecha*. Collegeville: Liturgical.
Flannery, A. (Ed.). (1975). *Vatican council II: The conciliar and postconciliar documents*. Northport: Costello.
Francis of Assisi (1223). (1999). The later rule. In *Francis of Assisi: The saint* (p. 103). New York: New City.
Garcia, M. (1981). *Desert immigrants*. New Haven: Yale.
Gregory, W. (2006). Hebrew benevolent congregation temple symposium. *Origins, 36*(26), 443–444.
Gutierrez, G. (1973). *A theology of liberation*. Maryknoll: Orbis.
Gutierrez, G. (1991a). *We drink from our own wells*. Maryknoll: Orbis.
Gutierrez, R. (1991b). *When Jesus came the corn mothers went away*. Stanford: Stanford University.
John XXIII. (1963). *Pacem in Terris*. Retrieved from http://www.vatican.va/holy_father/john_xxiii/encyclicals/documents/hf_j-xxiiii_enc_11041963_pacem_en.html
John Paul II. (1986). *Letter to Brazilian bishops*. Esp. par. 5. Retrieved from http://www.vatican.va./holy_father/john_paul_ii/letters/1986/documents/hf_jp-ii_let_19860409_conf-episcopale-brasile_po.html
John Paul II. (1990). *Lenten message*. Esp. par. 3. Retrieved from http://www.vatican.va./holy_father/john_paul_ii/messages/lent/documents/hf_jp-ii_mes_19890908_lent-1980_en.html
John Paul II. (1995). *Message for world migration day*. Retrieved from http://www.vatican.va./holy_father/john_paul_ii/messages/migration/documents/hf_jp-ii_med_19940810_world-migration-day-1995_it.html
John Paul II. (1999). *Ecclesia in America* (p. 108). Vatican City: Libreria Editrice Vaticana.
Kerwin, D. (2006). Speech at Archdiocese of Hartford social justice dinner. *Origins, 36*(26), 445–447.
Leo XIII. (1897). *Rerum Novarum*. Retrieved from http://www.vatican.va/holy_father/leo_xiii/encyclicals/documents/hf_l_xiii_enc_15051881_rerum_novarum_en.html. Pars. 47ff.
Mahony, R. (2007). *Panel discussion on immigration*. Retrieved from http://al.nd.edu/news/13081-nd-forum-panelists-express-frustration-over-lack-of-federal-immigration-reform/
National Conference of Catholic Bishops Committee on Migration. (1996). *From newcomers to citizens: All come bearing gifts*. Retrieved from http://www.nccbuscc.org/mrs/citizenship.shtml/
Pius XII. (1952). *Exsul Familia Nazarethana*. Retrieved from www.papacyencyclicals.net/Pius12/p12exsul.htm
Pontifical Council for the Pastoral care of Migrants and Itinerant People. (2004). *Erga migrantes Caritas Christi*. Retrieved from http://www.vatican.va/roman_curia/pontifical_councils/migrants/documents/rc_pc_migrants_doc_20040514_erga_migrantes_caritas_christi_en.html
Rivera, L. (1992). *A violent evangelism*. Louisville: Westminster/John Knox.
Rodriguez, R. (2002). *Brown: The last discovery of America*. New York: Penguin.
Romo, D. (2005). *Ringside seat to a revolution*. El Paso: Cinco Puntos.
Sandoval, M. (1990). *On the move: A history of the Hispanic church in the United States*. Maryknoll: Orbis.
United States Conference of Catholic Bishops (USCCB) and Conferencia del Episcopado Mexicano. (2003). *Strangers no longer*. Washington, DC: USCCB.

Part III
Problems and Opportunities on the US-Mexico Border

Chapter 6
Housing, *Colonias*, and Social Justice in the U.S.-Mexico Border Region

Guillermina Gina Núñez-Mchiri

The places and spaces in which people live and build community reveal the consequences of what Paul Farmer (2003) refers to as structural violence associated with poverty, marginalization, and underdevelopment. Many such settlements are located in southwestern states along the US-Mexico border. In this chapter, I bring attention to unmet needs and challenges currently faced in these communities, given the type of development strategies pursued on the periphery of large urban centers. *Colonia* residents face pressing issues, among them, the need for public health-care facilities, social and physical infrastructure, and employment opportunities. I develop these ideas in this chapter based on 10 years of ethnographic research in two large counties, in Texas and New Mexico, located along the US-Mexico border.

Colonias, a word that means "neighborhoods" in Spanish, are nonincorporated communities located on the rims of larger urban centers throughout the US-Mexico border. *Colonias* provide temporary and permanent housing for residents and transnational sojourners crossing the US-Mexico border. They are significant for understanding the inequities associated with life in the margins in one of the most important migration corridors in the world: the El Paso del Norte Metropolitan region (Ward 1999). Donaldson and Esparza (2010) estimate *colonias* are comprised of about 2,500 villages, towns, and cities with well over one million residents primarily concentrated in the state of Texas and in smaller numbers in New Mexico, Arizona, and California. *Colonias* have both rural and urban characteristics, depending on their history, size, population density, location, and community development trajectories (Núñez 2006). Although factors such as the *colonia's* history and completed infrastructure will vary, most of these communities lack basic infrastructure and public services (Staudt 1998). In El Paso County, Texas, there are 144 officially recognized *colonias with,* in 2007, 56,671 households (personal communication with Jessie Acosta, El Paso County Planning Department, 2009)

G.G. Núñez-Mchiri (✉)
Department of Anthropology, University of Texas at El Paso, El Paso, TX, USA
e-mail: ggnunez@utep.edu

M. Lusk et al. (eds.), *Social Justice in the U.S.-Mexico Border Region*,
DOI 10.1007/978-94-007-4150-8_6,

Fig. 6.1 Image of *Colonia* household without potable water taken by Ms. Vera Norez, undergraduate research assistant at UTEP, during the Fall 2010 (Photo taken with *colonia* residents' permission)

(see Fig. 6.1). Many of these *colonias*, some with idealized names, have subsections or extensions, such as Agua Dulce ("Sweet Water," but located in the semiarid desert with limited access to water), which show how these communities have expanded over time.

This work provides an anthropological perspective to the study of *colonias*, housing, and social justice issues in these communities. My research has been mostly in Doña Ana County, New Mexico, on the US-Mexico border and immediately adjacent to El Paso County. I lived in Las Cruces, New Mexico, from 2002 to 2005, and commuted daily to conduct ethnographic and applied research in the *colonias* in northern Doña Ana County, spending 3 years conducting household interviews and participating in community-planning meetings with residents, nonprofit organizations, and government agencies. During this time, I conducted ethnosurveys in 75 *colonia* households from 2002 to 2003, and multiple household visits conducting oral histories from 2003 to 2005. However, since I began teaching at the University of Texas at El Paso since 2005, I have done multiple site visits to *colonias* in east and west El Paso and have met and interviewed with similarly situated residents and community organizers in order to gain comparative perspectives in two counties that are part of two states along the US side of the international borderline. Over the years, I visited *colonia* families and households, as well as weddings, graduations, funerals, baby showers, community meetings, community cleanups, and numerous meetings pertaining to *colonia* housing, health, and community development issues. Moreover, I met with county employees including the urban planner and the county attorney responsible for putting forward much of the *colonias* legislation in Austin, the capital city of Texas, and working with US Census personnel so they could have a better account of *colonia* populations. I have also mentored and supervised undergraduate and graduate students with research interests in *colonias* in El Paso County, accompanying them to field visits and to interviews with *colonia* residents and the people who work in these communities as community partners.

In seeking to understand the growth and development of *colonias* along the US-Mexico border, Núñez and Klamminger (2010) have previously examined how urban cores and peripheries are engaged in both mutually beneficial and exploitive relationships of power. It is on the fringes of larger urban centers of power, such as *colonias*, where residents' rights and humanity are often adversely affected by economic depression, social isolation, political alienation, and repression. It is specifically in such places situated outside of centers of economic and political power where scholars, policy makers, and social service providers may observe the consequences of international trade policies, immigration regulation policies, and the surveillance and protection of the nation-state at the cost of civil and human rights. Although change is slow and gradual, *colonia* settlements and communities usually undergo continuous processes of transition.

The various types of industries located along the US-Mexico border have drawn migrants from Mexico's central and southern states who are enticed to move to the border in hopes of higher wages. In the El Paso-Ciudad Juárez border region, the service sector and manufacturing plants or *maquiladoras* have drawn migrants to the border region for more than four decades. Ganster and Lorey (2007:123) indicate that migrants settled in larger urban concentrations due in part to jobs in manufacturing, construction, hotels, restaurants, and services. Other more rural parts of the border attract migrants to emigrate across the border in search of work in agricultural and dairy industries. The supply and demand for low-cost agricultural goods, manufactured goods, and services in the US-Mexico border region are shaped by national and international markets and by local demands for seasonal and year-round labor. Economic dynamics influence the growth of *colonias*, primarily because employers that recruit labor are not necessarily responsible for providing housing. As such, individuals become responsible for finding affordable housing within a relatively close proximity to their place of employment.

This chapter is divided into five sections. First, I focus on the historical forces and the public policies that have shaped *colonia* development and underdevelopment. Then, I discuss the structural violence caused by the relative lack of visibility and attention given to *colonias* along the US-Mexico border. I argue that this "out of sight, out of mind" adds to the marginalization and exclusion of *colonias* in public policy debates associated with border industrialization and urban growth.

I follow with a discussion of *colonia* household characteristics, which provides readers with a more nuanced understanding of the benefits and challenges of life in *colonias,* including the self-help practice of home building and the clustering of *colonia* households as a strategy of resilience and as a source of conflict. Next is a section on community development efforts that address how *colonia* residents contribute to community development efforts via neighborly relations and relationships with people and institutions of power. I argue here that development efforts that add to the skills and employment opportunities of *colonia* residents are as important as place-oriented development efforts. I follow by a discussion on the social stigmas associated with *colonias* and the need to reexamine how these communities are defined as communities of lack versus communities that add value to our border region. This chapter concludes with thoughts for future research and policy recommendations to address the need for additional policy and scholarly attention to *colonia* communities.

Historical Forces and Public Policies That Shape *Colonia* Development

Colonias on the US-Mexico border are situated within one of the most important migration corridors in North America. This region plays a significant role in the movement of people and goods. Migration and population settlement processes along the US-Mexico border are deeply rooted in historical, economic, and political processes affecting the El Paso del Norte region. The massive migration of peoples throughout the world and in the US Southwest specifically involves processes of displacement, movement, and incorporation. The lives of immigrants are often characterized to the processes of migration and incorporation in host nations that are often hostile to these populations. Leo Chávez, in *Shadowed Lives* (1992), analyzes immigrants who live in the shadows hoping to go unnoticed while seeking work in the United States. As communities located on the border, the growth and development processes of *colonias* are inextricably linked to historical, political, and economic forces influencing human migration and immigrant population settlement and accommodation processes.

The concentration of the Mexican and Mexican American population in the US Southwest, their stigmatization, and their marginalization are tied to a number of historical events dating to the origins of the US-Mexico border. In 1848, Mexican populations inhabited this region when the Treaty of Guadalupe Hidalgo and the Gadsden Purchase led to the creation of the US-Mexico border (Del Castillo 1990). Some of the *colonias* date back to the 1800s when the border was under negotiation (Núñez 2006). Migration from Mexico to the United States originated in the southwestward expansion of the United States in the nineteenth century and the deliberate recruitment of Mexican laborers by US employers in the twentieth century (Castles and Miller 1998; citing Portes and Rumbaut 1996). More recent accounts of Mexican migration to the United States indicate how binational labor programs, such as the Bracero Program of 1942 to 1964, resulted in the recruitment of 2.2 million laborers to the United States to assist with farm work while US service men and women participated in World War II, leading to the border's population explosion (Vélez-Ibáñez 1997; Ganster and Lorey 2007).

In the 1950s, rural land in El Paso County, TX, was marketed nationally and internationally as estate communities prime for investment and for retirees. However, the high costs associated with developing these communities discouraged investors from providing the necessary infrastructure for these properties to become full-fledged communities. This failed marketing strategy to market rural land in El Paso County to local and foreign investors contributed to the high rates of absentee owners of *colonia* properties. The lack of attention given to vacant lands in *colonias* further adds to the "out of sight, out of mind" attitude that persists about *colonia* underdevelopment issues. Absent landholders are people who do not dwell on a permanent basis in these communities (Ward et al. 2000). The number of empty lots within *colonias* contributes to the accumulation of desert brush and of illegal dumpsites used to discard used tires, old furniture, and industrial and household waste. The lack of attention to illegal waste disposal practices in *colonias* creates not only problems with vermin and pests but also fire hazards and unappealing landscapes.

One *colonia*-specific policy leading to the creation and leading to the creation and classification process of *colonias*, the González National Affordable Housing Act (NAHA) was passed in 1990, which defined a *colonia* as an "identifiable community in Arizona, California, New Mexico, or Texas within 150 miles of the U.S.-Mexico border, lacking decent water and sewage systems and decent housing and in existence as a *colonia* before November 28, 1989." This definition, and in particular the cutoff date of November 28, 1989, generated a rushed effort among local communities throughout the border region's counties to reclassify those in need of physical infrastructure as "*colonias*." Although this classification would bring federal and state funding to local border communities, the "*colonia*" label also contributed to racialized stigmatization as low-income communities of color in need of federal and state "set aside" funding—much like an affirmative action approach to border community development efforts. In Texas, a number of *colonia*-specific pieces of legislation have deterred the development of new *colonias*. However, much of this legislation has constrained what residents and sometimes unscrupulous developers have been able to do with current *colonia* plots of land. Future policy researchers should consider examining legislative efforts to banish regulations, while examining ties between legislative officials and developers.

In 1994, the passing of the North American Free Trade Agreement (NAFTA) marked a significant shift in the manufacturing activities of the border region. Many of these shifts have their historical precedence in the 1960s Border Industrialization Project, which aimed to lay the groundwork for *maquiladoras* (Fernández Kelly 1983). Large textile plants were relocated to Mexico and elsewhere, displacing thousands of workers from manufacturing jobs in the city of El Paso. As people lost their jobs, they were unable to pay for high rents or mortgages in the city and were forced to look for affordable housing options in the *colonias*. In El Paso County, Riley (1998) cites the US Department of Labor report that indicates that 10,000 workers in El Paso lost their jobs as a result of NAFTA, more than any other city in the country. These manufacturing jobs in El Paso had offered laborers wages of about US $400 a week, while *maquiladoras* across the border in Ciudad Juárez paid an average of US$50 a week (Mauleon and Ting 2000). As corporations exported their production-related jobs across the border into Mexico and elsewhere, laborers have been left stranded without opportunities to apply their job skills in new industries.

More contemporary policies have affected the movement of Mexican-origin populations. For example, border enforcement and protection policies that came about after September 11, 2001, made it more difficult for unauthorized immigrants to migrate back and forth across the border. In many border households, family members have sought to become legally authorized US residents and citizens. However, the long, tedious, and costly naturalization process has forced many families to stay put in the border region until family members become documented. Movement past US Border Patrol checkpoints has become increasingly more dangerous for individuals and families who are seeking legalization (Núñez 2006; Núñez and Heyman 2007; Talavera et al. 2010). More recently since 2007 to 2011, the narco-war violence in Ciudad Juárez, Chihuahua, Mexico, has forced residents to relocate to other places in Mexico and across the border into El Paso. Middle and business class residents found options in the city, while the working poor have sought refuge in *colonias*. The 2010 Census data, not yet released at the time of this publication, is likely to show the rise in the foreign born population of El Paso County. City officials have given earlier guesstimates of 30,000 new residents moving in from Ciudad Juárez; however, the actual numbers are unknown. Schools have more children from Juárez, new businesses have opened throughout the city, and more residents are self-identifying as originally being from Ciudad Juarez who came to El Paso as “visitors” or as “refugees” seeking to escape the violence.

Out of Sight, Out of Mind: The Structural Violence of Living in the Margins

In *Centering the Margins*, Núñez and Klamminger (2010) discuss how *colonias* serve as a “buffer” for a number of clashes taking place at the boundaries of two nations: the clash between rural and urban, immigrants and citizens, authorized population settlement and unauthorized development, as well as many other social, political, and ecological outcomes associated with rapid urbanization and inadequate infrastructure. These populations on the margins of urbanized settings function as spaces and places of social tension and transformation. As buffers, *colonias* serve as the safety nets for the border region’s low-income and working poor residents, migrants, and local residents, people who are pushed to the margins because they are employed at or below the national poverty levels in the border region's metropolises and surrounding rural communities. Without *colonias*, the border region would arguably experience much higher rates of visible homelessness and despair. Yet, because of *colonias*, many of the US-Mexico border region's working poor, and their accompanying socioeconomic and environmental conditions, are less visible and less noticeable (Núñez-Mchiri 2009).

Colonias represent an example of contemporary inequality in the US-Mexico borderlands. The social and geographic distance of *colonias* contributes to the challenges of everyday life through the marginalization of *colonia* families and households. Family dynamics are influenced by a number of factors describing the family's life cycle, educational levels, language(s) spoken at home, social economic status, work experience, social networks, and citizenship status. There are, at any given time, a number of these categories that affect families in *colonias* and their ability to face the challenges of daily life. For example, a single parent who has several children needs to balance the ability to seek work or go to work while figuring out what to do in the event a child gets ill. In a *colonia*, this is a complex dilemma particularly because of limited resources in these communities, including health-care facilities, child-care centers, public transportation, language barriers, and limited financial resources. Having one child become ill complicates the parent's ability to pick up other children from school if transportation is an issue. So what usually happens in this case is that a parent will take all of the children from school to accompany the ill child to the nearest health-care center. Given the limited financial resources in most *colonia* households, it was common for residents to take their children across the Mexican border to seek health care. The high incidences of violence in Ciudad Juarez have surely affected the cross-border practice of border residents seeking medical care in Mexico; this is a topic for future research and inquiry. The lack of affordable and accessible health clinics in Texas contributes to high absentee rates among *colonia* school-aged children, who are often pulled out of school to accompany their families in search of medical services in the city or across the border. This is a significant concern primarily because if children miss too much school, parents face fines and court hearings before a judge to explain school absences.

While *colonias* offer a place where workers can live inexpensively and create their own homes and communities, they do so at the high costs of jeopardizing the human and civil rights and quality of life of low-income residents, the majority of whom are of Mexican descent. Colonia residents constantly move in and out of zones of development and underdevelopment, negotiating everyday life in search of employment in the city and in search of refuge, repose, and shelter in their *colonia* populations. Life in *colonias* is often complicated because residents and their communities are usually outside of the visual horizons and mental landscapes of those operating within centers of power that are making decisions on the livelihoods of others. *Colonias* provide an outlet for low-income and working poor residents who are funneled away from the urban core and into the rural periphery. As opposed to other large urban cities, where the affluent have sought to escape urban poverty by moving out to the suburbs or into gated communities, on the border it is poor people who are pushed out, primarily because they are not able to find well-paying jobs and affordable housing in the city.

Previous ethnographic research (Núñez 2006; Núñez and Heyman 2007; Heyman et al. 2009; Talavera et al. 2010) has revealed that marginality in *colonias* is multiplied by the structural violence associated with wider political issues, such as immigration raids, poor access to education and health care, unemployment, and underemployment. These challenges are further aggravated by personal and individual experiences, such as lack of transportation, physical mobility, limited social networks, and lack of credit. Poverty and limited economic mobility in the border region then provide people with few opportunities. Those with the financial means to move out of *colonias* will often opt to do so, while other residents have limited options to live elsewhere.

The spatial distance of *colonias* and other rural communities from potable water lines and the extensive plots of empty space between *colonias* make for the delivery of piped water a highly costly ordeal (Bath et al. 1994). In 2009, for example, there were approximately 10,000 residents[1] in El Paso County without water services. This estimate may be compared to 1998 figures in which an estimated 75,000 residents living in El Paso County's *colonias* lived without potable water services (Staudt 1998:114). There are 144 *colonias* in El Paso County; of these, there are approximately 11 neighborhoods that are still in need of potable water (personal communication Jessie Acosta El Paso County Planning Department, 2009). In an interview conducted in east El Paso County, Texas, by Vera Norez (2010), one *colonia* resident indicated "I have nothing here, no gas, electricity, and NO water. I have nothing. I live worse here than I did in Mexico" (Fig. 6.2).

Many *colonia* communities continue to wait for potable water to be delivered to their homes; unfortunately, the decision to deliver water to many *colonias* lies in the hands of local water boards who must decide on whether or not this service will be eventually delivered. Water boards are quasi-government entities that deliver services to specific neighborhoods located within districts. Communities that are more developed have been clustered and are concentrated in their population densities are more likely to have water delivery services expedited. The major challenge for *colonia* residents and for water districts involves the cost of delivering water and laying in the adequate pipelines and infrastructure to deliver the water. If a community is far from the nearest water connection and there are relatively few households that require services, these will be on a waiting list for a much longer period of time. Densely populated settlements with economic and political resources and organization are more likely to seek out the delivery of water with greater expediency. Another significant concern is the use of septic tanks, which often overflow and cause significant health risks to residents. The high cost of clearing up a backed up or overflowing septic tank is one more expense residents must contend with.

---

[1]This estimate was provided by an El Paso Water Utilities representative during a "Drink Up?" Water Quality and Resources in the Texas-New Mexico Region Panel discussion at the University of Texas, El Paso, during Earth Week—Tuesday, May 21, 2009.

Fig. 6.2 Image of water containers outside a mobile home owned by an 82-year-old grandmother who is the sole caretaker of three grandchildren in a *colonia* in East El Paso, Texas. Photo taken in 2010 by Ms. Vera Norez, undergraduate research assistant UTEP (Photo taken with colonia resident's permission)

Characteristics of Colonia Households

Homes in *colonias* are usually built according to a family's creativity, needs, and economic possibilities. Most *colonias* are not usually built like track neighborhoods according to one of a few standardized floor plans. Housing structures in *colonias* range from mobile homes known locally as *trailas*, site-built homes, and manufactured homes. Residents often purchase a plot of land and then bring to it a mobile home or a trailer home they can situate on their property. As families grow, so do their needs for additional rooms. Thus, it is quite common for trailer homes to be modified with added-on rooms, kitchens, living rooms, and car ports. Among the sturdier housing structures are the site-built homes, which are homes built on the ground, as opposed to elevated trailer homes placed on cinder blocks or other usually unstable platforms.

Colonia households are usually comprised of any number of combinations of single-family units, multi-family units, and clustered households. Single-family homes usually have one or two parents and children. Multi-family units may have two or more generations of family members living in one home. Clustered households are usually members of two or three generations living in separate household structures within a plot of land or homes located immediately adjacent to one another in neighboring lots. Each of these family household units and arrangements have their benefits and challenges, as families in *colonias* negotiate their living spaces according to their financial means and life cycles. For example, a young couple might need to live with one of the spouse's parents until they have enough money of their own to buy their own plot of land or their own home elsewhere. These household accommodations lead to collaboration and the pooling of resources that contribute to a family's resilience and strategic negotiations to meet a family's daily needs. Familial networks and the social, economic, and political obligations these create can and often do assist *colonia* families in times of need. However, these same networks often complicate life for residents as individuals within households compete for space, food, autonomy, and privacy.

From my own ethnographic work in the border region, I have found that to a great extent, the market economy weighs heavily in a family's ability to purchase a property and build a home in a *colonia*. Residents in *colonias* either rent or buy what they can afford to live in. To a great extent, I would argue *colonias* provide an alternative to visible homelessness in our border region. Unlike life in a city, in *colonias*, a family is likely to buy land by making a small down payment and then making modest payments on their property on a monthly basis. On average, *colonia* lots range from three-quarters of an acre of land to one acre per lot. Once a plot of land is acquired, a small trailer is usually placed on the property until a family is able to afford a site-built home. Some families have lived in mobile homes their entire lives, while other families modify their mobile homes to have added-on rooms to accommodate growing families. Families usually gather their resources to purchase construction materials to then build on to their homes. These household structures thus represent a transition from the ephemeral to the permanent, as residents become rooted in *colonias*. In spite of these challenges, *colonias* have higher homeownership rates than mainstream Americans.

Given the "organic" nature of *colonia*-household structures, there are a number of characteristics that tend to define owner-built homes. Residents must often rely on their own self-help construction skills and those of their most immediate friends, relatives, or neighbors. While many residents have professional construction, electrical, plumbing skills and experiences, many other residents do not. Self-help housing represents the best option to building homes from whatever materials, skills, and resources residents have at their disposal. Thus, it is common for many homes in colonias to have problems with leaky roofs, faulty wiring, and unfinished projects that make these housing units unsafe to live in.

Many *colonia* residents must rely on their own skills and knowledge to repair their homes as best as possible. As Esperanza Hernández (pseudonym), a *colonia* resident in east El Paso, Texas, noted:

> As a single-mom, I had to figure out how to fix things around my home. I cannot afford for someone else to come in and do things for me. Now, I even teach other women, especially single-mothers how to fix their homes by laying their own tile, changing a water heater, and making other small repairs around their homes.

One *colonia* housing specialist expressed concern about *colonia* residents' self-help efforts, particularly when these efforts do not follow safe housing codes, especially when dealing with electrical outlets and other home-safety practices. As this specialist in Texas noted, "self-help efforts seem ideal, except when people are not informed about the safety hazards they create when trying to do the repairs by themselves. We have seen several unfortunate events, in which people's homes have burned because of faulty electrical jobs." In spite of these risks, residents tend to take pride in what they have been able to build through their own financial and personal investments. As one resident noted:

> Do you see this room? We added it when we got our income tax return a few years ago. Then another year, we used our income tax return to purchase our living room set. We have built our home as we have had the money to do so. Sometimes we have had to borrow from our family, but we pay them in time. This is our home and we like it just as it is.

A home is not simply a built structure; rather, it is a result of a family's economic assets, personal skills, and social/familial networks. Without these family and friends, many residents would not have the homes they currently live in. A major reason for this is because there are no banks in *colonias* to help offer residents affordable loans to purchase or build their homes. Thus, residents turn to their own sources of financial support—their friends and family members. The building of *colonias*' homes intricately involves reciprocal relationships and obligations among residents. *Colonias* are places in which people build their families, create memorable experiences, and articulate their values, aspirations, and the desire to achieve their goals. That is, homes in *colonias* represent the history of families, the investment of their collaborative efforts, and the edification of dreams and aspirations to be part of the nation state.

Community Development Efforts in *Colonias*

Particular attention to household and community interactions is important for understanding the building of community at a local level. In *Colonias and Public Policy* (1999), Peter Ward refers to the processes of community building among *colonia* residents as "horizontal integration," which refers to the amount of interactions at the local level among individuals within a community or settlement to access services that help solidify a sense of place and unity among residents. Residents' experiences organizing community events, political meetings, prayer groups, and formal and informal neighborhood organizations add to their horizontal community-building experiences in *colonias*. Community building is also made possible by the interaction and negotiations of power and resources between *colonia* residents, local leaders, nonprofit organizations, and government organizations and their representatives. This negotiation of power relationships is defined by Ward (1999) as the vertical integration of community, which often involves tapping into influential actors outside of *colonias*, primarily in the city, region, state, and federal government entities through numerous meetings, projects, and political events. Understanding *colonia* development through the analysis of horizontal and vertical integration provides key insights on the development of *colonias* as this process takes place through the efforts of social change agents, who build partnerships and coalitions with nonprofit organizations and government agencies.

Recent research on community development efforts in *colonias* has identified place-based development and people-centered development approaches (Arizmendi et al. 2010). In the past, *colonias* as places have been invested in by federal and state programs. One federal employee working with housing issues on the border expressed interest in having her agency's funding be "visible" to political officials who wanted evidence of where their support went to and what was built from government funds. This means that the place or location of the *colonias* seem to be important for funders who want to see and show constituents what they supported. By examining how *colonias* homes and communities are built, we can appreciate the value created by residents of *colonia* communities. Evidence of *colonia* residents expressing interest in staying to live in *colonias* indicates that they seem to be better invested in participating in local efforts aimed toward improving their communities, which is an important factor for understanding and facilitating community-building processes (Núñez 2006). A sense of ownership and stewardship is evident in residents who aim to become permanent homeowners and residents in *colonias* and who care to see their communities improve over the long run. As one informant currently working with the *colonia* of Agua Dulce in east El Paso, Texas, indicated, "*colonia* residents are here to stay" and they want to improve their homes for their children. An example of community partnerships supporting residents' efforts to fix their homes is the Agua Dulce Self-Help Center. As children in *colonias* graduate from high school, and move out, their parents remain in *colonias*. One of the major challenges faced by *colonia* youth is the lack of transportation to leave their homes in search of higher education and employment opportunities in the city because many cannot afford personal transportation (personal communication with a *colonia* community partner in Agua Dulce).

Problematizing *Colonias* as Stigmatized Social Spaces

In understanding *colonias* as social spaces, this work builds on Setha Low's approach for *spatializing culture* by "locating, both physically and conceptually, social relations and social practices in social place" (2005:111). The social production of community entails the analysis of all those factors (social, economic, ideological, and technological) that constitute the physical creation of the material setting. The social construction of community addresses the phenomenological and symbolic experience of space as mediated by social processes such as exchange, conflict, and control. Understanding how *colonias* are socially produced and socially constructed is significant for understanding how larger issues of urbanization, migration, displacement, and settlement processes are experienced at the local level. The social production of *colonias* entails the population settlement processes that influenced people to seek land and homeownership in rural or peri-urban regions of the US-Mexico border. The social construction of community deals more directly with the processes that *colonia* residents engage in to add value to the social relationships they have with each other as neighbors and with institutions of power in seeking recognition as legitimate communities. For outside observers, scholars, and policy makers, *colonias* may be viewed and defined in a deficit-model framework, for it is through definitions of what these communities lack (paved roads, water, wastewater systems, etc.) that the term *colonias* has been coined in public policy frameworks. In this case, the concept of spatializing culture is helpful in understanding how residents add value to their homes and properties by linking their historical trajectories and personal narratives of their community development struggles toward the inscription of memory and pride in homeownership in communities previously viewed as marginal and peripheral.

Colonias have historically been described in the literature within a highly stigmatizing "social problem" framework associated with poverty and with Mexican and Mexican American populations in the United States (Hill 2003; Mukhija and Monkkonen 2007). In spite of their social, geographic, and political distance and invisibility, *colonias* are strategically located within one of the most important migration corridors in the world. As such, international policies have a direct impact on *colonias* located on the US-Mexico border. Furthermore, the geographic location of *colonias*, as suburbs for the poor, is central to the discussion of social justice issues in the border particularly because of these populations' racialized, class-based, and linguistic associations with all things associated with "Mexicanness" on the border (Vélez-Ibáñez 1997; Vila 2000). Residents in *colonias* are often plagued by social stigmas, such as illegitimacy and illegality. The peripheral location of *colonias* both in a geographical sense (meaning the physical distance from the nearest cities) as well as in a sociopolitical context (mainly the political distance from centers of power) contributes to the marginalization of these settlements on various levels.

In "Metaphoric Enrichment and Material Poverty: The Making of *Colonias*," Sarah Hill (2003) provides examples of factors contributing to the stigmatization of *colonias* in El Paso County as places associated with poor hygiene, illegality, and disease. Working as a journalist in the 1990s, Saenz's work (2011, Personal Communication of his 1992 radio news report on the threats of cholera outbreaks in El Paso County, Texas.) supports Hill's research, indicating that *colonias* in El Paso County faced the threat of cholera outbreaks primarily because of poor water quality issues. The fears associated with illness and contagious diseases have historically contributed to the stigmatization and alienation of *colonia* populations. In *Batos, Pochos, and Bolillos,* Chad Richardson (1999) discusses the social stigma associated with *colonias* and notes that many university students who live in *colonias* hide the fact they live in these communities for fear of being rejected by their university peers. Richardson provides a counternarrative that discusses the pride people in *colonias* have about their homes and how they create community through collective mobilization and shared activities within local community centers, thus showing that *colonias* are spaces where people negotiate their everyday existence with limited services while building relationships and building families that enrich their everyday existence.

The emergence of *colonias* has also been described in the public policy literature within an affordable housing framework, as *colonia* residents often seek refuge in these communities as "alternatives to affordable housing" in rural and peri-urban population centers (Vélez-Ibáñez 2004). *Colonia* residents are often involved in the informal labor market, as day laborers and as seasonal migrant laborers. Coronado (2003) notes that one of the primary reasons *colonia* residents are pushed to live in underdeveloped regions of the border is because many immigrants and low-income populations lack access to credit lines offered by formal financial institutions. The lack of employment opportunities and underemployment make *colonia* residents less likely to be able to maintain their lines of credit. In a capitalist system, *colonia* residents are often affected by poverty and lack of financial support (low-interest credit lines, affordable home loans, etc.), and yet, they heavily subsidize economic growth and development in the US-Mexico borderlands, primarily as *colonias* house thousands of laborers that may be accessed as a labor pool seasonally and all year round to support industries that thrive on the backs of a low-wage workforce, a workforce that has very little time to expend trying to organize themselves to improve their living conditions.

Concluding Remarks and Policy Recommendations

Building opportunities for creating visibility and awareness to *colonias* is a first step toward cultivating compassion, empathy, and collaborative efforts to support the humane and dignified living conditions in *colonias*. Most ventures require partnerships between residents, nonprofit organizations, researchers, and government officials at the local, county, state, and federal levels (Staudt and Coronado 2002). Integrating efforts and resources at various levels of governance can contribute toward building stronger relationships and practical projects that meet the needs and priorities of *colonia* communities. Investments in the social infrastructure via people-oriented projects are as important as investments in physical or place-based projects. One specific strategy that invests in people and infrastructure projects could include training, certifying, and hiring local residents to help build their own infrastructure in the form of roads, sidewalks, parks, businesses, and homes (Núñez 2010). Supporting residents who want to make improvements to their homes as well as those who are seeking to build safe and long-lasting housing structures through programs that offer hands-on trainings and professional certifications are likely to enhance self help efforts. Programs and financial institutions that offer affordable financial options could help address the affordable housing needs of thousands of *colonia* families. Supporting the creative and resourceful spirit of *colonia* residents through microloans and microenterprise development would seem like an optimal opportunity to invest in *colonias* without necessarily creating dependency on external agencies and institutions. Supporting businesses and home-based enterprises would also benefit men and women in *colonias.*

The social and geographic distance that exists between larger urban centers and rural regions on the US-Mexico border contributes to the invisibility and lack of coherent planning and investments in *colonia* populations. The time to reexamine how we view *colonias* through a public policy and academic lens is necessary to support a more equitable distribution of resources along the US-Mexico border. Additionally, the time seems ripe for the definition of *colonias* to be reconsidered and redefined so that the three major federal agencies that have previously funded projects in *colonias*, Housing and Urban Development (HUD), the US Department of Agriculture (USDA), and the Environmental Protection Agency (EPA), may work together in a more consistent and systematic approach to *colonia* development efforts. As one *colonia* specialist in El Paso notes, "the money has been there, the Community Development Block Grant (CDBG) funds from HUD, *colonias* have been impacted by these federal agencies not working together to address water and other issues. You need to work with ten different agencies to try to get anything done." The bureaucratic complexities of working through various federal, state, and county agencies cripple collaborative and sustainable community development efforts. Social justice for *colonia* communities requires comprehensive analysis of poverty, racism, inequality, and power, as much as the disentanglement of bureaucratic obstacles and collaborative efforts, for social and structural change and justice to take place.

Acknowledgement The author would like to acknowledge the research efforts of Vera Norez and Justin Anthony Monarez, undergraduate research assistants who assisted with ethnographic fieldwork and policy research conducted in the colonias of El Paso, Texas in 2010. A special appreciation to the women leaders of the colonias of Texas and New Mexico, Mr. Jessie Acosta from El Paso County's Planning Department for assistance with colonia enumeration data, and to Georg Klamminger for his contributions to this research as a graduate intern at UT El Paso in 2009.

References

Arizmendi, L., Arizmendi, D., & Donelson, A. (2010). Housing in Texas Colonias. In *The colonias reader: Economy, housing, and public health in U.S.-Mexico border colonias*. Tucson: University of Arizona Press.

Bath, C. R., Tanski, J. M., & Villarreal, R. E. (1994). The politics of water allocation in El Paso county colonias. *Journal of Borderland Studies, 9*(1).

Castels, S., & Miller M. J. (1998). The age of migration: International population movements in the modern world. 2nd ed. London: Macmillan Press.

Chávez, L. R. (1992). In G. A. Spindler (Ed.), *Shadowed lives: Undocumented immigrants in American society* (Case studies in cultural anthropology). Orlando: Harcourt Brace Jovanovich College Publishers.

Coronado, I. (2003). La vida en las colonias de la frontera Life in colonias on the border. *Latino Studies, 1*(1), 193–197.

Del Castillo, R. (1990). The Treaty of Guadalupe Hidalgo: a legacy of conflict. Norman: Univeristy of Oklahoma Press.

Donaldson, A., & Esparza, A. X. (2010). *The colonias reader: Economy, housing, and public health in the U.S.-Mexico border*. Tucson: The University of Arizona Press.

Farmer, P. (2003). *Pathologies of power: Health, human rights, and the new war on the poor*. Berkely: University of California Press.

Fernández Kelly, M. P. (1983). *For we are sold, I and my people: Women and industry in Mexico's frontier*. Albany: Suny Press.

Ganster, P., & Lorey, D. E. (2007). The U.S.-Mexican border into the twenty-first century (2nd ed.). Lanham: Rowman & Littlefield.

Heyman, J. M., Núñez, G. G., & Talavera, V. (2009). Health care access and barriers for unauthorized immigrants in El Paso county, Texas. *Family and Community Health, 32*(1), 4–21.

Hill, S. (2003). Metaphoric enrichment and material poverty: The making of "colonias". In P. Villa (Ed.), *Ethnography at the border*. Minneapolis/London: University of Minnesota Press.

Low, S. M. (2005). Spatializing culture: The social production and social construction of public space in Costa Rica. In *Theorizing the city: The new urban anthropology reader*. New Brunswick/London: Rutgers University Press.

Mauleon, V., & Ting, C. (2000). *At the breaking point: U.S. Mexico border.* Texas Colonias: El Paso. Retrieved from http://journalism.berkeley.edu/projects/border/elpasocolonias.html

Mukhija, V., & Monkkonen, P. (2007). What's in a name? A critique of 'colonias' in the United States. *International Journal of Urban and Regional Research, 31*(2), 475–488.

Norez, V. (2010, December 1). *A day without water: Negotiating everyday life in a colonia*. Final paper presented at the fifth student research symposium, University of Texas, El Paso.

Núñez, G. G. (2006). *The political ecology of colonias in the Hatch Valley: Towards and applied social science of the U.S.-Mexico border*. Riverside: University of California.

Núñez, G. G. (2010, March 8). *Personal commentator at the border network for human rights listening session with the U.S. State Department*, Department of Justice, U.S Department of Health and Human Services, the United States Housing and Urban Development, and the United Nations Human Rights Council Universal Periodic Review, as part of a Civil Society Consultation session, El Paso, Texas.

Núñez-Mchiri, G. G. (2009). The political ecology of the colonias on the U.S.-Mexico border: Human-environmental challenges and community responses in southern New Mexico. *Southern Rural Sociology, I*(24), 67–91.

Núñez, G. G., & Heyman, J. M. (2007). Entrapment processes and immigrant communities in a time of heightened border vigilance. *Human Organization: Journal of the Society for Applied Anthropology, IV*(66), 354–365.

Núñez, G. G., & Klamminger, G. (2010). Centering the margins: The transformation community in *colonias* on the U.S.-Mexico border. In K. Staus, C. M. Fuentes, & J. E. Monárrez Fragoso (Eds.), *The Paso del Norte metropolitan region: Global inequalities, cities, and citizenship at the Mexico-U.S. border*. New York: Palgrave Macmillan.

Portes, A., & Rumbaut, R. G. (1996). Immigrant America: A Portrait. 2nd ed. Berkeley and Los Angeles: University of California Press.

Richardson, C. (1999). *Batos, bolillos, pochos, and pelados: Class and culture on the south Texas border*. Austin: University of Texas Press.

Riley, M. (1998). NAFTA restructures border economies. Retrieved from *News World Communications*, Inc.

Staudt, K. (1998). *Free trade? Informal economies at the U.S.-Mexico border*. Philadelphia: Temple University Press.

Staudt, K., & Coronado, I. (2002). *Fronteras no más: Toward social justice at the U.S.-Mexico border*. New York: Palgrave Macmillan.

Talavera, V., Núñez-Mchiri, G. G., & Heyman, J. M. (2010). Deportation in the U.S.-Mexico borderlands: Anticipation, experience, and memory. In N. De Genova & N. Peutz (Eds.), *Deportation regime: Sovereignty, space, and the freedom of movement*. Durham, NC: Duke University Press.

Vélez-Ibáñez, C. G. (1997). *Border visions: Mexican cultures of the southwest United States*. Tucson: The University of Arizona Press.

Vélez-Ibáñez, C. G. (2004). Regions of refuge in the United States: Issues, problems, and concerns for the future of Mexican-origin populations in the United States. Malinowski award lecture. *Human Organization, I*(63), 1–20.

Vila, P. (2000). *Crossing borders, reinforcing borders: Social categories, metaphors, and narrative identities on the U.S.-Mexico frontier vila*. Austin: University of Texas Press.

Ward, P. M. (1999). *Colonias and public policy in Texas and Mexico: Urbanization by stealth*. Austin: University of Texas Press.

Ward, P. M., Stevenson, R., & Stuesse, A. (2000). *Residential land market dynamics, absentee lot owners and densification policies for Texas colonias*. Austin: LBJ School of Public Affairs.

Chapter 7
Achieving Health Equity and Social Justice in the US-Mexico Border Region

Nuria Homedes

Health Status at the US-Mexico Border

It is now widely accepted that people's health status is determined by their genetic makeup and access to health services but, even more importantly, by their level of education, socioeconomic status and income inequalities, environmental and employment conditions, and lifestyle. As it has been described in the different chapters of this book, the border region[1] has experienced a phenomenal population growth that has outpaced the ability of border communities to provide the necessary physical and social infrastructure to allow for the healthy development of the population. More recently, the health of the borderlanders has been further challenged by high and increasing income inequalities, between and within the border communities in both countries (George 2010), and by increasing levels of insecurity and violence. Although economic and health indicators tend to converge at the US-Mexico border, the average per capita income in the United States is about four times higher than in Mexico. This huge difference will be reflected in the living conditions and services offered to residents in either side of the border.

In 2007, per capita income in US-southern border counties was about two-thirds the average national income (US$26,842 vs. 39,013), the percent of residents living in poverty was almost twice as high as in the United States (25.2% vs. 13%), the levels of educational attainment were lower, and unemployment rates were higher than in the rest of the country (11.5% vs. 5.6% in 2008) (USMBHC 2010). Not

[1] Unless otherwise specified, the statistics cited are from the border counties, as defined by the US-Mexico Border Health Commission.

N. Homedes (✉)
Management, Policy and Community Health, School of Public Health, The University of Texas Houston Health Sciences Center, El Paso Regional Campus, TX, USA
e-mail: nhomedes@utep.edu

M. Lusk et al. (eds.), *Social Justice in the U.S.-Mexico Border Region*,
DOI 10.1007/978-94-007-4150-8_7, © Springer Science+Business Media B.V. 2012

surprisingly, most health indicators are poorer at the US-Mexico border than in the border states and the nation's average. In 2006, the Border Counties Coalition affirmed that if the border was considered a 51st state, it would have the "lowest level of health and wellbeing in the United States" (International Community Foundation 2006: 5).

The border population tends to have higher rates of infectious diseases such as hepatitis A, *campylobacter*, *salmonella*, *shigella*, and tuberculosis and, except for California, have lower rates of sexually transmitted infections (Chlamydia, gonorrhea, syphilis, hepatitis B, and HIV) than the other residents of the border states and the United States (The Epilink 2008a; Homedes 2010). Disability and chronic disease rates are high in the border counties. One in seven border residents is disabled; the prevalence of diabetes at the border almost doubles that of the United States (16.1% vs. 9%) and experts predict that, given the obesity epidemic, it will continue to increase (PAHO 2004; Texas Department of State Health Services 2007). Other chronic diseases, such as cardiovascular problems, cirrhosis of the liver, and certain types of cancer, are present at similar rates than in the rest of the country, except for cancer of the cervix, which despite being fully preventable continues to disproportionally affect Hispanic women and those residing in border counties (USMBHC 2010).

The Mexican communities bordering the United States, until very recently, offered better socioeconomic conditions than the rest of Mexico. Lured by low unemployment, economic opportunities, higher average incomes than in the rest of the country, and the possibility of migrating to the United States, residents in other Mexican states and Central America migrated toward the border municipalities. Like in the United States, the physical and social infrastructure in the Mexican border municipalities was unable to cope with the population influx but they managed to offer similar or better conditions than the rest of Mexico. This relative advantage of the border residents explains why the Mexican government diverted its attention away from the border and focused on other more disadvantaged and politically important states. Compared with the rest of Mexico, border residents have lower rates of maternal and infant mortality and infectious diseases, similar rates of diabetes and cancer, and higher rates of tuberculosis, HIV/AIDS, mental health problems (addictions and suicides), and accidents (see Chap. 9 by Moya, Loza, and Lusk, this volume) (Comisión Fronteriza Mexico-Estados Unidos, n.d. circa 2010). As in the United States, Mexico and the Mexican border states are experiencing a significant increase in the rates of obesity and diabetes.

Resolving the economic and environmental border problems,[2] improving nutrition and reducing the high obesity rates, and controlling violence would have a very significant and sustainable impact on the health of the borderlanders. However, even if we managed to eliminate all these environmental and social contributors to disease and illness, people will continue to get sick and will be in need of medical attention.

[2]For instance, water scarcity, air pollution, water and land contamination, inadequate waste disposal, and degradation of natural resources.

In this chapter, we describe how border residents use the Mexican and US health-care systems and the advantages and disadvantages of accessing providers on both sides of the border, and we explore different policy options that are being considered to maximize the opportunities that both health-care systems offer to borderlanders.

The US and Mexican Health-Care Systems

Contrary to the United States, in Mexico, access to health care is a constitutional right. Until recently, all those who did not have social security insurance[3] (about 50% of the population) or private insurance (about 3%) could receive services in the facilities of the Health Secretariat, and about 10% of the population residing in dispersed rural areas was served through an outreach program (OECD 2005). In 2004, the Mexican health-care system underwent a profound reform. It is expected that by the end of 2011, all Mexican residents that were previously served by the Health Secretariat will be covered by a voluntary insurance program, largely financed by the federal government and administered by the State Health Secretariats, called *Seguro Popular*. All Mexicans are eligible to enroll in *Seguro Popular*, but if they are not in the first two income deciles, they have to pay premiums commensurate with their income (Homedes and Ugalde 2009). The organization of the *Seguro Popular* resembles the Medicaid program, and much as it happens with Medicaid, it covers a limited number of services and medications, is cofinanced by the states, and its implementation strategies vary from state to state. Until all uninsured are enrolled in the *Seguro Popular*, the State Health Secretariats will continue to provide services to the uninsured using a sliding fee-for-service scheme.

Currently, in most states (22 of 31 and the Federal District), the *Seguro Popular* beneficiaries can access services in the state-run health infrastructure or through private providers contracted by the state for this purpose (Gonzalez-Block and Nigenda 2008). This program, along with rumors that social security institutes may start subcontracting with private providers, and the intent to develop medical tourism have contributed to the development of private health infrastructure, especially in areas closest to the US-Mexico border and in large Mexican cities (Medical Tourism Corporation 2012). Several of these new facilities have been accredited by US institutions, a very attractive feature for US insurance companies and residents who cover and seek services in Mexico. This is especially important because Mexico

[3]Workers in the formal economy enroll in the social security system that corresponds to the worker's line of employment. There are different social security systems in Mexico, the largest being IMSS (for the private sector), ISSSTE (for the state and federal employees), and PEMEX (for workers in the oil industry), and medical insurance for the worker and his/her family is among the many social services they provide. Each social security system has its own infrastructure and salaried employees. All social security services, including pharmaceuticals, are free of copayments and deductibles.

does not have a formal accreditation system for health professionals and the system to accredit training centers and facilities is very young and heavily influenced by the opinions of physicians.

The US health-care system is the most expensive in the world, with a per capita expenditure of 7,285 Purchasing Power Parity Dollars (PPP$) in 2007, compared to PPP $819 in Mexico (The Henry K. Kaiser Foundation 2007), and in both countries, about 50% of the expenditure is private. In contrast to the United States, in Mexico most (95%) of the private expenditures are out of pocket, only 5% is spent in private insurance premiums. Insured Mexicans often prefer to use private ambulatory services for reasons of convenience, easier geographical access, or trust.

The range of per capita expenditures varies widely in both countries, with those in the highest income brackets, covered by private insurance, and residing in large urban areas having easier access and accounting for higher expenditures than those in the lower socioeconomic strata, residing in rural areas or low-income neighborhoods, and relying in subsidized insurance (Medicaid and SCHIPs in the United States, and *Seguro Popular* in Mexico).

Access to Medical Care

In 2000–2003, US borderlanders had a lower probability of accessing a physician (56.7%), a specialist (19.9%), or a dentist (61%) than the US population, whose probability of seeing a provider were 68.2%, 25.7%, and 64%, respectively. They also had lower probabilities of accessing mental health services, and women were less likely to see an obstetrician than residents in the rest of the country (Notzon and Albertorio-Diaz 2008). Results of a community-based survey aimed at documenting the prevalence of diabetes on both sides of the border illustrate the deficiencies in meeting the health needs of the border population. This study revealed that 22% of the type II diabetic patients were unaware of their condition (PAHO 2007). Similarly, prior studies had shown that diabetes control was deficient in the region; diabetes mortality rate was 83% higher in the border states than in the United States (US-Mexico Border Counties Coalition 2006), and the age-and-sex-adjusted rate of amputations at the Texas-Mexico border was almost double than in Texas (CDC 2003).

The uninsured of both countries experience the greatest barriers to health care, especially in the United States where they often have to resort to emergency rooms. In the United States, about 26.5% of the border residents younger than 65 and 18% of those younger than 19 years of age are uninsured, and in some counties, the proportion of uninsured is even higher. According to Bastida et al. (2008) the uninsured rates in Texas-border counties can be as high as 38% and, on average, these families would have to spend 43% of their income on family health insurance premiums to cover all family members, almost twice the percentage of what the residents in the United States would have to pay. In contrast, the uninsured Mexicans can access the services provided by the State Health Secretariats and have their fees

Table 7.1 Rates of health professionals per 10,000 residents in the US counties bordering Mexico and in the United States, 2007

	US border counties with Mexico	United States
Physicians (per 10,000 people)	16.3	26.1
Psychiatrists (per 10,000 people) (2003)	0.32	1.42
Dentists (per 10,000 people)	5.1	6.5
Nurses (per 10,000 people)	43.1	57.6
Auxiliary nurses (per 10,000 people)	1.4	2.3
Pharmacists (per 10,000 people)	4.4	5.3

Source: US-Mexico Border Health Commission (2010)

drastically reduced or even waived. However, despite having easier access, about 30% of the Mexican population self-medicates (Pagán et al. 2006) or others are not able to access the needed services due to limited supply.

Access is hampered, on both sides of the border, by the scarcity of health-care providers. The Health Resources and Services Administration (HRSA) has designated most US border counties as medically underserved, which means that they have a shortage of primary health-care physicians, high mortality and poverty rates, and/or a high proportion of elderly population. As can be seen in Table 7.1, the rate of health professionals per 10,000 people is much lower in the border counties than in the rest of the country. Especially acute are the shortages of mental health professionals (counselors, psychiatrists, psychiatric nurses, psychologists, social workers, etc.) particularly considering the upsurge of violence in the region.

The rates of health professionals per population in Mexican border counties, although insufficient by international standards, used to be higher than for the rest of Mexico; however, the situation has changed in recent years, and if a census was made today, we would probably document severe shortages.[4] Unfortunately, the violence in Mexico, especially in Ciudad Juárez, has targeted physicians, and it is estimated that about 30% of them have fled the city and a similar percentage of clinics and pharmacies have been closed (O'Connor and Booth 2010).

Population-based studies have documented that a significant proportion of US border residents, especially the uninsured, seek health services in Mexico, where services are considerably cheaper, more convenient and timely, and culturally more appropriate. The extent of US residents crossing the border to receive medical or dental services and to purchase medicines is not well documented, but it is not negligible. For instance, during 2005 and 2006, 17% of the insured and 63% of the uninsured over 35 years of age residing in the Lower Rio Grande Valley (Cameron, Hidalgo, Willacy, Starr and Zapata counties) received services in Mexico, and the uninsured were three to seven times more likely to receive Mexican services than

[4] Some of the displaced Mexican health professionals reside on the US side of the border and are illegally offering services in their residences. Mexican pharmaceuticals are being illegally sold in US border cities by individuals and in selected convenience stores.

the insured (Bastida et al. 2008). In Laredo (Texas), 27% of the insured and 41% of the Hispanics sought medical care in Mexico (Landeck and Garza 2002). For years, Presidio (Texas, 6,000 inhabitants) did not have a single medical provider and most residents relied on the pharmacies and the medical services of Ojinaga (Mexico).

About 22% of people at the New Mexico Southern border sought medical care in Mexico (Escobedo and Cardenas 2006), with the percent of uninsured being higher at 37% (Macias and Morales 2001). A study conducted two decades ago in the small border community of Sunland Park, New Mexico, revealed that two-thirds (65%) of the residents had received Mexican medical services (New Mexico State University 1991).

Using the 2001 California Health Interview Survey, Wallace et al. (2009) documented that almost half a million Mexican-immigrant adults residing in California had sought medical and/or dental services and/or prescription drugs in Mexico during the prior year, and half of them had traveled more than 120 miles. Proximity to the border, lack of insurance, and cultural issues were the main predictors for traveling to Mexico for medical reasons.

US residents with insufficient or without prescription-drug coverage can purchase their medicines in Mexico at lower prices and without a prescription. About one-third of the El Paso residents regularly cross the border to purchase medicines in Ciudad Juárez, Mexico (Rivera et al. 2009), and among the indigent, the proportion is even higher. A survey of low-income migrant families, 50% of them undocumented, revealed that 85% had bought medicines in Mexico and 64% had purchased Mexican antibiotics (Homedes 2008). A pharmacy in Nuevo Progreso (Mexico) said that 95% of their clients were US residents (Calvillo and Lal 2003), and a survey of US residents who purchased medicines in Ciudad Juárez revealed that 71% of the medicines were purchased without a prescription, 96% of the prescriptions were written by Mexican doctors, and 66% of the medicines were self-prescribed. The study concluded that although Mexican pharmacies are a solution for low-income US residents with chronic conditions who cannot afford the US prices, a few of the medicines dispensed without a prescription could have deleterious long-term effects if inappropriately used. Despite that concern, more than half of the products purchased were of limited therapeutic value and did not pose a threat to the user (Homedes 2009). Undocumented migrants are for obvious reasons unable to cross the border to seek care, although they often use surrogates to consult with a Mexican physician or pharmacist (Homedes 2008).

Arizona's retirement communities organize regular bus tours to Mexico for dental work and inexpensive drugs, and dentists in border towns are marketing and providing services to residents from as far as Alaska (Roig-Franzia 2007; Avila 2009).

Some US-based insurance companies recognize this behavior and cover services rendered in Mexico, but none of the government-sponsored US insurance does. It is conceivable that, with the recent upsurge in violence, the number of people seeking services in Mexico has decreased, but unfortunately, there are no data to document by what proportion. It does appear that those who require services, have crossing documents, and do not have US health insurance continue to seek care in Mexico, but they choose providers that are closest to the border, where the risk of being caught in crossfire is lowest.

Mexican residents also cross the border to receive services in the United States, but these crossings are less frequent, and with a few exceptions, Northbound border crossers represent a net gain for US providers and facilities because they are affluent and pay out of pocket or through private Mexican or US insurance. On the other hand, Mexicans of lower socioeconomic status who come to the United States due to a serious medical emergency or to deliver a baby may be taxing the United States and the US-border municipalities. Some of them may leave unpaid bills, including for emergency transportation, and the newborns become eligible to receive US-subsidized services (Hammes Company 2011). In contrast to the United States, some Mexican public insurance programs can cover services rendered in foreign soil. IMSS offers a special program for Mexicans working anywhere in the United States that entitles the beneficiaries to receive services on either side of the border, and there is discussion about expanding the benefits of the *Seguro Popular* to Mexicans residing in the United States.

Physicians and dentists on the US side of the border are aware that many of their patients are also receiving care in Mexico. A survey conducted in El Paso, Texas, documented that more than half (53%) of those who seek care in Mexico also have US health-care providers (Byrd and Law 2009), but generally there is no communication between the providers in either side of the border and mistrust among them runs high (Homedes and Ugalde 2003).

US health providers often criticize the quality of care provided in Mexico and, as a group, have opposed attempts to better integrate and coordinate the provision of services at the US-Mexico border. The health systems on both sides of the border operate in silos, and border crossers become the main coordinators of their own health, a risky situation when taking in consideration that they tend to be poor and presumably have low levels of health literacy. As it is, border crossers are exposing themselves to duplicate health exams, some of which may be intrusive and have the potential of producing adverse effects; may receive contradictory information and be ill equipped to discern what might be best for their health; and expose themselves to an excess consumption of pharmaceuticals, which at the very least would result in a waste of their scarce resources but might also generate serious drug interactions with deleterious consequences to their health.

Binational Collaboration at the US-Mexico Border

The need to foster binational collaboration, especially to contain infectious diseases at the border, dates from the first part of the twentieth century and has led to the creation of binational entities to facilitate it. During World War II, soldiers stationed in bases along the border traveled to Mexico for sex and alcohol. At that time, venereal diseases were considered a national security threat, and there was a need to contain them on both sides of the border.

Since the United States did not have any jurisdiction on Mexican territory, the US Public Services invited the Pan American Health Organization (PAHO) to open a field office in El Paso, Texas, in 1942. PAHO organized the first binational campaign to prevent, control, and treat the spread of venereal diseases at the border (Collins-Dogrul 2006). A year later, professionals from both sides of the border created a membership association, the US-Mexico Border Health Association (USMBHA). The USMBHA held a yearly meeting in one of the major border cities (alternating between Mexico and the United States), which congregated hundreds of health experts from both sides of the border and, in 1985, started to publish *The Journal of Border Health*.

The USMBHA and PAHO generated a series of working groups on different issues of binational interest (i.e., environmental health, community health, health professions, and communicable diseases) that brought together health professionals, academicians, administrators, public employees, and politicians from both sides of the border. Until the late 1990s, PAHO acted as the secretary for the USMBHA and provided financial support for its maintenance; however, the USMBHA felt that PAHO had too much control and was too slow to respond to the needs of the association. Eventually, the USMBHA became organizationally and financially independent, but after a few years, it was unable to sustain itself and was dissolved in early 2010.

Members of the USMBHA were instrumental in the creation of a binational organization, the US-Mexico Border Health Commission (USMBHC). The idea was formulated during a USMBHA meeting in 1990, the US Congress approved its creation in 1994 and funded it in 1998, but it was not formally constituted until July 2000 due to disagreements between the Mexican and US government.

The Commission has always had a US and a Mexican section; each section has its own executive director and is composed of the Health Commissioner (in the case of Mexico, the Secretary of Health) and 12 additional members appointed by the corresponding government, including the commissioners of health from each border state. On December 21, 2004, the Commission was designated as a Public International Organization by Executive Order of the US President. All executive directors of the US section have been fully bilingual; the first two were very committed to work in a binational manner and with some independence from the US government. However, both of them were invited to resign in part because when it comes to international relationships, the federal governments have the last word.

Much as the other US-border organizations that have sprung up on the US side of the border since the signature of NAFTA, currently the US section of the USMBHC is involved mainly on issues affecting the residents of US side of the border and the Mexican section concentrates on the interests of the Mexican side. The two USMBHC sections meet regularly to coordinate programs and research projects of interest for both nations. However, as the main health policy–making organization for the region, the USMBHC remains underfunded and it is operating below the expectations of border advocates.

The USMBHC has failed to become the broker that on behalf of border residents would attract the attention and funding from both federal governments and foster collaboration between US and Mexican health professionals to solve the major public health problems and health inequities of the region. For the US federal government, possibly due at least in part to the increasing anti-immigrant atmosphere and the events of September 11, 2001, the Southern border has received heightened interest but mainly to tighten its security, limit the flow of Mexican residents and illegal drugs into US territory, and avoid the spread of infectious diseases and bioterrorism.

In addition to the two international organizations, USMBHC and PAHO, on the US side of the border, there are over a hundred federal and state agencies and nongovernmental organizations involved in health issues, with very little coordination among themselves. Most of these groups have projects that require different levels of communication with Mexico, but usually they do not engage their Mexican counterparts in the design and implementation of their programs.

Some border public health workers consider that there is binational collaboration because Mexican and US organizations have jointly designed and implemented some community health educational activities and conducted trainings and workshops for personnel on both sides of the border, and municipalities have approved fairly limited emergency response plans. Others observe that, given the amount of resources invested in border collaboration, the number of binational initiatives, with tangible positive impacts, that have been sustained over time is limited. The best examples of collaborative programs are for the diagnosis and treatment of tuberculosis (TB) and Border Infectious Disease Surveillance (BIDS). As we will discuss, these projects have in common that they have been designed in collaboration with Mexican health authorities, financed largely by the Centers of Diseases Control (CDC), and aimed at controlling the spread of infectious diseases.

TB Cooperation Programs

During the 1990s, border experts observed that Mexico had a high incidence of TB and the disease was being transported back and forth through the US-Mexico border. In response, three binational TB programs managed by the Texas Department of Health and their Mexican counterparts, and financed by the CDC were established along the Texas-Mexico border: *Project Juntos* in El Paso and Ciudad Juárez; *Grupo Sin Fronteras* in the Rio Grande Valley, Reynosa, and Matamoros; and *Los Dos Laredos* in Laredo and Nuevo Laredo.

These programs raised awareness of TB, trained professionals, harmonized diagnosis and treatment protocols, provided direct observed therapy (DOTS), and financed the treatment of patients with multidrug resistance tuberculosis. The Department of Immigration and Health Services also works with the Department of Homeland Security to provide TB therapy for detainees diagnosed with TB until they are deported or released.

In 1995, the USMBHA established the 10 Against TB Program, later absorbed by the USMBHC and whose name expresses the commitment of the 10 US-Mexico border states to fight TB. This program has been instrumental in garnering political support for TB, expanding the DOTS program, strengthening the diagnostic capacity of Mexican laboratories, and continuing to improve TB management and tracking procedures.

One of its accomplishments was the design and adoption of a binational TB card, which is a wallet-size bilingual TB card that includes toll-free phone numbers for patient referrals and to access patient treatment information. The card is used by other TB initiatives (TBNet, Meet and Greet, and Cure TB) that specialize in ensuring continuity of care among patients who travel to Mexico. TBNet operates through the migrant clinics and facilitates the coordination of care as patients move through Texas and Mexico. Meet and Greet is the result of an agreement between Arizona and Sonora by which Sonoran health officials meet individuals with tuberculosis who are being deported to Mexico. Cure TB operates in San Diego and provides referrals for patients with active TB moving between the United States and Mexico.

The BIDS Program

In 1997, with the support of the USMBHA, the CDC, the Mexican Secretariat of Health, and state health officers began the development of infectious disease surveillance protocols. Both countries agreed on the infectious diseases to target, harmonized the criteria for the diagnosis of infectious diseases, standardized laboratory procedures, strengthened the public health infrastructure, and created protocols for data sharing (Weinberg et al. 2003). This project has been considered a model for true binational cooperation along the border, but it encountered financial, administrative, logistical, and political impediments that limited its speedy implementation and expansion.

The BIDS program paved the way for the implementation of the Early Warning Infectious Diseases Surveillance (EWIDS) program in the Southern US border. The EWIDS was initiated by the Department of Health and Human Services in 2003 in the states that border Canada and Mexico with the aim of preventing and controlling a potential bioterrorism attack.

The United States is interested in continuing to sponsor these programs to avoid the spread of infectious diseases in the US territory because, ultimately, they can lower the cost of disease control and treatment in the United States. Schwartzman et al. (2005) demonstrated that if the United States invested US$34.9 million to help implement DOTS in Mexico, there would be 2,591 fewer cases of TB in the United States, 349 fewer TB deaths, and a net present value discounted savings of US$108 million over a 20-year period.

The US-border history proves that collaboration between the bordering nations has not been easy. Researchers have identified legal, administrative, logistical, political, and cultural barriers to binational collaboration (Collins-Dogrul 2006; Homedes and Ugalde 2003; Weinberg et al. 2003), and little has been done to overcome them. In fact, the opposite could be true; observers have suggested that health collaboration between the two countries has been decreasing over time, especially after NAFTA (Homedes and Ugalde 2003), and it is possible that additional difficulties have emerged recently with the increased presence of security forces on both sides, the exacerbation of the war against drugs, and the shrinking of the US public budgets that in the past financed some public health activities on the Mexican border.

Fostering Equity and Better Quality of Care for US Border Residents

As we have seen, the border health-care infrastructure is insufficient to respond to the need of health services in the border region, but we can also affirm that the lack of coordination of services across the border further challenges the region's ability to respond to existing health challenges. In this section, I will focus primarily on options to promote equity in access to health services on both sides of the US-Mexico border, but the reader should not forget that investments in public health and in improving the socioeconomic and environmental conditions of the border will have a very significant impact on the health status of the borderlanders.

All of the proposed policies that I outline below require investments in attracting and retaining health professionals to the region. The US policy makers need to be especially vigilant because the Obama reform,[5] if implemented, will increase the demand for health professionals and may lure providers away from the US-border counties. Most health professionals prefer to work in more lucrative markets, where insurance reimbursements are highest and the proportion of patients who are poor, uneducated, and uninsured or covered by government subsidized insurance is lowest. The US border has been chronically underserved and, although there are tools that the US government could use to attract providers to the underserved areas, little has been done to remedy the border situation. The need to attract more health professionals to the region cannot be overemphasized, but it cannot be done at the expense of Mexico, as some entities have attempted to do. Importing Mexican health-care providers, especially nurses, would only exacerbate the crisis on the Mexican side of the border.

Municipalities on the Mexican side of the border have traditionally been more successful at attracting health professionals than the US side, but due to insufficient government positions, the provider to population ratios have remained below international standards. Similar to health care reform in the United States, the *Seguro Popular* has increased the demand for services and has generated employment

[5]Officially known as the Patient Protection and Affordable Care Act of 2010.

opportunities to formerly unemployed health professionals. Currently, the challenge for the municipalities in Northern Mexico is to appease the violence so that health professionals can safely return or migrate to the region, especially mental health providers.

Other strategies that could increase equity in access to services in border region include:

1. Decrease the number of US uninsured by allowing border residents to purchase Mexican insurance policies
2. Improve coordination of services among providers of both sides of the border
3. Develop more cross border projects
4. Establish systems to limit the use of Mexican services by US residents

1. Decrease the number of uninsured by allowing border residents to purchase Mexican insurance policies. US hospitals and health providers blame the undocumented Mexican residents for overcrowded emergency rooms, and they attribute a large proportion of the 800 million of uncompensated care that is being provided in the region to the undocumented and the Mexicans who cross the border to receive care (US/Mexico Border Counties Coalition 2006). However, available data do not appear to support this claim. A national study demonstrated that uninsured US citizens are more responsible for high emergency room use than the noncitizens are (Cunningham 2006), and a study conducted in the Lower Rio Grande Valley proved that when children have health insurance, the demand for pediatric services increases, and the number of children requiring hospitalization or the use of emergency services is drastically reduced (The Epilink 2008b). In addition, the Texas Comptroller (2006) concluded that the taxes paid by the undocumented exceed the cost of all the services provided by local and state welfare agencies.

To decrease the number of uninsured, in 1998, the California legislature allowed employers in Southern California to offer employees a choice of US or Mexican health insurance. The only Mexican insurance plan licensed in California is *Sistemas Médicos Nacionales,* or SIMNSA. SIMNSA's beneficiaries, about 30,000, can use Mexican or US providers, the latter only in case of emergency or obstetric care. SIMNSA also facilitates access to Mexican providers for an additional 100,000 enrollees in US private insurance plans who elect to be treated by Mexican providers. The Paso del Norte Group[6] is studying the implementation of a similar model for the Paso del Norte Region for several reasons: (1) Mexican insurance is cheaper than US insurance and therefore would minimize the negative effect that the Obama reform could have in formal employment, (2) respects the preferences of borderlanders who for years have been using Mexican services, and (3) avoids penalizing the border residents who prefer Mexican providers and, if the Obama reform is enacted, would have to avail themselves of US insurance and continue to pay for services when they cross the border.

[6] A coalition of Mexican and US business persons who have interest in the Paso del Norte Region (Western Texas, Ciudad Juarez, and Southern New Mexico).

The disadvantages of this model is that it does not resolve the problem of the undocumented who reside in the United States and could result in Mexican providers deciding that it is more profitable for them to serve US residents to the detriment of Mexicans, especially those of lower socioeconomic status, as it has happened in countries that have promoted medical tourism (Johnston et al. 2010). The Mexican government has expressed interest in improving access to services for the uninsured Mexicans who reside in the United States. To that effect, it is pursuing three strategies: (1) promote the IMSS program that covers services provided in the United States, (2) extend the benefits of the *Seguro Popular* to Mexican citizens working in the United States, and (3) expand the *Ventanillas de Salud* (Health Windows) program that is operating in some Mexican consulates. It is envisioned that in addition to health education and linkages to US providers, this program will offer some clinical services. These initiatives would benefit all Mexicans, regardless of their US-residency status, but their viability is constrained by the financial situation of the Mexican government.

2. Improve coordination of services among providers of both sides of the border. As we have seen, most of the collaboration across the US-Mexico border has been led by the US and the Mexican government, PAHO, USMBHA, and more recently the USMBHC. Throughout the years, there have been hundreds or even thousands of meetings, reports, agreements, and projects, but unfortunately only a handful of truly binational programs, of strategic interest for the United States, have been successfully implemented. The reasons why some programs succeed and others fail are not entirely clear.

Currently Medicare, contrary to other government insurance programs such as Tri-Care, only pays for services delivered on US territory, denying access to health services to Medicare beneficiaries who retire overseas. In order to access services, these retirees either purchase additional insurance or they postpone treatment and they return to the United States when the need for medical attention is urgent. In the latter case, Medicare will cover for emergency transportation. A few years ago, there were attempts to carry out a pilot study of a program that would allow Medicare to pay for services rendered in Mexico to US retirees. Cost-effectiveness simulations determined that allowing retirees to access services in Mexico would be cheaper than treating them in the United States, and yet to this date, the US government has not allowed the experiment to take place.

As mentioned, there are legal, administrative, economic, political, and cultural barriers to collaboration between the two countries, and few efforts have been undertaken to overcome them. Until those are leveled, border collaboration will remain difficult.

Even if there is little formal collaboration between the health systems of both countries, border crossers could enjoy better continuity of care if there was communication among health providers from both sides of the border. As I have mentioned, there is mistrust between US and Mexican providers, but this could change if US and Mexican medical schools and professional organizations decided to jointly organize professional development activities. It is also conceivable that, if the proposed private initiatives to develop cross border insurance and medical tourism progress, Mexican and US providers may have to collaborate and use the same diagnosis and treatment protocols and even share electronic medical records.

These private sector plans will benefit mostly the US employers, some Mexican providers, and some uninsured US workers, but they can also trickle down to low-income Mexican immigrants, especially if health providers from both nations are able to enroll and receive credit for participating in binational continuing education activities. Through these exchanges, US health professionals may become more familiar with Mexican norms and culture and might adopt patient communication models that are culturally more appropriate.

Collaboration among nongovernmental organizations operating on both sides of the border could be another alternative, but even if successful, it would only have a peripheral effect. Nongovernmental organizations are not the major players in either health system, and they tend to be strapped for resources.

3. Develop more cross border projects. Most efforts and successes in binational cooperation revolve around controlling the spread of selected infectious diseases. Additional programs could be developed to cover other infectious diseases such as HIV/AIDS, and some medical care programs. There is some evidence that Mexican migrants to the United States have disproportionally contributed to the spread of AIDS throughout Mexico, and yet we do not have a system to facilitate the screening and treatment of Mexican migrants as they return to Mexico.

Because a number of Mexican women and US citizens or residents who live on the Mexican side of the border cross the border to have children delivered in the United States, it will be desirable to develop a program that would coordinate the care provided by attending physicians on both sides of the border during prenatal/delivery/postnatal care. Instituting a bilingual prenatal care and delivery card containing clinical information as well as physicians' recommendations, that pregnant women could carry at all times, would provide critical information to any health provider responding to an emergency or at the time of delivery. All women in the region could benefit from this initiative, not just those crossing the border.

The advantage of persons having and transporting a medical information card is that it has already been tested in the binational TB programs, and once the binational card is developed, it is an affordable strategy and relatively easy to sustain. In addition, the cards empower the patients, who will be in possession of information that can be highly useful if their usual provider is out of reach, or if they want to have a second opinion, may help them avoid duplicative testing and the prescription of unnecessary drugs (or drugs that might interact with ongoing treatments) and can also be used as a reminder of providers' recommendations and boost patients' compliance.

4. Establish systems to limit the use of cross border services. It has been mentioned that the US hospitals and some border municipalities would like to stop or reduce the flow of Mexicans who use medical services in the United States and leave their bills unpaid. Some border municipalities say that they incur significant transport expenditures when Mexicans cross the border and, once in the United States, reveal that they have a medical emergency and need to access the "closest" hospital. Hospitals complain about losing large amounts to uncompensated care. US taxpayers have difficulty understanding the reasons why border communities subsidize the care rendered to Mexicans and at the same time leave thousands of US residents unattended.

However, the option of denying health services to Mexicans is unenforceable. It is not possible to distinguish the Northbound border crossers who are coming to use the health system without having the means to pay the bills from those who come for other reasons. Health providers cannot determine if the patient crossed the border to take advantage of the US system or if an emergency occurred while the person was residing in the United States. Distinguishing emergencies while a person is visiting the United States from abuses of the health system is difficult. Ethically, a medical emergency, workers cannot deny care to persons regardless of their place of origin and residency. In fact, it is useful to be reminded that US citizens without health insurance travel to the European Union seeking emergency care and surgeries they cannot afford back home.[7]

US health providers, including dentists, would also like to see the sealing of the border for other reasons. They claim that when US residents receive services or purchase medicines in Mexico, they expose themselves to substandard care and may require additional and more expensive treatments in the United States. In fact, they may not like potential clients to find cheaper services elsewhere. On the other side of the border, Mexican communities can also have grievances because when patients cross the border seeking medical care and are able to pay a higher fee, the availability of human health resources for Mexicans is reduced and prices may increase.

Given that neither side of the border has an excess number of health professionals, it could be argued that both countries could benefit if they seek solutions to their health problems within their own borders. As it is, Mexico, being poorer and having much lower prices offers a safety net for US residents, mostly the poor and uninsured who are left unattended by the US health-care system.

This situation would be reversed if, in accordance to the WHO Constitution, the UN Human Rights Conventions, and Obama's health reform, the US and Mexico's health system offered comprehensive quality health care to all their residents. Until this occurs, precluding people from crossing the border could be made more difficult but cannot be avoided.

Governments could decide to stop or discourage projects that require binational collaboration, US providers could adopt policies that further dampen residents from crossing the border to seek care and medicines, US private insurance companies could deny the reimbursement for services rendered in Mexico, etc. Such policies would be detrimental to some uninsured US residents. In my opinion, it would be better to leave things as they are rather than to attempt to close the border for those seeking medical care on the other side. After all, this is how the border has operated for centuries.

[7]Conversation with a Spanish physician in July 2007.

Conclusion

I have presented the very special situation of the US-Mexico border regarding health conditions and accessibility to health services. On the US side of the border, health conditions are worse than in the rest of the country. We have also shown the limited efforts to cooperate on health matters by the two governments. The only programs that have been successful are those that address the control of a handful of communicable diseases and were funded by the United States. In the area of medical care, apart from the TB programs, nothing has been done in spite of the fact that a large number of US citizens and residents cross daily the border to seek medical services and medicines. The lack of policies to reduce the constraints that the border creates or to take advantage of the border offerings is unfortunate, namely, lower costs in Mexico and more cultural affinity for the Hispanics who reside in the United States, and for the Mexicans the availability of services that they do not find at home or that they prefer to seek in the United States.

I have outlined four nonexclusive policy options. Another option is to leave things as they are. The data has shown that the claims that Mexican patients are bankrupting US hospitals are exaggerated, and the situation is not likely to worsen since crossing the border has become more difficult due to the efforts to limit illegal migration, drug trafficking, and bioterrorism.

The spread of infectious diseases into the United States through Mexican travelers has also become more unlikely because in order to prevent and control bioterrorism threats, the US government has established systems (The EWIDS Program) to identify and if necessary quarantine patients who cross the border and are potential carriers of infectious diseases.

The violence in Mexican border cities is deterring patients from seeking services in Mexico, and the number of people seeking care in Mexico will decrease if Obama's health reform is implemented. As we have seen, private sectors of both countries are interested in allowing US employers to offer the choice of Mexican or US insurance to their employees in order to comply with the potential obligation to insure all their workers. In my view, if the plan became effective, the Mexican government would need to weigh and carefully monitor the impact of such strategy on the availability and cost of services for the Mexican population.

Leaving things as they are does not preclude the incremental expansion of cross border projects to ensure continuity of care when the patients travel to and from Mexico, including increased communication among providers on both sides of the border.

References

Avila, O. (2009, March 24). Mexico the new dental destination. Americans flock to border town that takes bite out of high prices found in US clinics. *Chicago Tribune.*

Bastida, E., Brown, S. H., & Pagán, J. A. (2008). Persistent disparities in the use of health care along the US-Mexico border: An ecological perspective. *American Journal of Public Health, 98*(11), 1987–1995.

Byrd, T., & Law, J. (2009). Cross-border utilization of health care services by United States residents living near the Mexican border. *Revista Panamericana de Salud Pública, 26*(2), 95–100.

Calvillo, J., & Lal, L. (2003). Pilot study of a survey of US residents purchasing medications in Mexico: Demographics, reasons and types of medications purchased. *Clinical Therapeutics, 25*(2), 561–577.

Centers for Disease Control. (2003). Geographic disparities in diabetes-related amputations – Texas-Mexico Border. *Morbidity and Mortality Weekly Report, 55*(46), 1251–1253, November 24, 2006. Retrieved from http://www.cdc.gov/mmwr/preview/mmwrhtml/mm5546a3.htm

Collins-Dogrul, J. (2006). Managing US-Mexico border health: An organizational field approach. *Social Science and Medicine, 63*, 3199–3211.

Comisión de Salud Fronteriza Mexico-Estados Unidos. (2010). *Frontera Saludable 2010.* Reporte de medico plazo. Frontera Norte de Mexico. Mexico: Comisión de Salud Fronteriza Mexico-Estados Unidos. Sección Mexico.

Cunningham, P. J. (2006). What accounts for differences in the use of hospital emergency departments across US communities? *Health Affairs, 25*(5), w324–w336.

Escobedo, L., & Cardenas, V. M. (2006). Utilization and purchase of medical care services in Mexico by residents in the United States of America, 1998–1999. *Revista Panamericana de Salud Pública, 19*(5), 300–305.

George, R. (2010). *Social determinants of health and the United States-Mexico border.* Unpublished document.

Gónzalez-Block, M. A., & Nigenda, G. (2008). *Sistema de protección social en salud evaluación de procesos administrativos.* Cuernavaca (Mexico): Instituto Nacional de Salud Pública, Secretaría de Salud. 54 p.

Hammes Company. (2011). *Background documents used in the preparation of the Blue Ribbon Committee Regional Strategic Health Framework Gap Document.*

Homedes, N. (2008). *The health seeking behavior of undocumented immigrants in El Paso county.* El Paso: Center for Border Health Research. 145 pp.

Homedes, N. (2009). *The impact of pharmacies in Ciudad Juarez on the health of the borderlanders. Final report.* El Paso: Center for Border Health Research.

Homedes, N. (2010). *El sistema de salud y la inequidad en el lado estadounidense de la frontera entre EE.UU. y Mexico.* El Paso: Border Office of the Pan American Health Organization.

Homedes, N., & Ugalde, A. (2003). Globalization and health at the US-Mexico border. *American Journal of Public Health, 93*, 2016–2022.

Homedes, N., & Ugalde, A. (2009). Twenty-five years of convoluted health reforms in Mexico. *PLoS Medicine, 6*(8), e1000124. doi:10.1371/journal.pmed.1000124.

International Community Foundation. (2006). *Shared destiny: Sharing a binational agenda for health priorities in the San Diego-Baja California border region.* San Diego: International Community Foundation.

Johnston, R., Crooks, V. A., Snyder, J., & Kingsbury, P. (2010). What is known about the effects of medical tourism in destination and departure countries: A scoping review. *International Journal of Equity and Health, 3*(9), 24–37.

Landeck, M., & Garza, C. (2002). Utilization of physician health care services in Mexico by U.S. Hispanic border residents. *Health Marketing Quarterly, 20*, 3–16.

Macias, E. P., & Morales, L. S. (2001). Crossing the border for health care. *Journal of Health Care for the Poor and Underserved, 12*, 77–87.

Medical Tourism Corporation. (2012). Retrieved from http://www.medicaltourismco.com/mexico-hospitals/medical-tourism-mexico.php. Accessed 8 June 2011.

New Mexico State University. (1991). *Sunland Park community survey: Summary.* Las Cruces: Geography and Urban Planning Programs, Earth Sciences Department, New Mexico State University.

Notzon, F. S., & Albertorio-Diaz, J. (2008). *Access to and use of health care. In Border lives: Health status in the United States Mexico border region.* El Paso: United States-Mexico Border Health Commission.

O'Connor, A. M., Booth, W. (2010, November 19). Trying to save lives amid relentless drug violence: Mexican medical workers put their own on the line. *The Washington Post.* Retrieved from http://www.washingtonpost.com/wp-dyn/content/article/2010/11/18/AR2010111806504.html

Organization of Economic Cooperation and Development (OECD). (2005). *OECD reviews of health systems.* Mexico/ Paris: OECD.

Pagán, J. A., Ross, S., Yau, J., & Polsky, D. (2006). Self-medication and health insurance coverage in Mexico. *Health Policy, 75*, 170–177.

Pan American Health Organization (PAHO). (2004). *The US-Mexico border diabetes prevention and control project: First report of results.* El Paso: Author.

Pan American Health Organization (PAHO). (2007). *Diabetes increasing along US-Mexico Border.* Press Release. El Paso: Author.

Rivera, J. O., et al. (2009). Cross-border purchase of medication and health care in a sample of residents of El Paso (Texas) and Ciudad Juarez (Mexico). *Journal of the National Medical Association, 101*(2), 167–173.

Roig-Franzia, M. (2007, June 18). Discount dentistry, south of the border. *The Washington Post,* June 18.

Schwartzman, K., Oxlade, O., Barr, R., Grimard, F., Acosta, I., Baez, J., Ferreira, E., Melgen, R., Morose, W., Salgado, A., et al. (2005). Domestic returns from investment in the control of tuberculosis in other countries. *The New England Journal of Medicine, 353*, 1008–1020.

Texas Department of State Health Services. (2007). *2007 Health risk factors in the Texas-Mexico border.* Austin: TDSHS.

Texas Office of the Comptroller. (2006). *Undocumented immigrants in Texas: A financial analysis of the impact on the state budget and economy* (pp. 96–1224). Austin: Texas Comptroller of Public Accounts Publication.

The EpiLink. (2008a). Infectious diseases along the Texas-Mexico border. *The EpiLink, 65*(1).

The EpiLink. (2008b). Emergency department use among Hispanic children plummets with health insurance. *The EpiLink, 65*(1).

The Henry J. Kaiser Foundation. (2007). *U.S. global health policy: Health expenditure per capita (PPP; International).* Retrieved from http://www.globalhealthfacts.org/topic.jsp?i=66

US/Mexico Border Counties Coalition. (2006). *At the crossroads: U.S.-Mexico border counties in transition.* El Paso: Institute for Policy and Economic Development and US/Mexico Border Counties Coalition. Retrieved from http://www.bordercounties.org/index.asp?Type=B_BASIC&SEC=62E3532757C74978-A39A-36A8E00387B6

US-Mexico Border Health Commission. (2010). *Border lives: Health status in the United States-Mexico Border Region.* El Paso, Texas: United States Border Health Commission.

Wallace, S. P., Mendez-Luck, C., & Castañeda, X. (2009). Heading south: Why Mexican immigrants in California seek health services in Mexico. *Medical Care, 47*(6), 662–669.

Weinberg, M., Waterman, S., Alvarez Lucas, C., Carrion Falcon, V., et al. (2003). The US-Mexico border infectious disease surveillance project: Establishing binational border surveillance. *Emerging Infectious Diseases, 9*(1), 97–102.

Chapter 8
Mental Health Disparities and Social Justice in the US-Mexico Border Region

Griselda Villalobos and Arthur A. Islas

Overview of Hispanic Mental Health

One of the indicators of a country's overall well-being is the mental health status of its people. The World Health Organization defines mental health as "a state of well-being in which an individual realizes his or her own abilities, can cope with the normal stresses of life, can work productively and is able to make a contribution to his or her community. In this positive sense, mental health is the foundation for individual well-being and the effective functioning of a community" (WHO Fact Sheet No. 220 2010). The most extreme absence of mental health is mental illness. The National Alliance on Mental Health (2010) defines mental illness as "medical conditions that disrupt a person's thinking, feeling, mood, ability to relate to others and daily functioning." Unaddressed mental health needs can have an enormous adverse impact on a country both financially and on its human capital.

Mental health disparities exist in the United States in varying degrees; however, they are even more evident in the US-Mexico border region due to access issues, utilization rates, and the lack of culturally and linguistically competent mental health providers. Disparity results from provider practice patterns, uninsured rates, and other health-care factors. The Institute of Medicine (2002) defines disparity as "a difference in treatment provided to members of different ethnic groups that is not justified by the underlying health conditions or treatment preferences of patients" (p. 32). Disparities can be discussed broadly when examining the

G. Villalobos (✉)
Department of Social Work, University of Texas at El Paso, El Paso, TX, USA
e-mail: Gvillalobos1@utep.edu

A.A. Islas
Department of Family and Community Medicine, Paul L. Foster School of Medicine, Texas Tech University, El Paso, TX, USA
e-mail: arthur.islas@ttuhsc.edu

M. Lusk et al. (eds.), *Social Justice in the U.S.-Mexico Border Region*,
DOI 10.1007/978-94-007-4150-8_8, © Springer Science+Business Media B.V. 2012

magnitude of variation across all groups. Disparities can also be defined narrowly when examining how different a specific group is from the overall population (Pearcy and Keppel 2002). Service disparities involve issues of prevalence, access, availability, and uninsured rates. Treatment disparities include inconsistencies in diagnosis, treatment, and outcomes for an ethnic minority group (McGuire et al. 2006; U.S. Department Health and Human Services 2001).

The supplement to the 1999 Surgeon General's report titled *Mental Health: Culture, Race, and Ethnicity* addresses the issue of mental health treatment disparities for minorities, including Mexican Americans and the larger Hispanic population (U.S. Department Health and Human Services 2001). This comprehensive report explores the complexity of the impact of culture on attitudes about seeking mental health services, who seeks treatment and what types of services they seek. Two important implications emphasized in this report were that using traditional and mainstream mental health practices have resulted in disparities (Sue 2003), and that untreated mental illness results in ethnic minority communities suffering more than non-Hispanic White communities (U.S. Department Health and Human Services 2001). Four major disparities in mental health treatment are identified in the supplement:

- Minorities have less access to, and availability of, mental health services.
- Minorities are less likely to receive needed mental health services.
- Minorities in treatment often receive a poorer quality of mental health care.
- Minorities are underrepresented in mental health research.

The State of Mental Health in the United States

Utilization and Access

Despite being among the more advanced countries in the world, in many respects the United States lags behind in its identification and treatment of mental disorders and in addressing its mental health needs. In 2007, 33.3% of Americans reported they had poor mental health in the last 30 days (CDC 2007). Kessler et al. (2005) report that an estimated 26.2% of Americans aged 18 and older suffer from a diagnosable mental disorder in a given year. Further evidence of America's mental health problems can be inferred from the $85 billion spent in 2001 in treating mental illness (SAMHSA 2005).

Aggregate data show that between the years 2003 and 2005, 27.9 million adults (13.0% of the total adult population) received treatment or counseling for mental health problems during the preceding 12 months. Of these individuals, 19.2% perceived an unmet need for treatment or counseling (SAMHSA 2006). During 1998, an estimated 829.3 million visits were made to physician offices, of which 24,496,000 were for psychiatric diagnoses. Psychiatric visits represented 3% of the total physician office visits. Based on an assumed need of 10%, there should have been almost 83 million psychiatric visits. Many mental disorders are treated by primary care physicians because of lack of access or availability of mental health professionals. As a result, 6–10% of patients in primary practice have major depression. In other studies, the frequency of mental disorders in general practice varies from 11% to 36%. The National Institute for Mental Health (NIMH) estimates that 12% of women and 7% of men are affected by a depressive disorder each year. The prevalence of major depressive disorder (MDD) in the primary care setting has been estimated at between 4.8% and 8.6%. Lifetime risk of major depression in women is 20–25% and 7–12% in men. Given these statistics, it is logical to infer that mental health needs are great within the United States (AAFP 2001).

Providers

An important factor that determines adequate mental health service delivery is the number of mental health providers available to provide services. This is also a problem in the United States. A study conducted by Thomas et al. (2009) showed that 77% of US counties had a severe shortage of mental health professionals with over half of their needs unmet. In this same study, nearly every county had some unmet needs. The study found that rural location and per capita income were the most significant indicators of unmet needs.

Mental Health and Mexican Americans in the United States

The mental health disparities that plague our nation are magnified for minority groups such as Mexican Americans. Several treatment issues related to mental health services for Mexican Americans specifically have been the subject of empirical analysis. Research studies support the existence of disparities in mental health treatment utilization for Hispanics in general. For example, research shows that they tend to seek mental health treatment from primary care physicians rather than from specialty mental health providers such as psychiatrists, psychologists, social workers, psychiatric nurses, or other mental health professionals (Vega et al. 1999). The Quality Improvement for Depression project, which involved a sample of Whites ($n = 994$), Latinos ($n = 200$), and African Americans ($n = 127$) aged 18 and older, found that Latinos were less likely than Whites to obtain specialty mental health care even though they reported that their primary care providers recommended depression treatment at rates similar to those of non-Hispanic White patients (Miranda and Cooper 2004). These researchers propose that this may be due to barriers such as language and lack of culturally responsive providers.

Alegria and her collaborators (2002) analyzed data from the 1990 to 1992 National Comorbidity Survey with the purpose of exploring whether there were disparities in the rates of specialty mental health care for Latinos and African

Americans compared to non-Hispanic Whites. The sample included 695 Hispanics, 987 African Americans, and 6,026 non-Hispanic Whites aged 15–64. There were no significant differences between ethnic groups when the overall rates of use of any mental health, general health, or human services were analyzed. However, when specialty care was examined specifically, Hispanics, like African Americans, reported lower rates of obtaining specialty care than did non-Hispanic Whites. Reported rates were 7.2%, 5.9%, and 11.8%, respectively. Based on the findings from these empirical studies, evidence suggests that Hispanics in general are less likely to obtain specialty mental health care when compared to non-Hispanic Whites.

Two major studies support the underutilization of mental health services for people of Mexican descent. The Los Angeles Epidemiologic Catchment Area Study (ECA) conducted by the National Institutes of Health showed that Mexican Americans are less likely to use mental health services than White Americans at rates of 11% for Mexican Americans compared to 22% for Whites (Hough et al. 1987). The ECA looked at prevalence in the past 6 months and sampled 3,132 individuals from two distinct mental health catchment areas (Burnam et al. 1987). Half the sample was of Mexican descent (Mexican or US born) and the remaining half was largely non-Hispanic Whites. Vega and his colleagues (1999) found that only 9% of their Fresno, California, sample of 508 Mexican Americans who had mental disorders in the prior 12 months sought services from a mental health specialist. They also found that Mexican Americans were two times more likely to seek treatment for mental disorders in general medical settings than in specialized mental health agencies (Vega et al. 1999). Alegria et al. (2007) reported that one out of every ten Mexican Americans reported past-year mental health service utilization. Utilization rates were significantly lower when the differences between US-born and foreign-born Mexican Americans were examined. Vega et al. (1999) found that US-born Mexican Americans were more than twice as likely to seek mental health services as their foreign-born counterparts. These results indicate the utilization rates for Mexican Americans are low, but they are even lower for Mexican Americans who report a foreign-born status. At the same time, Sue et al. (1991) documented a dropout rate of 14.6% after one session for Mexican Americans and group averages for length of treatment of 5.1 sessions. Some of the reasons that were identified as contributing to dropout rates were socioeconomic factors, perceptions of mental health, cultural commitment, and lack of culturally appropriate mental health services (U.S. Department Health and Human Services 2001).

Cultural Factors

Mexican Americans comprise approximately 66% of all Hispanics within the United States (Hispanic Americans: Census Facts 2011). In the year 2000, 60% of the Hispanics in the United States lived in five southwestern states which include California, Arizona, New Mexico, Colorado, and Texas (United States Census

Bureau 2010b), creating a majority Mexican American culture along the US-Mexico border region. For example, Brownsville Texas is 91% Hispanic and El Paso County is 81% Hispanic (U.S. Census Bureau 2010). The Mexican American culture can be characterized as an amalgamation (a fusion of two groups to form a new culture) that results when the Mexican culture and the US-Mexican culture intersect. Despite the wide range of cultural characteristics that are seen in Mexican Americans, several key characteristics are described in the literature. It is important to consider, however, that Hispanics as a whole, as well as Mexican Americans, are heterogeneous in nature. Mexican Americans in the US border region range in acculturation levels from the newcomer who is a monolingual Spanish speaker to the highly acculturated monolingual English speaker, with bilingual and bicultural individuals falling somewhere in between. Similarly, individuals in the US border region fall on a continuum from those who are completely underserved to those who receive the best care possible. This continuum is highly correlated with income and education as in other ethnic groups.

Familism or *familismo* is characterized by strong family closeness and loyalty in Mexican American families (Alvidrez and Bean 1976; Mindel 1980). For some traditional Mexican Americans, family includes a network of formal and informal relations that are considered the center of an individual's psychosocial world (Holleran and Waller 2003). This phenomenon is demonstrated in family members' behavior (behavioral familism) in the amount of visiting that takes place, particularly in the home of the matriarch (either mother or grandmother). It is not uncommon for Mexican American families to live in close proximity and visit one another several times per week. A second way in which familism is demonstrated is what is called attitudinal familism in which families make decisions in a collective manner, and they protect one another from outside forces. Familism includes the sharing of caretaking and disciplining of children, financial responsibility, companionship, emotional support, and problem solving (Falicov 1982).

Deference to authority, also known as abiding by a rigid hierarchical structure, is another prominent cultural characteristic of traditional Mexican Americans. Mexican American children are raised with very strict boundaries between themselves and their parents (Falicov 1982). Respect (*respeto*) is expected and is defined as a relationship involving a "highly emotionalized dependence and dutifulness, within a fairly authoritarian framework" (Diaz-Guerrero 1975, p. 140). This way of relating to those considered to be in power is later translated into having a high deference to authority in school and in the work place (Hofstede 1980). For some Mexican Americans, this characteristic may lead them to be passive toward authority figures. Similarly, a high degree of deference may lead Mexican Americans to expect healthcare professionals to be highly directive and to act as experts (Poonam 2002).

Two other cultural characteristics associated with Mexican Americans are *present-orientedness* and *fatalism*. Poonam (2002) writes that unlike the dominant US culture, Hispanic cultures generally focus more on the past (tradition) and present, rather than the future. In addition, the idea of fatalism can be seen in some more traditional Mexican Americans who do not feel they have control over their environment. One author proposes that historically, people in Mexico have been in a position of powerlessness and have learned to accept things as they come. He adds that the term "*ni modo*" (oh well) has become a culturally conditioned attitude, reinforced by religion (Lafayette De Mente 1996).

Three cultural characteristics that describe how some Mexican Americans relate to others are *formalidad* (formality), *simpatía* (congeniality), and *personalismo* (personalism). Lafayette De Mente (1996) writes that just as Americans pride themselves on their informality, Mexicans are proud of their more formal behavior and regard it as one of the most important aspects of their culture. This formality is evidenced by Mexican Americans who prefer to be greeted with a handshake and by the use of the more formal version of "you" in the Spanish language (*usted*) that is customarily used initially to address new acquaintances. S*impatía* emphasizes the need for behaviors that promote pleasant and nonconflicting social relationships (Triandis et al. 1984). The term *personalismo* has to do with Mexican Americans' focus on relationships rather than on tasks (Levine and Padilla 1980).

Predominant cultural characteristics associated with gender roles for traditional Mexican Americans are *machismo* and *marianismo.* Machismo refers to the male role that is demonstrated by some Mexican American men, although patriarchal and masculinist behaviors by men are in no way limited to the Mexican culture. The negative aspects of machismo are bravado, physical aggression, womanizing, and philandering. The positive aspects of machismo are identified as honor, being a good provider, being a good protector, moral courage, and responsibility (Torres and Solberg 2002). *Marianismo* is a concept that portrays women as spiritually superior to men and therefore can endure all suffering inflicted by men. This concept takes its name from the cult of the Virgin Mary in the Catholic tradition and was first identified by Stevens in 1973 (Marsiglia and Holleran 1999).

Mental Health Along the US-Mexico Border

There is a paucity of literature addressing the state of mental health along the US-Mexico border. However, because mental health is determined by socioeconomic, biological, and environmental factors (WHO Fact sheet #220 2010), the mental health disparities that abound throughout the country become compounded and of greater complexity when we examine mental health access and delivery along the US-Mexico border. The US-Mexico border region suffers as an economically and educationally depressed area. These factors set the stage for a wide range of access issues that result in mental health disparities for the Mexican Americans who predominantly reside in this area. As a consequence, there is a tendency for US border residents to cross over into Mexico to obtain mental health services because it is less expensive and is considered more culturally responsive. Similarly, there are numerous reports of continuing visits into Mexico to obtain prescription medication that can be obtained there without a prescription. This creates a situation where people self-diagnose and self-treat symptoms related to health and mental health.

In addition, a connection can be made between the number of mental health providers in an area and the prevalence of mental illness. A study conducted by Mark et al. (2007) found that the higher the number of psychiatrists, social workers, and psychologists per capita, the lower the suicide rate. This study also found that the more educated the population and the greater the percentage with health insurance, the lower the suicide rate. The border region has deficiencies in each of these areas.

Access

Understanding the barriers to access is complex as it is difficult to isolate any one barrier. The best way to tackle this feat is to focus on how these barriers intersect and result in underutilization, premature termination, and short lengths of treatment for Mexican Americans. The Surgeon General's Supplement identifies language, lack of Spanish-speaking mental health providers, and lack of insurance as the major access barriers (U.S. Department Health and Human Services 2001). Snowden et al. (2006) list cultural misunderstanding and culture-based alienation, economic barriers, mistrust, stigma, clinician bias, and language as important factors to consider when examining lack of access to mental health services. Other reasons that are identified are lower levels of acculturation (Wells et al. 1989), different beliefs about the need for ongoing treatment (Anderson 1995), a cultural heritage that makes use of different methods of treatment (Rogler and Cortes 1993), and extensive support systems that may mitigate the acuity of the need for treatment (Briones et al. 1990).

The movement to provide culturally and linguistically competent mental health services has been growing in recent years; however, there is much work to be done. The importance of providing culturally and linguistically competent mental health services should not be underestimated as there is evidence to support that people are able to express emotional aspects of their lives more effectively in their native language and that a person's language influences the way they express thoughts, feelings, and emotions (Malgady and Zayas 2001). In addition, caution must be used when providing mental health services to people with limited English proficiency as the risk of misdiagnosis is increased. Furthermore, Hispanics have identified access to mental health services in their preferred language as being the biggest barrier to receiving quality care. The Pew Hispanic Center (2002) reported that three of every ten Hispanics report problems communicating with their providers. The need for increasing the number of bilingual and bicultural mental health providers in the US-Mexico border region is supported by research findings that Mexican Americans with ethnically matched therapists tend to remain in treatment longer and have better outcomes (Sue et al. 1991).

Utilization

When Texas State Senator Eliot Shapleigh examined mental health estimated needs and those served throughout the Texas border counties, he found that for most counties, less than 50% of the population in need was served (see Table 8.1; Shapleigh 2010). This situation is clearly linked to lack of funding for mental health services. El Paso County, for example, has always experienced less proportionate funding than the rest of Texas. The geography of Texas plays a role in this. There are more than 500 miles between El Paso and the power centers of Austin, San Antonio, Dallas, and Houston, respectively.

Providers

The national shortage of mental health professionals is accentuated along the US-Mexico border. Table 8.2 depicts the number of mental health professionals per Texas County and compares these figures with nonborder Texas counties to show the glaring discrepancy between the two.

Culture and Mental Health

Perhaps one of the factors that is most overlooked is the importance that culture may play in addressing issues of mental health access and utilization. An important development in the understanding of culture and mental health came as a result of the work of national experts in the field who in their supplement (U.S. Department Health and Human Services 2001) to the Surgeon General's 1999 Report concluded that it is critical to consider culture in planning interventions for minority groups. Culture bears upon what people bring to the clinical setting, if they seek treatment and where they seek treatment. In addition, culture influences how people communicate their symptoms. Furthermore, culture influences the meaning people give to their illness, affecting whether they seek help, types of coping styles, social supports, and how much stigma is connected to mental illness (U.S. Department Health and Human Services 2001).

Along the US-Mexico border, providing mental health services requires that mental health providers understand the Mexican American culture with its varying degrees of acculturation. Mental health providers should consider that some Mexican Americans may attribute mental illness to supernatural causes and seek help from traditional healers (*curanderos*) who are more familiar with their culture (Altarriba and Bauer 1998). They may present other culturally appropriate beliefs such as talking with deceased relatives, seeing religious visions, and worrying about hexes (Miranda et al. 1996). In addition, studies have found that Mexican Americans may present more somatic symptoms of depression than exhibit sadness or depressed mood (Escobar et al. 1987; Kolody et al. 1986; Mezzich and Raab 1980). Furthermore, some Mexican Americans may believe that others will think they are crazy if they are depressed and may view antidepressants and other medications as addictive (Lewis-Fernandez et al. 2005). In addition, the lack of

Table 8.1 Estimated at risk, eligible, and served by TDMHMR in 2002

	Adults			Children		
	Estimated adults at risk and eligible for MHMR	Adults served	Percent of adults who were served (%)	Estimated children at risk and eligible for MHMR services	Children served	Percent of children who were served (%)
Brewster	180	144	80	49	27	55
Cameron	5,979	2,199	37	2,965	417	14
Culberson	55	27	49	23	*	*
Dimmit	180	76	42	85	20	24
El Paso	12,343	5,705	46	5,577	1,322	24
Hidalgo	10,033	1,993	20	5,331	613	11
Hudspeth	59	14	24	28	*	*
Jeff Davis	44	21	47	12	6	48
Kinney	65	10	15	21	*	*
Maverick	797	315	40	451	129	29
Presidio	130	86	66	61	11	18
Starr	902	212	24	526	201	38
Terrell	21	*	*	7	*	*
Val Verde	804	259	32	373	96	26
Webb	3,371	1,250	37	1,861	535	29
Zapata	216	96	44	103	69	67
Borderlands	35,182	12,407	35	17,473	3,446	20
Texas	*397,166*	*150,241*	*38*	*151,464*	*39,591*	*26*

*Counties with fewer than 5 adults or 5 children receiving services were not reported to safeguard the identity of those individuals

Source: Texas Department of Mental Health and Mental Retardation

Estimated at risk and eligible for services was defined using the proportions in the 2003 Strategic Plan for TDMHMR

Table 8.2 Licensed professionals

Texas border county	Population	Psychiatrists[a]	Psychologists[b]	Social workers[a]	LMFT[a]	LPC[a]	Total	MH provider per 100,000 population
Brewster	9,408	1	4	4	2	12	23	244
Cameron	408,951	14	30	154	13	106	317	78
Culberson	2,733	0	0	0	0	0	0	0
Dimmit	9,816	0	0	1	0	5	6	2
El Paso	763,712	27	66	405	47	278	823	107
Hidalgo	768,405	17	75	375	10	220	697	90
Hudspeth	3,772	0	0	0	0	0	0	0
Jeff Davis	2,777	0	0	2	0	3	5	2
Kinney	3,447	0	1	0	0	1	2	58
Maverick	54,461	0	1	13	1	10	25	46
Presidio	8,542	0	0	0	0	1	1	12
Starr	65,944	1	1	12	0	11	25	38
Terrell	1,103	0	0	0	0	0	0	0
Val Verde	49,616	0	2	15	1	8	26	529
Webb	251,096	3	20	64	0	58	145	58
Zapata	14,944	0	0	0	0	1	1	7
Texas nonborder county								
Harris	4,016,367	353	1,144	2,689	561	2,126	6,873	171
Lubbock	265,963	17	91	248	67	245	668	251
Tarrant	1,780,892	105	377	1,595	220	1,158	3,455	194
Travis	974,427	160	688	1,800	212	1,073	3,933	403
Texas Total	*24,873,773*	*1,634*	*6,316*	*16,574*	*2,789*	*14,876*	*42,189*	

Source: Texas Department of State Health Services, Professional Licensing and Certification Unit-September 10, 2009
Estimated licensed health professional by county September 2009
[a]By county of practice
[b]By county of residence

mental health providers who are bicultural and bilingual adds to the problem of providing mental health services that effectively meet the needs of the US-Mexico border population.

Political Context

Mental illness, because of the nature of the disorders and the social stigma they carry, is a very controversial political topic. The mentally ill are often victimized by the political process. Because persons affected by mental disorder are known to be less likely to advocate for themselves and are also less likely to take an active role in the political process, they have little or no influence on elected officials. Through victimization, this segment of society suffers undue and detrimental cuts when financial and other resources are scarce and cutbacks are needed. Mental health is often the first and most deeply affected by programmatic cuts because the recipients of mental health services are less likely to complain.

International Factors

A recent phenomenon that affects the US-Mexico border at a higher rate is the influx of Mexican refugees due to the recent drug war–related violence in Mexico. It is estimated that 230,000 Mexican nationals have fled violence in Cuidad Juárez, Mexico, and 124,000 of those settled in El Paso, Texas. Most of these Mexican nationals remain "underground" due to their undocumented status and fear of being sent back to Mexico. As a result, they may be unable to secure employment or access to health or mental health services. These recent events have bombarded mental health agencies with unfunded individuals in need of intense mental health services. Hundred of individuals are presenting to mental health agencies with severe symptoms of depression, anxiety, and posttraumatic stress disorder (Lusk et al. 2011). This further adds a burden on a mental health system that cannot meet the needs of its own residents.

Future Challenges

One of most significant challenges is to increase the amount of mental health providers along the border. Recruitment and retention is often difficult given the population and amount of uninsured individuals along the border. Additionally, the need to increase culturally and linguistically competent mental health professionals exists and is often not addressed in the mental health education programs. For example, a Center for Mental Health Services (2000) report shows that there are

29 Latino mental health professionals per 100,000 Latinos compared to 173 non-Hispanic White mental health professionals per 100,000 White patients. To help with this need, the border must look within itself to create its own mental health providers who are familiar and culturally comfortable with working within this unique population.

In addition, changes to the existing system can be made to help increase access and attain appropriate care in a timelier manner such as the creation of better training programs for all practitioners in the identification and treatment/referral of mental health patients as needed.

An increase in representation of minority groups in mental health research is also a needed component to increasing and improving mental health along the US-Mexico border. Funding opportunities to conduct research on mental health and Mexican Americans should be strategically sought.

Access to and utilization of mental health professionals and services is directly related to the ability of patients to appreciate the need for care and their ability to access that care. Within the current US health system, the mental health client who because of the very nature of their disorders may find that they are left out of the insurance pool as most Americans achieve insurance status through employment. As a result, these individuals are often dependent upon an overutilized and underfunded safety net system that is insufficient in resources, both fiscal and physical, to meet the needs of the population. Along the border, the facets of poor social economic attainment, low educational achievement, and a culturally different society add extra burden to the mental health patient, creating a social injustice for the border mental health population. We believe that true social justice can only be achieved if access to health care, especially mental health care, is obtainable not only by those who have means but by the most fragile and vulnerable in society.

References

Alegria, M., Canino, G., Rios, R., Vera, M., Calderon, J., Rusch, D., et al. (2002). Inequalities in use of specialty mental health services among Latinos, African Americans, and non-Latino Whites. *Psychiatric Services, 53*(12), 1547–1555.

Alegria, M., Shrout, P. E., Woo, M., Guarnaccia, P., Sribney, W., Vila, D., et al. (2007). Understanding differences in past year psychiatric disorders for Latinos living in the US. *Social Science & Medicine, 65*, 214–230.

Altarriba, J., & Bauer, L. M. (1998). Counseling the Hispanic client: Cuban Americans, Mexican Americans, and Puerto Ricans. *Journal of Counseling and Development, 76*(4), 389–397.

Alvidrez, D., & Bean, F. D. (1976). The Mexican family. In C. Mindel & R. Habenstein (Eds.), *Ethnic families in America*. New York: Elsevier.

American Academy of Family Physicians. (2001). *Mental health care services by family physicians (position paper)*. Retrieved on December 22, 2010, from www.aafp.org/online/en/home/policy/policies/m/mentalhealthcareservices.html

Anderson, R. M. (1995). Revisiting the behavioral model and access to health care: Does it matter? *Journal of Health and Social Behavior, 36*, 1–10.

Briones, D. F., Heller, P. L., Chalfant, H. P., Roberts, A. E., Aguirre-Hauchbaum, S. F., & Farr, W. F. (1990). Socioeconomic status, ethnicity, psychological distress and readiness to utilize a mental health facility. *The American Journal of Psychiatry, 147*, 1333–1340.

Burnam, M. A., Telles, C. A., Hough, R. L., & Escobar, J. I. (1987). Measurement of acculturation in a community population of Mexican Americans. *Hispanic Journal of Behavioral Sciences, 9*, 105–130.

Centers for Disease Control and Prevention, Behavioral Risk Factor Surveillance System Survey Data (BRFSS). (2007). Unpublished data. Information about the BRFSS is available at http://www.cdc.gov/brfss/index.htm

Center for Mental Health of the Substance Abuse & Mental Health Services Administration (1998). *Cultural Competence Standards in managed care for four underserved/underrepresented racial ethnic groups*. Retrieved from http://wiche.edu/culturalCompetenceStandards/gen/abstract

Diaz-Guerrero, R. (1975). *Psychology of the Mexican: Culture and personality*. Austin: University of Texas Press.

Escobar, J. I., Burnham, M., Barno, M., Forsythe, A., & Golding, J. (1987). Somatization in the community. *Archives of General Psychiatry, 44*, 713–718.

Falicov, C. J. (1982). Mexican families. In M. McGoldrick, J. K. Pearce, & J. Giordano (Eds.), *Ethnicity and family therapy* (pp. 134–163). New York: The Guilford Press.

Hispanic Americans: Census Facts. (2011, February 3). *Infoplease. 2000–2007 Pearson education*, publishing as Infoplease. http://www.infoplease.com/spot/hhmcensus1.html#ixzz1CqmQju70

Hofstede, G. (1980). *Culture's consequences: International differences in work-related values*. Beverly Hills: Sage.

Holleran, L. K., & Waller, M. A. (2003). Sources of resilience of Chicano/a youth: Forging identities in the borderlands. *Child and Adolescent Social Work Journal, 20*(5), 335–350.

Hough, R. L., Landsverk, J. A., Karno, M., Burnam, M. A., Timbers, D. M., Escobar, J. L., & Regier, D. A. (1987). Utilization of health and mental health services by Los Angeles Mexican Americans and non-Hispanic whites. *Archive of General Psychiatry, 44*, 702–709.

Institute of Medicine. (2002). *Unequal treatment: Confronting racial and ethnic disparities in health care*. Washington, DC: National Academy Press.

Kessler, R. C., Chiu, W. T., Demler, O., & Walters, E. E. (2005). Prevalence, severity, and co-morbidity of twelve-month DSM-IV disorders in the National Comorbidity Survey Replication (NCS-R). *Archives of General Psychiatry, 62*(6), 617–627.

Kolody, B., Vega, W., Meinhardt, K., & Bensussen, G. (1986). The correspondence of health complaints and depressive symptoms among Anglos and Mexican-Americans. *Journal of Nervous Mental Disorders, 174*, 221–228.

Lafayette De Mente. (1996). *NTC's dictionary of Mexican cultural code words*. Chicago: NTC Publishing Group.

Levine, E. S., & Padilla, A. M. (1980). *Crossing cultures in therapy*. Belmont: Wadsworth.

Lewis-Fernandez, R., Das, A. K., Alfonso, C., Weissman, M. M., & Olfson, M. (2005). Depression in US Hispanics: Diagnostic and management considerations in family practice. *Journal of the American Board of Family Medicine, 18*(4), 282–296.

Lusk, M., McCallister, J., & Villalobos, G. (2011). Mental Health Sequelæ among Mexican Refugees Fleeing Violence and Trauma. *Comparative Social Welfare*. In press.

Malgady, R. G., & Zayas, L. H. (2001). Cultural and linguistic considerations in psychodiagnosis with Hispanics: The need for an empirically informed process model. *Social Work, 46*(1), 39–49.

Mark, T. L., Shern, D. L., Bagalman, J. E., & Cao, Z. (2007). *Ranking America's mental health: An analysis of depression across the states*. Alexandria: Mental Health America.

Marsiglia, F., & Holleran, L. (1999). I've learned so much from my mother: Narratives from a group of Chicana high school students. *Social Work in Education, 21*(4), 220–238.

McGuire, T. G., Alegria, M., Cook, B. L., Wells, K. B., & Zaslavsky, A. M. (2006). Implementing the Institute of Medicine definition of disparities: An application to mental health care. *Health Services Research, 41*(5), 1979–2005.

Mezzich, J., & Raab, E. (1980). Depressive symptomatology across the Americas. *Archives of General Psychiatry, 37*, 818–823.

Mindel, C. H. (1980). Extended families among urban Mexican Americans, Anglo and Blacks. *Hispanic Journal of Behavioral Sciences, 2*(1), 21–34.

Miranda, J., & Cooper, L. A. (2004). Disparities in care for depression among primary care patients. *Journal of General Internal Medicine, 19*, 120–126.

Miranda, J., Azocar, F., Organista, K. C., Muñoz, R. F., & Lieberman, A. (1996). Recruiting and retaining low-income Latinos in psychotherapy research. *Journal of Consulting and Clinical Psychology, 64*, 868–874.

National Alliance on Mental Illness. (2010). *Mental illness: Facts and numbers* [Fact sheet]. Retrieved from http://www.nami.org/Template.cfm?Section=About_Mental_Illness&Template=/ContentManagement/ContentDisplay.cfm&ContentID=53155

Pearcy, J. N., & Keppel, K. G. (2002). A summary measure of health disparity. *Public Health Reports, 117*, 273–280.

Pew Hispanic Center and Henry J. Kaiser Family Foundation. (2002). *2002 National survey of Latinos: Survey brief.* March 2004, pp. 1–5.

Poonam, S. (2002). Suggestions for psychologist working with Mexican American individuals and families in health care settings. *Rehabilitation Psychology, 47*(2), 230–239.

Rogler, L. H., & Cortes, D. E. (1993). Help-seeking pathways: A unifying concept in mental health care. *The American Journal of Psychiatry, 150*, 554–561.

Shapleigh, E. (2010). Texas 29th Senatorial District. *Texas borderland: Frontier of the future*. Retrieved October 31, 2010, from http://dnn.epcc.edu/portals/0/Borderlands/Texas_borderlands.pdf

Snowden, L., Masland, M., Ma, Y., & Ciemens, E. (2006). Strategies to improve minority access to public mental health services in California: Description and preliminary evaluation. *Journal of Community Psychology, 34*(2), 225–235.

Substance Abuse and Mental Health Services Administration. U. S. Department of Health and Human Services. (2005). Mental health services expenditures, 2001. In *National expenditures for mental health services and substance abuse treatment 1991–2001* (Chapter 3). Retrieved from http://www.samhsa.gov/spendingestimates/toc.aspx

Substance Abuse and Mental Health Services Administration, Center for Behavioral Health Statistics and Quality (2010). *Mental Health, United States, 2010*. Retrieved from http://www.samhsa.gov/data/

Sue, S. (2003). In defense of cultural competency in psychotherapy and treatment. *American Psychologist, 58*(11), 964–970.

Sue, S., Fujino, D. C., Hu, L. T., Takeuchi, D. T., & Zane, N. W. S. (1991). Community mental health services for ethnic minority groups: A test of the cultural responsiveness hypothesis. *Journal of Counseling Psychology, 59*, 533–540.

Thomas, K. C., Ellis, A. R., Konrad, T. R., Holzer, C. E., & Morrissey, J. P. (2009). County-level estimates of mental health professional shortage in the United States. *Psychiatric Services, 60*(10), 1323–1328.

Torres, J. B., & Solberg, S. H. (2002). The myth of sameness among Latino men and their machismo. *The American Journal of Orthopsychiatry, 72*(2), 163–181.

Triandis, H. C., Marin, G., Lisansky, J., & Betancourt, H. (1984). Simpatia as a cultural script of Hispanics. *Journal of Personality and Social Psychology, 47*, 1363–1375.

U.S. Department Health and Human Services. (2001). *Mental health: Culture, race, and ethnicity-a supplement to mental health: A report of the surgeon general*. Rockville: Public Health Service, Office of the Surgeon General.

U.S. Census Bureau (2010). State & County Quick Facts. Retrieved from http://quickfacts.census.gov/qfd/states/4800.html

United States Census Bureau. (2010b). *Income* [Data file]. Retrieved December 19, 2010, from http://www.census.gov/hhes/www/income/data/historical/people/index.html

Vega, W. A., Kolody, B., Aguilar-Gaxiola, S., & Catalano, R. (1999). Gaps in service utilization by Mexican Americans with mental health problems. *The American Journal of Psychiatry, 156*(6), 928–934.

Wells, K. B., Golding, J. M., Hough, R. L., Burnam, M. A., & Karno, M. (1989). Acculturation and the probability of use of health services by Mexican Americans. *Health Services Research, 24*, 237–257.

World Health Organization. (2010). *Mental health: Strengthening our response* [Fact sheet No. 220]. Retrieved from http://www.who.int/mediacentre/factsheets/fs220/en/

Chapter 9
Border Health: Inequities, Social Determinants, and the Cases of Tuberculosis and HIV

Eva M. Moya, Oralia Loza, and Mark Lusk

> *Off all the forms of inequality, injustice in health is the most shocking and inhumane.*
>
> – Martin Luther King, Jr.

Setting the Stage

The study of borders includes the study of social inequalities. At borders, diseases travel and kill at will. When the borders in question are between a rich and a poor country, as in the case of the US-Mexico border, we have two very different types of health-care systems, each with disproportionate share of risks and diseases. Warner (1991: 242) notes that "it is unlikely that any other bi-national border [U.S.-Mexico] has such variety in health status, entitlements, and utilization." Low socioeconomic and educational levels, immigration, and rapid industrial development accompanied by population growth for the implementation of the North American Free Trade Agreement (NAFTA) in 1994 help to explain

E.M. Moya (✉)
Department of Social Work, University of Texas at El Paso, 500 W. University Ave., 79968 El Paso, TX, USA
e-mail: emmoya@utep.edu

O. Loza
Department of Public Health Sciences, University of Texas at El Paso, 500 W. University Ave., 79968 El Paso, TX, USA
e-mail: oloza@utep.edu

M. Lusk
Department of Social Work, College of Health Sciences, University of Texas at El Paso, 500 W. University Ave., 79968 El Paso, TX, USA
e-mail: mwlusk@utep.edu

M. Lusk et al. (eds.), *Social Justice in the U.S.-Mexico Border Region*,
DOI 10.1007/978-94-007-4150-8_9, © Springer Science+Business Media B.V. 2012

the present complexity. All of these factors influence the health and quality of life of residents in the border region. Diseases and environmental hazards on one side of the border directly impact the other side because of the mobility and migration in both directions. The continuous flow of the border's population creates a unique zone with distinctive disease patterns and specific health characteristics (Brandon et al. 1997). Despite the obstacles and inequalities, we argue that cross-border cooperation can reduce injustices for healthier borderlanders, as we demonstrate in the analysis on tuberculosis and HIV.

Focusing on Social Determinants of Health

The values of a society are displayed in its willingness to secure better health, well-being, and quality of life for *all* (Healthy People 2020, 2010). Residents of the US-Mexico border, as in the rest of the globe, envision a day when preventable death, illness, injury, and disability, as well as health disparities and inequalities, will be reduced, and each citizen will enjoy the best health possible. This transformation will only occur when we change our thinking about "health," examine the societal determinants (root causes), and direct more resources and interventions to address primary, causal factors that affect health. Social determinants of health are defined as the conditions in the social, physical, and economic environment in which people are born, live, work, and age. The determinants consist of policies, programs, and institutions as well as other aspects of social structures, including the government and private sectors and community factors (Healthy People 2020, 2010).

Our rationale for focusing on social determinants includes the need to move beyond controlling disease to address the factors for the root causes of risk, vulnerability, and disease and the importance of achieving health equity, social justice, and human security. By addressing inequalities in social (e.g., socioeconomic status, gender, sex, age, ethnicity, and educational attainment) and physical environmental factors, we can increase health equity, decrease health disparities, and ensure social justice. Education is the best indicator of socioeconomic status (SES) as it shapes future occupational opportunities and earnings. An education provides knowledge and life skills that allow people to increase their access to information and resources to promote and protect health (Marmot 2009). Higher income can provide better nutrition, housing, schooling, recreation, and health care (Wilkinson and Marmot 2003). Another important measure that greatly affects health status is whether or not one is employed or has entitlement benefits, threat of unemployment, and job insecurity (Rodriguez 2001). Pathways by which SES influences health are those that affect health more generally (Elder and Newman 2002).

SES has cumulative effects (Baum et al. 2009) on health throughout the entire life course and reducing inequalities therein can meet numerous health objectives in both the United States and in Mexico. While SES is clearly linked to morbidity and mortality, the mechanisms responsible for the association are not well understood. Identifying these mechanisms is important as these would provide more options for policy and interventions as described in the Healthy People 2020 Action Framework. Healthy People is a comprehensive set of 10-year national public health and health objectives to guide planning and motivate action. The intent of Healthy People 2020 is to be useful and relevant to public health agencies and their partners at the state and local levels, as well as the national level (Fielding and Kumanika 2009).

The US-Mexico Border Context

The US-Mexico border region attracts individuals and migrants from other areas of Mexico and Latin America who seek economic opportunities and, in many cases, migration to the United States. These goals are not always achieved once they arrive to the region, thus creating populations that are displaced and vulnerable. When poor people migrate into developed countries like the United States, the risk of adverse health outcomes, such as TB and HIV, is increased. Also intriguing is the so-called "Hispanic or Latino health paradox" and the "immigrant advantage" referring to the contradictory finding that indicates that Latinos and immigrants in the United States tend to have significantly better health and mortality outcomes than the average population despite generally low socioeconomic status (Markides and Coreil 1986; Cho et al. 2004; Frazini and Ribbie 2001; Hayes-Bautista et al. 2002). Findings from the Tomas Rivera Policy Institute (Tamingco 2007) suggest that the Latino health paradox exists for mental health issues, asthma, and high blood pressure. Results from this study indicate that Hispanics immigrants are healthier in terms of these three health outcomes when they first arrive in the United States; however, they become less healthy after acculturation.

There are 26 US federally recognized Native American tribes and 7 Mexican indigenous peoples in the border region. Extensive family and cultural ties are shared by many of these peoples. Health inequalities along the border especially affect indigenous populations who are vulnerable as a result of socioeconomic status, lack of health insurance, linguistic and cultural barriers, and limited access to health care (PAHO 2007; USMBHC 2010).

The US-Mexico border is a semipermeable membrane; it is open to risk and disease but closed to the free movement of people, services, and cures. In the US-Mexico borderlands, separating a rich and poor country with different types of health-care systems, inequalities in access to health care are created or reinforced. The distributions of communicable diseases like TB and HIV are associated with other social disparities (e.g., wealthy versus poor, majority versus minority) in both access to medical care and treatment. In addition, considerable research in public health on the US-Mexico border has increased focus on individual behavior and social determinants (USMBHC 2010; Bliss 2010; PAHO 2007).

The following section summarizes some of the most significant health issues affecting the border communities, with an emphasis on TB and HIV, and provides recommendations about how to address these issues in social justice terms.

Health Issues

Health and environmental issues in the border region are challenging and difficult to resolve. This is due in part to the international nature of the US-Mexico border environment, the different levels of economic development, and asymmetrical economies and governments (see Chap. 10 by Grineski and Juárez, this volume). The challenges transcend political boundaries. Examples include air and water pollution, groundwater depletion, soil contamination, illegal outdoor burning, drug addiction, and infectious disease. In order to address these issues, it is important for multiple US and Mexican federal, state, and local agencies to coordinate, communicate, and cooperate over their coresponsibilities. The United States and Mexico recognize the international nature of the major issues on the border and have built a closer bilateral relationship (though see Chap. 7 by Homedes, this volume), but with Mexico fast approaching a failed state, the future of cooperation will be limited as Mexico's government grapples with more immediate issues.

Health conditions are similar on each side of the US-Mexico border. Of the ten leading causes of death for adults, six are the same in both nations: heart disease, malignant neoplasm, cerebrovascular diseases, diabetes mellitus, liver disease and cirrhosis, and motor-injury accidents. Tuberculosis (primarily pulmonary), substance abuse, HIV, and vector-, water-, and food-borne diseases are also important diseases along the border.

Nutrition and Metabolic Diseases

Childhood obesity is reaching epidemic proportions in the border region (USMBHC 2010). Diabetes mellitus, a chronic disease that is linked to lifestyle, is pervasive in the border region. Border people also experience high rates of obesity due to low levels of physical activity and poor nutrition choices. An alarming fact is that an estimated 11.6% of the people with diabetes in the US border states are not aware that they have diabetes. In Mexico, that percentage is 40 (Bliss 2010). Rates of diabetes were slightly higher for female than male on both sides of the border (PAHO 2007). Data on Hispanics, Mexican Americans, and Native Americans residing at the US-Mexico border suggest that some diseases such as diabetes are genetically linked, while other conditions are due primarily to access to health care and poverty (Koo 2002).

Challenges to effective diagnosis and preventive care include the fact that many people on the border do not have the skills or the health literacy to effectively manage their health condition. Many communities do not have adequate access to health services, and many persons living with diabetes and their families do not have the economic means to meet the challenges posed by the disease. Obesity, a chronic health condition, also disproportionately affects the border population. Obese individuals along the US side of the border have 2.8 times greater risk of developing diabetes (Bliss 2010; PAHO 2007). Cancer rates and their stages of diagnosis in the border region show that the most common cancers are breast, cervical, and prostate. These cancers are detected at later stages among Hispanics, African Americans, and Native Americans as compared to non-Hispanic whites. Poor populations are two to three times more likely to die of cancer, possibly due to delayed diagnosis, fewer screenings, lack of (or limited) health insurance coverage, and fewer treatment options (Suarez and Ramirez 1999). Cancer survival would be improved with increased screening and increased health insurance coverage so that treatment could be accessed soon after diagnosis.

Mental Health and Substance Abuse

Drug and alcohol abuse are serious public health problems along the border. Adolescents are the most vulnerable population groups at high risk for addiction, including drug abuse, tobacco use, underage drinking, and suicide. Easy access to illicit drugs leads to high rates of substance abuse and addiction in the Texas-Mexico border region, particularly among teenagers (Maxwell 2007). Individuals who live in unsafe environments are more likely to use illicit drugs than those who are in secure surroundings.

Access to Health Care

There are widespread documented inequalities in the availability and distribution of basic public health infrastructure and resources on the border. It is particularly noteworthy that US border states and counties have the highest uninsured rates in the country. Hispanics face greater socioeconomic vulnerabilities (e.g., poverty, low educational attainment, higher unemployment) and experience more disease burden from preventable health disparities such as TB, diarrheal diseases, poor nutrition, obesity, and diabetes.

Due to low rates of health insurance coverage, Mexican-origin immigrants in the border region have limited access to health services (see Chap. 7 by Homedes, this volume). Gaps in services can also affect treatment services (e.g., mental health, medical care, substance abuse treatment). The undocumented status of the significant number of Mexican immigrants (11–13 million) also contributes to their disadvantaged situation because under US law, undocumented individuals are not eligible for Medicaid, Women, Infant and Children (WIC) programs, Children Health Insurance Program (CHIP), or other federally funded health programs (Padilla et al. 2006). Medical health coverage rises with increased income level and education – both of which are lower among immigrants as compared to the general population.

Upgrading and enhancing health and mental health care in the border region requires attention to providing culturally and linguistic competent services with a focus on cultural values and language, utilizing appropriate assessment tools, provision of ongoing orientation to services, increasing appropriate evidence-based practices, emphasizing biculturalism, developing coalitions, and engaging community in outreach efforts.

The Cases of Tuberculosis and HIV

While a myriad of communicable diseases exist in the border region, TB, HIV and their comorbidity are of most concern. TB and HIV account for substantial morbidity and mortality, with great social and fiscal costs to individuals, families, and societies. The US-Mexico border still experiences a disproportionate burden of these conditions as compared to the rest of these countries and compared to other Western industrialized nations, with significant disparities observed across subgroups and geographical regions (CDC MMWR 2009).

There is recognition of the direct correlation between TB and HIV incidence and the incidence of poverty (Paluzzi 2004). Although these diseases cross class lines and geographical locations, its highest toll has always been among the working class poor and their families. The patterns of diseases found in Hispanics, African Americans, non-Hispanic whites, Native Americans, and Mexicans along the border create unique challenges for public health responses.

Tuberculosis

Every minute, four people die from tuberculosis and 15 more become infected worldwide (Harrington et al. 2009). In 2008, there were 11,095,750 people living with active TB globally (The Henry Kaiser Family Foundation Global Health Facts 2010). When complex forces move more poor people into the United States (from Mexico or any other underdeveloped country), an increase in TB incidence is inevitable. The US-Mexico border is at high risk of elevated TB and HIV incidence and other health issues due to socioeconomic stress, rapid and dynamic population growth, mobility and migration, and the interrelationship of cultures (Finch et al. 2001; Moya and Shedlin 2008) and a young population (Harrison and Kennedy 1994). TB is a subtle and complex chronic infectious disease. The extent of the disease is likely to be underreported because of mobility and migration across the border as well as the long latency of the condition after infection occurs. The incidence of TB at the border far exceeds national incidence rates in both countries (see Fig. 9.1).

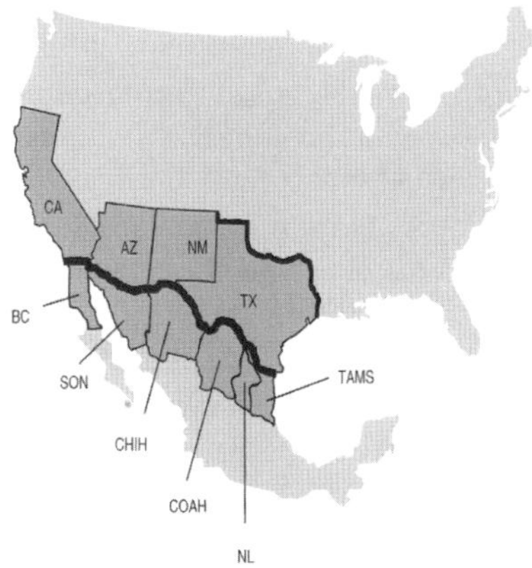

United States/Mexico border

- States: four in the U.S., six in Mexico
- Length: 1,952 miles (3,141 km)
- Border area[a] population ~17 million persons
- Annual northbound border crossings: ~264 million persons[b]

	2009 TB Cases	2009 TB Rate[c]	Cases of Persons Living with HIV (2008)[d]	HIV Prevalence (per 100,000)[d]
Arizona (AZ)	232	3.5	14,041	216.0
California (CA)	2,470	6.7	100,366	366.4
New Mexico (NM)	48	2.4	3,675	178.9
Texas (TX)	1,501	6.1	62,179	255.6
U.S. Border States	4,483	6.4	-	-
U.S. Total	11,545	3.8	580,371 (HIV) 459,594 (AIDS)*	275.4 (HIV) 152.5 (AIDS)*
Baja California (BC)	1,544	48.4	5,540	3.0
Chihuahua (CHIH)	691	20.4	3,366	5.0
Coahuila (COAH)	476	18.1	1,496	1.0
Nuevo Leon (NL)	974	21.9	3,506	2.0
Sonora (SON)	829	33.0	1,985	3.0
Tamaulipas (TAMS)	1,037	32.5	2,979	3.0
Mexican border states	5,551	28.7	-	-
Mexican National	18,011	16.7	124,505	2.0

a. Border area is defined as the area extending 100 kilometers (62 miles) north-south of the U.S.-Mexico border
b. United States Department of Transportation, Bureau of Transportation Statistics, 2010
c. Sources: Centers for Disease Control and Prevention. Reported Tuberculosis in the United States, 2009. U.S. Department of Healthand Human Services, CDC, 2010. Plataforma Unica de Inforamcion. Modulo Tuberculosis. DGE/Mexico/2010.
d. Sources: HIV data for U.S. (CDC, 2008a; CDC, 2008b, and CA, AZ, NM, and TX State Health Departments) and Mexico (CENSIDA, 2009)
* 2007 National Rates(CDC, 2008a)

Fig. 9.1 US-Mexico border tuberculosis cases and rates (2009) and HIV cases and prevalence (2008)

There is little discussion among health decision makers, researchers, and health practitioners about how to address poverty inequality in tuberculosis and migration (Farmer 2005). As shown in Fig. 9.1, in 2009, TB rates on each side of the border were 1.8 times their respective national averages according to published (CDC 2010) and unpublished sources (Castellanos 2010). Ongoing transmission, prolonged infection, delayed diagnosis, increased mobility, and increased drug resistance have been documented among persons residing along the US-Mexico border (Schneider et al. 2004). Poor socioeconomic conditions, limited access to health care, TB-related stigma, increased mobility, and migration make case management and completion of standard 6-month treatment more difficult (Moya and Lusk 2010; Alvarez-Gordillo et al. 2000; Jaramillo 2002). TB presents unique characteristics that have their origin in the fact that society is divided into SES-based groups or classes, and it is from this status that the resistance to the TB emerges. Mechanisms to reach out to educate and treat vulnerable populations for TB in both countries, including those that enter the United States legally, need to be addressed and implemented.

In Mexico, every day there are 54 new TB cases, and every 6 hours a person dies from TB (Castellanos 2009). TB continues to affect communities and individuals that are most vulnerable (e.g., poor, underserved, malnourished, HIV positive, diabetics). Mexico's national TB rate for 2009 was 16.7 per 100,000 (Castellanos 2010); this is over four times the rate in the United States of 3.8 per 100,000. Mexico's national TB prevalence rate for 2009 was 23 per 100,000 – eight times higher than the United States rate of 3 per 100,000 (The Henry Kaiser Family Foundation Global Health Facts 2010).

Each of the six Mexican states that border with United States has higher TB rates compared to the national TB rate. Combined, these represent 29% of the total cases for Mexico in 2009, with the border municipalities of the states of Baja California, Nuevo León, and Tamaulipas having the largest concentration of tuberculosis cases (Castellanos 2009; CDC MMWR 2009). According to the Centers for Disease Control and Prevention (CDC), in the United States in 2009, a total of 11,545 new TB cases were reported, and the TB rate declined by 4.2% from 2006 to 3.8% cases per 100,000 (CDC MMWR 2010). The national TB incidence rate in 2009 was the lowest since national reporting began in 1953. Despite this improvement, foreign-born persons and racial and ethnic minorities continue to bear a disproportionate burden of the disease in the United States. TB rates among Hispanics, Mexican-origin individuals, African Americans, and Asians were 7.8, 8.3, and 22.9 times higher than among non-Hispanic whites, respectively, in 2007 (CDC MMWR 2009). Beck (1992) suggests the defining feature of a "risk society" is the distribution of "dangers" and a move toward the increasing individualization of risk.

We live in a globalized society of risk and vulnerabilities. A core argument is that the discourses of "nation" are becoming more important in terms of globalization as an articulating device (Craig 2007), which serves to define the "insiders" from the "outsiders." This helps to create risk categories (e.g., foreign-born, Mexican-origin) to justify enhanced surveillance and serve to separate those who can manage the risk from those whose risks require management under supervision (Dean 1995; Castel 1991). Risk management consequently represents a localized response to the globalized problems of TB, HIV, and poverty. The risk of TB then becomes associated to particular social categories, such as foreign-born, rather than the structural inequalities and process that place people at risk and maintain positions. For example, TB is associated with poor-quality and overcrowded housing (Bhatti et al. 1995; Farmer et al. 1991, 1997; Farmer 2000), and minority ethnic groups are more likely to experience housing inequalities as well as reside in areas that experience disadvantage (Acevedo-Garcia 2000).

TB often coexists with HIV and, if not treated, can produce fatal consequences. TB is the leading killer of people with HIV. People who are HIV positive and infected with TB are 20–40 times more likely to develop active TB than people not infected with HIV in the same country (WHO 2009). The focus on TB and HIV in the US-Mexico border is timely given the evidence of increasing burden and worsening health disparities for these conditions, the evolution in the understanding of the social and structural influences of disease epidemiology, and the implications of the global economic downturn. The global trends and impacts on health of HIV, TB, and sexually transmitted infections (STIs) remain among the most urgent public health challenges of our time (WHO 2009).

HIV and Sexually Transmitted Infections

HIV and some STIs can be transmitted through unprotected sex, perinatal transmission (e.g., mother-to-child), parenteral transmission (e.g., needle sharing during injection drug use), blood/plasma transfusion, and organ transplantation. Risky sexual behavior and drug use contribute to the spread of HIV. Social, economic, and cultural factors, which may enhance the spread of HIV, include urbanization, migration, poverty, homelessness, and poor education. These factors may play differential roles in the risk of infection across populations and subgroups such as migrants, female sex workers, injection drug users (IDUs), men who have sex with men, and high-risk heterosexuals. Not only do these populations engage in high levels of HIV risk behaviors but they are prone to stigma and blamed for spreading the disease (Kaisernetwork.org 2007; Magis-Rodriguez et al. 2010; Larios et al. 2009; Brouwer et al. 2009; Strathdee et al. 2008; Patterson et al. 2006; UNAIDS 2004).

The mobility and dynamics of the US-Mexico border also complicate the control and reduction of HIV and STIs. Migration, mobility, socioeconomic status, lack of educational resources, intravenous drug use, and high sexual risk behaviors and practices are among the primary factors that facilitate the spread of HIV in the region. Studies have highlighted the role of intravenous drug use, men that have sex with men, sex work, mobility, and migration in HIV transmission (Kaisernetwork.org 2007; Magis-Rodriguez et al. 2010; Larios et al. 2009; Brouwer et al. 2009; Strathdee et al. 2008; Patterson et al. 2006; UNAIDS 2004). HIV counts and rates along the US-Mexico border are shown in Fig. 9.1. As we indicate in this chapter, though HIV prevalence in Mexico border states is considerably lower than for the US border states, the epidemic is concentrated among high-risk populations in large cities and hence has not yet generalized. Without proper prevention, Mexico border states are facing an emerging epidemic. In most border communities, there are programs and initiatives addressing HIV and STIs using border binational approaches.

High-Risk Populations on the US Side of the Border Region

Presently, there are over 156,700 women and girls living with HIV in the United States, and they account for 27% of all adults and adolescents living with HIV (CDC 2008a). Of these, 73% had been exposed through high-risk heterosexual contact and 26% through injection drug use (CDC 2008b). Hispanics are disproportionately infected with HIV; although comprising 13% of the US population, they account for 17.5% of US AIDS cases (U.S. Census Bureau 2004; CDC MMWR 2008b). After the continental United States (35%) and Puerto Rico (25%), the majority of AIDS cases among the Hispanic population were concentrated among those born in Mexico (13%) (CDC 2000).

"Counties along the U.S.-Mexico border are among the poorest economically in the United States" (Lobato and Cegielski 2001). Migrant workers and families of low SES living on the border experience food insecurity known to lead at least one member in the family to suffer from depression, learning disorders, and gastrointestinal complications (Weigel et al. 2007). Almost half of counties along the US-Mexico border are medically underserved and of low socioeconomic status (Lobato and Cegielski 2001).

High-Risk Populations on the Mexican Side of the Border

HIV is considered a low prevalence but emerging epidemic in Mexico. There are over two million cumulative cases of HIV in Mexico (CENSIDA 2009) ranking 23rd in HIV prevalence among Latin American nations (UNAIDS 2004). When prevention strategies for high-risk populations are not implemented, the epidemic tends to spread. Dr. Remedios Lozada, HIV/STI coordinator for Baja California State, observes that intravenous drug users are "a vulnerable population, and sometimes people think it's a small group – those using drugs … but really, as we've seen in other countries where they didn't address the problem immediately, it could spread. And so we have to be careful and we have to intervene" (Kaisernetwork.org 2007). The at-risk populations for HIV include female sex workers (FSWs), injection drug users (IDU), FSW-IDU, female sex partners of IDU, men who have sex with men (MSM), migrants and deportees, and persons with other STIs.

Tijuana and Ciudad Juárez, the two largest cities on the US-Mexico border, have a high concentration of IDUs, FSWs, and migrants that mirror many of the interrelated environmental factors that make these cities prime cities for an HIV epidemic. For example, Tijuana and Ciudad Juárez are situated on major drug trafficking routes for heroin, marijuana, cocaine, and methamphetamine, resulting in drugs being highly available and cheap.

Mobility is another important driver in Mexico's HIV epidemic, especially for migrant males who are more likely to have sex with other men and to pay for sex with males and females, compared to nonmigrants (Ramos et al. 2009). The amount of movement and growth in bordering US and Mexican cities has led to an increase in the incidence of certain infectious diseases (Espinoza et al. 2009). In Tijuana, Baja California, the most populated city along the border with over 1.5 million residents (INEGI 2010), migration history has been found to be associated with "unique economic and social stressors," current risk behaviors, and access to health care and new drug use trends (Brouwer et al. 2009). When migrants reach these border cities and cannot migrate into the United States or are deported to the border region, many find themselves displaced and at risk for working in the sex industry or using drugs. Young women are particularly vulnerable to becoming sex workers in this region, especially since prostitution is legal in many Mexican municipalities. Migration to the region, a search for better pay, or a search for means to survive or raise families plays a role in their initiation into sex work. Given the high availability of drugs in the region, drug use patterns may be influential factors relating to their decision to enter sex work.

Historically, these two cities have been known spots for sexual tourism. Prostitution is regulated, but not prohibited. In both Juárez and Tijuana, there are "tolerance zones" where sex work is quasi-legal. In 2006, it was reported that 4,850 FSWs were registered with the Municipal Health Service in Tijuana and as many as 4,000 FSWs work without permits (Patterson et al. 2006). Among all sex workers, only 38% reported often or always using condoms for vaginal sex with clients. Many female sex workers reported that men are willing to pay about twice as much for unprotected sex (Larios et al. 2009). FSWs have high rates of STIs with prevalence of active syphilis (titer >1:8), chlamydia, and gonorrhea in Tijuana and Ciudad Juárez at 26.9%, 13.0%, and 6.4%, respectively (Loza et al. 2010a, b). For all three infections, drug-using behaviors, rather than sexual behaviors, were independently associated with infection (Loza et al. 2010a, b). FSW-IDU also have higher rates of HIV and STI compared to other FSW (i.e., HIV 16% versus 4%; syphilis 49% versus 22%; gonorrhea 15% versus 4%; and chlamydia 24% versus 10%) (Strathdee et al. 2008). Given the extent of migration and deportation between the United States and Mexico and the elevated risk of HIV transmission that accompanies mobile populations, a multilevel response for HIV prevention programs among high-risk and mobile populations is necessary (AIDSTAR-One 2010).

Structural Interventions

The US-Mexico border needs public health structural interventions that promote health by changing the structural context within which health is promoted. Structural interventions implicitly address the cause of public and social health problems in the context and environment that influence risk behaviors, or other determinants of infection and morbidity, rather than the characteristics of the individuals who engage in risk behaviors. Prevention efforts must take into account the structural sources of risk and address them as part of a broader effort to end social inequality and engender social change. Implementation of structural interventions involves struggle, consensus building, and conflict resolution. There are various effective examples of structural interventions for TB and HIV prevention (Aggelton et al. 2003; Farmer et al. 1991; De Heer et al. 2008; Ramos et al. 2009; Stop TB Partnership 2006). In this chapter, we consider existing approaches gaining prominence.

Advocacy, Communication, and Social Mobilization in Mexico: The SOLUCION TB Case

From 2006 to 2010, Project Concern International (PCI) implemented the USAID-funded TB prevention and control initiative in Mexico called SOLUCION TB (*S*trengthening *O*bserved therapy *L*inking *U*p *C*ommunity-based *I*ntegrated *O*utreach *N*etworks for *TB* control).[1] These experiences led PCI to combine an "Empowering Directly Observed Therapy, Short-course (Empowering DOTS)" approach with practical and creative advocacy, communication, and social mobilization (ACSM) activities. As a result, TB case management and treatment improved, and social mobilization and community participation in TB activities increased, resulting in an average cure rate in the 13 participating states of 90.7%, compared to a national rate of 84.1% (PCI 2010). The successful integration of health, medical, and social models and the strategic combination of DOTS and ACMS have given rise to a series of lessons learned, promising practices, approaches, and implementation models which hopefully, when shared and adapted to local contexts, will help move the TB state-of-the-art efforts in prevention and control further along, in Mexico, the United States, and around the globe. PCI learned that ACMS strategies need to effectively raise awareness, mobilize community members, and empower and engage persons affected by TB, to successfully prevent and control TB and its repercussions. As an important aspect of its ACSM work, PCI carried out the first national Knowledge Attitudes and Practices study for TB control in Mexico (for additional information, visit www.solluciontb.org). The core findings demonstrate that prior education efforts have resulted in a majority of the population at large being aware of the fact that (1) TB exists, (2) it is a public health problem, (3) it is a disease serious enough to require immediate attention and medical care, and (4) adherence to TB treatment is a key aspect of TB care (Lomeli et al. 2010). Findings also made evident the fact that more detailed and in-depth information needs to be provided to persons affected by TB community at large to combat misconceptions that might lead to poor health-care seeking practices, stigma, and its resulting discriminatory behaviors (Moya 2010).

[1]The initiative started in one state and expanded nationally. The initiative (also referred to as program) includes three basic components: (1) recruitment and training of dedicated TB workers, (2) capacity-building interventions and (3) advocacy, communication, and social mobilization strategies (ACMS). This intervention has the person affected by TB (PATB) at the center of the design and implemented within the infrastructure of the Ministry of Health, TB Program. The program targeted 35 health jurisdictions in 13 Mexican priority states, which account for 65% of all TB cases in the country.

HIV Interventions

Mexican nongovernmental organization such as *Programa Compañeros* and *PrevenCasa* have applied various approaches to HIV harm reduction, prevention, and services to the most-at-risk populations in Ciudad Juárez and Tijuana, respectively (AIDSTAR-One 2010). Prevention programs in both cities have promoted protective behaviors among IDUs such as needle-exchange programs (NEPs), obtaining syringes at pharmacies, and disinfection of used syringes with bleach. The first NEP was introduced in Ciudad Juárez in the early 1990s by the nongovernmental organization *Programa Compañeros*, A.C., funded by the Border AIDS Partnership, an affiliate of the National AIDS Fund. Between 2004 and 2008, over 120,000 syringes were distributed in Ciudad Juárez. Through *PrevenCasa* since 2006, Patronato Pro-COMUSIDA runs a NEP and distributes *PreveKits* or safe injection kits to users (Kaisernetwork.org 2007).

Educational Interventions

The Cross-Border HIV/AIDS Prevention Training Program, part of the US-Mexico Training, Internships, Exchanges, and Scholarship (TIES) Initiative through the El Colegio de la Frontera Norte, Universidad Autónoma de Baja California, San Diego State University (SDSU), and University of California, San Diego (UCSD), is a recent example of an educational HIV training intervention along on the border. This partnership has been developing a binational infrastructure for training of Mexican nationals by visiting scholars program at UCSD and SDSU for researchers from Mexico in HIV prevention and program evaluation to meet the demands of the emerging HIV border pandemic among the mobile, migrant, and other high-risk groups (TIES 2008).

Recommendations for Policy Action

The following recommendations will help move the state of the art in prevention and control forward along the border. Therefore, TB and HIV can finally and ultimately be eliminated as a major social public health crisis:

- Address the social and structural sources of TB and HIV vulnerability. Enact broader, socioeconomic reforms, particularly those focused at improving child development, school nutrition programs, and the working and living conditions of the working classes to make significant inroads into the epidemiological patterns of TB and HIV.
- Address the socioeconomic inequalities that create vulnerability and foster the spread of diseases. No single country or society can resolve the origins and

consequences of the greatest social disease "poverty." However, some countries like the United States are in a better position to globalize resources and social actions.
- Need macro binational dimension policies to respond to communicable and noncommunicable diseases to understand social factors and income inequality and its relation to health.
- Person- and community-centered aspects should be effectively combined with the more medical aspects in a way that is comprehensive and seamless, resulting in an integrated approach to prevention, care, and support and encourage the use of qualitative data in the biomedical discourse.
- Refocus health promotion and education to collective empowerment and community mobilization to create a critical perception of the social, cultural, political, and economic forces that structure reality and to address the factors that are oppressive.
- Build on community capacities and existing knowledge and recognize the legitimacy of indigenous knowledge and capability (e.g., HIV, women's health, maternal and child health).
- Document and share practical and creative experiences, lessons learned, and promising practices in addressing health disparities. It is important that resources are devoted to rigorously documenting and providing an evidence base in order to transform some of these "promising" practices into "best" practices.
- Building strategic partnerships within and outside the health sector are essential for success, for maximizing limited resources, for ensuring sustainability, and for optimizing what ultimately needs to be social mobilization around issues of stigma, discrimination, gender inequalities, and other key social drivers of health disparities.

Acknowledgments We want to thank our colleagues SOLUCION TB Project Concern International; *Programa Nacional de Tuberculosis en Mexico*; CDC Division of HIV/AIDS, STI, TB and Hepatitis; New Mexico Department of Health; Texas Department of State Health Services; Arizona Department of Health Services; and California Department of Health for their contributions to this chapter.

References

Acevedo-Garcia, D. (2000). Residential segregation and the epidemiology of infectious diseases. *Social Science & Medicine, 51*, 1143–1161.

Aggelton, P., Parker, R., & Malawa, M. (2003). *Stigma, discrimination and HIV/AIDS in Latin America and the Caribbean*. Washington, DC: Inter-American Development Bank.

AIDSTAR-One. (2010). *UNAIDS. Case study: HIV prevention on the U.S.-Mexico border*. http://www.aidstar-one.com/case_study_hiv_prevention_us_mexico_border. Accessed 4 Dec 2010.

Alvarez-Gordillo, G. D., et al. (2000). Perceptions and practices of tuberculosis patients and non-adherence to their therapy in Chiapas, Mexico. *Salud Pública de Mexico, 40*, 520–528.

Baum, F. E., Begin, M., Houwelling, T. A. J., & Taylor, S. (2009). Changes not for the fainthearted: Reorienting health care systems toward health equity through action on the social determinants of health. *American Journal of Public Health, 99*(11), 1967–1974.

Beck, U. (1992). *Risk society towards a new modernity*. London: Sage.
Bhatti, N., Law, M. R., Morris, J. K., Halliday, R., & Moore-Gillon, J. (1995). Increasing incidence of tuberculosis in England and Wales: A study of likely causes. *British Medical Journal, 310*, 967–969.
Bliss, K. (2010). *The challenges of chronic diseases on the U.S.-Mexico border*. Washington, DC: Center for Strategic and International Studies.
Brandon, J., Crespin, F., Levy, C., & Reyna, D. (1997). Border health issues. In J. Bruhn & J. Brandon (Eds.), *Border health: Challenges to the United States and Mexico*. New York: Gardland Press.
Brouwer, K. C., Lozada, R., Cornelius, W. A., Firestone Cruz, M., Magis-Rodríguez, C., Zúñiga de Nuncio, M. L., et al. (2009). Deportation along the U.S.-Mexico border: Its relation to drug use patterns and accessing care. *Journal of Immigrant and Minority Health, 11*(1), 1–6.
Castel, R. (1991). From dangerousness to risk. In G. Burchell, C. Gordon, & R. Miller (Eds.), *The Foucault effect: Studies in governmentality* (pp. 281–297). London: Harvester-Wheatsheaf.
Castellanos, M. J. (2009). Situación Actual de la Tuberculosis en Mexico. *Reunión Anual de SOLUCION TB* (pp. 4–7). Mexico: Secretaria de Salud, Plataforma Única de Información Móduló de Tuberculosis.
Castellanos, M. (2010, September 29). Situación Actual de la TB/VIH y TB/DM en Mexico. *Reunión Nacional de SOLUCION TB y Programa Nacional de Micobacteriosis*. Mexico: Programa Nacional de TB en Mexico.
CDC (MMWR). (2009, March 20). *Tuberculosis trends in the United States, 2008*. Retrieved January 4, 2010, from Centers for Disease Control and Prevention: http://www.cdc.gov/mmwr/preview/mmwrhtml/mm5810a2.htm
CDC (MMWR). (2010, March 18). *Centers for Disease Control and Prevention*. Retrieved March 23, 2010, from http://www.cdc.gov/media/mmwrnews/2010/n100318.htm#2
Centers for Disease Control and Prevention (CDC). (2000). *HIV/AIDS surveillance report*. Year end edition. http://www.cdc.gov/hiv/stats/hasr1202.htm. Accessed 9 Dec 2010.
Centers for Disease Control and Prevention (CDC). (2008a). *HIV surveillance report. Diagnoses of HIV infection and AIDS in the United States and dependent areas, 2008* (Vol. 20). http://www.cdc.gov/hiv/surveillance/resources/reports/2008report/. Accessed 9 Dec 2010.
Centers for Disease Control and Prevention (CDC). (2008b). HIV prevalence estimates – United States, 2006. *Morbidity and Mortality Weekly Report, 57*(39), 1073.
Centers for Disease Control and Prevention (CDC). (2010). Retrieved October 26, 2010, from CDC Tuberculosis Statistics: http://wwww.cdc.gov.tb/statistics/tables.htm
Centro Nacional para la Prevención y el Control del VIH/SIDA (CENSIDA). (2009). *El VIH/SIDA en Mexico 2009*. http://www.censida.salud.gob.mx/descargas/2009/VIHSIDAenMexico2009.pdf. Accessed 11 Nov 2010.
Cho, Y., Frisbie, W. P., Hummer, R., & Rogers, R. (2004). Nativity, duration of residence, and the health of Hispanic adults in the United States. *International Migration Review, 38*(1), 184–211.
Craig, G. M. (2007). 'Nation', 'migration' and tuberculosis. *Social Theory & Health, 5*, 267–284.
De Heer, H., Moya, E., & Lacson, R. (2008). Voices and images tuberculosis photovoice in a binational setting. *Cases in Public Health Communication and Marketing, 2*, 55–86.
Dean, M. (1995). Governing the unemployed self in an active society. *Economy and Society, 24*, 559–583.
Elder, N. E., & Newman, K. (2002). Socioeconomic disparities in health: Pathways and policies. *Health Affairs, 21*(2), 60–75.
Espinoza, L., Hall, H. I., & Hu, X. (2009, October). Increases in HIV diagnoses at the U.S.-Mexico border, 2003–2006. *AIDS Education and Prevention, 21*(5 Suppl), 19–33.
Farmer, P. (2000). The consumption of the poor: Tuberculosis in the 21st century. *Ethnography, 1*, 183–216.
Farmer, P. (2005). Never again reflections on human values and human rights. In *The Tanner lectures on human health* (pp. 139–179). Utah: University of Utah.
Farmer, P., Ramilus, S., Robin, S., & Kim, J. Y. (1991). Tuberculosis, poverty, and "compliance": Lessons from rural Haiti. *Seminars in Respiratory Infections, 6*(4), 254–260.

Farmer, P., Bayona, J., & Becerra, M, et al. (1997, February 27–March 2). Poverty, inequality and drug resistance: Meeting community needs in the global era. *International union against tuberculosis and lung disease, North American region* (pp. 88–101). Chicago.

Fielding, J., & Kumanika, S. (2009). Recommendations for the concepts and forms of Healthy People 2020. *American Journal of Preventive Medicine, 37*(3), 255–257.

Finch, B., Vega, W., Hummer, R. A., & Kolody, B. (2001). The role of discrimination and acculturative stress in the physical health of Mexican-origin adults. *Social Sciences and Medicine, 23*, 399–429.

Frazini, L., & Ribbie, J. K. (2001). Understanding the Hispanic paradox. *Ethnicity & Disease, 11*(3), 496–518.

Harrington, M., Morgan, G., & Syed, J. (2009). *Tuberculosis research and development.* Stop TB Partnership. TB/HIV Project. New York: Treatment Action Group.

Harrison, L. D., & Kennedy, N. J. (1994). Drug use in the U.S.-Mexico border area: Is there an epidemic waiting to happen? *Hispanic Journal of Behavioral Health Sciences, 26*(3), 281–295.

Hayes-Bautista, D. E., Hsu, P., Hayes-Bautista, M., Iniguez, D., Chamberlin, C., Rico, C., et al. (2002). An anomaly within the Latino epidemiological paradox: The Latino adolescent male mortality peak. *Archives of Pediatric and Adolescent Medicine, 156*, 480–484.

Healthy People 2020. (2010, July 11). *Healthy People 2020: An opportunity to address societal determinants of health in the U.S.*. Washington, DC: Department of Health and Human Services.

Henry Kaiser Family Foundation. (2010). Retrieved June 19, 2008, from Globalhealthfacts.org: http://www.globalhealthfacts.org

Instituto Nacional de Estadistíca Geografia e Informatica (INEGI). (2010). Censo de Población y Vivienda 2010. Población total segun sexo, viviendas habitadas e indicadores seleccionados por zona metropolitana. http://www.censo2010.org.mx/. Accessed 14 Dec 2010.

Jaramillo, E. (2002). *Contribución de la comunidad a la atención de la tuberculosis: Una perspectiva Latinoamericana.* Geneva: World Health Organization.

Kaisernetwork.org. (2007). *Migrant workers contributing to spread of HIV along U.S., Mexico border, researchers say.* http://www.kaisernetwork.org/daily_reports/print_report.cfm?DR_ID=43814&dr_cat=1. Accessed 6 Dec 2010.

Koo, R. (2002). Poverty and health on the border. *Texas Journal of Rural Health, 20*(3), 38–51.

Larios, S. E., Lozada, R., Strathdee, S. A., Semple, S. J., Roesch, S., Staines, H., et al. (2009). An exploration of contextual factors that influence HIV risk in female sex workers in Mexico: The social ecological model applied to HIV risk behaviors. *AIDS Care, 21*(10), 1335–1342.

Lobato, M., & Cegielski, P. (2001). Preventing and controlling tuberculosis along the U.S.-Mexico border. *Recommendations and Reports, 50*(RR1), 1–2.

Lomeli, B., Ramos, R., Gallegos, N., Moya, E., & Rangel, G. (2010). *From cough to cure: KAT TB study in Mexico*. San Diego: PCI.

Loza, O., Patterson, T. L., Rusch, M., Martinez, G. A., Lozada, R., Staines-Orozco, H., et al. (2010a). Drug-related behaviors independently associated with syphilis infection among female sex workers in two Mexico-US border cities. *Addiction, 105*(8), 1448–1456.

Loza, O., Strathdee, S. A., Martinez, G. A., Lozada, R., Ojeda, V. D., Staines-Orozco, H., et al. (2010b). Risk factors associated with chlamydia and gonorrhoea infection among female sex workers in two Mexico-USA border cities. *International Journal of STD and AIDS, 21*(7), 460–465.

Magis-Rodriguez, C., De Luca, M., Bravo-Garcia, E., Rivera-Reyes, P., Ortiz-Mondragon, R., & Gayet, C. (2010). The AIDS epidemics in Mexico up to 2008. *Gaceta Médica de Mexico, 146*(1), 45–49.

Markides, K., & Coreil, J. (1986). The health of Hispanics in the Southwestern United States: An epidemiologic paradox. *Public Health Reports 101*(3), 253–265.

Marmot, M. G. (2009). Action on health disparities in the United States: Commission on social determinants of health. *Journal of the American Medical Association, 301*(11), 1169–1171.

Maxwell, J. C. (2007). *Substance abuse trends in Texas: June 2007.* Retrieved November 15, 2010, from http://www.utexas.edu/research/cswr/gcattc/documents/June2007_000/pdf

Moya, E. M. (2010, January 1). Tuberculosis and stigma: Impacts on health-seeking behaviors and access in Ciudad Juárez, México and El Paso, Texas. *ETD collection for University of Texas, El Paso.* (Paper AAI3409176).http://digitalcommons.utep.edu/dissertations/AAI3409176

Moya, E., & Lusk, M. W. (2010). *Trans-border research on stigma and treatment adherence in tuberculosis.* El Paso: University of Texas at El Paso.

Moya, E., & Shedlin, M. (2008). Policies and laws affecting Mexican-origin immigrant access and utilization of substance abuse treatment. *Substance Use & Misuse, 43*, 1747–1769.

Padilla, Y. C., Radey, M. D., Hummer, R. A., & Kim, E. (2006). The living conditions of U.S.-born children of Mexican immigrants in unmarried families. *Hispanic Journal of Behavioral Sciences, 28*(4), 331–349.

Paluzzi, J. (2004). A social disease/a social response: Lessons in tuberculosis from early 20th century Chile. *Social Science & Medicine, 59*, 763–773.

Pan American Health Organization (PAHO). (2007). United States-Mexico border area. In PAHO, *Health in the Americas* (Vol. II-Countries, pp. 733–744). Washington, DC: PAHO.

Patterson, T. L., Semple, S. J., Fraga, M., Bucardo, J., de la Torre, A., Salazar, J., et al. (2006). Comparison of sexual and drug use behaviors between female sex workers in Tijuana and Ciudad Juárez, Mexico. *Substance Use & Misuse, 41*(10–12), 1535–1549.

Project Concern International (PCI). (2010). *End of year project report to world learning*. Tijuana: PCI.

Ramos, R., Ferreira-Pinto, J. B., Brouwer, K. C., Ramose, M. E., Lozada, R. M., Firestone-Cruz, M., et al. (2009). A tale of two cities: Social and environmental influences shaping risk factors and protective behaviors in two Mexico-US border cities. *Health & Place, 15*(4), 999–1005.

Rodriguez, W. (2001). Keeping the unemployed healthy: The effect of means-tested and entitlement benefits in Britain, Germany and the United States. *American Journal of Public Health, 91*(9), 1403–1411.

Schneider, E., Laserson, K., & Wells, C. D. (2004). Tuberculosis along the United States-Mexico border, 1993–2001. *Pan American Journal of Public Health, 16*(1), 23–34.

STOP TB Partnership. (2006). *Advocacy, communication and social mobilization framework for action 2006–2015.* Geneva: World Health Organization.

Strathdee, S. A., Lozada, R., Semple, S. J., Orozovich, P., Pu, M., Staines-Orozco, H., et al. (2008). Characteristics of female sex workers with US clients in two Mexico-US border cities. *Sexually Transmitted Diseases, 35*(3), 263–268.

Suarez, L., & Ramirez, A. (1999). Hispanic/Latino health and disease: An overview. In M. K. R. Huff (Ed.), *Promoting health in multicultural populations: A handbook for practitioners* (pp. 115–136). Thousand Oaks: Sage.

Tamingco, M. T. (2007). *Revisiting the Latino health paradox.* Los Angeles: Tomas Rivera Policy Center.

The United Nations Joint Program on HIV/AIDS (UNAIDS). (2004). *2004 Report on the global AIDS epidemic.* http://www.unaids.org/bangkok2004/GAR2004_html/GAR2004_00_en.htm. Accessed 13 Oct 2008.

U.S. Census Bureau. (2004). *U.S. interim projections by age, sex, race, and Hispanic origin: 2000–2050.* Table 1a. Projected population of the United States, by race and Hispanic origin: 2000 to 2050. U.S. Census Bureau, Population Division. http://www.census.gov/population/www/projections/usinterimproj/. Accessed 13 Dec 2010.

U.S.-Mexico Border Health Commission (USMBHC). (2010, October 25). *A white paper: Health disparities and the U.S.-Mexico border challenges and opportunities.* El Paso: USMBHC.

U.S.-Mexico Training, Internships, Exchanges, and Scholarship (TIES). (2008). *Initiative (2010). Evidence of success: Results from higher education for development sites to six partnerships.* Cross-Border HIV/AIDS Prevention Training Program: El Colegio de la Frontera Norte/Universidad Autónoma de Baja California/San Diego State University (SDSU)/University of California, San Diego (UCSD). http://www.hedprogram.org/LinkClick.aspx?fileticket=27bzZpP6fTk=&tabid=60. Accessed 13 Dec 2010.

Warner, D. (1991). Health issues at the US-Mexico border. *Journal of the American Medical Association, 265*, 242–247.

Weigel, M. M., Armijos, R. X., Hall, Y. P., Ramirez, Y., & Orozco, R. (2007). The household food insecurity and health outcomes of U.S.-Mexico border migrant and seasonal farmworkers. *Journal of Immigrant and Minority Health, 9*(3), 157–169.

WHO. (2009). *World Health Organization's 2009 report on global tuberculosis control.* Retrieved December 4, 2009, from World Health Organization: http://www.who.int/tb/publications/global_report/en/

Wilkinson, R., & Marmot, M. (2003). *Social determinants of health: The solid facts* (2nd ed.). Copenhagen: World Health Organization.

Chapter 10
Environmental Injustice in the US-Mexico Border Region

Sara E. Grineski and Patricia M. Juárez-Carrillo

Given the inescapable physical connection between humans and nature, the future path of the ecological turn will be to merge social and environmental justice into one agenda.

– (Hazlett 2003, p. 416)

Introduction

The academic literature has demonstrated countless cases of disproportionate negative environmental impacts on socially marginalized people (i.e., environmental injustices), including those living in the US-Mexico border region (Carruthers 2007, 2008). The border region has been characterized as having a higher prevalence of chronic diseases, infections, pollution, and environmental health hazards that are coupled with high rates of poverty and joblessness, and low rates of literacy and access to affordable health care (Rao 2009). The antonym of environmental injustice is environmental justice (EJ), which Robert Bullard (1996, as cited in Mohai et al. 2009, p. 407) has defined as the principle that "all people and communities are entitled to equal protection of environmental and public health laws and regulations." The US Environmental Protection Agency (EPA) eventually elaborated on this principle, after years of consideration, and further defined EJ as:

> Fair treatment and meaningful involvement of all people regardless of race, color, national origin, or income with respect to the development, implementation, and enforcement of environmental laws, regulations, and policies. Fair treatment means that no population,

S.E. Grineski (✉)
Department of Sociology, University of Texas at El Paso, 500 W. University Ave., 79968, El Paso, TX, USA
e-mail: segrineski@utep.edu

P.M. Juárez-Carrillo
Project Concern International, 5050 Murphy Canyon Road, R-110 San Diego, CA 92123
e-mail: PJuarez@pciglobal.org

M. Lusk et al. (eds.), *Social Justice in the U.S.-Mexico Border Region*, DOI 10.1007/978-94-007-4150-8_10, © Springer Science+Business Media B.V. 2012

> due to policy or economic disempowerment, is forced to bear a disproportionate share of the negative human health or environmental impacts of pollution or environmental consequences resulting from industrial, municipal, and commercial operations or the execution of federal, state, local and tribal programs and policies (as cited in Mohai et al. 2009, p. 407).

This definition has served as *de facto* official policy under the Clinton, Bush, and now Obama administrations, and it serves as "the legal bar that EJ groups must reach to receive government attention" in the United States (Mohai et al. 2009, p. 407). According to Walker (2009), the language and concepts of EJ are highly applicable in international settings because EJ framing transcends boundaries through international alliances, coalitions, and networks.

Environmental injustices are prevalent in the border region, given the social and physical landscape of the region. Socially, the border is home to 13 million people, approximately a third of whom are under 15 (US-Mexico Border Health Commission [USMBHC] 2003). There are significant disparities, in terms of development and wealth, on both sides of the border. The US side is home to some of the poorest counties in the United States (e.g., Starr), but San Diego is more affluent than the average US county. On the Mexican side, three municipalities (*municipios*) containing half the Mexican border population (i.e., Ciudad Juárez, Mexicali, Tijuana) are ranked highly in terms of human development, but they also house poor rural migrants in semi-urban neighborhoods without access to basic services (USMBHC 2003).

The geography of the border region exacerbates the region's environmental problems (Heyman 2007). The region is generally semiarid, with more rainfall on the coasts, and the dry conditions heighten concerns about water and air quality (Liverman et al. 1999). Outstanding cases of environmental injustices include the Sunland Park Landfill (in southern New Mexico) in the small, Hispanic, low-income village of the same name, which handles hazardous waste from El Paso and Juárez (Rosell 1999; Roberts 2011); the increase in truck traffic and diesel particulates since the NAFTA (North American Free Trade Agreement) burdening residents in Tijuana-San Diego and Ciudad Juárez-El Paso (García and Simpson 2004); the 100-year existence of the ASARCO copper smelter located at the confluence of Texas, New Mexico, and Chihuahua within 5 km of 70 schools (Collins et al. 2008); the anencephaly clusters during the late 1990s that drew attention to the *Dren Cinco de Marzo*, a wastewater channel and *de facto* repository for industrial and chemical sludge which snakes through *colonias* in Matamoros (Simon 2006); and the concentration of TV manufacturing plants suspected of illegally discharging waste in the Chilpancingo neighborhood in Tijuana (Garcia and Simpson 2004), featured in the 2006 documentary *Maquilapolis: City of Factories*.

Within the border region, we can conceptualize environmental injustices occurring at multiple scales, such as between the United States and Mexico and within communities located in each country. This chapter will focus on exploring injustice at both of those scales, before exploring community responses to injustice along the border.

Environmental Injustice in the Border Region

Transnational Environmental Injustices Between the United States and Mexico

Environmental injustices in relationships between less developed countries (LDCs) and more developed countries (MDCs), like Mexico and the United States, have been well documented. Over the last four decades, social scientists have recognized the transnational shifting of environmental burdens, in terms of the hazards associated with production and waste disposal, from MDCs to less powerful LDCs (Adeola 2000; Pellow 2007). This global transference of risk has been framed as an environmental injustice because it is directly related to a global system of stratification whereby powerful states (e.g., Unites States) are able to impose their economic will on less powerful LDCs (Frey 2003; Pellow 2007; Newell 2005). LDCs are saddled with environmental burdens because they are marginalized within the global political economic order and represent a path of little resistance (Pellow 2007); the ideology that any development in a LDC is better than no development at all also justifies MDCs in making LDCs convenient depositories for their toxic wastes (Newell 2005). LDCs can also lack adequate environmental policy and/or enforcement of current policies and can be desperate for the economic gain that comes from the toxic waste trade (Adeola 2000).

It can be argued that nowhere is the movement of hazardous production from powerful to less powerful states more readily visible than along the US-Mexico border. Here, hazardous production processes are transferred to Mexico through transnational corporations operating *maquiladoras* (i.e., export-oriented final assembly plants) (Frey 2003), and 67 of the top 100 *maquiladoras* in Mexico (based on number of employees) are owned by US companies (Maquila Portal 2011). The level of industrial hazard, measured by the density of facilities, was 24 times higher in the average Ciudad Juárez, Chihuahua, neighborhood in the year 2000, as compared to the average neighborhood in its American sister city, El Paso, Texas (Grineski and Collins 2010), representing a clear injustice between the two countries. The difference in the level of hazard between the two cities is evidence of the importance of uneven power relations between powerful and less powerful nations in determining who is placed at risk. This represents a global environmental injustice, as it reflects how unequal political-economic relations between the United States and Mexico have produced divergent trajectories of industrialization. Specifically, deindustrialization in El Paso combined with a *maquiladora* boom in Ciudad Juárez has resulted in a highly disparate cross-border industrial risk profile. The NAFTA appears to have accentuated these divergent trajectories in El Paso and Juárez (Grineski and Collins 2010). The lower level of factory risk experienced by El Pasoans relative to *Juarenses* is largely a product of economic globalization, whereby factories based in the United States have moved to other countries in search of reduced production costs (Grineski and Collins 2010).

The combination of lower production costs and lax environmental policies and enforcement attracts industry to LDCs. For example, a US-owned thermoelectric plant sited near Mexicali (capital of Baja California) in 2003 generates power primarily for southern California. This plant is located in Mexico because of the streamlined permitting process, limited political space for popular resistance, lower wages, lower land costs, and a more favorable political and investment community (Carruthers 2008). Another advantage for the United States is that Mexico must bear the burden of the plant's substantial carbon dioxide footprint.

Despite the fact that electric power plants are the largest source of toxic air pollution in North America and the Mexicali Valley-Salton Sea binational air shed was already recognized as seriously polluted, Mexican authorities approved the installation of this plant in 2001 (Carruthers 2008). After intense public pressure to meet California air standards, the US-based corporation installed nitrogen oxide scrubbers at the plant to reduce air emissions. However, when activists demonstrated the scrubbers were only partially installed, the US Department of Energy pressured the plant to comply with US law. Nonetheless, the plant reopened in 2004 after learning that the scrubbers were not needed to comply with Mexican law (Carruthers 2008).

The transfer of industrial hazards from the MDCs toward LDCs, such has happened in this Mexicali case, has not gone unnoticed (Widener 2007; Williams and Mawdsley 2006). In the Mexicali case, a multistakeholder coalition fought the plant at every step in the process (Carruthers 2008). All along the US-Mexico border, social movements have formed in response to the exploitation of Mexican environmental and human resources by the United States (Carruthers 2007, 2008; Garcia and Simpson 2004; Peña 1997), with some being successful. These will be discussed in more detail later in the chapter.

Environmental Injustices: Mexico

In addition to these transnational injustices present between the US and Mexican sides of the border, there are finer scale injustices occurring within border communities, including those on the Mexican side. In Tijuana (Baja California), researchers demonstrated that *maquiladoras* were located in more densely populated areas with higher concentrations of children. In a survey of 800 *maquiladora* workers, they found that the newest workers (usually migrants) lived closer to the plants than more senior workers and were thus exposed to greater residential risks (Kopinak and Barajas 2002). In Nogales (Sonora), researchers found significantly higher proportions of educated and affluent residents living within 500 and 1,000-m buffers of hazardous waste-generating facilities (using correlation analysis), with no significant differences in the proportions of recent immigrants living within as compared to outside the buffers (Lara-Valencia et al. 2009).

Fig. 10.1 The low-rise fringes of Ciudad Juárez, Chihuahua (Source: Timothy Collins)

Ciudad Juárez (Chihuahua), the fifth largest city in Mexico and a key center of *maquiladora* employment, has been studied more frequently from an EJ perspective than other Mexican border cities. In Juárez, both socially advantaged and disadvantaged residents are at increased risk from environmental hazards, depending on the hazard of focus. Similar to the patterns in Nogales (Lara-Valencia et al. 2009), neighborhoods with higher mean levels of education (higher social class), lower proportions of migrants, and lower proportions of young children had significantly higher *maquiladora* hazard densities (Grineski and Collins 2010). This is because in Juárez, more affluent residents live in the central city to access social, infrastructural, and market-based services (e.g., secondary schools, hospitals, paved roads, sewer systems, and retail) (Grineski and Collins 2010). Different than US cities, Mexican cities like Juárez tend to have well-developed central cities served by basic infrastructure (e.g., piped water, sewage treatment, paved roads, and electricity), whereas the fringes (where suburbs would be in an American city) contain informal settlements of low-rise, self-constructed homes without access to this infrastructure (Davis 2006) (see Fig. 10.1), which impose health and environmental risks on residents (Graham et al. 2005).

Transnational corporate owners of *maquiladoras* choose to set up operations in the developed areas, on high rent land, because it has either been offered as an incentive by state officials (Zeisel et al. 2006) or is otherwise relatively inexpensive from a global perspective (it is a bargain compared to land in Detroit, Michigan). Such industrial siting decisions are made possible by the inequalities that exist between transnational corporations from MDCs and LDC cities. The clustering of formal development in the central city means that this area is disproportionately

Fig. 10.2 A *maquiladora* located in a formally developed neighborhood of Ciudad Juárez, Chihuahua (Source: Sara Grineski. A version of this photo was previously published in Grineski et al. 2010)

home to more affluent residents and transnational industrial development (see Fig. 10.2). In contrast, domestic industries (e.g., brick kilns) cannot afford to compete in a transnational land market and thus are sited in less privileged areas, where more socially marginalized residents live (Grineski et al. 2010).

However, when formal development is considered (i.e., a variable including strong roof, strong walls, floors, public sewer lines, piped water indoors, and hot water heaters) in the statistical analysis, the patterns of environmental injustice in Juárez change. Within the formally developed residential-industrial landscape that is characteristic of the more affluent parts of Juárez, it is the less affluent (i.e., lower social class) that reside most proximate to *maquiladoras* (Grineski and Collins 2008). The most affluent *Juarenses* live at greater distances from *maquiladoras* while remaining within formally developed portions of the city. The areas closest to the *maquiladoras* are left for the relatively less affluent fortunate enough to live in formally developed built environments (Grineski and Collins 2008).

Given that *maquiladoras* are not the only environmental hazard facing Juárez residents, researchers have also examined risks associated with brick kilns and the rail line (Grineski et al. 2010). Risk associated with brick kilns (or *ladrilleras*) represents a clear case of environmental injustice in the city (see Fig. 10.3). Romo Aguilar et al. (2004) estimate that there are 369 brick kiln burns per month in Juárez and approximately 391 kg of air contaminants are released during every burn. Brick kilns are owned by local residents, and the majority of the bricks are sold domestically (Romo Aguilar et al. 2004). Those of lower social class and a disproportionate number of children reside in neighborhoods with higher brick kiln density (Grineski et al. 2010). Locals make very small profits from their kilns, and

Fig. 10.3 Traditional-style brick kiln in Ciudad Juárez, Chihuahua (Source: Sara Grineski)

they have been facing pressure to sell out to larger operators because they cannot afford to support their families (Romo Aguilar et al. 2004). The disproportionate presence of children near the kilns, which is related to family-owned nature of the business, is a serious health concern given the air pollution generated by the low-technology wood and sawdust fired kilns.

Environmental injustices are also found in relation to the rail line. Residence near the rail line is especially risky in Juárez because one of the world's most dangerous chemical plants (i.e., Solvay) ships hydrofluoric acid along it (Mackler 1999; Morales et al. 2012) and areas near the rail line are disproportionately inhabited by poor residents (Grineski et al. 2010). In addition to posing an acute risk, the rail line is noisy and a personal safety hazard for residents and pedestrians.

In addition to these hazards, there are also inequalities with regard to access to potable water. The lack of urban planning and informal, rapid growth, common in Mexican border cities, creates health risks for low-income residents who inhabit the urban fringes and are less likely to have municipal water or sewage connections. Health risks are present because poor water quality is common when residents have to store and treat their own supplies and because untreated sewage can cause contamination (Graham et al. 2004). Moreover, connections between environmental contamination and health effects have been made on the Mexican side. In Ciudad Juárez, researchers found a positive association between environmental pollution, specifically ozone, and emergency room visits for asthma and acute respiratory diseases, especially for children under 5 (Hernández-Cadena et al. 2000). Exposure to vehicular traffic also decreased lung volumes in children with asthma (Holguin et al. 2007). In terms of workplace risks, *maquiladoras* are a key source of exposure to hazardous chemicals, as many have documented (Moure-Eraso et al. 1997; Quintero and Romo 2001; Williams and Homedes 2001).

Environmental Injustices: The United States

Far fewer quantitative studies of unequal risks have been conducted in US border cities. The lack of quantitative studies belies a tradition of community organizing for environmental justice. However, several quantitative studies have been conducted in El Paso (Texas), the sister city of Ciudad Juárez. When relating residential risk from factories (i.e., those regulated through the US EPA's Toxic Release Inventory) with census data, El Paso neighborhoods with lower social class and higher proportions of residents that had recently migrated to the city had significantly higher densities of factory-related hazards (Grineski and Collins 2010). Increased health risks, in the form of residential exposure to hazardous air pollutants that are known to cause cancer, are also found for El Paso neighborhoods with higher-than-average percentages of Spanish speakers with limited English language proficiency, foreign-born residents, and non-US citizens (Collins et al. 2011). El Paso's pattern of environmental injustice reflects a typical MDC process of environmental inequity formation. In the United States, features of urbanization (e.g., subsidization of the suburbs, see Gottdiener and Hutchison 2006) have influenced the marginalization of disadvantaged populations in urban locations near industrial sources of pollution (Pulido 2000).

However, semirural socially marginalized residents along the US side of the border are also subject to an environmental injustice that is more commonly found in LDCs: the lack of access to piped water and sewage systems. This is a critical injustice, given the generally high levels of infrastructure accessible to residents living in the United States. Residents lacking access to water reside in the low-income, predominately Mexican and Mexican American *colonias* (Bath et al. 1998). *Colonias* are mostly unincorporated communities located in California, Arizona, New Mexico, and Texas along the border characterized by high poverty rates and

Fig. 10.4 Two residences without access to piped water sharing a lot in a *colonia* near Fort Hancock, Texas (Source: Yolanda McDonald)

substandard living conditions (see Fig. 10.4). For example, in El Paso County in 2010, 86,472 residents lived in 321 *colonias*; 56 of these *colonias*, housing 5,529 residents, still lacked access to piped drinking water (Office of the Texas Secretary of State 2010). Most of these residents rely on water delivery trucks and store their water in reused drums or water tanks; however, this water typically has low levels of chlorine and sometimes coliforms, representing a health risk for users (Graham and VanDerslice 2007). The lack of access to water represents a clear case of environmental injustice, especially considering the racist history of water policymaking in El Paso County which has led them to be excluded from this basic right (Bath et al. 1998). Conditions in *colonias* are further discussed in Chap. 6 of this volume.

Given that El Paso is a minority-majority city (i.e., the majority of residents are Hispanic), researchers have examined intraethnic variations in exposure to health risks from cancer-causing toxic air pollutants to see how risks for disadvantaged whites compare to those for disadvantaged Hispanics. Cancer-causing toxic air emissions in El Paso are a serious problem; in 2002, they were over 20 times higher than the regulatory threshold. On-road sources (like cars and trucks) represent 60% of the total lifetime cancer risk burden from environmental sources in El Paso (Collins et al. 2011). Researchers found that mutually reinforcing disadvantages multiply cancer risk disparities from air toxics for Hispanics in El Paso County, while disadvantages associated with class, age, and gender status have little influence on cancer risks from air toxics for white people. For example, the cancer risks from air toxics for lower-class Hispanics (based on poverty status and education) were much greater than the risks for upper-class Hispanics, whereas for whites, class was not a significant determiner of risk. In sum, the study found that Hispanic ethnicity intensifies exposure to environmental cancer risks while whiteness alleviates cancer risk disparities based on other dimensions of social disadvantage (Collins et al. 2011). This supports the presence of white privilege in this predominately Hispanic border city.

While there are only a few quantitative EJ studies on the US side, several studies have quantified environmental contamination and its relation to health. Researchers found that levels of traffic-related pollution (nitrogen oxides) were higher near the international bridges (Gonzalez et al. 2005), an area that is predominately inhabited by Hispanic residents. When predicting children's hospitalizations for respiratory infections in El Paso, environmental respiratory health risks from hazardous air pollutants were associated with a 16% increase in admissions (Grineski et al. 2012). Taken together, these findings for El Paso demonstrate a rather traditional pattern of environmental injustice in the United States, whereby disadvantaged residents face increased risk.

However, health and environmental agencies on both sides of the border have directed scarce attention to these disproportionate impacts. Reviewing the issues addressed by Border 2012 (e.g., binational program involving environmental agencies) suggests that more attention is paid to air, water, and soil pollution; infrastructure; and emergency response (see http://www.epa.gov/Border2012/) as opposed to the social inequalities in exposures and environmentally associated health conditions. Globalization and global inequalities, binational political complexities, patterns of urbanization, and demographic dynamics contribute to an explanation for the patterns of injustice found in the US-Mexico border region. This understanding alone is insufficient to create social change. It must be translated into social activism and governmental responses, which are the focus of the next section.

Addressing Environmental Injustice

Strategies for Success

A key strategy to fighting environmental injustices in the border region has been to link "local struggles for a safer environment to global claims for justice" (Carruthers 2008, p. 152). This strategy fits the border landscape especially well because of the transference of risk from MDCs to LDCs that is readily evident on the Mexican side. For example, residents of the Chilpancingo *colonia* in Tijuana, along with their allies from the Environmental Health Coalition, based in San Diego, successfully fought for the closure and cleanup of a San Diego-based company's lead smelter (Carruthers 2008). After operating for more than 20 years in the *colonia*, the *Metales y Derivados* smelter was closed due to public pressure in 1994 (Carruthers 2008), leaving 42,000 tons of lead behind (Environmental Protection Agency [EPA] 2010a). EJ activists filed a petition through North American Commission for Environmental Cooperation, a NAFTA organization, in 1998, which caused the case to gain an international profile as an example of the failures of NAFTA

(Carruthers 2008). Finally, in 2004, the US EPA and Mexico's environmental ministry, *Secretería de Medio Ambiente y Recursos Naturales*, agreed to fund the cleanup, which was completed in 2009 (EPA 2010a).

Community organizing, critical in the *Metales y Derivados* case, has been central to the EJ movement along the border more generally. Historically, Mexican Americans advocated for environmental justice as they fought for improved occupational conditions and reduced risks from pesticides for Hispanic migrant farm workers in the United States during the 1960s, led by Cesar Chavez, Dolores Huerta, and Jessie Lopez (Taylor 2002). San Diego's Environmental Health Coalition represents a more contemporary example of a border-based grassroots EJ organization focused on advocating for a clean environment, safe working conditions, a decent standard of living for all border residents, and for democratic governance (García and Simpson 2004).

Nonprofit organizations also have a role to play in advocating for EJ. While not focused on EJ directly, Sabet (2008) argued that nonprofit organizations are critical to addressing the environmental problems of disadvantaged populations, and that the organizations' social networks are important for success. For example, the nonprofit *Asociación de Colonias Populares* in Nuevo Laredo (Tamaulipas) has worked to mobilize neighborhood residents in informally settled areas to support particular political candidates in exchange for neighborhood improvements, such as water and sewage infrastructure. However, this organization has been criticized because "leaders have had to put the needs of the party before the needs of their neighborhoods" (Sabet 2008, p. 73). As opposed to building networks with politicians, other groups, such as *Organización Popular Independiente* and *Aqua 21* in Ciudad Juárez, have remained nonpartisan and networked with community organizations and universities in order to improve community capacity and obtain resources to address water and environmental health issues (Sabet 2008). The Center for Environmental Resources Management at the University of Texas at El Paso has partnered with community organizations through the *Agua Para Beber* project, which served over 5,000 families in the United States and Mexico without access to piped water by providing educational materials on safe water practices and drinking water storage containers (1994–2008) (CERM 2008) and through the *When Water Works for Health* initiative (1998–2000), which provided 800 families in the United States and Mexico with education and improved water/sewage infrastructure (CERM 2000).

One model through which academic researchers and community groups can work for EJ in the border region is through community-based participatory research (CBPR). CBPR connects research, action, and education while prioritizing democratic processes and continual exchange between researchers and community members (Wallerstein and Duran 2003). CBPR has been successful in addressing environmental injustice through leadership and skills enhancement, active participation in problem-solving and action, and policy changes (Minkler et al. 2008), and it can be effective on the border.

Using a CBPR framework, the Community Health Worker (CHW) or *promotoras* model has been applied to address issues of environmental health disparities

(U.S. Department of Health and Human Services [DHHS] 2007). In the border region, CBPR partnerships using the CHW model have been successful in reducing household-level environmental risks (Liebman et al. 2007; Carrillo Zuniga et al. 2009). Moreover, through the awareness-raising efforts of CHWs, community-based organizations have emerged to conduct activities beyond education and outreach, by advocating for safe environmental conditions and infrastructure for the people they serve while engendering community agency in isolated neighborhoods, such as in semirural *colonias* (May et al. 2003). As such, CHWs integrate social justice principles into their work (Spencer et al. 2010).

Another cooperative approach to addressing environmental injustice has been to bring together four types of actors: government officials, academics, nongovernmental organizations, and capitalist interest groups (i.e., economic development groups and industrial associations) (Córdova Bojórquez 2009). This type of action can be seen in the *Plan Estratégico* in Ciudad Juárez and the *Water Task Force of the Paso del Norte*, which advises the Border 2012 program. The goals of these collaborations are to "make agreements collegially and consensually, with the aim of sensitizing those who really make decisions: the government, in the first place, and the interest groups, secondly (*toma acuerdos colegiados y consensuados con el ánimo de sensibilizar a quien en realidad toma las decisiones: el gobierno, en primer lugar, y los grupos de presión, en segundo*)" (Córdova Bojórquez 2009, p. 49).

Nonprofit organizing and community mobilizations can lead to the creation of new EJ policy which can aid future groups in their struggles. In Chaparral (New Mexico, near El Paso), which is a primarily low-income and Hispanic community, developers wanted to site a new landfill. The *Colonias* Development Council, a local nongovernment organization, helped residents mobilize to oppose this. This opposition movement framed a new legal reference in the State of New Mexico as Governor Richardson signed the Environmental Justice Policy Order 2005–056 in response to this case (Henkel 2009). The Executive Order states that all residents, including communities of color and low-income communities, will receive fair treatment and meaningful involvement in environmental decision-making; that New Mexico will address the disproportionate exposure of low-income and minority communities to environmental hazards; and that the State will create an EJ taskforce to take actions to reduce environmental injustice (New Mexico Environment Department 2005). The order will give future potentially affected communities a powerful tool to use to advocate for EJ in New Mexico.

Nonetheless, efforts to address environmental injustices are hampered by the complicated jurisdictional, legal, political, social, and economic conditions that exist on the US-Mexico border, both between countries and between states (Henkel 2009). For example, the economic conditions of the brick kiln operators have made it difficult for brick kiln–related advocacy to be effective. In the 1990s, the Ciudad Juárez chapter of the national organization *Federación Mexicana de Asociaciones Privadas* (FEMAP), which has an El Paso-based partner foundation, began working to reduce air pollution by targeting brick production (Staudt and Coronado 2002;

Romo Aguilar et al. 2004). As previously mentioned, brick kilns are a key source of air pollution and environmental injustice in Juárez. FEMAP worked to introduce propane gas as a source of fuel for the brick kilns instead of scrap wood and toxic materials like tires. The strategy was not successful because of the high cost of gas and the lack of infrastructure to deliver it to the kiln sites; no kilns were using gas as of 2004 (Romo Aguilar et al. 2004). Then, working to further address this issue, the municipal government created a "brick kiln park" outside of town in 2004 using a more earth-friendly design to reduce air pollution. Given the challenges and costs of moving operations, learning a new technique, and transportation to the park, few operators (i.e., 6 in 2004) have chosen to make bricks there (Romo Aguilar et al. 2004). These strategies were designed without much input from kiln operators, which may have contributed to their failure.

In addition, linguistic, cultural, and economic barriers to binational collaboration have combined with increasing concerns about national security to make cross-border environmental organizing difficult (Staudt and Coronado 2002). More specifically, Staudt and Coronado (2002) identified monolingualism, limited resources, border crossing requirements (e.g., passports), fear, stereotypes, wait times to cross international bridges, competition, and previous bad experiences as potential blocks to transnational collaborations. There may also be a lack of awareness, on the part of border residents, about environmental injustice and a lack of interest in environmental topics, which hampers advocacy. When El Paso's ASARCO copper smelter tried to reopen in 2007 and was permitted in 2008 to emit 4.7 tons of lead annually (more than any other US facility) (Collins et al. 2008), EJ framing was never evoked during protest events or even during planning meetings of the local opposition group, despite an obvious connection in a city that is majority-minority and working class. More pressing issues like economic insecurity and violence may take precedence, especially on the Mexican side. A recent survey of 1,000 residents in Ciudad Juárez found that 88% of residents did not participate in any group or community organization, and 47% said that they did not want to participate in a group to improve the city's environment (Romo Aguilar et al. 2009). In another study, one-third of 177 surveyed *Juarenses* living near parks have never used them, with poor families being more likely to report not using the parks (Romo Aguilar and Córdova Bojórquez 2009). This makes environmental organizing difficult, although not impossible, as cross-border environmental collaboration does occur (see Chapter 4 in Staudt and Coronado 2002).

This lack of awareness may be facilitated and maintained by the technical way in which environmental conditions are addressed in this region. A Web of Science search related to the US-Mexico border environment reveals that much more attention is given to documenting and assessing environmental conditions than associating these risks with disadvantaged populations and increased rates of adverse health outcomes. This may relate to the minority-majority condition in the region, as agencies, communities, and researchers are blind to the inequities that exist within this largely Hispanic border population.

Important Resources

Institutionally, various agencies focus on implementing programs and providing funds to address environmental injustice issues in the US-Mexico border region. Major US agencies are listed in Table 10.1. Additional resources in the United States include "The Citizen's Guide to Using Federal Environmental Laws to Secure Environmental Justice" (Environmental Law Institute 2002), the "Toolkit for Assessing Potential Allegations of Environmental Injustice" (EPA 2010b), the Health Impact Assessment (Mindell et al. 2008), and health and environmental departments of the border states, some with programs specifically addressing EJ issues. See also a list of community and nonprofit organizations from both sides of the border that are addressing environmental issues in Sabet (2008, pp. 240–247 [Mexican organizations] and pp. 252–253 [US organizations]).

Achieving Environmental Justice

To achieve environmental justice in the border region, we offer several recommendations. First, community groups, researchers, and health/environmental professionals should address public health, policy, education, and outreach through the lens of EJ because it is a powerful tool to locate, address, and monitor environmental and health inequalities. Second, EJ groups need to be able to access information and tools to use in their struggle, as well as have access to influence the regulatory process. Legal tools, like New Mexico's Environmental Justice Policy Order, which was based on President Clinton's Executive Order 12989 (Bullard 2005), can be particularly useful, as can tying into broader framing that can galvanize support beyond the EJ community, such as antiglobalization, anticorporate power, and anti-NAFTA movements (Carruthers 2008). Others have demonstrated that linking local movements with global environmental organizations is an effective strategy to gain resources and power (Pellow 2007; Walker 2009). Right-to-Know legislation has been a powerful tool for EJ groups in the United States, allowing communities to learn about toxic releases at all regulated factories in the United States (see www.rtknet.org). However, the same sort of data is not presented in an Internet portal for Mexico. In addition, health and environmental agencies can improve their communication and education strategies so that border communities can better understand risks and trust and participate in protection programs (Byrd et al. 2001).

Third, because social inequities impact health and are highly intertwined with environmental risks (Commission on Social Determinants of Health 2008; Pearce et al. 2010), social and economic policies that work toward achieving health equity and well-being for all are needed (Marmot and Wilkinson 2006). On the border, an integrated system to track social disparities in health and environmental health risks is especially important, given the complex obstacles resulting from differential laws, policies, and jurisdictions among border states and between Mexico and the United States (Henkel 2009).

Table 10.1 US-based agencies and collaborative programs addressing EJ issues

Name	Issues addressed	Link
United States		
Environmental Protection Agency (EPA)	Enforcement, education, funding for EJ programs	http://www.epa.gov/compliance/environmentaljustice/
Interagency Working Group in Environmental Justice (IWG EJ)	Federal work group to address EJ issues under Plan EJ 2014	http://www.epa.gov/compliance/environmentaljustice/interagency/index.html
Agency for Toxic Substances and Disease Registry (ATSDR)	Remediates hazardous sites; addresses citizen concerns; public health assessments; environmental health education; emergency response	http://www.atsdr.cdc.gov/
National Institute on Minority Health and Health Disparities (NIMHD)	Research, training, and funding to address minority health disparities	http://www.ncmhd.nih.gov/
National Environmental Public Health Tracking Network	Links environmental measurements with health outcomes in CA and AZ	http://ephtracking.cdc.gov
Border region		
Commission for Environmental Cooperation (CEC)	Agreement between Canada, United States, and Mexico; environmental law, policy and trade issues	www.cec.org
US EPA Border 2012 – Next Generation	Binational agreement between United States and Mexico; taskforces, work groups, funding, and research to protect border environment health	http://www.epa.gov/usmexicoborder/
Border Environment Cooperation Commission – *Comisión de Cooperación Ecológica Fronteriza*	Binational agreement; infrastructure projects; research on environmental improvement and well-being	http://www.cocef.org/
US Geological Survey – US-Mexico Border Environmental Health Initiative (BEHI)	GIS maps and databases related to transboundary environment/health issues	http://borderhealth.cr.usgs.gov
Centers for Disease Control and Prevention (CDC) US-Mexico Border Health	Collaborative programs to improve health	http://www.cdc.gov/nceh/hsb/borderhealth/
Pan American Health Organization – US-Mexico Border Office	Regional office of the World Health Organization; environmental health issues	http://www.fep.paho.org/eng/

Fourth, given the disproportionately young population that resides on the US-Mexico border (USMBHC 2003), attention must be paid to reducing children's environmental exposures, especially because of their increased susceptibility to environmental conditions and greater health impacts. EJ concerns related to children's well-being require urgent attention because population well-being in the future depends heavily on the efforts made in the present to preserve and ensure healthy environments for them (World Health Organization [WHO] 2004).

Lastly, we advocate for the adoption of the precautionary principle in environmental policymaking along the border because in many cases, the nature and impacts of risks are unknown. This principle states that "in the case of serious or irreversible threats to the health of humans or the ecosystem, acknowledged scientific uncertainty should not be used as a reason to postpone preventive measures" (WHO 2004, p. 1). In many cases, the science regarding potential cumulative, complex, and synergetic interactions between toxics is not known, and that should not keep us from acting to create a safe and just environment.

Acknowledgments We acknowledge Yolanda McDonald for sharing the information about El Paso County *colonias* with us.

References

Adeola, F. (2000). Cross-national environmental injustice and human rights issues: A review of evidence in the developing world. *The American Behavioral Scientist, 43*(4), 686–706.

Bath, C., Tanski, J., & Villarreal, R. (1998). The failure to provide basic services to the colonias of El Paso county: A case of environmental racism? In D. Camacho (Ed.), *Environmental injustices, political struggles: Race, class and the environment* (pp. 125–137). Durham: Duke University Press.

Bullard, R. (2005). Introduction. In R. Bullard (Ed.), *The quest for environmental justice: Human rights and the politics of pollution* (pp. 1–16). San Francisco: Sierra Club Books.

Byrd, T., VanDerslice, J., & Peterson, S. (2001). Attitudes and beliefs about environmental hazards in three diverse communities in Texas on the border with Mexico. *Pan American Journal of Public Health, 9*(3), 154–160.

Carrillo Zuniga, G., Donnelly, K., Cortes, D., Olivares, E., Gonzalez, H., & Cizmas, L. (2009). Border health 2012: Binational collaboration to develop an outreach environmental education program. *Public Health Reports, 124*(3), 466–471.

Carruthers, D. (2007). Environmental justice and the politics of energy on the US-Mexico border. *Environmental Politics, 16*(3), 394–413.

Carruthers, D. (2008). Where local meets global: Environmental justice on the US-Mexico border. In D. Carruthers (Ed.), *Environmental justice in Latin America: Problems, promise and practice* (pp. 136–160). Cambridge: MIT Press.

Center for Environmental Resource Management. (2000). *When water works for health.* Final report (Unpublished report). El Paso: The University of Texas at El Paso.

Center for Environmental Resource Management. (2008). *Agua para Beber: Program for the provision of safe drinking water along the U.S.-Mexico border* (Unpublished report). El Paso: The University of Texas at El Paso.

Collins, T., Grineski, S., & Flores, M. (2008). Environmental injustice in the Paso del Norte. *Projections, 8*, 156–171.

Collins, T., Grineski, S., Chakraborty, J., & McDonald, Y. (2011). Understanding environmental health inequality through contextually-relevant and comparative intracategorical analysis: Cancer risks from air toxics in El Paso, Texas. *Health and Place, 17*, 335–344.

Commission on Social Determinants of Health. (2008). *Closing the gap in a generation: Health equity through action on the social determinants of health.* Final report. Geneva: World Health Organization.

Córdova Bojórquez, G. (2009). La gestión del agua en Ciudad Juárez, Chihuahua: Líderes y miembros de ONG. In *Gestión ambiental y participación ciudadana en el estado de Chihuahua: Cuatro estudios de caso (Brevarium)* [Environmental negotiation and citizen participation in the state of Chihuahua: Four case studies (Brevarium)], Direccion Regional Noroeste (1st ed., pp. 37–63). Tijuana: El Colegio de la Frontera Norte.

Davis, M. (2006). *Planet of the slums.* New York: Verso.

Environmental Law Institute. (2002). *A citizen's guide to using federal environmental laws to secure environmental justice.* Washington, DC: Environmental Law Institute.

Environmental Protection Agency [EPA]. (2010a). *Metales y Derivados cleanup.* Retrieved November 23, 2010, from http://www.epa.gov/Border2012/metales-cleanup.html

Environmental Protection Agency [EPA]. (2010b). *Environmental justice.* Retrieved November 17, 2010, from http://www.epa.gov/environmentaljustice/resources/policy/index.html

Frey, R. (2003). The transfer of core-based hazardous production processes to the export processing zones of the periphery: The maquiladora centers of northern Mexico. *Journal of World Systems Research, IX*, 317–354.

Garcia, C., & Simpson, A. (2004). *Globalization at the crossroads: Ten years of NAFTA in the San Diego/Tijuana border region.* Retrieved June, 2010, from Environmental Health Coalition: http://www.environmentalhealth.org/BorderEHC/BT_Globlztin2CrossRds.html

Gonzalez, M., Qualls, C., Hudgens, E., & Neas, L. (2005). Characterization of a spatial gradient of nitrogen dioxide across a United States-Mexico border city during winter. *The Science of the Total Environment, 337*(1–3), 163–173.

Gottdiener, M., & Hutchison, R. (2006). *The new urban sociology.* Boulder: Westview.

Graham, J., & VanDerslice, J. (2007). The effectiveness of large household water storage tanks for protecting the quality of drinking water. *Journal of Water and Health, 5*(2), 307–313.

Graham, J., Gurian, P., Corella-Barud, V., & Avitia-Diaz, R. (2004). Peri-urbanization and in-home environmental health risks: The side effects of planned and unplanned growth. *International Journal of Hygiene and Environmental Health, 207*, 447–454.

Graham, J., Corella-Barud, V., Avitia-Diaz, R., & Gurian, P. (2005). The in-home environment and household health: A cross-sectional study of informal urban settlements in northern Mexico. *International Journal of Environmental Research and Public Health, 2*(3), 394–402.

Grineski, S., & Collins, T. (2008). Exploring environmental injustice in the global south: Maquiladoras in Ciudad Juárez, Mexico. *Population and Environment, 29*(6), 247–270.

Grineski, S., & Collins, T. (2010). Environmental injustice in transnational context: Urbanization and industrial hazards in El Paso/Ciudad Juárez. *Environment and Planning A, 42*(6), 1308–1327.

Grineski, S., Collins, T., Romo Aguilar, L., & Aldouri, R. (2010). No safe place: Environmental hazards & injustice along Mexico's northern border. *Social Forces, 88*(5), 2241–2266.

Grineski, S., Collins, T., Chakraborty, J., & McDonald, Y. (2012). Environmental health injustice: Exposure to air toxics and children's respiratory hospital admissions in El Paso, Texas. *The Professional Geographer.* DOI: 10.1080/00330124.2011.639625

Hazlett, M. (2003). The story of Silent Spring and the ecological turn. *Dissertation UMI Number 3100215.* University of Kansas, Lawrence.

Henkel, D. (2009). Upholding environmental justice in the colonias: A New Mexico approach. *Journal of Borderlands Studies, 24*(1), 62–75.

Hernández-Cadena, L., Téllez-Rojo, M., Sanin-Aguirre, L., Lacasaña-Navarro, M., Campos, A., & Romieu, I. (2000). Relación entre consultas a urgencias por enfermedad respiratoria y contaminación atmosférica en Ciudad Juárez, Chihuahua [Relationships between emergency room visits for respiratory disease and atmospheric pollution in Ciudad Juárez, Chihuahua]. *Salud Pública de Mexico, 42*(4), 288–297.

Heyman, J. (2007). Environmental issues at the US-Mexico border and the unequal territorialization of value. In A. Hornberg, J. McNeill, & J. Martinez-Alier (Eds.), *Rethinking environmental history: World-systems history and global environmental change* (pp. 327–343). New York: Altamira Press.

Holguín, F., Flores, S., Ross, Z., Cortéz, M., Molina, M., & Molina, L. (2007). Traffic-related exposures, airway function, inflammation, and respiratory symptoms in children. *American Journal of Respiratory and Critical Care Medicine, 176*, 1236–1242.

Kopinak, K., & Barajas, M. (2002). Too close for comfort? The proximity of industrial hazardous wastes to local populations in Tijuana, Baja California. *Journal of Environment and Development, 11*(3), 215–246.

Lara-Valencia, F., Harlow, S., Lemos, M., & Denman, C. (2009). Equity dimensions of hazardous waste generation in rapidly industrialising cities along the United States-Mexico border. *Journal of Environmental Planning and Management, 52*(2), 195–216.

Liebman, A., Juárez, P., Leyva, C., & Corona, A. (2007). A pilot program using promotoras de salud to educate farmworker families about the risks from pesticide exposure. *Journal of Agromedicine, 12*(2), 33–43.

Liverman, D., Varady, R., Chavez, O., & Sanchez, R. (1999). Environmental issues along the United States-Mexico border: Drivers of change and responses of citizens and institutions. *Annual Review of Energy and the Environment, 24*, 607–643.

Mackler, A. (1999/2000, December 1999–January 2000). *Norflour S.V. under investigation.* Retrieved from Frontera Norte Sur Newsletter: http://frontera.nmsu.edu/dec99jan00/feat2.html

Maquila Portal. (2011). *100 top maquilas*. Retrieved June 21, 2011, from http://www.maquilaportal.com/index.php/page/top100.html

Marmot, M., & Wilkinson, R. (2006). *Social determinants of health* (2nd ed.). Oxford: Oxford Press.

May, M., Bowman, G., Ramos, K., Rincones, L., Rebollar, M., Rosa, M., et al. (2003, October). Embracing the local: Enriching scientific research, education, and outreach on the Texas-Mexico border through a participatory action research partnership. *Environmental Health Perspectives, 111*(13), 1571–1576.

Mindell, J., Boltong, A., & Forde, I. (2008). A review of health impact assessment frameworks. *Public Health, 122*, 1177–1187.

Minkler, M., Breckwich Vazquez, V., Tajik, M., & Petersen, D. (2008). Promoting environmental justice through community-based participatory research: The role of community and partnership capacity. *Health Education & Behavior, 35*(1), 119–137.

Mohai, P., Pellow, D., & Roberts, J. (2009). Environmental justice. *Annual Review of Environment and Resources, 34*, 405–430.

Morales, O., Grineski, S.E., & Collins, T.W. (2012). Structural violence and environmental injustice: The case of a US-Mexico border chemical plant. *Local Environment, 17*(1), 1–21.

Moure-Eraso, R., Wilcox, M., Punnett, L., MacDonald, L., & Levenstein, C. (1997, May). Back to the future: Sweatshop conditions on the Mexico-US border. II. Occupational health impact of maquiladora industrial activity. *American Journal of Industrial Medicine, 31*(5), 587–599.

New Mexico Environment Department. (2005). *Environmental justice executive order 2005–056.* Retrieved November 23, 2010, from http://www.nmenv.state.nm.us/justice/EO_2005_056.pdf

Newell, P. (2005). Race, class and the global politics of environmental inequality. *Global Environmental Politics, 5*(3), 70–94.

Office of the Texas Secretary of State. (2010, December 1). *Tracking the progress of state funded projects that benefit colonias.* The Colonia Initiative Program. Austin: Office of the Texas Secretary of State.

Pearce, J., Richardson, E., Mitchell, R., & Shortt, N. (2010). Environmental justice and health: The implications of the socio-spatial distribution of multiple environmental deprivation for health inequalities in the United Kingdom. *Transactions of the Institute of British Geographers, 35*(4), 522–539.

Pellow, D. (2007). *Resisting global toxics: Transnational movements for environmental justice.* Cambridge: MIT Press.

Peña, D. (1997). *The terror of the machine: Technology, work, gender, and ecology on the U.S.-Mexico border*. Austin: University of Texas at Austin.

Pulido, L. (2000). Rethinking environmental racism: White privilege and urban development in southern California. *Annals of the Association of American Geographers, 90*(1), 12–40.

Quintero, C., & Romo, L. (2001). Riesgos laborales en la maquiladora. La experiencia Tamaulipeca [Occupational risks in the maquiladora. The experience of Tamaulipas]. *Revista Frontera Norte, 13*(2), 11–46.

Rao, S. (2009). The health and well-being of individuals, families, and communities that make up the US-Mexico border region. *Family & Community Health, 32*(2), 2–3.

Roberts, C. (2011, January 21). Ten more years approved for the Camino Real Landfill. *El Paso Times*, p. A1.

Romo Aguilar, M., & Córdova Bojórquez, G. (2009). Áreas verdes y participación ciudadana en Ciudad Juárez, Chihuahua [Green spaces and citizen participation in Ciudad Juárez, Chihuahua]. In *Gestión Ambiental y participación ciudadana en el estado de Chihuahua: Cuatro estudios de caso (Brevarium)* [Environmental negotiation and citizen participation in the state of Chihuahua: Four case studies (Brevarium)], Direccion Regional Noroeste (pp. 11–35). Tijuana: El Colegio de la Frontera Norte.

Romo Aguilar, L., Cervera Gómez, L., & Córdova Bojórquez, G. (2004). Estudio urbano ambiental de las ladrilleras en el municipio de Juárez [Urban environmental study of the brickmakers in the municipality of Juárez]. *Revista Estudios Fronterizos, 5*(9), 9–34.

Romo Aguilar, M., Córdova Bojórquez, G., Bruguez Rodríguez, A., Rubio Salas, R., & Ochoa Lozano, L. (2009). Proceso de gestión en el ordenamiento ecológico y territorial del municipio de Juárez, Chihuahua [Process of negotiation on the environmental order and territorial of the municipality of Juárez, Chihuahua]. In G. Bocco (Ed.), *Nuevas formas de gestión ambiental: Agua y ordenamiento ecológico territorial* [New forms of environmental negotiation: Water and environmental territorial order] (pp. 133–165). Tijuana: El Colegio de la Frontera Norte.

Rosell, E. (1999). The Sunland Park/Camino Real partnership: Landfill politics in a border community. In M. Loustaunau & M. Sanchez-Bane (Eds.), *Life, death, and in-between on the U.S.-Mexico border* (Vol. 24, pp. 191–208). Westport: Bergin & Garvey.

Sabet, D. (2008). *Nonprofits and their networks: Cleaning the waters along Mexico's northern border*. Tucson: The University of Arizona Press.

Simon, S. (2006). Environmental justice as place-making: A study of Mexican migrants, transnational advocacy, and urban rehabilitation in Matamoros, Mexico. *Social Justice: Anthropology, Peace and Human Rights, 6,* 1–30. Retrieved from http://digilib.gmu.edu:8080/xmlui/bitstream/1920/1333/1/Simon.pdf

Spencer, M., Gunter, K., & Palmisano, G. (2010). Community health workers and their value to social work. *Social Work, 55*(2), 169–180.

Staudt, K., & Coronado, I. (2002). *Fronteras no más: Toward social justice at the U.S.-Mexico border*. New York: Palgrave Macmillan.

Taylor, D. (2002). *Race, class, gender, and American environmentalism* (Gen. Tech. Rep. PNW-GTR-534). Portland: U.S. Department of Agriculture, Forest Service.

U.S. Department of Health and Human Services [DHHS]. (2007). *Community health worker national workforce study.* Washington, DC: Bureau of Health Professions, Health Resources and Services Administration (HRSA).

U.S.-Mexico Border Health Commission [USMBHC]. (2003). *Healthy border 2010.* Retrieved July 10, 2007, from http://www.borderhealth.org/files/res_63.pdf

Walker, G. (2009, December). Globalizing environmental justice: The geography and politics of frame contextualization and evolution. *Global Social Policy, 9*, 355–382.

Wallerstein, N., & Duran, B. (2003). The conceptual, historical, and practice roots of community based participatory research and related participatory traditions. In M. Minkler & N. Wallerstein (Eds.), *Community-based participatory research for health* (pp. 27–52). San Francisco: Jossey-Bass.

Widener, P. (2007). Benefits and burdens of transnational campaigns: A comparison of four oil struggles in Ecuador. *Mobilization, 12*(1), 21–36.

Williams, D., & Homedes, N. (2001). The impact of the maquiladoras on health and health policy along the US-Mexico border. *Journal of Public Health Policy, 22*(3), 320–337.

Williams, G., & Mawdsley, E. (2006). Postcolonial environmental justice: Government and governance in India. *Geoforum, 37*(5), 660–670.

World Health Organization [WHO]. (2004, June 23–25). *Dealing with uncertainty-how can the precautionary principle help protect the future of our children?* Working document. The precautionary principle. Public health, protection of children and sustainability. Background document (pp. 15–29). Budapest: Secretariat for the Fourth Ministerial Conference on Environment and Health.

Zeisel, K., Paredes, N., & Brunelle, D. (2006). *The North American Free Trade Agreement (NAFTA): Effects on human rights.* Retrieved July 10, 2008, from http://www.fidh.org/IMG/pdf/Mexique448-ang2006.pdf

Chapter 11
Migration and Discrimination: Contradictory Discourses Regarding Repatriations in Ciudad Juárez, Chihuahua, Mexico

Hector Antonio Padilla and Irasema Coronado

> *...the infinitely complex red-tape existence of stateless persons*
> *...the outsourcing of huge masses of people and their deprivation to pariahs...*
>
> (Hannah Arendt 2003)

In this chapter, we analyze social discourses that have emerged in Ciudad Juárez, Chihuahua, Mexico, against people that have migrated to Ciudad Juárez from southern Mexico; we give most attention to discourse against Mexicans that have been deported from the United States. We offer a critical view of the practices and the public and private discourses taking place within broad sectors of the community; these discriminate against and marginalize migrants by blaming them for local problems, such as the lack of public services, overcrowding in public schools, lack of employment opportunities, and, more recently, the increase in violence and public insecurity.

We present historical antecedents to the way this migratory phenomenon has triggered these contradictory discourses. Rhetorical contradictions and inconsistencies abound regarding the presence of migrants. Some argue that the repatriated are deserving of humanitarian assistance; however, there is a division of opinion regarding how much to help and whether helping others is a good use of resources. Some believe that funding for services to migrants is too small and thus that migrants exert pressure on a political system with serious financial limitations. Another idea is that migrants without roots in the community are a potential danger. We discuss the

H.A. Padilla (✉)
Department of Social Science, Universidad Autónoma de Ciudad Juárez,
Ciudad Juárez, Chihuahua, Mexico
e-mail: hpadilla@uacj.mx

I. Coronado
Department of Political Science, University of Texas at El Paso, El Paso, TX, USA
e-mail: icoronado@utep.edu

M. Lusk et al. (eds.), *Social Justice in the U.S.-Mexico Border Region*,
DOI 10.1007/978-94-007-4150-8_11,

actions and discourses that the government and nongovernmental organizations have launched in response to the arrival of repatriated migrants and their presence in the city. This discourse occurs amid an unstable political and social panorama, an unprecedented crime wave, and violence that converts the repatriated into scapegoats.

The Cases of Ricardo, Arturo, and Efrain[1]

Ricardo

Ricardo left his community of origin in the state of Durango and settled in New Mexico. He married Susana, who is a permanent legal resident, and together they formed a life. Ricardo was able to obtain a driver's license in the state of New Mexico. Susana and Ricardo saved enough money to make a down payment on a plot of land with a trailer and arranged to make monthly payments with the owner. Ricardo and Susana added on to the trailer and slowly but surely were constructing a nice house; they even had a nice porch decorated with plants and flowers. They purchased money orders to make the monthly payments on their property because they avoided banks for obvious reasons. Monthly, they deposited their money order in a locked box outside the owner's home. One day, they were shocked to learn that they were in arrears and that the owner was taking back the property and the trailer along with all of the improvements. Susana and Ricardo had receipts to prove that they had made the payments with money orders. In spite of the fact that a friend provided legal counsel, unfortunately, they were not successful in making their case because no one tracks who cashes money orders, and it is tantamount to dealing in cash.

The sheriff's department set up a roadblock in order to check for car registration and proof of car insurance. Ricardo was stopped and was able to provide the necessary documents, and as he was driving off, the officer asked him, "What is your social security number?" Unable to answer, Ricardo found himself in border patrol custody and agreed to a voluntary return to Mexico. He tried to stay in Ciudad Juárez but found it difficult to find work and returned to his community in Durango where he is working on a pig farm. Susana is heartbroken and has subsequently lost contact with him and laments that *"mi corazón esta en Durango"* (my heart is in Durango).

Efraín

Efraín legally came to the United States as a small child. He attended public schools in the United States, spoke English very well, and Spanish rather poorly.

[1] Pseudonyms.

He was a legal permanent resident in the United States. He never applied for US citizenship. For all intents and purposes, Efraín can be described as a de facto US citizen. His allegiance to the United States is strong. Efraín's family all resides in the United States. Prior to his deportation, he attended the university and took out student loans to pay for his education. Efraín was caught shoplifting at a luxurious department store and later was caught driving under the influence of alcohol twice. Subsequently, he was classified an excludable alien and deported to Ciudad Juárez. There he lives in a home that his parents owned before they moved to El Paso. He is the only member of his family to live in Ciudad Juárez and lives there alone. His family visits him occasionally. Once he arrived in Ciudad Juárez, he did not have any documents: driver's license, *Clave Unica de Registro de Población* (CURP), voting registration card, passport, etc. He has not been successful at finding employment for a variety of reasons: his Spanish is poor; he expresses critical comments about Mexico that rub his friends and acquaintances the wrong way. He finds that he is discriminated against because he does not speak proper Spanish and his Mexican friends tell him that he has feelings of superiority and that if he loves the United States so much, he should go back; of course, if he does, he would face a long prison sentence and would then be redeported. He could possibly find employment at a call center in Ciudad Juárez that requires people to speak English fluently, but the wages are very low.

Arturo

In December 2008, Arturo was deported to Ciudad Juárez, Chihuahua, Mexico, after a 5-month stay in a detention center located in Sierra Blanca, Texas. He arrived at the detention center after a local police in El Paso, Texas, stopped him when he was driving to pick up his daughter from school and was unable to produce a driver's license. Arturo was deported to Ciudad Juárez, a city that was totally alien to him. He left behind his wife and three children, all US citizens.

In Ciudad Juárez, he was greeted by aunts and uncles and his grandmother who provided him with boarding—a home that they are leaving behind—because they are all legally moving to El Paso, Texas. Arturo set up his new home and closed a chapter in his migration cycle. His new home is on the outskirts of Ciudad Juárez, in an area with a high crime rate, historically, and like other parts of the city, it is currently experiencing an unprecedented increase in violence. In 2008, more than 1,600 people were murdered in Ciudad Juárez, many of them shot with AK 47 rifles. Arturo has been deported into a city that has been identified as one of the most dangerous cities in the world, and it does not seem welcoming.

Arturo was born in Ciudad Juárez and raised in El Paso, Texas; he has been expelled by a country that does not want him. In his new city, he feels alone and lives behind closed doors. He is vulnerable, in a precarious situation, socially and personally; Ciudad Juárez is not a welcoming community and therefore Arturo feels excluded. Like every other resident of Ciudad Juárez, Arturo feels the wave of violence that has swept the city. Additionally, several social groups and a sector of the political and business classes see deportees as potentially contributing to this violent wave. These social and political sectors seek to impede the entry of the deportees practically and discursively or to shorten the stay of those recently repatriated by sending them back to their communities of origin in Mexico. Latching onto the "*Repatriación Ordenada y Segura*" (orderly and safe repatriation), a policy of the Mexican federal government, these social and political forces demand that deportees leave Ciudad Juárez immediately or as soon as possible.

These deportees have been expelled three times—first, when they leave their communities of origin in Mexico because they cannot find employment or educational opportunities; the second time is when they are detained in the United States and deported to Mexico; and the third time is when they arrive into the border city to which they have been deported and are "encouraged" to return to their community of origin.

But Arturo does not have any other place to go. After spending 6 months in Ciudad Juárez, he decided to go back "home" to El Paso, Texas. He was successful but was apprehended again and sent to detention for a longer period of time—he felt jail was a better place to be than Ciudad Juárez. His story is one of many that one hears—a clear example of immigration laws creating and punishing criminals and violators of the law, who later on, reenter society, carrying with them the stigma of "delinquents," undesirable people, and failures, people that no one wants.

The stories of Ricardo, Efraín, and Arturo summarize the history of deportations, the social discourses surrounding the immigration debate, and the different levels at which government and society in general react to centuries of migration flow into and out of Ciudad Juárez and into and out of El Paso, Texas, a border community that has been touted as the largest borderplex on the US-Mexico border. It is a historical pattern marked by the ebb and flow of the US economy and the social and political crises in Mexico, evidenced as a historical process of movement and demographic displacement of people from the south of Mexico to the north and into the United States. This migratory movement, once a one-way street, is now a two-way street as Mexicans are expelled from the United States with the possibility of staying in a border city or returning to the interior of Mexico.

The Emergence of the Double Discourse

The precursor of migration to Ciudad Juárez lies in the basis of US immigration policy occurring at the beginning of the twentieth century when the United States imposed restrictions on the entry of Mexican and other foreigners entering the United States (Martínez 1982; Gonzáles 2007; González de la Vara 2002; Orozco 2007; Romo 2005). In those years, like today, many Mexicans opted to migrate in order to find better employment and economic opportunities. Mexican migration into the United States took place in spite of the fact that the Mexican government tried to retain migrants in the country by creating free trade zones in major border cities, hoping that these free trade zones would encourage foreign investment, stimulate the economy, and create jobs. These free trade zones, rather than keeping Mexicans from migrating north, became magnets attracting more migrants from southern Mexico to come north.

The migration of Mexicans to northern Mexico and the southwestern United States was uncontainable during the last two decades of the nineteenth century and the early twentieth century. Facilitating this migration was the expansion of economic activities on both sides of the border and establishment of railroads between the countries and across US southwest. The internal migration from southern Mexico to northern Mexico led to the growth of Mexican border cities. Likewise, Mexican migration contributed to the growth of US border cities. Mexican Americans residing in El Paso did not benefit from the growing economy in the city. For example, in the Chihuahuita neighborhood, Mexican Americans were the poorest of the poor; their neighborhood lacked public services, and little was done to improve their living situation. In 1910, more than 10,000 Mexican Americans lived in El Paso, Texas, making it one of the cities with the largest Mexican origin population (Martínez 1982).

But the economic crisis in the United States in the decade following 1900 led the United States to close its border and provoked the first wave of deportees to Mexico. Simultaneously, the first discursive expressions and policies resulting in the deportation of Mexicans back to their country of origin began. This discourse reiterated what residents of Ciudad Juárez had been expressing against the newly arrived immigrants from the southern part of Mexico, in "their" city, who were not successful in their attempts to enter the United States. Hence, Ciudad Juárez was becoming a city of "outsiders" those from the southern part of Mexico.

Faced with this reality, the Mexican government attempted to implement several measures; on one hand, they would discourage the migration of people from the south of Mexico into cities like Ciudad Juárez, and on the other hand, they would encourage their compatriots repatriated from the United States to return to their communities of origin and not stay in border cities. Government officials attempted to find employment for deportees and newly arrived migrants from the South. Several newspapers of that era, such as *El Clarín del Norte*, warned people from other parts of Mexico not to travel to northern Mexico because the demand for their labor had waned in the United States (Martínez 1982).

Specifically, Mexican workers returning from work in the US railroad and mining industry without any money and lacking in other basic necessities could apply to the Mexican government, through their consulate offices in El Paso, Texas, to provide food and free transportation in order to return to their communities of origin in southern Mexico. Similar support services were promised to those wanting to bring their families residing in the United States to Mexico.

Examples of these measures abound and even in cities in central Mexico such as Guanajuato. In Guanajuato, ads and posters were placed warning people of the precarious situation that prevailed in Ciudad Juárez, so they would be discouraged from migrating to northern Mexico. In 1910, perhaps for the first time, discourse that looked at Mexican deportees with jealousy and suspicion described them as masses of deportees congregating in the city center. The Mexican consul general in El Paso declared that if this situation continued, the "deported immigrants" could shortly become a menace to public security. Consequently, the federal government managed to find employment for 200 people outside of Ciudad Juárez, thus creating a fortunate or unfortunate forced reintegration of these people (Martínez 1982).

In the 1920s, the US Congress passed anti-immigrant legislation and waves of deportations occurred. The next decade, the deportations of immigrants from the United States continued, but this time it was due to the impact of the crash of the stock market and the economic debacle that ensued (Balderrama 2005). The situation changed in the 1940s when the United States needed cheap labor because men were fighting in World War II and women were working in factories. The United States and Mexico negotiated a labor agreement, the Bracero Program, whereby Mexican men would work in the fields. In the 1960s, the Bracero Program ended and the repatriation of Mexicans once again ensued.

Therefore, during these years, a scheme was configured: with the arrival and reception of migrants, authorities, and privileged sectors of society, some sectors conceived of the migrants as a problem that needed to be addressed through charity on the one hand and, on the other hand, as potential social danger in the region that urgently needed addressing by limiting their stay in the city. In the case of Ciudad Juárez, the business leaders wanted the federal government to dissuade migrants from coming to the border through the implementation of educational campaigns.

At this juncture, the official Mexican government responded by using measures to reincorporate the deportees. The Mexican government allowed them to import their personal effects and work tools without paying import taxes, offering free transportation to the country's interior and promising employment opportunities and free or discounted land. The Mexican government faced many challenges as they attempted to promote regional, economic development strategies and take advantage of the competitive advantage of the border to retain Mexicans wanting to migrate to the United States and reincorporate those that had been deported.

Overwhelming evidence suggests that the Mexican government's development strategies did not work. Clearly, over time, the migratory flow was irreversible—one form of migration had fomented another. Many Mexican workers in the United States, who returned to Mexico, had established family ties in the United States and once repatriated to Mexico, instead of returning to their place of origin, stayed in northern border cities, such as Ciudad Juárez, intending to return to the United States; they were labeled "*la población flotante*," the floating population. Others made Ciudad Juárez their permanent home, provoking with their presence the same actions, worries, and discriminatory discourses of the past.

With the policies contemplated in the Border Industrialization Plan, many of the repatriated were expected to find employment in manufacturing; as migrants to the United States, they would be absorbed into the labor force, stopping the exodus of Mexicans into the United States. It became evident that the Bracero Program contributed to the establishment and strengthening of migratory social and familial networks. While the Bracero Program, a binational agreement, had facilitated migration, this migration was later stigmatized and criminalized (Delgado 2004). In these circumstances, migration was far from being stopped but rather was facilitated and encouraged by US-based employers that continued to hire cheap Mexican labor.

The following decades, one can observe a growing generalized migration to the United States stimulated by not only the migratory networks that had been established but by fundamental economic and structural changes in Mexico. Mexico deepened its economic development policies that privileged the urban industrial sector, negatively impacting the agricultural sector. The adverse effect in the rural areas and the agricultural sector was compounded in 1986 when Mexico joined GATT and later, in 1994, with the North American Free Trade Agreement (NAFTA). All of this reinforced on a greater scale the migratory process toward the United States and the growth of the population in border cities, among them Ciudad Juárez, a city where the expansion and growth of the *maquiladora* industry is an attractive force for many Mexicans from southern Mexico. The anti-immigrant sentiment in Ciudad Juárez toward people from Veracruz was especially virulent in the late 1990s. Then Mayor Gustavo Elizondo wrote to the governor of Veracruz asking him to inform his citizens that deceitful recruitment for employment was taking place in Ciudad Juárez and that many women were asking for financial assistance and/or turning to prostitution out of desperation. There was even discussion of organizing a "Border Patrol" that would preclude migrants from the south to come to Ciudad Juárez (Staudt and Coronado 2002: 145–148).

Public Policies and the Criminalization of the Repatriated

The schema of reception into Ciudad Juárez and transporting the deportees to other places in Mexico did not vary much during the last decade (2000–2010). During the presidency of Vicente Fox, the exodus of Mexicans into the United States reached very high levels. This high number of immigrants was used as an argument by President George W. Bush to launch harsher measures in order to stop the (illegal) entry of Mexicans into the United States and to capture and deport as many as possible. In this new context, like in the past, Ciudad Juárez experienced growth in the number of deportees and with that the same discourse was reiterated that discriminates against and criminalizes them.

According to the *Instituto Nacional de Migración* (INM) (The National Migration Institute), over 571,401 people were deported annually through different delegations that exist in Mexico. Between 2001 and 2008, over 4,571,209 undocumented people were deported from the United States into Mexico; 706,575 were deported into the State of Chihuahua; of those 539, 316 were deported to Ciudad Juárez (www.inami.com.mx). Yet, today's negative discourses regarding these people reproduce those of the past. For example, a local newspaper's headline reads: "Assassinated by six bullets in his home, Arrived from the U.S." In the body of the article, it states that the deceased had just been deported from the United States 2 months earlier and that he had been in prison for drug trafficking (*El Mexicano* 7-22-2009).

In this same manner, another newspaper article reads: "A man that has recently been deported from the U.S. was assassinated yesterday along with a woman who was originally from Durango." The article reports "that several residents of El Paso, Texas, family members of the deceased arrived at the scene and stated that their relative had been deported for reasons that they did not want to elaborate on. The victim had several Aztec symbols tattooed on his body but his link to an Azteca Gang could not be confirmed" (*El Diario* 08-06-2010).

In 2008, according to the US Department of Homeland Security (DHS), 97,133 migrant criminals were deported; 73% of the criminal migrants were Mexicans, and 36% had committed drug-related crimes (*Reforma* 09-06-2009). With negative reporting, a negative social construction of the deportees is being created without taking into account that most of the deportees, 68% that live in the United States, do not commit violent acts; rather they do not have driver's licenses, car insurance, or have committed traffic violations. Approximately 34% have not committed a crime save being in the United States without proper documents (Paris 2010).

Locally, it is feared that the repatriated with criminal pasts will only increase the rates of crime in the city. The local press perpetuates these sensationalist discourses without any empirical evidence regarding the probability of this, or the actual impacts. If indeed these deportees decide to stay in Ciudad Juárez, the possibility that they will commit crimes is relatively low. According to population estimates provided by the Mexican government agency, *Consejo Nacional de Población* (CONAPO), in 2004, of the total number of deportees, only 30% indicated that they did not want to return to the United States. Of this 30%, only 20% indicated that they had intentions of staying in a border city. So one can surmise that of the 525,000 deportees from 2001 to 2008, only 31,542 stayed in Ciudad Juárez; that is only 3,942 people a year. According to Rodolfo Rubio, only 3% of the deportees actually stay in Ciudad Juárez. This is approximately, 15,000 people—a relatively low number in relation to the possible impact that these people could have on the delinquency rates of the city and the demands on public and social services.

The problems regarding the deportees in Ciudad Juárez are not so much in the medium or long term, but in the short term. Local authorities should be concerned with providing immediate medical, legal, and humanitarian attention, and not in expressing their concern regarding the possible increase in violent crimes because of their arrival in the city. Regarding the crime rates in Ciudad Juárez, several academics and members of NGOs agree that the increase in violence is due to the strategy that the federal government has implemented against organized crime. This issue has been covered extensively in the local press since President Felipe Calderón's visit in February of 2010 with the launch of a reconstruction project/campaign, *"Todos Somos Juárez"* (We are all Juárez); some feel that this campaign will save the social fabric of the city.

In order to attend to social demands that emanate from the presence of the repatriated, a handful of public and private institutions exist that coordinate work under the framework of the "*Programa de Repatriación Humana*" (Human Repatriation Program) that the federal government (2006–2012) has implemented. The goals of this program are to receive the deportees; to provide them with food and shelter, and medical attention, in cases of an emergency; and to formally validate the skill set that they learned while working in the United States, assist in temporary job placement and put them in touch with loved ones. All of these actions portend to guarantee "human and dignified treatment to half a million Mexicans that are deported every year" (www.inm.gob.mx 2007).

Institutions at several levels implement these public policies: local government, the *Coordinadora de Atención a Los Migrantes* (CAM) (Coordinating Office of Attention to Migrants), created in 2007 by the Municipality of Ciudad Juárez; the *Secretaría de Fomento Social* (Secretariat of Social Development), by the state government; and the federal government agency, *Instituto Nacional de Migración.* Civil society is represented by the *Casa del Migrant*e (Home of the Migrant) and the Mexican affiliate of the *Asociación de Jóvenes Cristianos* (YMCA).

In order to meet the deportees' needs, these institutions offer immediate assistance by providing legal assistance, shelter, and help in obtaining official identifications such as voter registration cards, the main form of ID used in Mexico, and the only valid ID that can be used to deal with government agencies or banks.

Also, since deportees seldom have money, but may have checks, the groups intercede on deportees' behalf at banking institutions. Additionally, these institutions provide bus transportation vouchers and money for meals during trips to deportees' cities of origin. Because of several agreements between the two federal governments, there is an orderly and safe deportation process that allows the Mexican government to provide these services (Núñez 2008). Likewise, though not acknowledged openly by the authorities, but by social service organizations, the fact that members of these institutions "greet" the deportees means they too provide a safeguard against gangs and other criminal elements that operate the international ports of entry. Additionally, police officers have also been accused of being discriminatory in their treatment of the deportees and have violated their human rights. The *Centro de Derechos Humanos De Los Migrantes* (CDHM, Center for the Human Rights of Migrants) considers that the repatriated migrant "since his/her arrival in Ciudad Juárez is subjected to being victimized by the municipal police, the taxi drivers that want to overcharge them to take them to the central bus station, and the money exchange businesses that want to charge them a lot for cashing their checks" (Blanca Navarrete 2008).

The collaboration among these different institutions reveals the double discursive dimensions and contradictions that have been long established. On one hand, they emphasize the humanitarian and altruistic aspect of the attention they provide to the deportees. On the other, the negative aspect is highlighted—the risk to public security that deportees pose and the judgmental prejudices that label them a priori as delinquents. This double-sided discourse is found among those that are advocates for the migrants. For example, a person working for CAM stated:

> We help them obtain their *Clave Unica de Registro de Población* (CURP), national ID card, we tell them the requirements that they need to fulfill in order to obtain a birth certificate,

a voter registration card, we provide advice on everything they need to do when they arrive into our country. We explain to them the actual state of affairs of the nation. A lot of them do not know who Felipe Calderón is; he is our president.

Later on she adds: "At times those of us who live in Ciudad Juárez or that are originally from Ciudad Juárez have an erroneous concept of the people that are deported from the U.S. They think that they are delinquents, that they are people that are not capable of anything, they have a badly placed stereotype, I believe that the people, due to the U.S., are our most valuable people, I think that these people are risking everything and they leave behind what they love the most in this life, their children and their families, looking for a better life to provide for their children" (Adriana Cruz 2008).

Later, though there is a contradiction when she affirms that the deportees that they work with: "A few of them, yes they are rapists, assassins or delinquents that are Mexicans that went to commit crimes in the U.S. and they were deported, we do not want those people in Ciudad Juárez for nothing, we want for them to leave, we do not want more rapists or assassins in the city, and that is why we help them leave the city; we do not want those types of people to stay" (Adriana Cruz 2008).

The discourse analyzed above deals with two irreconcilable dimensions: one is the perception that deportees are potentially criminals and at the same time that the deportees are worthy of social services. It does seem that the perception that deportees are criminals carries more weight because the business community, municipal authorities, and the middle class use media outlets to express their sentiments vis-à-vis the deportees. The media reports give credence and validity and weight to their perspective.

In this case, the best and most clear example is the discourse that criminalizes the deportees; one can observe that this polemic that unfolded locally in response to the comments made by then governor Arnold Schwarzenegger in April of 2008. Schwarzenegger warned and threatened to deport close to 20,000 Mexicans that were in detention in California jails and prisons. Ciudad Juárez Mayor Jose Reyes Ferriz, a member of the PRI party that served from 2007 to 2010, immediately responded that "If one third of those 19,000 delinquents stay in the city, while is it a big amount, thousands of delinquents that are going to have and continue to receive in our city, with very negative effects." In his capacity as president of the US-Mexico Border Mayors Association, and at his behest, he organized a meeting where this topic was discussed.

At that meeting, along with other mayors, he proposed as a principal measure to develop a legal strategy and solicit the support of the *Secretaría de Relaciones Exteriores* (Ministry of Foreign Relations) so that they could avoid the possible massive deportation and in this case that the deported would be sent directly to Mexico City. "So that from there they can then go to their places of origin, and not have the temptation to want to stay in Ciudad Juárez, so that they can cross back into the U.S." (*El Diario* 05-19-2009). In the mayor's opinion and judgment, "... thousands of delinquents in just one moment in any community represent a grave danger to society; it is a situation that must not occur; we should fight so that it does not happen; and we need to take the necessary measures" (*El Diario* 2009) in thc alarming headline "*Alarma a alcaldes fronterizos deportación de miles de presos indocumentados de California*" (US-Mexico Border Mayors Alarmed by the deportation of thousands of undocumented prisoners in California).

The position of the mayor is shared and expressed in a radical and aggressive manner by other social sectors that maintain their discriminatory and xenophobic attitudes regarding the deportees. For example, on the website of a digital newspaper, *El Diario Digital*, a reader comments:

It is truly unheard of that always this and other borders are seen as areas where human trash can be discarded, *the worst of the worst* is delivered to our border and the worst case is that they stay here and commit more crimes and cause more harm than that has already been done to our *Juárez*, and worse yet is that Mexican elected officials do not have a plan to counteract this risky situation. They only worry about their salaries, and we the citizens are the ones that will pay the consequences of these inhumane acts of the *Gubernator* and his minions.

This social discourse that emphasizes the potential danger of the presence of the deported in Ciudad Juárez resonates with the escalation of extreme criminal violence that the city has experienced in the past decade (2000–2010). The apex of this criminal activity that clearly began in 2008, when the number of violent deaths in the city escalated drastically, especially homicides committed by "commandos" with high-powered weapons, continue to this day. In 2008, 1,623 homicides were reported in the city and in 2009, 2,657, and in 2010, 3,042. In addition to the violent deaths, the indices of criminal activity have increased dramatically; for example, stolen vehicles and robberies and also new phenomena have developed that never or seldom occurred in the past: extortions of private businesses and kidnappings.

Even though the majority of these deaths are associated with, or attributed by the government authorities to, the war between rival cartels of organized crime, and the war on drugs that was launched by president Felipe Calderón since he assumed power in December of 2006, to the authorities, it is easy to link the presence of those repatriated with this problem. Not only are the repatriated seen as possible delinquents that can be recruited by organized crime and gangs in the city, but also the discourse is one of "*localista*" and xenophobic by extolling the virtues of being a *Juarense* or a *Chihuahuense.*

This discourse vindicates people from Ciudad Juárez and Chihuahua as being peaceful, hospitable, and productive and the protectors and defenders of the "image of the city" entrepreneurial, powerful, and strong. This is about making this discourse the lens that sees the repatriated as having an identity that is "not *Juarense*," the other, and the other is a threat and a menace to what is *Juarense.* Evidently, a pure ideological posture is present in sectors of the population that claim the city for themselves and suppose that the repatriated damage or harm the image of the city (Manuel Arroyo 2008).

Governor Rick Perry expressed his unhappiness with the fact that people that had been detained in Arizona were being deported through Texas. According to US government officials, their goal is to break the smuggling cycle in the Arizona-

Sonora region and deport people through other cities. The spokesperson for the governor's office stated that if the goal was to return the deportees to Mexico, the fastest route is not through Texas (Grissom 2010).

Conclusions

In the complex social context that we have outlined in this chapter, the official local government discourse contributes to the perpetuation of negative social constructions of deportees. Government officials tend to highlight the fact that the deportees are vulnerable people because they do not have money, food, clothes, etc., and that this desperate situation that they find themselves in leads to them turning to crime, stealing in order to eat and that in turn they become potential targets for the drug dealers to do their dirty work because the deportees are in such a vulnerable state. It is another step in the sequence of vulnerabilities that have affected the lives of these people. First, they were forced to abandon their places of origin, where they suffered the first expulsion. Later, they arrived to the United States, a country where they faced discrimination and rejection that led to another expulsion when they were detained, jailed, and deported. The third expulsion, when they arrived to Ciudad Juárez, occurred in a city where criminal violence is coupled with insensitivity and the rejection by the authorities and certain sectors of society that do not want to receive them. In this way, the main purpose of the government policy centered on the safe and orderly repatriation converts to a contradiction that pushes the repatriated to a yet another expulsion: from a city that once more rejects them.

This stance is not shared by all, and certainly not by human rights activists that collaborate neither with the local government nor with the consular authorities of the Mexican consulate in El Paso, Texas, that have declared that it is a myth that all the deported are delinquents. In this respect, it is said that the impact on Ciudad Juárez of these deportations depends on the strategy that is utilized by the immigration authorities but that only 3% of the deportees opt to stay in the city; the majority accept the offer and support of social organizations and other agencies that participate in the *Programa de Repatriación Humana* (Program of Humane Repatriation). In this same way, it is clarified that while some are ex-convicts, the majority of the deportees had been arrested for minor infractions such as driving without a license, auto insurance, or not paying traffic tickets or plainly because they were undocumented (Rubio 2008).

One cannot demonize migration when one has a public policy that generates employment that depends on migrants. What would the Border Patrol do? In fact, it would be better if one understood the undocumented as consumers of services. On the contrary, "one sees the immigrants as a unit, as a collective in order to sanction them" (Arroyo 2008). This attitude is worse and is more evident in times of economic crisis that lends itself stigmatize the immigrant. It is about, one can add, a constant in history, in which the immigrant always appears as the responsible culprit as viewed by middle-class conservative people and sectors that are tied to the land and that deal with speculations and not empirical evidence (Chavira 2008).

Underlying this is that the policy toward immigrants and the official discourse about them has a double meaning and in the final analysis is discriminatory and in reality hides the inefficiency of public policies. This is what causes the creation of scapegoats that has converted the immigrants in Ciudad Juárez, into what is revealed as a big problem of discourse, of sensibility (Rubio 2008). In this manner, the way that one sees the immigrant also indicates that "it is a reflection of cultural immaturity of certain sectors of the community, the region that is not sufficiently capable to recognize, accept or analyze; or be able to accept the reality that we are a composition of many, that we are different and very rich" (Arroyo 2008).

That is how one can see the repatriated as a possible criminal, some maintain; one also needs to see the anger, blame, and impotence that these people feel and that certainly, many of them have reached the point that they have internalized that they are criminals and that they possibly develop a criminal consciousness. This should take us all to recognize that there is a continuity of criminalization; there is also a continuity of the lack of opportunity in both countries (Paris 2010). In sum, as a recent article warns, one takes the deportee as an economic product, a criminological factor, and as an object of public and private charity, but never as a taxpayer or as a citizen (Trapaga 2009). In other words, the repatriated migrants, in large measure, continue to be a "labor force whose members lack basic rights, as citizens, and in their own country of origin and that in the future they cannot count on the backing of the U.S. or Mexican government; both will deny them their rights, and therefore they will continue to be vulnerable and subjected to labor exploitation" (Sandoval 2009).[2]

References

Arendt, H. (2003). That infinitely complex red tape existence: From a letter to Karl Jaspers. In *The portable Hannah Arendt* (pp. 25–29). New York: Penguin Classic.

Balderrama, F. E. (2005, Fall). The emergence of unconstitutional deportation and repatriation of Mexicans and Mexican Americans as a public issue. *Radical History Review, 93*, 107–110.

Delgado Wise, R. (2004). Globalización y migración laboral internacional. Reflexiones en torno al caso de Mexico. en *Nuevas tendencias y desafíos de la migración internacional Mexico-Estados Unidos*. Comps. Raúl Delgado Wise y Margarita Favela. Ed. Universidad Autónoma de Zacatecas, Universidad Autónoma de Mexico y Centro de Investigaciones Interdisciplinarias en Ciencias y Humanidades. 2004.

González de la Vara Martín. (2002). *Breve historia de Ciudad Juárez y su región*, Ediciones eón, Ciudad Juárez. Retrieved from: http://www.inm.gob.mx/index.php/page/Estadisticas_Migratorias

[2]An earlier version of this chapter was presented at the Latin American Studies Association Meeting in 2009 in Rio de Janeiro, Brazil. The authors acknowledge and thank Leobardo Alvarado for his assistance in the gathering of data for this work.

González Herrera, C. (2007). *Racismo, eugenesia y salud pública en la formación de la frontera Estados Unidos-Mexico, 1900–1930*. en Memorias del 2° Coloquio Carl Lumboltz de Antropología e Historia del Norte de Mexico. Chihuahua: Escuela Nacional de Antropología e Historia Unidad Chihuahua.

Grissom, B (*The Texas Tribune*). (2010). *Program to deport migrants from Ariz. Through Texas still irks Perry*. Reprinted December 10, 2010 *El Paso Times* front page and continues to 9A.

Heuer, W. (2007). Europe and its refugees: Arendt on the politicization of minorities. *Social Research, 74*(4), 1159–1172.

Martínez, O. (1982). *Ciudad Juárez: El auge de una ciudad fronteriza a partir de 1848*. Fondo de Cultura Económica.

Orozco, V. (2007). *Una narración histórica: los primeros cien años en las relaciones Juárez-El Paso*. Chihuahua Hoy 2007, Tomo V, ICHICULT, UACJ, UACH, Mexico (pp. 37–58).

Paris, D. (coord.). (2010). *Mesa Derechos Humanos y procesos de repatriación de Estados Unidos a Mexico,* Mesa redonda con especialistas de El COLEF y la RECCI, 18 de agosto del 2010.

Romo, D. (2005). *Ringside seat to a revolution, an underground cultural history of El Paso and Juárez: 1893–1923*. El Paso: Cinco Puntos Press.

Sandoval, J. M. (2009). Integración regional subordinada, saqueo de recursos estratégicos, migraciones forzadas y lucha por la soberanía en el continente americano. en *Alternativas de regionalización versus integración subordinada en América latina*. Compiladores Raquel Álvarez de Flores y Juan Manuel Sandoval Palacios. *Ed.* Consejo de Desarrollo Científico, Humanístico y Tecnológico (CDCHT), Centro de Estudios de Frontera e Integración (CEFI) y Consejo Nacional para la Cultura y las Artes-Instituto Nacional de Antropología e Historia (CONACULTA-INAH).

Staudt, K., & Coronado, I. (2002). *Fronteras no Más: Toward social justice at the U.S.-Mexico border*. New York: Palgrave USA.

Trapaga, I. (2009). Tesis de maestría: *Y TUVE UN PINCHE FRACASO. Migrantes deportados por Ciudad Juárez: la Frontera como sistema de clasificación y regulación económica y moral y su impacto en la construcción de las subjetividades dentro de los circuitos migratorios Mexico-Estados Unidos*. ENAH.

Walters, W. (2002). Deportation, expulsión and the international police of aliens. *Citizenship Studies, 6*(3), 265–292.

Newspapers

El Continental, n.a. Deportados en Ciudad Juárez. April 4, 1933, p. 1, no section.

El Diario, Castañon, A. Exigen los alcaldes fronterizos que deportaciones de reos sean por D.F. *El Diario*, May 5, 2009, p 1, sección A.

El Diario, Olivas, J. D. Impacto a la ciudad depende de estrategia de repatriación. *El Diario*, May 16, 2009, p 6, Section A.

El Diario, Roban y matan a hombre recién deportado de EU. *El Diario*, August 6, 2010, p. 1, Section B.

El Mexicano, Ramírez, C. Asesinado de 6 balazos en su casa. Llegó de EU. *El Mexicano*, July 22, 2009, p. 1, no section.

Reforma, Garduño, S, Reclutan polleros a adolescentes. *Reforma*, September 6, 2009, p 1, Section A.

Interviews

Adriana Cruz Hernández, directora del Centro de Atención a Migrantes del Municipio de Juárez (CAM), 2007–2010 December 1, 2008, by Jorge Breceda.

Blanca Navarrete, directora del Centro de Derechos Humanos del Migrante (CDHM). October 29, 2008, by Leobardo Alvarado.
Julieta Núñez, delegada del Instituto Nacional de Migración en Ciudad Juárez. December 5, 2008, by Jorge Breceda.
Manuel Arroyo, Universidad Autónoma de Ciudad Juárez (UACJ). November 14, 2008, by Leobardo Alvarado.
Ramón Chavira, Universidad Autónoma de Ciudad Juárez (UACJ). November 26, 2008, by Jorge Breceda.
Rodolfo Rubio, Colegio de la Frontera Norte (COLEF), de Ciudad Juárez. December 1, 2008, by Jorge Breceda.

Internet Sites

www.conapo.gob.mx
www.inami.com.mx
www.inm.gob.mx/repatriacionH/Informacionavances.pdf

Part IV
Moving Forward: Steps in Achieving Border Justice

Chapter 12
Education Policies: Standardized Testing, English-Language Learners, and Border Futures

Pauline Dow and Kathleen Staudt

So obvious it is rarely stated, educational historian David Tyack declared that while students represent 20% of the population, they will be 100% of the future (cited in Hochschild and Scrovonick 2003, p. 9). With youthful demographics, border communities contain an even larger portion of young people, but the same totalistic figures hold for the future of border economic development and democracy (or lack thereof). Students' talents and skills, if underdeveloped, predict a border future with an overrepresentation of low-wage earners and a "brain drain," boding poorly for a prosperous border economy wherein border voices can determine their futures. Good-quality education for all children is a key strategy for border economic development and political voice.

Public education is a prism through which to examine youth in all its diversity: gender, ethnicity, income, and class. At the border, one must add language and nationality. Angela Valenzuela, critic of "subtractive schooling" and its devaluation of Spanish language and family-based cultural assets, refers to Texas-style accountability systems that fail Latino students (1999, 2005). All along the approximately 1,000-mile Texas border with Mexico, Hispanic students comprise more than 80% of the student population, a population with 44% of children living in poverty, a rate twice that of non-border Texas children (CPPP 2009). Recent research at the border criticizes the "business model" applied to education, operating in ways that construct significant numbers of student failures and thereby produce

P. Dow (✉)
Division of Academics, Ysleta Independent School District, 9600 Sims, 79925 El Paso, TX, USA
e-mail: pdow@yisd.net

K. Staudt
Department of Political Science, University of Texas at El Paso, 500 W. University Ave., 79968 El Paso, TX, USA
e-mail: kstaudt@utep.edu

M. Lusk et al. (eds.), *Social Justice in the U.S.-Mexico Border Region*,
DOI 10.1007/978-94-007-4150-8_12,

disengagement, high rates of school "dropouts" (known in Mexico as desertion [*deserción*]), especially in poverty communities in order to staff service and factory jobs (Cervera Gómez et al. 2008; Staudt 2010; Staudt and Méndez 2010).

In this chapter, we discuss the challenges associated with public education on the Texas side of the border along with the opportunities that educators, parents, and constituents have seized to create better educational experiences for border students, a quarter of whom the school bureaucracy classifies as "Limited English Proficient" (LEP). Our special focus is Ysleta Independent School District (YISD 2010b), with 44,729 students, 92% of whom are Hispanic, 24% English-language learners, and 81% economically disadvantaged (2010 figures). We also address the district's two-decade struggle to create spaces for school choice, two-way bilingual programs, language magnet schools, and pathways to higher education. Despite the constraints of a grid-like state and federal system that locks all students—despite their complex heritages and diverse household incomes—into a one-way-fits-all educational structure, various community-oriented leaders, educators, and parents designed local policies that we examine in this chapter. Local policies tempered the problems and obstacles in Ysleta, El Paso's second-largest urban district: student graduation plans (including the subsidy of college entrance exams), service-learning policies, and bilingual language programs that feed expectations to enhance the border gateway region of the Americas. First, however, we briefly examine historical trends in educational policy and the effects of poverty on genuinely equal educational opportunity.

Historical Perspectives: 40 Years of Educational Policies in Texas

Texas and El Paso's once relatively autonomous school districts, in the historic context of educational decentralization in the United States, have given way to greater state authority over schools and, more recently, to the federal imposition of standardized testing regimes under No Child Left Behind. Prior to the civil rights era of the 1960s, by no means did decentralized policymaking provide for high learning expectations and quality education, especially for Hispanic students who have always constituted the largest student population in El Paso (Rippberger and Staudt 2003). As the sole numerical baseline for five southwestern states including Texas from 40 years ago (U.S. Commission on Civil Rights 1969–1974), the Mexican American Education Study (MAES) documented that Mexican American children had the highest rates of school dropout (what it called "low school holding power"), class repetitions, and reading scores below grade level. In the context of few Hispanic educators, administrators, and school board trustees, MAES also documented how teachers ignored Mexican American students in classrooms (Volume 4). Until the development of minimum expectations, one sometimes heard teachers and administrators express dismaying comments about poor kids: "What do you expect? Look at the neighborhood."

With the alarming Reagan-era report of 1983, called *Our Nation at Risk*, many states moved toward educational reforms intended to raise learning expectations for all students, to increase students' time in core curricular requirements, and to improve the preparation of teachers (see Shirley 1997, Chapter 2, for an analysis of the 1980s reforms in Texas). The strategies to implement reforms occurred through accountability tests and scores: exit exams for teachers and students as well as students' standardized tests, known as the TAAS in the 1990s and the TAKS in the 2000s (soon to be revised as the STAAR in 2012 and beyond; see http://www.tea.state.tx.us/student.assessment/staar/).

With bipartisan support, the US Congress passed No Child Left Behind Act (NCLB) in 2002, imposing a high-stakes version of accountability tests and other funding formulas. NCLB marked the death of Title VII of the Elementary and Secondary Education Act, thus transforming the teaching of English learners in the United States. Title VII promoted equal access to the curriculum, trained a generation of teachers in best-bilingual-education practices, and promoted achievement among students. NCLB meant that federal monies would no longer be administered via competitive grants designed to reward excellence and ensure quality control. Beginning in the 1990s, the Ysleta District acquired federal support under VII, attributed in part to the achievement of "recognized status" by the Texas Education Agency (TEA) in 1998. Under NCLB, subsidies (Title III) are distributed on a formula-grant basis to states based on enrollment of English learners and immigrant students. Gradually, however, since the 1960s and beyond, federal funding (known as Title VII, later changed to Title III, and Title I) became available to support school district funding for bilingual education (Title VII then Title III) programs and *supplemental* funding for schools with a high percentage of economically disadvantaged (Title I) students. In El Paso ISD, the biggest urban district in the region with 62,000 students, nine of ten high schools receive Title I funding (Staudt and Méndez 2010).

English-Language Learners, Testing, and Bilingual Education

In the border region, including El Paso, bilingual education (rather than English immersion) is crucial for students' ability to succeed in education. "Bilingual education is a simplistic label for a complex phenomenon" (cited in Crawford 2004, p. 32), and this chapter will not address the complexities, except to make the important distinction between programs that use and promote two languages to foster bilingualism and programs that do not. In 1994, Congress provided a description of the term "bilingual education program," which included the use of both English and the student's native language for instruction to enable students to achieve English proficiency and to learn subject matter content and higher-order thinking skills. This definition also included the option of developing English learners' native language or ancestral languages of American Indians, Alaska Natives, Native Hawaiians, and native residents of the outlying areas of the United

States. Finally, the Congress' definition provided for the option to include the participation of non-English learners (or English-proficient students) if the program was designed to promote proficiency in English and another language.

Researchers in education generally refer to the two groups of programs as "weak" forms of bilingual education (subtractive) and "strong" forms of bilingual education (additive). Weak, or subtractive, programs for English learners (ELs) are those that emphasize English, such as English-as-a-Second Language (ESL) pullout, Content ESL, and Transitional Bilingual Education, and do not sufficiently close the achievement gap. Stated another way, they do not provide English learners with the same access to education as their native English-speaking peers. These subtractive programs are remedial in nature because students are submersed in English and struggle to learn academic and cognitive skills. Because students receive instruction only in English, or receive only minimal support in their native language, students in these programs are not working on grade level and are often years behind their native-English-speaking peers.

Enrichment or additive program models, on the other hand, promote the acquisition of academic and cognitive skills in students' native language while they are acquiring English. These additive models include one-way and two-way dual-language programs (the difference between one-way and two-way is that in the latter, both non-English-proficient and English-proficient students are included). Because the model emphasizes the use of the native language as a medium of instruction, the expectation is that students are working on grade level in all content areas in their primary language, while simultaneously acquiring English (or Spanish in the case of the English-proficient students in two-way program) in a sequential and developmentally appropriate way.

A major difference between additive and subtractive forms of bilingual education is that in a subtractive model (such as ESL pullout), the program ends as quickly as possible, sometimes as early as second grade. Because the goal is solely the acquisition of English, no attention is given to maintaining the native language. In the additive or enrichment form of bilingual education, however, the goal is bi-literacy. Therefore, maintenance of the native language is a key element of the program model, and students do not "exit" the program. In Texas, when students meet state-imposed "exit" criteria, the district reclassifies the student and it no longer receives supplemental state or federal funding. However, the student, with parental permission, continues to be served in the dual-language program. In both one-way and two-way programs, students have the opportunity to continue building their academic skills in the native language beyond the elementary years and throughout middle and high school. For new immigrant students who enter US schools in the secondary years, and where additive programs are in place, students may enroll in content courses in Spanish, as well as courses in English which are content-based ESL courses. Unfortunately, these programs are rare. In districts that implement subtractive programs, ESL pullout is the norm at both the elementary and secondary levels. Research has shown that students in bilingual and English-as-a-second-language (ESL) programs require 4–7 years to achieve grade-level academic performance in English (Hakuta et al. 2000; Thomas and Collier 2002).

In Texas, depending on school district policies, children obtain as little as 2–3 years of the recommended amount of 4 or more years. Elementary education provides accountability standardized tests in English and Spanish in grades 3, 4, and 5, but middle and high school students must pass English-language tests regardless of the type of language support they receive.

Language specialists posit interdependence between students' performance in the first language with performance in their second acquired language (Cummins 1984, 2000). Studies also show that students who can read well in their first language typically do well in reading in their second language (Cummins 1979; Krashen 2003). In a 6-year longitudinal study comparing 109 children, all English learners, enrolled in bilingual programs (both one-way and two-way) in the El Paso area, students were tested in Spanish on the APRENDA in grade 2 in 2004 and in English on the SAT-10 in grade 6 in 2008 (intermediate level). The study documented that demonstrated earlier performance in reading in the first language is related to subsequent performance in the second language (Dow 2008; also see Dow et al. 2010). The same study looked at long-term (6 years) performance of 200 students participating in one-way and two-way bilingual programs. Students were tested using both norm-referenced (SAT-10) and criterion-referenced (Texas Assessment of Knowledge and Skills (TAKS)) tests. Students in the two-way program scored significantly better on the SAT-10 in both reading and math in grade 6. Two-way students also did better on the TAKS reading and math tests (Dow 2008).

The results of this one study do not, of course, confirm the superiority of two-way bilingual programs, but they do provide reason for optimism. Implementing more two-way bilingual programs can help border students to acquire content knowledge and proficiency in English and Spanish for school success and for a prosperous future in the interdependent borderlands of the United States and Mexico.

Accountability Testing Amid Unequal Funding

As noted earlier, for over two decades, both Texas and subsequently the federal government imposed a narrow curriculum, assessed through specialized standardized testing regimes on mainstream and border communities. With near-obsessive attention to "pass rates," disaggregated by ethnicity, gender, special education, LEP, and economic disadvantage, the accountability regime caught educators in an incentive system that led toward "teaching to the test," with low pass rates resulting in increasingly stiff consequences including school closure for total restructuring. The punitive nature of the bureaucratic system gave less and less time to classroom teaching (given the many benchmark and testing days), multiple assessment strategies, and broader context-rich curriculum so that students would co-construct their learning and move on pathways to higher education or meaningful work at living wages. For thorough analysis of the distortions to teaching and learning, including the "gaming" of the system, see McNeil (2005, 2008), McNeil et al. (2008).

Without a state income tax, funding for Texas schools was once based almost entirely on the property tax base. "Property-poor" districts spent lower amounts per pupil than "property-rich" districts (Rocha and Webking 1993). All of El Paso County's nine ISDs—three of them urban and six of them semi-urban/semirural including *colonia* settlements—were property poor. Thanks to a lawsuit that former San Antonio area ISD Superintendent James Vásquez filed in 1984, *Edgewood v Kirby*, (which other ISDs joined, including one from El Paso County), the courts declared the funding system to be unconstitutional and moved the state legislature toward budgetary formulas that improved equity in educational funding, culminating in the so-called Robin Hood system from 1993 to 2005. During his term, Texas State Comptroller John Sharp, in *Bordering the Future*, provided graphs that showed the connection between more equitable funding and a rise in border students' test scores during the 1990s (1998, Chapter 3). Robin Hood "captured" property tax funding from approximately 10% of the state's more than 1,000 ISDs for reallocation to the majority of school districts until a lawsuit by rich districts moved the legislature to adopt yet another funding formula.

Since 2005, the Texas legislature capped school-based property tax and mandated increased teacher salaries in a complex formula-funding system that requires districts to generate support for increased taxes from their voters. To increase funding at significant levels, school districts must get voters' approval through tax ratification elections. With the national economic recession, and especially in high-poverty/high-unemployment regions like the border, voters have been reluctant to vote for tax increases. According to the Texas Association of School Boards (TASB), the average expenditure per student in Texas is $8,000. In Ysleta ISD, that per student outlay is $5,903 (TASB 2008).

While the second Bush administration deepened the high-stakes accountability system, the Obama administration has consolidated and expanded the system even more with rhetoric about poor-performing schools, nods to taxpayer subsidized privatized schooling, and moves toward tying teachers' evaluations to improved test scores under the "Race to the Top" funding initiatives. During eras of budgetary constraints, school districts in fast growing border regions cut back programs like bilingual education or mandate "early exit" from bilingual education. Moreover, while schools have not yet become "English only," the budgetary cuts to bilingual education and standardized testing in middle and high school make it difficult for Spanish-language students to succeed or even to graduate from high school. Even federal funding to schools under Titles I and III have decreased or have been used less as supplementary funding and more to *supplant* regular salaries.

At the border, many Hispanic (the category used in the Texas Education Agency) students are double, sometimes triple counted in the categories of ethnicity, language (LEP), and economically disadvantaged (ED) (i.e., eligible for school lunch subsidies). Hispanic and LEP students achieve lower pass rates than White students at the border and Texas wide. While the definition and measurement of high school completion rates differ, the dropout figures of 20–35%, with Hispanic overrepresentation, are far too high for a prosperous future (Texas Education Agency Academic Indicator System [www.tea.state.tx.us/aeis, 2011a, b]; Intercultural Development Research Association [IDRA] 2010).

Poverty and Insecurity: Their Impact on School Funding and Households

While talent and potential are distributed equally among children, poverty and insecurity can reduce children's achievement in schools. Poverty occurs in spatial patterns, with low-income residents living in neighborhoods with low-rent housing or older housing stock. The neighborhood school feeder pattern reinforces these housing patterns. Low property values depress the tax yield and the ability of school districts to secure adequate budgets. While laws, policies, and court cases intervene to reduce ethnic and racial segregation in schools, similar attention to class, income, and poverty has not yet occurred, except for Title I (as noted above) but with marginal effects on overall funding per pupil.

The Southern Education Foundation (SEF) examined the rates of children living in families of four, both in poverty ($22,000) and in extreme poverty ($11,000), drawing on 2007–2008 figures (SEF 2010). The SEF documented higher rates of extreme poverty in southern states, including Texas. Texas poverty is concentrated along the border where several border counties fall among the bottom five counties of national per capita income ranks. The figures show that although Title I supplements funding, its contribution to equitable funding per pupil is meager, given the strikingly different funding bases in districts with high, medium, and low levels of extreme poverty (Title I funding is shown in the second figure): high poverty (10%+): $6,889→$8,049 (per pupil), medium (5–9.9%) ($9,132→$9,891), and low (<5%) ($13,790→$14,201) levels of extreme poverty (SEF 2010, p. 22). School funding matters for various features relating to school quality: teacher pay and credentials and support services among many others. Nevertheless, a discussion of poverty cannot focus solely on *school* funding alone.

Budgetary figures like those above conceal the meaning of poverty for children outside of school. Without adequate income, parents may frequently move in the search for lower-cost housing, meaning that children transfer from one school to another, leaving children to continuously adjust to new friends and teachers. Children in poor households may be hungry, live in crowded conditions without private space for studying, and lack discretionary money for books, computers, and Internet access. Poor teens may leave school in order to generate income to supplement family earnings. We could go on.

Additional insecurity at the border occurs at the border from migration, citizenship, and legal status or lack thereof. Estimates for the number of immigrants, both legal permanent residents and the undocumented, are difficult to make, especially given the exodus from Mexico and given Mexico's inability to provide safety since 2008, when Ciudad Juárez acquired the infamous distinction as the world's murder capital. Besides these refugees, El Paso is home to immigrant children and especially significant numbers of citizen children (born in the United States) who live in households with at least one undocumented parent (mixed status families). The fear of deportation forever hangs over these households and the children therein.

Some Promising Border Policy Initiatives: The Ysleta Case

Like most school districts in Texas and at the border, Ysleta ISD leaders enjoyed white privilege until the 1980s. Alicia Chacón was the first Hispanic to be elected to the school board in 1970, and during the 1990s, more attention began to be paid to schools south of the "invisible border" (Interstate Highway 10). Like most districts at the border, Ysleta teachers now more accurately reflect the student population they serve, with the majority Hispanic (76%).

Ysleta's vision statement, noted prominently on its website (www.yisd.net) and staff calling cards, has long focused on both pathways to higher education and bilingual capability. This sets Ysleta apart from the other districts in the region:

> All students who enroll in our schools will graduate from high school, fluent in two or more languages, prepared and inspired to continue their education in a four year college, university or institution of higher education so that they become successful citizens in their community.
>
> *Todos los estudiantes que se inscriben en nuestras escuelas se graduarán de la preparatoria, con fluidez en dos o más idiomas, preparados e inspirados para continuar su educación en un colegio, universidad o instituto de educación avanzada con el fin de lograr ser ciudadanos exitosos en su comunidad.*

Although the public and political space for border policy initiatives has shrunk over recent decades, Ysleta ISD established several that we analyze below.

Pathways to High School Completion and College

Ysleta ISD policy, unlike those of most districts in the region, proactively prepares students to treat middle and high school as pathways to higher education. Throughout the 1990s, Texas school bureaucracies made it easier to drop out of school (Romo and Falbo 1996), but Ysleta instituted Project Volver (Return) to use proactive strategies to contact students for return. Ysleta was the first district in the region to provide open access to schools within schools, namely, the Socratic Teacher Training magnet, as well as within-district student choice to attend any high school where space was available (thus moving beyond the neighborhood feeder system which can perpetuate the segregation of impoverished students). In the late 1990s, Ysleta initiated a Go College user-friendly computer center to encourage ninth graders to analyze options in higher education at Ysleta High School, close to the border, and now operate in all eight high schools in Ysleta. Below we highlight two aspects of Ysleta's approach: Student Graduation Plans and No Senior Left Behind.

Rather than merely report graduation rates in accountability systems, Ysleta requires counselors and language arts teachers to work with students to take concrete steps toward graduation and applications to higher education institutions. Students must complete at least one application to higher education institutions. Students must prepare an essay in their junior language arts class to include with college application forms, where needed. And the district subsidizes all students to take the Preliminary Scholastic Aptitude Test (PSAT) and SAT placement exams for admission to higher education unlike the other big urban districts in the region, with the PSAT to be taken no later than October of their junior year, thus avoiding the last minute, possibly lower scores of senior-year preparation. Data from Ysleta ISD shows that the more times (one vs. two) students take the PSAT, the better their scores on SAT.

A total of 2,939 YISD students participated in the SAT in order to meet graduation requirements and graduate in 2009 (2,395 participated in SAT as seniors, 368 as juniors, and 3 as sophomores). In 2010, the number of seniors tested on the SAT totaled 2,766, a decrease of 173 students. Group mean scores increased in all subjects from 2009 to 2010. The mean in critical reading increased from 381 to 390, 402 to 408 in mathematics, and 380 to 385 in writing.

The percentage of seniors participating in the SAT increased from 87% in 2009 to 89% in 2010 (Source: YISD DataMart; see computation below). When these data are disaggregated by ethnicity, it is estimated that the percent Hispanics tested in 2010 was 74% compared to 79% in 2009. Although the percent Hispanics tested decreased by five points, Ysleta ISD Hispanic students continue to test at two-and-a-half times higher than the average rate as compared to other large urban public school districts. Hispanic students represent the largest and fastest-growing minority group taking the SAT and now account for 13.5% of all SAT takers compared to 7.8% 10 years ago. The number of Hispanic testers over 10 years has more than doubled (College Board 2009).

Year	Number participated in SAT	Number of seniors in class	Percent participated in SAT
2009	2,939	3,381	0.869269447
2010	2,766	3,113	0.888531963

No Senior Left Behind (NSLB) was begun in 2007 to reduce the number of students that were ineligible to graduate at the end of their senior year due to failure on the state assessment, insufficient number of credits, and/or attendance issues. To ensure that timely and appropriate intervention is provided, counselors, teachers, and administrators at every high school monitor at-risk students on a weekly basis. For example, students can be referred to the Acceleration, Remediation, and Credit Recovery Program to obtain tutoring, alternative assignments, and other assistance to help complete assignments and pass courses. Every student is expected to follow through, and if they do not, parents are called, counselors intervene, and every effort is made to help the student make progress. The district also utilized response to intervention (RtI), a tiered system of escalating interventions, to address the assistance and intervention needs of students that are underperforming. Other intervention programs include Advancement via Individual Determination (AVID), a program designed to motivate and prepare students for college; Gear

Up; and Twenty-first Century Schools after school programs. An external nonprofit organization with social work professionals, Communities in Schools, also has a presence at many schools in Ysleta District.

Community-Based Experiences

An innovative approach to active learning involves the cultivation of students' experiences as volunteers outside of school. Moreover, early exposure to developing an ethic of service among students will prepare them for engaged public life. Beginning with the 2009–2010 school year, Ysleta adopted a policy requiring all students in grades 9–12 to accumulate 20 volunteer service hours per year, so that by the school year 2012–2013, and thereafter, all seniors will graduate with an accrued total of 80 volunteer service hours. Each campus designates one person per grade level to monitor the documentation of service hours and ensures the inclusion of accumulated hours in the student's personal graduation plan.

Ysleta ISD defines volunteer service to the community as service performed for approved persons, organizations, or agencies outside of the student's home and/or family. The service must be performed without monetary compensation, and hours shall be accumulated in the form of time. Services cannot be performed as part of the regular school day, unless students are participating in a school-sponsored community service project. Examples of approved agencies include Humane Society, Senior Centers, Habitat for Humanity, Battered Women's Shelter, and Child Crisis Center.

Bilingual Education

In 1994, Ysleta ISD established the first two-way dual-language Spanish-English program in El Paso County at Eastwood Heights Elementary School. In 1995, Ysleta opened Alicia R. Chacón International Language Magnet School with 282 students in grades kindergarten through third grade learning English, Spanish, and their choice of a third language—German, Russian, Chinese, or Japanese. Today, 772 students are enrolled at the school (expanded in subsequent years to include grades kindergarten through eighth grade), and many are on a waiting list. In 2001, the first cohort of students from Alicia Chacón entered Del Valle High School, and they graduated in 2005 with dual-language honors.

In 1997, Hacienda Heights Elementary School opened a communications program offering a dual-language Spanish-English program with a third-language experience in Japanese or French. In subsequent years, the district initiated an expansion of the dual-language Spanish-English programs across the district.

In 2010, 24 elementary, 6 middle, and 4 high schools offer dual-language programs, including Eastwood Knolls, Ysleta ISD's newest international school adding Mandarin Chinese as a third language to their existing exemplary dual-language program. Ysleta plans to establish a third international school in the next 2–3 years.

Conclusion

In this chapter, we have analyzed national, state, and local policies and practices related to accountability testing, focusing especially on border resident English-language learners and students in poverty. Once a decentralized education system, and not necessarily one that offered quality education to all students, the United States and the State of Texas have increasingly centralized educational policy-making, offering some budgetary resources but also imposing requirements that burden students and teachers in the border region. High-stakes accountability testing systems create burdens for students and sustain achievement gaps (as measured by the tests), particularly for English-language learners.

Despite these burdens imposed upon districts, teachers, and students, promising educational practices occasionally emerge, such as those associated with strong dual-language programs. This chapter has also focused on promising local policy initiatives that address issues in the border region. Ysleta Independent School District proactively supports students' pathways through high school graduation into higher education in concrete and effective ways, as detailed in this chapter. The district also adopted policies that support civic engagement and volunteerism, sustaining active learning approaches. Finally, the district is expanding innovative campus models within the district that incorporate evidence-based research on bilingual education that meshes with the importance of multiple-language speakers in the border gateway of the Americas. The local policies we analyzed illustrate models that might be adopted not only by other districts along the border but also in schools elsewhere in the United States as the nation deals with the confluence of language learners, poverty, and budgetary difficulties in an increasingly rigid national educational accountability system.

Our chapter also illustrates the importance of access points for improved policies in the pluralist democratic institutions of a federal system of government. Under federalism, with its divided authority between federal, state, and local governments, decision-making is complex, fragmented, and time-consuming. However, the system also opens space for innovative initiatives to be put into practice at various points, accessible to the voices of educators, parents, and other constituencies. Parents, educators, and school-board members in Ysleta used the open access points to establish effective policies which improve educational achievement, civic engagement, and pathways to higher education in and beyond the border region.

References

Center for Public Policy Priorities [CPPP]. (2009). *Kids living on the border more than twice as likely to live in poverty.* Retrieved from http://www.cppp.org/files/KC/BKC_McAllen.ppt# 270,12.

Cervera Gómez, L., Lizárraga Bustamante, G., & Sánchez Guillen, C. (2008). Estudio georeferencial de la Evaluación Nacional de Logro Académico en Centros Escolares [ENLACE] en el municipio de Ciudad Juárez, Chihuahua: Análisis especial [Georeferenced study of the National Evaluation of Academic Achievement in School Centers [ENLACE] in the municipality of Ciudad Juárez, Chihuahua. Special analysis]. *Revista Electrónica de Investigacióon Educativa [REDIE], 10*(1). http://redie.uabc.mx/vol10no1/contenido-cervera.html.

College Board. (2009). *College-Bound seniors are most diverse group ever to take SAT as more minority students prepare for higher education.* Retrieved from http://press.collegeboard.org/releases/2009/2009-college-bound-seniors-are-most-diverse-group-ever-take-sat174-more-minority-students-pr.

Crawford, J. (2004). *Educating English learners: Language diversity in the classroom* (5th ed.). Los Angeles: Bilingual Education Services, Inc.

Cummins, J. (1979). Cognitive/academic language proficiency, linguistic interdependence, the optimum age question and some other matters. *Working Papers on Bilingualism, 19*, 121–129.

Cummins, J. (1984). *Bilingualism and special education.* Clevedon: Multilingual Matters.

Cummins, J. (2000). *Language, power and pedagogy.* Clevedon: Multilingual Matters.

Dow, P. (2008). *Dual-language education: A longitudinal study of students' achievement in an El Paso County, Texas school district.* Unpublished doctoral dissertation, The University of Texas at El Paso.

Dow, P., Krashen, S., & Tinajero, J. (2010, Winter). A longitudinal confirmation of the interdependence hypothesis. *The International Journal of Foreign Language Teaching, 5*(2): 2–3.

Hakuta, K., Butler, Y., & Witt, D. (2000). *How long does it take English learners to attain proficiency?* (Policy Report). Berkley: The University of California Linguistic Minority Research Institute.

Hochschild, J., & Scrovonik, N. (2003). *The American dream and the public schools.* New York: Oxford University Press.

Intercultural Development Research Association [IDRA]. (2010). Retrieved from www.idra.org.

Krashen, S. (2003). Three roles for reading for language-minority students. In G. Garcia (Ed.), *English learners: Reaching the highest level of English proficiency* (pp. 55–70). Newark: International Reading Association.

McNeil, L. (2005). Faking equity: High-stakes testing and the education of Latino youth. In A. Valenzuela (Ed.), *Leaving children behind: How 'Texas-Style' accountability fails Latino youth* (pp. 57–112). Albany: State University of New York Press.

McNeil, L., Coppola, E., Radigan, J., & Vazquez Heilig, J. (2008, January). Avoidable losses: High-stakes accountability and the drop-out crisis. *Educational Policy Analysis Archives, 16*(3). http://epaa.asu.edu/epaa.v16n3.

Rippberger, S., & Staudt, K. (2003). *Pledging allegiance: Learning nationalism in El Paso-Juárez.* New York: Routledge/Falmer.

Rocha, G., & Webking, R. (1993). *Politics and public education: Edgewood v. Kirby and the reform of public school financing in Texas* (2nd ed.). Minneapolis: West Publishing.

Romo, H., & Falbo, T. (1996). *Latino high school graduation.* Austin: University of Texas Press.

Sharp, J. (1998). *Bordering the future: Challenge and opportunity in the Texas border region.* Austin: Texas Comptroller of Public Accounts.

Shirley, R. (1997). *Community organizing and urban school reform.* Austin: The University of Texas Press.

Southern Education Foundation [SEF]. (2010). *The worst of times: Children in extreme poverty in the south and nation.* Retrieved from http://www.southerneducation.org/pdf/TWOT-Extreme%20Child%20Poverty%20Rpt-Final.pdf.

Staudt, K. (2010). Texas accountability tests: Standardizing disengagement for Latino students? In D. Leal & K. Meier (Eds.), *Politics of Latino education* (pp. 43–57). New York: Teachers College Press/Columbia University.

Staudt, K., & Méndez, Z. (2010). Schooling for global competitiveness in the border metropolitan region. In K. Staudt, C. Fuentes, & C. Monárrez Fragoso (Eds.), *Cities and citizenship at the U.S.-Mexico border: The Paso del Norte metropolitan region* (pp. 173–194). New York: Palgrave.

Texas Association of School Boards [TASB]. (2008). *A cost analysis for Texas public schools.* Retrieved from http://www.tasb.org/legislative/legislative/reports/documents/costanalysis09.pdf. Accessed 30 Dec 2010.

Texas Education Agency [TEA]. (2011a). *Academic excellence indicator system.* Retrieved January 15, 2011, from www.tea.state.tx.us/aeis.

Texas Education Agency [TEA]. (2011b, April 22). *State of Texas Assessments of Academic Readiness (STAAR™) resources.* Retrieved from http://www.tea.state.tx.us/student.assessment/.staar/.

Thomas, W., & Collier, V. (2002). *A national study of school effectiveness for language minority students' long-term academic achievement.* Santa Cruz/Washington, DC: Center for Research on Education, Diversity & Excellence.

U.S. Commission on Civil Rights. (1969–1974). *Mexican American Education Study [MAES]. Vols. 1–6.* Washington, DC.

Valenzuela, A. (1999). *Subtractive schooling: U.S.-Mexican youth and the politics of caring.* Albany: State University of New York at Albany Press.

Valenzuela, A. (2005). *Leaving children behind: How 'Texas-Style' accountability fails Latino youth.* Albany: State University of New York Press.

Ysleta Independent School District [YISD]. (2010a). *YISD Datamart,* password protected – Dow access. Retrieved from https://datamart.yisd.net/.

Ysleta Independent School District [YISD]. (2010b). *YISD statistics.* Retrieved from http://www2.yisd.net/education/components/scrapbook/default.php?sectiondetailid=26&.

Chapter 13
Border Challenges and Ethnic Struggles for Social Justice in Arizona: Hispanic Communities Under Siege

Rosalía Solórzano Torres

This chapter focuses on border challenges, ethnic struggles, and the responses of Latina/o communities in Arizona. The Arizona's immigration reform, SB 1070, and the anti-ethnic studies law, HB 2281, attempt to streamline undocumented migration and the erasure of La Raza and Mexican-American Studies at the Tucson Unified School District. The dissemination of political hateful discourses guides the militarization of the border as an important social location and the creation of communities under siege. These laws dehumanize and create misguided and a blatant climate of racial hostility against Mexican and Hispanic communities, particularly those situated on the US-Mexico border. This chapter concludes with a brief examination of the repercussions of Republican political vitriol, a dissemination of an "ecology of fear," and the assassination attempt launched against Congresswoman Gabrielle Giffords, which brutally ended the lives of six individuals and left 14 others wounded in Tucson, Arizona.

Border Challenges

The border is a dynamic space where social, cultural, economic, and a political multiplicity of paradoxical scenarios emerge and are recycled only to reemerge again (James Hernandez 2007). It is critical to acknowledge and focus on the borderscapes of paradox: the points of emergence, sustenance, and connection, but also those of discontinuities and fragmentation between and within the border, but from a perspective of the people who live there, as a "shared community and unified space" (James Hernandez 2007, p. 21). The US-Mexico border becomes

R.S. Torres (✉)
Pima Community College, Tucson, Arizona, USA
e-mail: solorzanoros@hotmail.com

M. Lusk et al. (eds.), *Social Justice in the U.S.-Mexico Border Region*,
DOI 10.1007/978-94-007-4150-8_13,

the site of people's reactions to binational dictates at local and state levels. I focus on the SB 1070 and the HB 2281 particularly from the impacts upon Mexican and Hispanic communities and how these and dominant communities at large engage in the paradoxes brought about by political and cultural challenges to all people. "The border is not only the place of danger, pollution, violence, and transgression of dominant representations. Here, collective and individual efforts to heal, rehabilitate, and celebrate also renew community ties daily" (James Hernández 2007, p. 21). At the core of this metaphor, the fluidity of social interaction, human resources, and capital are continually enforced by a binational diversity of complex levels of bureaucracies and institutions. The issues of immigration and border economies are woven into complex national political scenarios where individuals become involved in the forging and creation of laws, and the ways that these laws are also prioritized and then enacted.

The US-Mexico border becomes a space of transformation and resistance. It is also a compelling social and political location for "marginalizing and unifying practices that constitute the border as paradox" (James Hernandez 2007, p. 22). Although the US-Mexico border is socially located at the "margins – the edge, it may also be conceptualized as a center of global and political economic change" (Staudt 1998, p. 10). The border, as a borderscape of paradox and a localized entity, becomes a most fluid social and cultural spatial entity defining the situated lives of its border citizens' lives. Through daily social and economic interaction, individuals sustain their cultural and political identities on both sides of the border.

Mexicans, Chicanas, and Chicanos historically have become ethno-racially defined, politically disempowered, and economically marginalized communities throughout the Southwest, and especially on the US-Mexico border (see Chap. 1). Mexicans, Chicanas, and Chicanos have continued a history of struggles and resisted the "melting pot" and cultural erasure designed and guided by Anglo-American ideology. The historical experiences of conquest, whether as internal colonies, annexation, or as a result of a war, have deeply affected and weakened the sociopolitical and economic lives of minority groups in the United States.

Currently, some of the most salient social structural issues impacting US-Mexico border communities are national and state security. These issues have become a top priority for the state of Arizona legislators since the aftermath of September 11. Protecting the safety of the US-Mexico border has become one of the most heated political, social, and economic debates of this century. In terms of national security and political economic discourses, some of the most salient issues impacting Mexican and Hispanic communities on the US-Mexico border are immigration regulation of undocumented migrants by the Department of Homeland Security, Immigration and Customs Enforcement (ICE), the building of walls and fences, virtual and human surveillance, national nativism and xenophobia, a national environment of political vitriol (the proliferation of hate and violence scripted into Republican political campaigns), federal militarization of the border, economic issues, crime, drug trafficking, vigilantism of paramilitary groups like the Minutemen, education, international commerce and trade.

In this chapter, I focus on the impact of the militarization and the political discourses formulated by Arizona legislators in creating a militarized border zone between the US-Mexico through the immigration reform law, SB 1070. I recur to research findings that seem to indicate Arizona legislators have been successful in creating inflammatory policies fueled by insecurity and xenophobia targeting and maintaining Mexican and Hispanic communities under siege, particularly those closer to the US-Mexico border. Arizona's anti-immigrant legislation creates an apparatus of control targeting minority groups and harassing Mexican and Latino communities. The new immigration law SB 1070 and the anti-ethnic studies law HB 2281 enacted by politicians in the state of Arizona demonstrate the negative impacts of policies aiming to discredit, label, and ostracize Mexican and Latina/o communities.

Crucial in our understanding of borderscape paradoxes is that for Mexicans, Chicanas, and Chicanos, the US-Mexico Southwest and the borderlands are primordial cultural, demographic, and geographic spaces: a homeland. I agree that at the core of complex social structural subordinating dynamics driven by state economic, demographic, and political processes lie the possibilities of political transformation and agency by the less powerful (Staudt 2009). The study of these borderscapes of paradox creates long-term heuristic impacts and, at the short term, immediate responses to local, state, and national control imposed on individuals and communities.

The Effects of the Immigration Reform Law and the Anti-ethnic Studies Law in Arizona

On April 23, 2010, governor of Arizona, Jan Brewer, signed SB 1070, the immigration reform law that became effective in 2011. The passage of this law crystallizes political interests espoused by the right-wing agenda in Arizona. SB 1070, and much like HB 2281, aims to eliminate ethnic studies in schools and universities (National Institute for Latino Policy 2010). Other states such as Alabama and Georgia have followed Arizona with similar and even more draconian laws.

Three years before the passage of this law, Prince William County, Virginia, introduced a similar bill and created an environment of fear in the communities of color, as well as negatively impacting all the community. "Our county was severely hurt economically. Many, many people left this county," said Nancy Lyall, a Mexicans without Borders member. "Prince William County has had some of the biggest depreciation of homes of anywhere in this area" (McCarren 2010, p. 1).

National social and political elements have been very important in facing up to the Republican imposition of SB 1070. There is national discontentment and preoccupation of the citizenry on the various "unresolved" issues created by immigration legislative disputes. The Hispanic communities have historically voted in support of the Democratic Party, perhaps with the exception of the Cuban contingency which has tended to vote Republican. For Hispanics, the fact that Democrats have failed to prioritize Hispanic issues and that President Obama has failed, so far, to create and enact a national immigration law addressing "amnesty and legalization" of undocumented migrants in the country has constituted a serious concern. Early in his administration, President Obama shifted his call for bipartisan collaboration, particularly in addressing immigration issues, the creation of jobs, and the budget deficits.

In Arizona, the perceived "uncontrolled" undocumented immigration in the United States and the militarization of the US-Mexico border has been the core center of SB 1070. The perception by politicians of the "invasion of the border by undocumented migrants" both at the national and state levels has resulted in a "flooding" of border patrol agents, surveillance vehicles, and top-of-the-line technology—cameras and stadium lights, all along the 2,000 miles shared between Mexico and the United States. During a testimony to the Senate Committee on Homeland Security last year, Dennis Burke, US attorney for Arizona, noted that Arizona now has more than 6,000 federal law-enforcement agents, with the majority of them employed by the Border Patrol representing nearly ten agents for every mile of international line between Arizona and Sonora. The Border Patrol presence has been backed by increases in counter-smuggling technology and intelligence, the establishment of permanent highway checkpoints, and a dramatic increase in customs inspectors at US ports (Wagner 2010).

Wagner (2010) asserts that DHS has reported the construction of 347 miles of pedestrian fences and 299 miles of "vehicles barriers." Over 660 miles of border have been built along the US-Mexico border. These physical obstacles are constructed to disrupt and discourage undocumented migration. At the same time, these *borderscapes of paradox* have engaged in a potentially irreversible destruction of endangered species through partitioning their ecological habitat by the construction of walls and fences. Let us look at the findings that conclusively invalidate the "invasion of the border" position and its pro-militarization of the border arguments.

Doris Meissner (2010), senior fellow at the Migration Policy Institute, who served as a commissioner of the US Immigration and Naturalization Service, debunks the argument that immigration is at an all-time high, and that most new immigrants arrive in the country without documents. She calls these arguments "fabrications" against immigrants which "daily resonate" within legislative sessions. Today, about two-thirds of immigrants are documented, either as naturalized citizens or as lawful permanent residents. Of approximately 10.8 million of unauthorized immigrants who are in the country, about 40% arrived with authorization but overstayed their visas. Although the unauthorized immigrant population includes more people from Mexico than from any other country, Mexicans are also the largest group of lawful migrants.

The issues of militarizing and shutting off the border in order to keep its communities "safe" have also been contested by research. One of the most important findings presented is that "... apprehensions along the U.S.-Mexico border have declined by more than 50% over the past 4 years while increases in the size of the undocumented population continue and had been growing by about 50,000 a year" (Meissner 2010, p. 1). Although undocumented migration and anti-immigrant sentiments have been increasing throughout Arizona, the US-Mexico border has never been more secure. Sheriff Dupnik, responding to the militarization of the border, argued that "This is a media-created event." Dupnik said, "I hear politicians on TV saying the border has gotten worse. Well, the fact of the matter is that the border has never been more secure" (Wagner 2010).

The enactment of draconian laws, SB 1070 and HB 2281, had significant electoral consequences within Arizona. Sheriff Dupnik has denounced the Arizona's immigration reform law. This law has become a model for the rest of the country of "what not to do" (Dupnik 2010). Yet, there is an opposite reaction created by the alarming issues of militarizing and shutting off the border in order to keep its communities safe, an environment of fear and terror created by the media and the legislation. The immigration reform law, SB 1070, has mobilized anti-immigrant sentiment, not only at a state but also at national levels. The anti-immigrant policies endorsed by the governor of Arizona, Jan Brewer, have triggered a momentum for what I call the *cloneglomerization*, or the increased cloning and dissemination of SB 1070 throughout the United States by various states. A triggering effect of the immigration reform law is likely to have a multiplying effect during the next decade. Texas Representative Debbie Riddle is one of the politicians who lined up to be the first to file an Arizona style immigration bill for Texas. She filed on November 8, 2010 (Johnson 2010).

This cloneglomerization effect goes hand in hand and is likely an effect of the recent unprecedented national electoral power gained by the Republican Party. According to Johnson (2010), the following states are likely to consider SB 1070 policies in upcoming legislative sessions: Ohio, Tennessee, Colorado, Georgia, Mississippi, Oklahoma, South Carolina, Minnesota, Missouri, Nebraska, New Mexico, Pennsylvania, and Utah. Wessler (2010) contends that white anxiety about the rapidly growing Latina/o population may also fuel anti-immigrant laws. The manner by which extremist legislation operates is by labeling, blaming, ostracizing, and demonizing the immigrant. This modus operandi becomes the venue by which various counties, cities, and states have been crafting and passing equally draconian legislation across the country. The SB 1070 and HB 2281 laws have been crucial for the reelection of Arizona's Governor Jan Brewer to a second term in office.

The Anti-immigration "Scapegoat" Effect

Migrants have been blamed for a gamut of problems such as the high unemployment in the nation. What are the evidence-based findings in refuting this assertion? Research findings show that although immigrants account for 12.5% of the population, they make up 15% of the workforce. They are overrepresented among workers largely because the rest of the population is aging. For over two decades, migrants and their children have accounted for 58% of the US population. Immigrants tend to be concentrated in high- and low-skilled occupations that complement—rather than compete with—jobs held by native workers (Meissner 2010, p. 1). There is a widely shared belief among minority groups that SB 1070 leads to an expansion of invasive political control strategies used by the state apparatus in order to "control and cleanse" the border. The argument yields for protecting the region from potential national security attacks, crime, delinquency, the smuggling of drugs, and finally "shutting off or sealing" the US-Mexico border with walls, fences, surveillance, and the National Guard. In enacting all of these national safety measures, national and state governments target immigrant communities, which become under siege through the sum operation of all of these invasive processes. Latinas/os become scapegoats for the state.

Ethnic Struggles for Social Justice: Responses from Communities Under Siege

Numerous rallies and marches at local and state levels and national, political, economic, religious, educational, as well as law enforcement leaders from both sides of the border have denounced this law and have formed national and international coalitions to oppose it. MALDEF, ACLU, ACLU of Arizona, LULAC, and NILC are among a coalition of organizations legally challenging the immigration reform law (de La Torre 2010). Coalitions of civil rights groups and activists have condemned HB 2281 and the immigration reform law.

About 200 groups joined an economic boycott against Arizona including African American and Jewish organizations. They asked members and supporters not to endorse conferences, or planning conventions in Arizona, and to abstain from buying goods. Alessandra Soler Meetze, executive director of American Civil Liberties Union of Arizona stated that "If these laws were implemented, citizens would effectively have to carry 'their papers' at all times to avoid arrest. It is a low point in modern America when a state law requires police to demand documents from people on the street" (de La Torre 2010).

On May 6, 2010, an issue of the *New York Times* entitled "Latino Groups Urge Boycott of Arizona over the New Law" by Julia Preston informed the public that the National Council of La Raza, or NCLR, the League of United Latin American Citizens, or LULAC, as well the National Puerto Rican Coalition announced a business boycott against the state of Arizona. US Representative Raul Grijalva, Democrat from Arizona, joined the boycott at a cost of receiving numerous death threats on his life. Janet Murguía, president of the NCLR, announced that "The new (immigration reform) law is so extreme, and its proponents appear so immune to an appeal to reason, nothing short of these extraordinary measures is required" (Preston 2010).

The faculty, administrators, and staff of three of Arizona's universities—Arizona State University, Northern Arizona University, and the University of Arizona—voiced their strong opposition to SB 1070. Similarly, NACCS, the National

Association of Chicana and Chicano Studies, and MALCS, *Mujeres Activas en Letras y Cambio Social,* publicly denounced SB 1070 and HB 2281. NACCS and HACU joined and endorsed the economic boycott against Arizona.

At the University of Arizona, the Faculty Senate denounced SB 1070, and in a letter written by the president of the University of Arizona, Robert N. Shelton criticized SB 1070 as "flawed public policy that sends all the wrong messages about our state." He wrote, "The anger that has been generated by SB 1070 is understandable. Many on our campus-whether international students and visitors, or faculty and staff who fear their ethnicity will make them targets-are anxious about its implementation. It is the expectation of most legal experts that SB 1070 will be overturned by the courts. Whether or not this happens, I am certain that no one on our campus should fear that because of their ethnicity or national origin they will be accosted by our police" (Shelton 2010).

In Arizona, the *racialized* discourses brought about by SB 1070 and HB 2281 endorsed by Republicans, right-wing groups, administrators, and legislators continue to stir a collective awareness and actions from people across the nation (Rogers 2010). Ethnic Studies Week was a nationally coordinated event aimed to defend ethnic studies in Arizona and inspired by opposition to the passage of the HB 2281 in Arizona's Public Schools and the May 21 passage of new social sciences standards by the Texas State Board of Education. As of August 12, 2010, the group had over 1,300 members from across the nation. The University of Arizona Gender and Women Studies Department served as an organizational and leadership umbrella for the various community organizations, educators, and activists who organized and participated in celebrating Ethnic Studies Week in Tucson, Arizona, from October 4 to 10, 2010.

The Dehumanization Effect of the Immigration Reform Law

Arizona Senator Russell Pearce, author of SB 1070, has predicted that the law would discourage, stop, and eradicate undocumented migration and crime in order to *secure* neighborhoods throughout Arizona. However, a statistic disregarded by Mr. Pearce provided by the American Immigration Council of the Immigration Policy Center (IPC) shows that crime rates have systematically fallen in Arizona since 2005. Research findings gathered by the IPC on undocumented immigrants show that immigrants are less likely to commit crimes than native-born individuals (Immigration Policy Center [IPC] 2010). This report concludes that immigration policies are not effective ways of addressing crimes because the majority of those committing crimes are not immigrants.

The immigration reform law has been contested on the fact that some of its regulations seemed to be "unconstitutional" and restrictive of individuals' freedom. Pima County Sheriff Clarence W. Dupnik, in a guest opinion on May 6, 2010, harshly criticized and pointed to two stances by which the law would delegate the enforcement to in demanding documents from those individuals stopped when there may be "reasonable suspicion" that they may be undocumented (Dupnik 2010). The criminalization and dehumanization of communities of color is evident. They are likely to become under siege through the enforcement of this law, through physical, psychological, cultural, and political control.

Last year in Phoenix, Arizona, Sheriff Joe Arpaio of Maricopa County directed his officers to raid a local company, Lasermasters, and arrested 24 immigrants. The workers were charged with felony identity theft for working with false documents (Preston 2010). Opposition to the immigration reform law immediately triggered the responses of Latina/o communities throughout Arizona and created nationwide coalitions denouncing SB 1070. Communities of color launched rallies, protests, marches, and an economic boycott against the state of Arizona. In Los Angeles, California, more than a dozen protesters were arrested by police officers for chaining themselves together and blocking traffic in front of a federal immigration center for protesting against the Arizona law (Preston 2010). These forms of resistance are likely to increase in Arizona in the future, particularly before a new presidential election.

The Current State of the Immigration Reform Law, SB 1070

The immigration reform law went through litigation processes in challenging the legality and validity of its language and its impacts on communities of color and other communities as well. Arizona had spent over a million dollars defending its law in court by July of 2010. SB 1070 became a law on July 29, 2010. President Obama won an injunction against most of the SB 1070 law, except for the employer provisions. In November of 2010, Supreme Court arguments made it likely that the injunction against the law would be sustained (Johnson 2010). US District Court Judge Susan Bolton issued a preliminary injunction preventing several sections of Arizona's new immigration law from becoming law. Her decision impacts the immigration reform law by removing:

- The portion of the law that requires an officer to make a reasonable attempt to determine the immigration status of a person stopped, detained, or arrested if there is reasonable suspicion that they are in the country illegally
- The section that creates a crime of failure to apply for or carry "alien-registration papers." The portion that makes it a crime for illegal immigrants to solicit, apply for, or perform work. (This does not include the section on day laborers.)
- The section that allows for a warrantless arrest of a person where there is a probable cause to believe they have committed a public offense that makes them removable from the United States

The Arizona court decision affirmed the following aspects of the law: The ruling says that law enforcement still must enforce federal immigration laws to the fullest extent of the law when SB 1070 went into effect on Thursday, July 29, 2010. Individuals will still be able to sue an agency if they adopt a policy that restricts such enforcement. That section of the law creates misdemeanor crimes for harboring and transporting illegal immigrants. Her ruling followed hearings on three of seven federal lawsuits challenging SB 1070. Judge Susan Bolton also denied legal requests by Governor Jan Brewer, Maricopa County Sheriff Joe Arpaio, and several other defendants seeking to have the lawsuits dismissed because, they argued, the plaintiffs did not prove that they would be harmed by the law if it went into effect (Rau et al. 2010).

More of the Same Political Rhetoric of Fear and Cultural Erasure

On May 2010, Governor Brewer signed HB 2281 and the bill became a law on December 31, 2010. HB 2281 is widely interpreted as the banning of ethnic studies in the public schools of the state of Arizona. This law specifically targets the Raza and Mexican-American or Chicana/o Studies Program at the Tucson Unified School District. The author of this law is Tom Horne who at the time was the State Superintendent of Public Instruction. Although nearly half of Arizona's public school classrooms are filled by Hispanics, HB 2281 makes it illegal for these students to learn about the richness of their history and culture.

This law also includes the firing or reassignment of language teachers with "heavy accents" and "ungrammatical English." The law states: "That any course, class, instruction, or material may not be primarily designed for pupils of a particular ethnic group as determined by the State Superintendent of Instruction. State aid will be withheld from any school district or charter school that does not comply" (Calefati 2010).

HB 2281 is also a political interest disguised as an educational reform, an "Americanization" reform much like the ones established by the Federal Government in the beginning of the twentieth century for assimilating all people of color. Tom Horne argues, "Traditionally, the American public school system has brought together students from different backgrounds and taught them to be Americans and to treat each other as individuals, not on the basis of their ethnic backgrounds" (Calefati 2010). Under this statement lies the foundation of cultural erasure, as effective political right-wing rhetoric in creating collective historical amnesia and separating specifically Mexicans and Hispanics from their ethnic and cultural roots. It is a mechanism of racial supremacy and control. Delegitimizing the histories of individuals through economic control, instilling fear and xenophobia, creates subjugation and repression.

Tom Horne, Republican, won the seat for attorney general for the state of Arizona in 2010 defeating Democrat Felicia Rotellini. He is a strong supporter of the immigration reform law. The HB 2281 law also denies Hispanics their right to define the most important pedagogies to educate their youth. This borderscape of paradox juxtaposes the roles and rights that pedagogues have in educational institutions with those of politicians, individuals like Horne, and Huppenthal who use their political appointments and political power attempting to interpret educational pedagogies, as well as dictating erasure at those teachings perceived to be a threat to the status quo. Hence, Horne's interpretations of Raza and Mexican American Studies as a threat to American values shows a political "ethnic chauvinism" against Mexican American Studies.

Certainly under HB 2281, it is politicians in Phoenix who will issue the sanctions impacting not only students but pedagogues as well. The anti-ethnic studies law is yet another distinct manifestation of an "ecology of fear." Extreme right-wing, xenophobic politicians become the executors of education by exercising the law to censure educational materials—"legally mandating" administrators to enforce a racist law and enforcing sanctions on those who refuse to follow these mandates. Horne argued that students will still be exposed to other cultures and traditions within the state standards and dictated by the politicians (Strauss 2010).

Hence, it is not educators but politicians who will micromanage the teaching processes and say, what, who, when, and how to teach the children of minority groups (not only Hispanics) their cultural heritage. These are effective ways of cultural erasure through the removal of ethnic identity and cultural pride, or a "whitewashed" process impacting the future generations of educated Hispanic youth. The National Institute for Latino Policy announced on October 20, 2010, that 11 teachers were suing Arizona over the new "anti-Latino" schools law. According to Martinez and Gutierrez (2010), 11 Tucson, Arizona, educators sued the state board of education and the superintendent for what the teachers consider an "anti-Hispanic" ban looming on Mexican-American Studies. The teachers are suing because HB 2281, which went into law May of 2010, violates free speech, equal protection, and due process.

Meyers and Orozco (2010) of Oregon State University have studied educational gains by minority students. They argue that there is multidisciplinary evidence concluding that student learning is positively correlated to student success when students are offered culturally relevant and community-minded curriculum. These scholars argue that when students are encouraged to think critically from cultural differences to gender equity and transnational relations, they are more likely to be educationally engaged for higher levels of education (Meyers and Orozco 2010). In addition, targeting Raza and Chicana/o Studies program, in the Tucson Unified School district, could potentially negatively affect students' academic achievement and reverse the academic gains they have made over the last several years.

Grado (2010) reports that Senator John Huppenthal intends to take his fight against ethnic studies programs as elected superintendent of Public Instruction in Arizona, a position previously held by Tom Horne. Political xenophobia and educational micromanagement permeate in defining the content and approaches of what types of instruction are permitted at local and state levels in Arizona. The banning of ethnic studies continues the hostilities against the Mexican and Latina/o and people of color communities. Although the immigration reform and the anti-ethnic studies laws are effective in the state of Arizona, collective organization of Mexican and Latina/o groups is crucial in creating resistance in structuring counter-hegemonic transformation not only at local, state, but also at national levels. For the next decade, it is likely that public disobedience and transformative political coalitions will increase and continue providing strength resisting and increasing the struggles for representation and social justice. The more intense these hostilities are throughout Arizona, the more likely communities will continue the resistance and struggle against them. The more laws are created aiming to control and repress communities, the more likely these struggles for social justice would intensify beyond 2011.

Toward Political Representation of Hispanic Communities

Currently, Mexican and Latina/o communities continue to legally challenge, confront, and resist the socioeconomic structural inequalities affecting their living standards. They are proactively paving the way for increasing their political participation at local and national levels. According to the US Census (2009), the number of Hispanic citizens who reported voting in the 2008 presidential election reached 9.7 million. The most important priority for Mexican-Americans in Arizona is challenging and changing the present authoritarian and unconstitutional environments created by its legislation through a political voter agenda that includes and unites all Latino and Latina ethnic and national groups in the United States. The organized efforts create a direct and well structured, inclusive, political voter agenda for the future elections.

Historically, Hispanics have been voting overwhelmingly Democratic, particularly Puerto Ricans and Mexicans. For the right-wing Republican extremists, the Hispanic vote threatens their political control. Rodríguez et al. (2010) remind us that Republicans are threatened by the possibility of the Hispanic vote turning Arizona into a blue state. Hence, the rationale of the immigration reform and the anti-ethnic studies laws aim at minimizing and preventing the number of Hispanics who become US citizens, creating a displacement and removal of the Hispanic population, and the developing policies aiming to minimize and restrict social, health delivery systems in order to minimize the Hispanic political participation in Arizona.

The Hispanic vote is shifting electoral power and reinforcing national political representation. The way to electoral power is to choose from the "lesser of two evils" and move forward to structuring and gaining political representation and power within the Democratic Party. For example, the "Tequila Party" created by various business entrepreneurs, industrialists, educators, and professionals would "ideally" organize to influence the Democratic Party in order to advance Hispanic leadership, interests, pro-immigrant rights, and strengthening interethnic solidarity among Hispanic groups.

Transformative political coalitions are empowered with representation through leadership coalitions making Latina/o communities a priority on the national agenda. Currently, the level of political harassment and antagonism against immigrant communities throughout the United States would likely increase. This represents a serious concern for the Democratic Party in upcoming elections. Collective organization is necessary for resistance and to attempt social justice against state or global economic forces. The decade from 2010 to 2020 is undoubtedly a ripe historical time for Hispanics to become politically engaged, particularly for social demographic and economic issues—a decade to fulfill their own public political agendas.

The Ecology of Fear and the Repercussions of Political Vitriolic Rhetoric

Professor Gerardo Devón Peña's concept "ecology of fear" illustrates the Arizona political climate and how "the manipulation and creation of story lines which have a political and civic climate, deliberately manipulated by politicians, produce a climate of intolerance, fear, insecurity, and hatred that is hostile to any one appearing 'foreign' to the self-image of 'white Americans'—whether immigrants or people of color in general" (Peña 2010, p. 2).

Congresswoman Gabrielle Giffords is not separate from Hispanic communities because of her political priorities on health care and immigration. Since the attack on her person, a multiplicity of media sources has reported on her wellness process. Congresswoman Giffords' political labor on behalf of equitable representation for people potentially could have made her a "target" and a real threat to the Republican Party, Tea Party members, and its extreme Christian right wing which is vehemently anti-populist and antidemocratic, despite their political rhetoric and discourses.

There are social, cultural, and political consequences affecting Arizona's political environment as an aftermath of the shootings. Congresswoman Giffords's future representation in the Senate has been removed and stopped from a pathway of bipartisan civil dialogue and political momentum. Giffords is well loved by her constituents and is perceived by many as a leader who was attempting to bridge and connect the differences between constituents. She has tried to reach between the liberal and conservatives by weaving mutual political, economic, social, and cultural understandings that would ultimately serve for the benefit of the community at large.

The assailant, Jared Lee Loughner, shot Congresswoman Giffords at point blank. Although seriously wounding her, miraculously Giffords survived the attack. Loughner's shooting rampage that left six people dead and wounded 14 others changed the history of Arizona and the people of Tucson forever. Who is culpable for this atrocious act of violence? Whether the assailant is perceived as an isolated mental illness or insanity case, psychiatrists argue that it is entirely possible for such an individual with bizarre behavior, psychotic behavior, antisocial behavior, and "the belief that one's mind is being externally controlled could be provoked to violence by rising levels of vitriol in political discourse" (Billeaud and Watson 2011).

Dissemination of an "ecology of fear" by political extremist right-wing vitriol is likely to be correlated with the shootings. Gun imagery, talk of "targeting" elected officials and "taking out political opponents" espoused by individuals like Glenn Beck or Sarah Palin's March 2010 web graphic targeting congressional districts, among them Congresswoman Gabrielle Giffords, trigger real violent consequences. Tea Party Iraq veteran Jesse Kelly held an event advertised with a vocabulary of destruction creating a warlike environment, the words "Get on Target for victory in November. Help remove Gabrielle Giffords from office. Shoot a fully automatic M16 with Jesse Kelly," in taking the district for Republicans. This scenario depicts a warlike environment which is deliberately engineered to create terror and violence. It is irresponsible political vitriol rhetoric with a vocabulary of bellicose metaphors of fear and physical threats, psychological intimidation, and violent imagery.

Giffords had previously addressed the violence issue in an interview with Chuck Todd of MSNBC. She said that Palin had put the "crosshairs of a gun sight over our district" and that "when people do that, they have got to realize there are consequences to that action." According to Rich (2011), at least three others of the 20 members of Congress on Palin's map were also hit with vandalism or death threats. Palin's map read, *"Don't retreat, Instead-Reload!"*

The following two acts of violence were also happening in Tucson, Arizona, in what became one of the "most venomous campaign seasons in recent history" (Brodesky 2011). After the House passing of the health-care bill, vandals smashed the front door of Gifford's office in Tucson, Arizona. Seven months before Giffords' office had been vandalized, one of the attendees dropped a gun on the floor during a *Congress on your Corner* session as she addressed health-care issues in a gathering in the town of Douglas, Arizona.

White powder was sent to Congressman Raul Grijalva's congressional office last year during the month of October. He was compelled to temporarily close his Phoenix office as a result of increasing threats to his life. These threats resulted after he called for an economic boycott against the state of Arizona. His support of the boycott came as a direct opposition to SB 1070.

Since 2008, other violent acts of hatred have appeared at a national level. Rich (2011) argues that since Obama's ascension to the presidency, there have been repeated incidents of political violence, for example, the 2009 killing of three Pittsburgh law enforcement officers by a neo-Nazi Obama hater, and an attack on and an IRS office in Austin, Texas.

There has been a multiplicity of news coverage of the Tucson's tragedy joined by community voices challenging the continuing spreading of fear, terror, and the state of siege that was created by the shooting rampage that impacted all the community of Tucson, Arizona, and the state of Arizona as well. On Saturday, January 8, 2011, 75-year-old Sheriff Clarence W. Dupnik, a Democrat with more than three decades of law enforcement experience in Arizona's second most populous Pima County, linked the Tucson rampage to inflammatory conservative political rhetoric during a nationally televised news conference.

"When you look at unbalanced people, how they respond to the vitriol that comes out of certain mouths about tearing down the government. The anger, the hatred, the bigotry that goes on in this country is getting to be outrageous. And unfortunately, Arizona I think has become the capital. We have become the Mecca of bigotry and prejudice" (Riccardi 2011). This remark created a swift response from the right wing, Republicans, extremists, the Christian right, and Tea Party members. They started to discredit and partially blame Sheriff Dupnik for the shootings because he did not provide security to cover Congresswoman Giffords'event (Fischer 2011).

Another crucial issue of contemporary discontentment among people in Arizona is that Arizona currently is one of three states at a national level allowing people to carry concealed weapons without a permit. Goodman (2011) interviewed Sheriff Dupnik as he declared Arizona's gun law "insane." "We are the Tombstone of the United States of America ... I have never been a proponent of letting everybody in this state carry weapons under any circumstances that they want. And there is almost where we are."

Sheriff Dupnik call for civility on political issues currently resonates not only in the state of Arizona but throughout the nation as a result of President Obama's speech during his visit to Tucson, Arizona, on Wednesday, January 12, 2011.

Together We Thrive

On Wednesday 12, 2011, President Obama and his wife Michelle Obama attended a memorial event at the University of Arizona McKale Center. The President offered the nation's condolences to the victims of the shootings calling to "... usher in a new era of civility in their honor." President Obama's speech was nationally praised as a compassionate and powerful address. The city of Tucson and the state of Arizona were grieving the losses caused by the ominous act of hatred that left families without their loved ones. Many vigils and marches have been taking place outside of Gabrielle Giffords' office, and a memorial has been set outside of the University Medical Center for the citizenry to express their sentiments, grieving for the fallen and the actions of the heroes.

President Obama urged the citizenry to look inward but also prompted a collective response against "reflexive ideological and social conflict" (Cooper and Zeleny 2011). Thousands of people at the McKale Center sat silent listening and cheered at several points during President Obama's address. "It's important for us to pause for a moment and make sure that we are talking with each other in a way that heals, not a way that wounds," the President said. He added "let us remember that it is not because a simple lack of civility caused this tragedy. It did not. But rather because only a more civil and honest public discourse can help us face up to our challenges as a nation, in a way that would make them proud," referring to all those remembered in his eulogy: US Judge John M. Roll, Gabe Zimmerman, Dorwan Stoddard, Dorthy Murray, Phyllis Schneck, and 9-year-old Christina Taylor Green.

In conclusion transformative political and economic coalitions are empowering options for Latino comunities in making "visible" their political participation through leadership on the national agenda. Currently, the levels of political harassment and antagonism against immigrant communities throughout the United States would likely increase, as well as the cloneglomerization of SB 1070 across the nation. This becomes a serious concern for President Obama and the Democratic Party in upcoming elections for 2012 and 2014. Collective organization of the Latino community is crucial for representation and social justice in a global economy. The decade from 2010 to 2020 is undoubtedly a ripe historical time for Latinos and Mexicans to culturally, socially, economically, and politically engage in a decade of change and representation in the United States.

References

Billeaud, J., & Watson, J. (2011, January 11). *Arizona Giffords shooting: Parents of suspect devastated, neighbor says.* Retrieved from Arizona Central: http://www.azcentral.com/news/articles/2011/01/11/20110111gabrielle-giffords-arizona-shooting-suspect-neighbors.html

Brodesky, J. (2011, February 13). *While AZ circles the drain, legislators dream up ways to keep us laughing.* Retrieved from *Arizona Daily*: http://azstarnet.com/news/local/govt-and-politics/article_15815925330a-5e16-ac7b-78a5c87aab2c.html

Calefati, J. (2010, May 12). *Arizona bans ethnic studies.* Retrieved October 7, 2010, from *Mother Jones*: http://motherjones.com/mojo/2010/05/ethnic-studies-banned-arizona

Cooper, H., & Zeleny, J. (2011, January 11). *Obama calls for a new era of civility in U.S.- politics.* Retrieved January 13, 2011, from *The New York Times*: www.nytimes.com

de la Torre, A. (2010, April 29). *National Immigration Law Center, MALDEF, ACLU, ACLU of Arizona will challenge Arizona racial profiling law in court.* Retrieved from National Immigration Law Center. News Releases: www.nilc.org/pubs/news-releases/nr012.htm

Dupnik, D. (2010, May 5). Arizona's immigration mistake: Those who look suspiciously like illegal immigrants will find their liberty in severe jeopardy. *Wall Street Journal*, pp. Guest Opinion, 1.

Ethnic Studies in Arizona. (2010, September 16). *University of Arizona faculty senate unanimously passes resolution opposing House bill 2281!!!* Retrieved from http://www.ethnicstudiesarizona.com/2010/09/university-of-arizona-faculty-senate.html

Fischer, H. (2011, January 11). Dupnick's remark stir political debate. *Arizona Daily Star.* Tucson, AZ, p. A5.

Goodman, A. (2011, January 11). *A tale of two sheriffs.* Retrieved January 12, 2011, from Truthdig: http://trutdig.com/report/item/a_tale?of_two_sheriffs_20110111

Grado, G. (2010, October 29). *Senator Huppenthal would seek to restrict ethnic studies at the University of Arizona.* Retrieved January 11, 2011, from *Arizona Capitol Times.* Dolan Media Newswire Story: http://www.dolanmedia.com/view/cfm?recID=644652

Immigration Policy Center [IPC]. (2010, June 22). *Arizona's punishment doesn't fit the crime: Studies show decrease in Arizona crime rates over time.* Retrieved October 7, 2010, from American Immigration Council: http://www.immigrationpolicy.org/just-facts/arizona%E2%80%99s-punishment-doesn%%E2%80%99t-fit-crime-studies-show-decrease-arizona-crime-rates

James Hernandez, F. (2007, August). Marginalities and the democratic imaginary of the global borderlands. *Dissertation UMI 3281863.* Stanford University, Palo Alto, CA.

Johnson, L. (2010, December 28). *Many states look to Arizonas SB1070 as a model for new immigration legislation.* Retrieved January 20, 2011, from *Washington Independent*: http://washingtonindependent.com/104713/many

Martinez, M., & Gutierrez, T. (2010, October 20). *11 teachers sue Arizona over new 'anti-Hispanic' schools law.* Retrieved from CNN Story Highlights: http://www.sodahead.com/united-states/teachers-sue-arizona-over-anti-hispanic-schools-law/question-1290837/

McCarren, A. (2010, April 30). *Virginia official: Similar immigration law worked.*Retrieved from WUSA-TV, Washington, DC: http://www.azcentral.com/news/articles/2010/04/30/20100430arizona-immigration-law-virginia-law-similar.html
Meissner, D. (2010, May 2). *5 myths about immigration.* Retrieved May 7, 2010, from *The Washington Post*: htpp://www.washingtonpost.com/wpdyn/content/article/2010/04/30/AR2010043001106.html?wspisrc=nl_pmopinions
Meyers, S., & Orozco, R. (2010, May 12). *New Arizona law could be detrimental to students, according to OSU researchers.* Retrieved from Oregon State University [OSU]: http://oregonstate.edu/ua/ncs/archives/2010/may/new-arizona-law-could-be-detrimental-students-according-osu-researchers
National Institute for Latino Policy. (2010, April 30). *Arizona ethnic studies classes banned, teachers with accents can no longer teach English.* Retrieved from Huffpost Politics: http://www.huffingtonpost.com/2010/04/30/arizona-ethnic-studies-cl_n_558731.html
Peña, G. (2010, May 4). Letter to Gov. Honorable Jan Brewer on behalf of the National Association of Chicana and Chicano Studies. *National Association of Chicana and Chicano Studies.* San Jose, CA: http://www.naccs.org/images/naccs/ltrs/SB_1070.pdf
Preston, J. (2010, May 6). *Latino groups urge boycott of Arizona over new law.* Retrieved May 6, 2010, from *The New York Times*: http://www.nytimes.com/2010/05/07/us/07immig.html
Rau, A., Rough, G., & Hensley, J. (2010, July 28). *Arizona immigration law: Key parts struck down by judge.* Retrieved from Arizona News from *The Arizona Republic*: http://tucsoncitizen.com/arizona-news/2010/07/28/arizona-immigration-law-key-parts-struck-down-by-judge/
Riccardi, N. (2011, January 10). *After shootings, Clarence Dupnik is Arizona's new sheriff in town.* Retrieved from *Los Angeles Times*: http://articles.latimes.com/print/2011/jan/10nation/la-na-arizona-shooting-sheriffs-201101. Retrieves 11 Jan 2011.
Rich, F. (2011, January 16). *No one listened to Gabrielle Giffords.* Retrieved January 18, 2011, from *The New York Times*: http://www.nytimes.com/2011/01/16/opinion/16rich.html?_=language
Rodriguez, R., Mendez-Negrete, J., & Peña, D. (2010, May 27). *Deep impact: Three Mexican-American scholars discuss Arizona's immigration law and its ramifications on the state's colleges and universities.* Retrieved from http://goliath.ecnext.com/coms2/gi_0199-12949942/Deep-impact-three-Mexican-American.html
Rogers, I. (2010, June 22). *Assessing Arizona.* Retrieved January 11, 2011, from Issues in Higher Education: http://diverseeducation.com/article/13900/
Shelton, R. (2010, May 6). *Thank you. To the campus community.* Retrieved from The University of Arizona. Office of the President: http://president.arizona.edu/memos_letters/thank-you
Staudt, K. (1998). *Free trade: Informal economies on the U.S.-Mexico border.* Philadelphia: Temple University Press.
Staudt, K. (2009). Violence at the border: Broadening the discourse to include feminism, human security, and deeper democracy. In K. A. Staudt, T. Payan, & Z. A. Kruszewski (Eds.), *Human rights along the U.S.-Mexico border: Gendered violence and insecurity* (pp. 1–27). Tucson: University of Arizona Press.
Strauss, V. (2010, May 17). *Arizona officials go after Mexican studies program.* Retrieved from *The Washington Post*: http://www.washingtonpost.com/wp-dyn/content/article/2010/05/16/AR2010051603094.html?nav=emailpage
U.S. Census Bureau News. (2009, July 15). *Facts for features: Hispanic heritage month 2009.* Retrieved April 29, 2010, from Report CB09-FF.17: http://www.census.gov/mewsroom/releases/pdf/cb09-ff17.pdf
Wagner, D. (2010, May 2). *Violence is not up on Arizona border despite Mexican drug war.* Retrieved from *The Arizona Republic*: http://www.azcentral.com/news/articles/2010/05/02/20100502arizona-border-violence-Mexico.html
Wessler, S. (2010, November 12). *White anxiety fuels anti-immigrant laws.* Retrieved from *Color Lines.* News for Action: http://colorlines.com/archives/2010/11/in_the_shadows_of_arizonas.html

Chapter 14
Social Justice at the Border and in the Bordered United States: Implications for Policy and Practice

Mark Lusk, Kathleen Staudt, and Eva M. Moya

Borders are often understood in their simplest terms. They comprise a territorial line between two nation states. In this case, Mexico exists as an independent state to the south, and the United States is a sovereign power on the northern side. But, as we have seen, the border is immensely more complex than a line on a map. For over two centuries, the border was practically invisible to the naked eye, except as a shallow river in its eastern half and an occasional cattle fence on its western half. Unlike the Great Wall of China, which can be seen from outer space, this border has been indiscernible, changing, and, until recently, highly permeable.

In this chapter, we make the case that social injustice and surveillance are not only problematic at the border, but in the mainstream where the discourse of border security and surveillance practices spreads into and throughout national spaces. We begin first with an analysis of borders everywhere, followed with problematic public policies, and propose policy strategies to address these issues. While many of the problematic policies focus on the United States or Mexico, we also discuss binational policy issues or policy interventions that would affect both sides of the border, that is, the border zone. Among these policies, we advocate a demilitarization of the border, reoriented drug policies, a border economic investment zone, UN interventions to assist with refugees who flee from violence

M. Lusk (✉)
Department of Social Work, College of Health Sciences, University of Texas at El Paso, 500 W. University Ave., 79968 El Paso, TX, USA
e-mail: mwlusk@utep.edu

K. Staudt
Department of Political Science, University of Texas at El Paso, 500 W. University Ave., 9968 El Paso, TX, USA
e-mail: kstaudt@utep.edu

E.M. Moya
Department of Social Work, University of Texas at El Paso, 500 W. University Ave., 79968 El Paso, TX, USA
e-mail: emmoya@utep.edu

M. Lusk et al. (eds.), *Social Justice in the U.S.-Mexico Border Region*, DOI 10.1007/978-94-007-4150-8_14, © Springer Science+Business Media B.V. 2012

and poverty in Mexico, and trauma and recovery centers, such as those established in war zones, and post-conflict peace-building processes. The drug war has become an undeclared war, and national security discourse ignores attention to human security, with little end to the war in sight until other economic and social policies change. To make these changes, we discuss the importance of border voices in civil society activism.

The Border Is Everywhere

The conventional "Inside-Outside Model" of borders (Vaughan-Williams 2008) in which the border simply comprises "the edges of the physical territory" between states does not apply in a number of cases globally (Guild 2005, p. 1). Groundbreaking work by Guild on understanding borders within the European Union has changed our view of borders. It can now be said in Europe and in the United States that "the borders may be found anywhere" (Guild 2003, p. 103). In other words, borders are not necessarily consistent with the limits of a nation's physical perimeter.

In the United States, federal agents from myriad agencies can and do enforce immigration law in any location within the territory of the country. The jurisdiction of Immigration Customs Enforcement (ICE), for example, includes the entire country, and searches and seizures may be conducted anywhere. Traditionally, American borders and sea ports have been largely exempt from the provisions of the Fourth Amendment protection against unreasonable search. Border searches are not subject to the same provisos of reasonable search and/or probable cause as other federal searches. Border searches also do not require a warrant.

The Supreme Court has consistently upheld "specifically established exceptions" to the Fourth Amendment, among them border crossing points (Kim 2009). The border search is a long-established exception that actually precedes the Fourth Amendment, as it is based on the logic that the inspection of persons and goods upon entry into the country is a necessary element of sovereignty and safety. More recently, the "border exception" has been applied to the "functional equivalent of the border," which can include airports in the interior, crossroads of major routes, and interior ports, recognizing that people can enter the country at points other than the border (e.g., Salt Lake City Airport) (Kim 2009).

Another established exception includes the "extended border search," wherein warrantless searches are permitted beyond the functional equivalent of the border if there is reasonable certainty that a border was crossed, and there is reasonable suspicion that criminal activity was occurring (Kim 2009, p. 8). This is a type of "internal border" (Vaughan-Williams 2008).

Still another innovation in extending the reach of federal immigration enforcement is the Delegation of Immigration Authority Section 287(g) of the Immigration and Nationality Act—commonly called "287g." According to Immigration and Customs Enforcement (ICE), 287(g) "allows a state and local law enforcement entity to enter into a partnership with ICE, under a joint Memorandum of Agreement (MOA), in order to receive delegated authority for immigration enforcement within their jurisdictions" (ICE, n.d.). Over 70 local and state law enforcement agencies have entered into 287g partnerships, many of which are located far from a border. A 2010 US Department of Homeland Security (DHS) report on the performance of the 287(g) agreements found that "participating law enforcement agencies were not operating in compliance with the terms of agreement." Among them were "civil rights and civil liberty concerns" (Department of Homeland Security [DHS] 2010, p. 1).

In January 2011, Texas Governor Rick Perry, a former candidate for the presidential elections of 2012, challenged the state legislature to limit funding for what he called "sanctuary cities," using a broad, polarizing definition to include cities and counties that practice "community-oriented policing" strategies that do not inquire about citizenship status from crime victims or noncriminals. Even Harris County with its 287(g) agreement, containing Houston, the biggest city in Texas, was attacked during the gubernatorial campaign for being a sanctuary city (Grissom 2010). The Major City Chiefs Association—representing 56 big cities in the United States—has long advocated victim-friendly and community-oriented local police practices that enforce local and state laws, rather than federal laws. El Paso's former Police Chief, now El Paso County Sheriff Richard Wiles, argues that local residents, regardless of citizenship status, need to be able to trust local law enforcement. Moreover, local taxpayers can hardly afford unfunded state mandates and federalized law enforcement (see more on Wiles in Staudt 2008b).

The internal enforcement of immigration laws grew extensively during the decade following 9/11. Thousands of new agents were hired by Homeland Security and have been deployed throughout the country; there are now 20,700 border agents, double the number since 2004 (Napolitano 2011). They are not just assigned to the territorial borders, but now even bus and train commuters between cities in the east and Midwest have grown accustomed to being asked for proof of citizenship by the Border Patrol at train stops and bus stops in what has essentially become an "internal document check" (Bernstein 2010). Moreover, in places far from any border, international students are routinely detained for interrogation (Woodward 2011). In addition, private citizens have organized into anti-immigration and vigilante groups, such as the Minutemen who watch out for migrants without police oversight—serving as a sort of citizen-detective form of surveillance reminiscent of Orwell's *1984* (Vaughan-Williams 2008). Coupled with the remote sensing of the "Virtual Border," where military grade equipment, including both American and Mexican unmanned drones, patrol and surveil the border region 24/7, this could be called "the securitization of everyday life" (see selections in Bajc and de Lint 2011) on the border and beyond. As a result of the implementation of government policies that conflate immigration with terrorism, life on the border has been profoundly changed.

Federal policy on immigration, imports, contraband, law enforcement, terrorism, and drugs also knows no boundary. The reach of the Department of Justice, the Department of Homeland Security, Department of State, and the Drug Enforcement Agency is global. The DEA and FBI work extensively inside other countries in cooperation with foreign governments—particularly in Mexico. Wanted criminals, terrorists, drug traffickers, fugitives, smugglers, and criminal "aliens" are among the many groups that are tracked globally. Traveler watch lists detect suspicious persons well before they arrive in US airspace. This is what has been called an "external border" (Vaughan-Williams 2008).

State power is distributed through space, beyond borders—both internally and externally. The US border is everywhere. While the US-Mexico border is at the periphery of the American economy, it is also among the "centers" of national security policy. While the region lags in investments in human capital, it ranks very highly in military and national security capitalization. Spatial relations are an important way of understanding the ways in which power is deployed and the US-Mexico border is a case in point. As Shome argues:

> The U.S.-Mexico border relies heavily on the utilization and deployment of space for the enactment of state power and the production of territoriality. Since the passage of then-President Clinton's Operation Gatekeeper in 1994, the border has been turned into a militarized war zone—a deconstitutionalized zone where human rights have been suspended (2006, p. 45).

Moreover, the situation Shome describes has certainly not been attenuated during the post-9/11 decade. One clear example of this has been the Mérida Initiative (also called Plan Mexico), security cooperation between the United States and the government of Mexico and the countries of Central America to combat organized crime and narcotics. At some $1.4 billion, this program has sent the latest military, security and surveillance technology, and training to one of the most corrupt law enforcement systems in the world—the police and military of Mexico.

New Approaches to Policy, Practice, and Advocacy

An altogether new approach to policy and practice is needed in order to reshape the dynamics of the US-Mexico border region. The chapter authors have made several specific recommendations in the areas they discuss—ranging from redressing environmental injustice to equitably tackling health-care disparities. In this section, we present some overarching themes that would generate change on a larger scale. It has been argued throughout the book that the social and economic problems of the border region have their roots in the way in which the border is seen by residents and government policy makers on both sides of the border—images that sometimes border on caricatures—a violent place, with corrupt institutions, poor schools, and peopled in the majority by poor Hispanics. These images grow out of the economic and political isolation of the region and its location at the peripheries of power—politically and geographically distant from the policy makers that in many ways determine the region's destiny. In Chap. 1, we also have contended that the region is adversely affected by neocolonialism and the location of low value modes of production such as semi-modern agriculture, low wage manufacturing, and service labor.

It is also a region that is distorted by the presence of what Kathleen Staudt, Tony Payan, and Timothy Dunn have called the "border industrial security complex," a huge array of state and federal law enforcement and military organizations, a for-profit prison industry, and a misdirected "investment" of over a $1 billion in purchasing advanced weapons, high technology, and training in Mexico's security state (2009b). Thus, we propose some changes in policy and practice that address the big picture on how to turn the region around to one that will promise better lives for the area's children.

The Development and Militarization of the Mexican Border

Since the 1980s, the United States has militarized the border, using "low-intensity conflict" according to Timothy Dunn's landmark study (1996). What makes the border different two decades later is Mexico's militarization of its northern border with support from the United States against weapons that organized criminals smuggle from the United States, given the ease of purchase in border states. Militarization on either side of the border did not reduce the violence, given increases in murder rates in cities like Ciudad Juárez from 2007 to 2008, to 2009, and to 2010, continuing as we write in 2012. Indeed, Mexico's military and federal police share responsibilities for deaths, human rights abuses, and extortion, according to the many complaints made to both national and state human rights commissions. In the United States, few voice concerns for human rights and the weak-to-ineffective leverage from some in the US Senate to highlight abuses is the threat to withhold 15% of some part of Mérida Initiative funding. That is hardly enough, particularly in a flawed initiative that relies too much on sending money into corrupted institutions.

As its strategy for economic development at its northern border, Mexico has long depended on foreign investment. Since the 1960s Border Industrialization Program, foreign-owned export-processing factories have been established in Ciudad Juárez and other border cities, providing a magnet for northward internal migration to secure work in the formal economy and to obtain access to Mexico's health-care and social security system. At the high point of the turn of the twenty-first century, the city was home to approximately 300 export-processing factories (maquiladoras) that employed a quarter of a million workers (Ganster and Lorey 2005). However, employees are laid off or hired on temporary contracts in response to US economic slowdowns, such as the recession of 2008 and thereafter, thereby undermining job stability.

Worse yet is the pay scale in a city with a relatively high cost of living. Mexico's minimum wage is approximately US $3.50–4.00 per *day*, depending on the peso-dollar currency exchange and the location in Mexico (the northern states have higher minimum wages—amounting to approximately US 25 cents—than the central and south states), in contrast to the minimum wage in the United States of $7.25 per *hour* (2011 figures). Even factories that pay assembly-line workers "two times the minimum wage," the referent in Mexico, workers still bring home less than $50 weekly. These amounts are not adequate for sustaining families. Meanwhile, the Mexican state, which some scholars call the "absent state," has shrunk and deferred to the global corporations and their policies for a temporary workforce (see selections in Staudt et al. 2010).

President Felipe Calderón (2006–2012) invested large amounts of political and budgetary capital to fight organized crime, specifically drug-trafficking organizations (DTOs). This fight has been largely unsuccessful, as noted above. Murders have increased by tenfold from 2007 to 2010, at over 3,000 in a city of just over a million people. January 2009 was a turning point for *Juarenses* and the federal government, after gang members presumably affiliated with DTOs, massacred 15 teenagers at a birthday party in Villas de Salvárcar, a neighborhood in Ciudad Juárez. President Calderón finally visited the city not once, but three times, pledging "*Todos Somos Juárez*" along with a budgetary commitment to invest in the city's economy, education, and social infrastructure. Yet the amount pledged or allocated has not been transparent; at most it totals US $274,000 (Associated Press 2011). The so-called fourth pillar of the US Mérida Initiative is the Economic and Social Development Fund (ESDF), which is funded at $25 million. It is designed to stimulate social and economic investment, but was developed too late, with too little funding.

If the United States had been watching and learning from European countries, it would have realized that free trade stimulates migrant movement from low-income countries of the south to high-income countries of the north. Moreover, when large gaps in incomes between neighboring countries are as aggravated and wide as 10:1, such as the inequalities at the US-Mexico border, it should be no surprise that migrants move northward in search of decent-paying jobs, higher incomes, and futures for their families (Alba 2006). The North American Free Trade Agreement (NAFTA), put in place in 1994, only accelerated the income inequalities and movement northward (Portes 2006; Staudt and García 2011). In policy change terms, we believe that NAFTA ought to be renegotiated into an agreement that provides for higher wages in Mexico and that includes attention to migration. As migration scholars have noted, immigration policy cannot be developed in a unilateral way; rather, bilateral or multilateral approaches are essential (Alba 2006). Such was the approach initially taken by Presidents George W. Bush and Vicente Fox in 2001, prior to 9/11, after which bilateral negotiations broke down (Castañeda 2007) and President Bush issued Homeland Security Presidential Directive Number 2, "Combating Terrorism through Immigration Policy," which linked immigration and terrorism (in Staudt 2011, p. 115).

As solid and methodical research from Wayne Cornelius has documented many times, migration must be examined through the lens of supply and demand, rather than border controls (2006, 2007). In longitudinal research with migrant-sending communities in Mexico, Cornelius shows that despite the dangers of the journeys, the hundreds of annual known deaths in crossing from the elements and criminals, and the threefold increase in Border Patrol officers reinforced with physical barriers and technological surveillance, people without jobs or without living-wage jobs will migrate when they can get employment in the United States. Migrants who are apprehended at the border will make second and third attempts at crossing until they get into the United States.

Over the last century, immigration policies have been in constant flux. Among more recent turning points, we note the bipartisan Immigration Reform and Control Act (IRCA) of 1986, which established two major reform principles: amnesty for those undocumented immigrants who could prove residence and employer sanctions which would penalize employers for hiring people not authorized to work in the United States. Heretofore, only the immigrants had borne the penalty burdens. Still, immigrants face steeper and steeper penalties, including detention, deportation, and in some cases felony charges that would inhibit the possibility of future entry into the United States. Since 1986, employer sanctions have been enforced with miserly budgetary commitments, and amnesty has become a politically dirty word that hardly enters the discourse of immigration reform.

Since IRCA, many millions of migrants from Mexico and elsewhere have entered the United States illegally and found work. By 2008, the Pew Research Center estimated that the figure for undocumented immigrants was 11.9 million and that it had stabilized (Passel and Cohn 2009). The year 2004 was the last year that bipartisan cosponsored comprehensive immigration reform legislation (Senators Kennedy (D) and McCain (R)) was introduced but failed. A harsh immigration bill passed the US House of Representatives under James Sensenbrenner's HB 4437 in 2005, stimulating massive protests and rallies in 2006, but it did not pass in the US Senate. Sensenbrenner's bill would have deported millions of people, potentially separated parents from their citizen, US-born children, and stimulated even more massive growth in the for-profit detention prisons that already permeate the border region (not to mention exorbitant taxpayer costs). The surveillance and roundup measures would run contrary to seemingly constitutional protections and freedoms from surveillance. (We say "seemingly" given the creeping surveillance of all land and sea borders under "border security" procedures, that is, the bordering of the United States analyzed above.)

Bipartisan immigration reform efforts have broken down since 2004, except for massive spending on border security and the fence (aka wall) which added 670 barrier miles in a near-2,000-mile border. Funding for the "virtual fence," surpassing \$1 billion and providing just 53 miles of unreliable coverage, finally came to a halt (Bennett 2010). The border fence was contracted to Boeing Corporation and was plagued by cost overruns and delays. After 5 years, in 2010, Secretary Janet Napolitano, noting that the program was ineffective in reducing border enforcement, canceled the virtual fence (Napolitano 2011).

Comprehensive immigration reform was introduced by Representative Luis Gutiérrez (D), with nearly 100 cosponsors in 2009. The bill responded to the constituency interests of business, labor, immigrants, and the faith and human rights communities. However, the vitriolic party polarization in the US Congress inhibited its passage. Even the DREAM Act of late 2010, which would have provided a pathway to citizenship for nearly a million young people who grew up in the

United States, did not pass. In the meantime, politicians in state legislatures have alarmingly taken up state level "reforms" in this federal policy arena (see Chap. 13 by Solórzano, this volume).

For the sake of not only the border, but also for the rest of our bordered country, we advocate comprehensive immigration reform immediately and challenges to harsh measures in state legislatures. Some harsh measures are unconstitutional, such as prospective laws that would deny birthright citizenship, going so far as to challenge the 14th Amendment to the US Constitution which defines citizens as both those born in the United States and naturalized citizens. Besides state efforts to remove constitutional birthright citizenship, legislative efforts are in motion in Texas, Arizona, New Mexico, and elsewhere to require police to engage in racial (immigrant) profiling to require citizenship or legal permanent status for people to secure licenses to drive or to work in service occupations and to require citizenship for public school attendance (the latter, another challenge to a Supreme Court decision). The War on Immigrants is in full force at a time when the US population is aging coupled with the need to replenish Social Security funding. Immigrants, whether documented or not, pay Social Security and other taxes and fill needed jobs in the service, manufacturing, construction, and agricultural sectors. Current immigration policy is counterproductive to say the least.

The War on Drugs Has Failed

President Richard Nixon declared the War on Drugs in 1969. Over 40 years later, drug use not only continues unabated in the United States but also has reached historically high levels. The United States has become the world's largest illegal drug-consuming country. With the supply and demand binational lens, drug consumption in the US fuels and funds Drug Trafficking Organizations (DTOs) in countries to the south, including Mexico. Notable Latin American scholars and ex-presidents have called for changes in the US approach to drugs, focused primarily on the interdiction of drugs at land and sea borders and the de-criminalization of drug users in the United States (Latin American Commission on Drugs and Democracy [LACDD] 2009).

In the United States, drug laws have provided huge incentives for law enforcement, public and for-profit prisons to jail drug users, many of whom instead would benefit from treatment for addiction. Moreover, "persons of color" are disproportionately jailed, reflecting institutional racism and impoverishment among US "minority" groups (Staudt 2011, p. 118). Again, had the United States watched and learned from European countries, it would have realized that the criminalization of drugs invariably connects drug users of the so-called soft drugs like marijuana to the hard drug dealers who sell heroin, cocaine, and methamphetamine, that is, to organized crime. In places like the Netherlands and Portugal, where access to marijuana is available without criminal penalties, the incidence of drug use on episodic and regular bases is less than in the United States (Staudt et al. 2009c, including lengthy bibliography; Greenwald 2009).

We call for new approaches to the drug war, including far more budgetary allocations for treatment and addiction. Under President Barack Obama's administration, the terminology of "War on Drugs" was dropped in a new policy released in May 2010, as was a call for greater budgetary commitments to prevention and treatment. However, billions of dollars continue to be spent annually on interdiction and criminalization, despite the absence of documentation on the effectiveness of drug war policies. US drug czar Gil Kerlikowske has acknowledged that the War on Drugs has not worked. After 40 years and at a cost of over $1 trillion, the drug problem has actually been magnified (Associate Press 2010).

The War on Drugs has failed on other fronts. It has fueled a huge growth in the American prison population and has incarcerated hundreds of thousands of nonviolent offenders in expensive prisons where there are few or no drug treatment programs and little or no job training. The United States has the highest incarceration rate in the world and is well ahead of authoritarian states such as Russia, Iran, China, and Saudi Arabia. In 2010, 748 persons per 10,000 were incarcerated in federal, state, or local prisons and jails—a rate nearly equivalent to 1:100 (*The Economist* 2010). There are about 2.5 million prisoners in the United States, and a disproportionate percentage is African American and Hispanic. Most are incarcerated for nonviolent offenses such as possession of small amounts of illegal drugs. Some are sentenced to life imprisonment for convictions of three felonies, whether violent of not. And this is not without cost. The American Prison State—the largest in the world—costs from $18,000 per prisoner per year in Mississippi to $50,000 per year in California, the latter roughly equivalent to Ivy League tuition. Over a quarter of federal prisoners are incarcerated on drug charges (Drug Facts 2011). Most do not receive drug addiction treatment.

There are alternatives. The drug court system places nonviolent drug offenders into community-based corrections, wherein the probationer is required to be clean and sober, obtain employment, complete their education, and undergo extensive drug treatment. Recidivism rates for drug court graduates are markedly lower than for prison parolees—as low as 2–20% (Office of the National Drug Control Policy 2010). The average cost of drug court is less than $2,000 per person per year (US Department of Justice 2010).

Scrap Plan Mérida

As the violence associated with drug trafficking and organized crime in Mexico began to accelerate from 2005 onward, the United States began negotiations with Mexico to provide anticrime and counterdrug assistance to Mexico. Recognizing that Central American and Caribbean nations had also been caught up in the regional crime wave and were affected by alarming growth rates in homicide, negotiation included all of Central America and the Caribbean nations of Haiti and the Dominican Republic. The result, announced in October 2007, was the *Mérida Initiative for Mexico and Central America*. The announced appropriation was $1.4 billion for Mexico. In 2008, the approved supplemental appropriations for Central

American added $65 million. In 2009, Congress appropriated $300 million for Mexico and $110 million for Central America. The Obama Administration in 2009 requested $450 million for Mexico for Fiscal Year 2010, and the Congress added millions to the State Department Regional Security Initiative and the Caribbean Basin Security Initiative (Seelke 2010). The first tranches of funding went to the purchase of high-grade weaponry, helicopters, surveillance and communication equipment, and training in the technologies for the Mexican police and military.

Concerned by Mexico's poor record of human rights protection, notably the conduct of the police and military toward Mexican civilians, Congress began to insist on "soft-side" strategies and limiting the funding of the military. As a result, by 2009, supplemental funds were allocated toward institution building, rule of law, and anticorruption activities in Mexico. Funds were also freed up for a mere $25 million in Economic and Social Development Funds—resources that are allocated toward the support of micro-credit financing and job training (Seelke 2010). This can best be described as "too little, too late."

Since the beginnings of the Plan Mérida, Mexico's crime wave has not abated. Police corruption has not declined. Reports of human rights violations have not dropped, and the homicide rate has more than tripled. The wisdom of expending over a billion dollars on providing military and security equipment to one of the most corrupt military/law enforcement systems in the hemisphere seems as ludicrous as fighting a decade long and seemingly endless war in Afghanistan. It is, on the face of it, absurd.

In Chap. 1, we noted that the 2010 US Agency for International Development budget for Mexico was only $28 million—a far cry from the $2–3 billion in economic and military assistance annually to Egypt and Israel. Programs funded under this amount include strengthened rule of law, economic competitiveness, infectious disease control, and grants for higher education (US Agency for International Development [USAID] 2010a). Yet, as USAID itself points out, "Mexico still faces huge gaps between rich and poor, north and south, urban and rural. Over 40% of the country's population is poor (living on less than $2 per day), while close to 18% is extremely poor (living on less than $1 per day)" (USAID 2010b, p. 1).

We propose what would seem to be self-evident—that the ill-conceived Plan Mérida (which was modeled on the equally ill-fated Plan Colombia)—be scrapped altogether. The entire amount, over $1.5 billion, should be redirected and invested (rather than squandered) into long-term international development programs that create local employment within Mexico and provide funding for primary and secondary education (the fastest path to economic development). This would staunch the migration of Mexicans to the north where they are hunted and harassed and provide them with the means of supporting their families in their own home states.

From a Culture of "*ni nis*" to One of "*si sis*"

At the heart of high rates of violence and social and economic deterioration in Mexico is youth unemployment, which leads many young people to turn to organized crime for career opportunities. Mexican media have identified a new social phenomenon in Mexico known as *los "ni nis"* or *"ni trabajan, ni estudian"*—young people who neither work nor study. Mexico's National Autonomous University claims there are several million *"ni nis,"* although the government reports that there are only a few hundred thousand. One of the largest populations of *"ni nis"* is in Ciudad Juárez. A recent report (Comisión Nacional para Prevenir y Eradicar la Violencia Contra las Mujeres 2009) financed by the Mexican government found that 120,000 Juárez residents between the ages of 13 and 24—or 45% of this population—were neither enrolled in school nor working in the formal sector. Many live in slums spreading out over *colonias* or hills on the west side of the city, home to workers in *maquiladora* assembly plant industry. It is vital that the governments make services to children and youth a top priority.

The US-Mexico border needs a comprehensive social initiative for children and youth that includes school retention, substance abuse and violence prevention, and treatment interventions for fifth and sixth graders; an educational, vocational, and social reinsertion program to identify early on risk and vulnerability and help youth stay in school; and employment and workforce opportunities as well as community linkages to trigger social cohesion and economic development and deter youth from the dropping out of school, participating in gangs, engaging in delinquent behavior and practices, and drug trafficking. Community-based services and a program to address substance abuse especially among youth at risk and their families are vital. Programs that focus on nonviolent conflict resolution, respect, and peace are needed on both sides of the US-Mexico border. We recognize that this is unlikely over the short term as Mexico cannot assure even the most basic human needs as defined by Maslow—human security.

Finally, we observe that the failure of the US Congress to pass the Dream Act in 2010 has created a large population of immigrant *"ni nis"* in the United States. The Mexican and other immigrant children who have grown up in the United States and who call it their home will never be able to attend college or find legal employment—dooming them to *"ni estudian, ni trabajan."* Where is the wisdom in this? Without legal access to work or school, we have institutionalized their alienation and ensured a future for them of gangs, crime, and lifetime undocumented status.

US-Mexico Border Region Economic Investment Zone

At least since the 1960s, economically distressed cities, neighborhoods, and regions have benefitted from federal efforts to enhance economic development. These have included Regional Development Commissions, enterprise zones, and empowerment zones. Representing an example at the regional level is the Appalachian Regional Development Act of 1965 (40 U.S.C. App. 402), which created the Appalachian Development Commission. This bill authorized "federal assistance in the construction of an Appalachian development highway system; construction of multicounty demonstration health facilities, hospitals, regional health, diagnostic and treatment centers, and other facilities for health; seal and fill voids in abandoned mines and to rehabilitate strip mine areas; construction of school facilities for vocational education; and to assist in construction of sewage treatment works" (US Department of Labor 2011). Similar to the Appalachian Commission is the Delta Regional Authority (Mississippi Delta) (see Chap. 1, this volume, on pockets of poverty and underdevelopment in the United States).

An example of such federal assistance at the metropolitan level was the Housing and Urban Development Act of 1968 (including New Communities Act of 1968) (42 U.S.C. 3909) and its amendments, which provide for "guarantees, and commitments to guarantee, the bonds, debentures, notes, and other obligations issued by new community developers to help finance new community development projects" (US Department of Labor 2011).

Economic enterprise zones were first introduced under the Urban Employment Opportunities Development Act of 1967 (S. 2088). This bill, introduced by Senator Robert Kennedy, did not pass but for the first time introduced the idea of providing tax credits in return for private sector investments and job creation. Senators Jack Kemp and others introduced federal bills to fund federal enterprise zones under presidents Reagan and Bush, but the lack of success at the federal level led to state legislation. Louisiana established enterprise zones in 1981, and within a decade all but seven states had passed similar legislation.

During the Clinton administration (1993), the Federal Empowerment Zone/Enterprise Community Program was established. Under the auspices of the US Department of Housing and Human Development (HUD), the empowerment zones created tax incentives "to encourage businesses to open, expand and to hire local residents." Incentives include employment credits, zero capital gains tax, increased tax deductions, and accelerated property depreciation (Department of Housing and Human Development 2011).

In February 2003, a bipartisan group, Senators Bingaman (NM), Hutchinson (TX), and Boxer (CA), introduced legislation (S. 458) to create a Southwest Regional Border Authority to award grants to local communities, especially distressed communities, in support of local economic development projects. Noting the limited capital in the US-Mexico border region, the bill sought to develop business incubators. It also sought to acquire advanced technology for the region, fund infrastructure development, and develop entrepreneurship (Congressional Record—Senate, February 23, 2003, p. 4644). The bill was not passed. In 2007, Representative Silvestre Reyes (TX) introduced HB 2068: The Southwest Regional Border Authority Act to meet similar goals. It did not make it out of committee.

Finally, Representative Reyes from El Paso was able to revive the effort in 2008 when his request to establish a Southwest Border Regional Commission was included in the 2008 Farm Bill (HR 2419), which became law in June of 2008. The House and Senate overrode a veto by President Bush (personal communication, Luis Torres, January 27, 2011). The Farm Bill established three regional commissions modeled on the Appalachian Regional Development Commission—one on the US-Mexico border, another Northern Regional Development Commission in upper New England, and a Southeast Crescent Regional Development Commission in the southeastern states.

Unfortunately, while the commissions were authorized for $30 million per fiscal year for 2009–2012, the Southwest Border Regional Commission has never received any appropriations, appointed commissioners, established offices, or become operational.

We propose that regional efforts be mounted to secure appropriations for the Southwest Border Regional Commission on a par with the Appalachian Regional Commission, which requested $76 million for fiscal year 2010 (Appalachian Regional Commission 2009). The bill as currently written focuses on infrastructure assistance, assistance to distressed places in the form of grants, the development of multistate regional strategies, and the provision of administrative-expense support to local development organizations that are leading regional development efforts. We propose instead that it be modeled after the empowerment zone concept, which provides incentives to the private sector to build businesses, create jobs, and foster entrepreneurship through tax incentives such as zero capital gains tax, rapid capital equipment depreciation, and tax deductions for hiring local residents. This shifts the orientation of the agency away from grants and bureaucracy model of economic development to tax expenditures to attract private investment. In essence, tax expenditures are taxes that are not collected or revenue that is foregone by creating deductions, exclusions, tax deferrals, and preferential taxation rates. In contrast to direct government spending on regional development (a strategy that would not find much support among the conservative federal legislators of the border states), this would create huge incentives for industry and capital to relocate to the peripheral border economic zone—an approach that is more likely to be palatable in Washington. Such a strategy has been shown to be effective elsewhere. As early as the 1970s, Great Britain had established empowerment zones and enterprise zones with great success (Mulock 2002).

Refugees: Challenges and Opportunities

Clearly, most Mexican migrants to the United States do so for economic reasons. With a minimum wage of about $5 a day, less than the minimum hourly rate in the United States, and with the collapse of small-scale farming, people choose to move by the millions into a foreign country fraught with the dangers of crossing and the ever present threat of arrest, imprisonment in the immigration prison complex, and deportation to the bridge of a border city far from their home town or village. The fact that most Mexican emigrants are economic migrants overshadows the emergence of a completely different type of immigrant—the refugee.

Shortly after he was elected President of Mexico in 2006, Felipe Calderón declared a war on the drug cartels that are responsible for the huge illicit trade of drugs into the United States and throughout Mexico. The president mobilized thousands of federal police officers and deployed them to cities that had previously been patrolled almost exclusively by corrupt local police officers. In addition, he called up divisions of the Mexican Armed Forces who joined in the nationwide effort to clamp down on drug cartels and gangs. The result was paradoxical. Instead of reducing crime and limiting drug trafficking, the country was plunged into a progressively worsening state of disorder and crime, characterized by gang warfare and alarming rates of homicide, kidnapping, extortion, femicide, carjacking, opportunistic crime, social disorder, and the decline of civil society (Campbell 2009). The Mexican Centro de Investigación y Seguridad Nacional estimates that from the onset of the president's war on drugs in 2006–2010, approximately 28,000 people have died in Mexico in *la violencia* that has wracked the nation—particularly along its border with the United States (Smith 2010).

The situation in Mexico has created widespread fear. The streets of major border cities are nearly empty after dark. Opportunistic crime has emerged to fill the vacuum of security as police officers have been paralyzed by their incapacity to enforce the law in the face of daily murders of law enforcement by *sicarios* (assassins). Businesses have closed in cities like Ciudad Juárez by the thousands in the face of extortion and threats of death and arson. Thousands of Mexico border residents have fled to the United States for safe haven. Many thousands more have migrated to the interior of Mexico. The result of this state of chaos in Mexico is that uncounted numbers of persons and families have fled across the border to Texas and other border states as refugees, many of whom have directly experienced serious trauma prior to their migration.

As we noted in Chap. 1, the *Observatorio de Seguridad y Convivencia Ciudadana*, a think tank at the Autonomous University of Ciudad Juárez, estimates that over the past 3 years, 230,000 Mexicans have fled the violence in the city. They calculate that around half of the refugees have fled to the United States, a majority of whom now reside in or around El Paso, Texas (JRL 2010, September 20). These refugees are afforded no legal asylum in the United States and must blend in with relatives or go underground. When detained by the US Border Patrol, they are detained indefinitely in border immigration prisons, where their rights are extremely limited. Although they are afforded visits from the Mexican Consulate, the Texas Civil Rights Project, priests, and human rights groups, their detentions are lengthy, and the outcome is near certain deportation. Because so few Mexicans are granted asylum (2% according to US Department of Justice figures) yearly, only some 200 apply for political asylum (Becker and McDonnell 2009).

Under current US law, as defined by the 101(a) (42) of the Immigration and Nationality Act, a refugee is a person "who is unable or unwilling to return to his or her country of nationality because of persecution or a well-founded fear of persecution on account of race, religion, nationality, membership in a particular social group, or political opinion" (Department of Homeland Security 2010, p. 1). While there is no limit on the number of persons who may be granted refugee status, there is a limit on how many refugees or asylees may qualify for permanent refugee status—no more than 10,000 per fiscal year (Department of Homeland Security [DHS] 2010). In either case, the individual requesting permission to reside in the United States must demonstrate that he or she would be subject to persecution on the basis of "race, religion, nationality, membership in a particular social group, or political opinion" (Department of Homeland Security 2010, p. 1). Further considerations regarding refugee status include the provision that an applicant must be of particular humanitarian concern to the United States. A priority system governs the process. High priority is given to individuals identified by the United Nations High Commission for Refugees, secondary priority is given to groups of particular humanitarian concern as identified by the US government, and lower priority is given to the reunification of families (Department of Homeland Security 2010).

The number of persons admitted to the United States as refugees has been falling. In 1990, slightly over 120,000 were admitted. In 2009, 74,602 were admitted—mostly from Iraq, Burma, Bhutan, Iran, Cuba, and conflict zones in central Africa (Martin 2010). In 2009, 192 persons from Mexico were granted refugee status by the United States. The average number of refugees granted status in the United States from 2000 to 2009 was 86 individuals per year (Department of Homeland Security 2011). Several factors are at play in the limited number of asylum and refugee cases. In the strictest sense, persons fleeing mass violence due to the drug wars and breakdown of civil society in Mexico cannot generate a rationale for persecution on the basis of belonging to a group or category. An occasional journalist has been granted asylum. Second, unlike Iraq or Iran, Mexico does not qualify in the US humanitarian policy as an area of particular concern. Third, if the United States considered Mexicans to be potential refugees on the basis of being displaced or harmed by civil war, the precedent would be set to grant asylum to very many Mexican nationals—something that would not sit well with the body politic.

Under the 1951 Convention Refugee Convention, the United Nations defines a refugee as any person who "as a result of events occurring before 1 January 1951 and owing to well-founded fear of being persecuted for reasons of race, religion, nationality, membership of a particular social group or political opinion, is outside the country of his [or her] nationality and is unable, or owing to such fear, is unwilling to avail him [or her]self of the protection of that country; or who, not having a nationality and being outside the country of his [or her] former habitual residence as a result of such events, is unable or, owing to such fear, is unwilling to return to it" (United Nations High Commission for Refugees [UNHCR] 2011). The convention was drafted in the postwar years to protect displaced persons and individuals who were facing persecution in their home country. Of course, the original definition has evolved with time to include persons who are fleeing for their lives for other reasons. The United Nations High Commission for Refugees also serves internally displaced persons and stateless people. The UNHCR helps people safeguard their rights, helps them find refuge in other countries, and to prevent statelessness. The commission has established camps and relocation programs throughout the world to assist individuals to secure safety, provide health care, provide schooling, and relocation assistance. The UNHCR also provides visa assistance and international human rights oversight to assure the migrant's protection from government harassment and vigilantism. Over a 100 such camps and programs have been set up in Pakistan, Chad, Nepal, Zambia, Congo, Thailand, Ethiopia, and elsewhere.

Since the Unites States cannot come to terms with the large influx of Mexicans who are fleeing the threat of murder, kidnapping, extortion, torture, and internal displacement, could the country not turn to the United Nations for assistance? A UN-run refugee camp in Fort Stockton, Texas—home to hundreds of Mexican refugees—would send a message to the world that American immigration policy is built on human rights, social justice, or human welfare and not on national security. Nonetheless, the likelihood of the UNCHR setting foot in the US-Mexico border region is about the same as the government of Mexico requesting United Nations Peacekeeping Forces to bring order back to that country.

As a result, nongovernmental agencies in the border region are presently flooded with refugees. Those shelters in the El Paso region that do not require documentation are being inundated with transnational refugees. Agencies that provide mental health services to indigent clients are seeing huge increases in the population of persons affected by acute stress disorder, anxiety disorders, depression, and post-traumatic stress disorder. A few of the contributors of this volume are providing services to refugees who are experiencing trauma.

Toward Stronger Civil Society Activism with Border Voices

Social justice cannot and will not occur by waving magic wands, given the politics of fear and hate that have gripped the national and binational establishments in both the United States and Mexico. Stronger democracies in both countries require organized constituencies, informed voters, and higher voter turnout coupled with engaged citizens and residents. Along with the substantive chapters of this volume and their policy recommendations about health, the environment, and education, plus the broad-based policies we have proposed in this closing chapter, we call for civil society activism and explicit strategies to connect social justice research and action in ways that engage with decision-makers and make policy change. Such activism cannot only be grounded at the border but must also be mainstreamed, enriched, and strengthened with border voices. In a parallel way, neither can such activism follow the typical historical strategy of mainstream voices and capital city decision-making about the border without border voices.

In this, our closing section of this chapter, we highlight social justice activism in communities across the borderlands. We call attention to community non-government organizations (NGOs), nonprofit agencies, and litigation projects and strategies that have worked to strengthen social justice. Some of these organizations draw on faith-based perspectives (Chap. 5, Stowe, this volume) while others on principles, reasoned self-interest, and ideological commitment to social justice. Below, we highlight best practices in these organizations, many leaders of whom use the power of numbers—people working together and in alliance with other organizations—to counteract the power of money and hate, with the goal of shifting power relations.

Human rights groups along the border have mobilized people to stand up for their rights and negotiated with border enforcement agencies for more humane practices. For example, the Border Network for Human Rights (www.bnhr.org) has become the latest iteration of the handful of people who started the Border Rights Coalition in the 1980s and volunteers who helped document immigrant abuse with support from the American Friends Service Committee. BNHR now claims thousands of participants in El Paso and southern New Mexico; it is a strong member of the Texas-wide Reform Immigration for Texas Alliance (RITA)—a coalition of strong civil society organizations, such as labor unions and civil rights groups like the Mexican American Legal Defense and Education Fund (MALDEF).

At the Arizona border, two NGOs, Humane Borders and No More Deaths, also bring human rights perspectives to bear on their efforts to save migrants' lives while crossing the hot and treacherous desert landscape. Official blockades surrounding ports of entry around the major urban centers of El Paso and San Diego funnel migrants to underpopulated regions and have led to 4,600 identifiable deaths from 1994 to 2007 (Dunn 2009) (additional cadavers have no doubt yet to be discovered). Humane Borders documented the location of nearly half of these deaths in a southern Arizona map (http://www.humaneborders.org/news/news4.html). Both Humane Borders and No More Deaths try to save migrants' lives by leaving plastic containers with water. For this, members have been charged and fined for littering. As No More Death states on its website, with rotating pictures of the blistered and bloodied feet of migrants at shelters, "Humanitarian aid is never a crime" (http://www.humaneborders.org/news/news4.html).

Clergy often share leadership in these organizations, and support comes from people and institutions of faith. As far back as the 1980s, Presbyterian Reverend John Fife worked with the Sanctuary movement—a word with deep roots in the European medieval era when churches were sometimes the last refuge for those seeking protection from the state tyranny—which aimed to assist refugees fleeing from Central American military and death squads. It is a sad irony that politicians now use the word to brand cities negatively with community-based policing strategies.

In El Paso, the nonprofit organization Annunciation House has offered hospitality to those who pass through the border. Some 90,000 have been served over a quarter century. Loosely affiliated with Catholic teachings and support, the Annunciation House is usually granted a hands-off approach by the US Border Patrol. Nonetheless, devastating exceptions have occurred, such as when an officer shot and killed teenager Juan Patricio Peraza just outside the shelter on a Sunday morning in February 2003.

The Catholic Church is a strong advocate of immigrant rights. It helps organize events to remember migrant deaths with white crosses and personal names of the victims at various locations along the border. Drawing on Biblical references to "welcome the stranger," some clergy like Fr. Daniel Groody at the University of Notre Dame proclaim that "we see the face of Jesus in the migrant" (see, e.g., the documentary he produced, *Dying to Live: A Migrant's Journey*; http://dyingtolive.nd.edu/other.html). In El Paso, the Diocesan Migrant and Refugee Service provides legal assistance to migrants, citizenship classes, VAWA counseling (see Chap. 4 by Staudt, this volume), and asylum workshops to people. It recognizes, like many who live at the border, that immigration policy—contrary to policy discourse—separates families and puts members in mixed citizenship-undocumented households at economic risk. Likewise, the secular Las Americas Immigrant Advocacy Center provides legal assistance and VAWA counseling. The Texas Civil Rights Project (TCRP), including its border affiliates, the South Texas Civil Rights Project and the Paso del Norte Civil Rights Project, provides fine legal assistance involving US discrimination against persons with disabilities, citizens abused by law enforcement, and threats to free speech. TCRP has pursued litigation strategies that allowed workers to recover wages lost ("wage theft") and residents to enjoy homes free of Border Patrol invasion. Many of these nonprofit organizations are strapped for resources and engage in frenetic fund-raising to maintain their staffs and keep offices open. Occasionally, volunteers come from near and afar to assist, such as the Lutheran Border Servant Corps, college, university and law school interns, and others.

California, too, has its share of faith-based human rights activism. In Pierrette Hondagneu-Soto's book title on organizing efforts in Los Angeles, her title says it all: *God's Heart Has No Borders: Religious Activism for Immigrant Rights* (2008).

For all the clergy and faith leader activism, we cannot help but note two important themes that undermine the efficacy of these approaches. First, active church membership is both aging and declining in the United States. This does not bode well for faith principles applied to social justice. Second, many members' beliefs operate at great odds from their human rights institutional positions in many denominations and clergy leaders. Moreover, many people pride themselves for lives in a secular state. Mexican activists, too, operate with wariness about the relationship between church and state, given the historic alignment of the church and dictatorship in the nineteenth century.

The Industrial Areas Foundation (IAF) is a nationwide organization that uses principles developed first by the late Saul Alinsky to change power relations within communities. The base of IAF organizations consists of coalitions of congregations and nonprofit organizations that develop leaders who engage in relationships with public officials. Their objective is to pursue social justice through changing public policies and thereby change power relations in communities. These civil society organizations are nonpartisan. Texas IAF is a statewide coalition of regional affiliates from Dallas/Fort Worth and Lubbock to Houston, Austin, San Antonio, and the border: Valley Interfaith in South Texas and both the El Paso Interreligious Sponsoring Organization (EPISO) and Border Interfaith in El Paso. Institutions rather than individuals belong to each IAF organization, and IAF affiliates' agendas emerge from "house meetings" among individuals in those institutions. For example, Border Interfaith is a cross-class coalition of Protestant and Catholic congregations, a reformed synagogue, the Buddhist community, the Women's Intercultural Center (a nonprofit), the Westway neighborhood (a *colonia*), and the El Paso Federation of Teachers and Support Personnel. Once social justice agendas develop, leaders identify "winnable goals," organize civic and candidate forums, and meet with public officials. Leaders acquire social capital, that is, relationships of trust to accomplish public goals. It is often easier to build social capital within and across institutions than with strangers. The Texas IAF and its local affiliate track records include water and sewer systems in *colonias* during the 1980s, parent engagement in public schools (see Shirley 1997), workforce training for living-wage jobs, and negotiations with the border sheriff to end checkpoints that resulted in the harassment of those who "looked" Mexican and the deportation of hundreds of immigrants (Staudt 2008b).

While we have highlighted IAF in Texas, the same models exist in New Mexico, Arizona, and California. However, IAF rarely works nationally, a detriment to changing national policies (Drier and selections in Orr 2007).

Mexico also has its fair share of nonprofit organizations, NGOs, and perhaps more visible, social movement groups that highlight problems episodically but often disappear. Many people are wary of engagement with the state, concerned about cooptation (see this analyzed with respect to women and antiviolence activism in Staudt 2008a). The dividing line between genuinely independent NGOs and nonprofit organizations that lose their critical edge and turn into contractor groups is problematic throughout the Americas (see Alvarez 1998 on the "NGOization" of social movements). Nonprofit organizations probably struggle for resources in Mexico even more than in El Paso. Yet neighborhood-based, community organizations like *Las Hormigas* (the ants), born in 2002, generate solidarity, build social capital, and accomplish goals such as reforestation, counseling, and legal services for women (www.lashormigascomunidad.org).

Despite the current violence in Ciudad Juárez, people show courage and resilience in organizing peace and justice demilitarization movements and human rights advocacy. Women wear white *burkas* to protest the violence and protect their faces from state surveillance. Youth and students on both sides of the borders organized a large (estimated at 700 people) binational solidarity rally at the border fence, followed by a fast to remember the teen victims of the January 2010 massacre (see Bañuelas' speech (Afterword), this volume). The discourse of human rights is far stronger in Mexico, given its ironic embeddedness within the state through national and state human rights commissions and a constitution which promises much but delivers little by way of rights.

Cross-border activism faces many obstacles, but it is also facilitated with the existence of family, friend, and work relationships and ideologies of social justice that span the border. Staudt and Coronado (2002) discuss the obstacles and opportunities, providing best practice case studies and vignettes of cross-border organizing in the areas of environmentalism, work, business, and human rights. Several official bodies and commissions also exist, such as the International Boundary and Water Commission (and CILA-*Comisión Internacional de Límites y Aguas*, the Mexico counterpart) and health and specific disease commissions.

Colleges and universities could do a better job of civic education, defined as not only civic knowledge but also civic skills, motivations, and experiences. The Social Justice Initiative in the Department of Communications at the University of Texas at El Paso is an example. It is an action-based initiative that is deeply committed to issues of social justice, equity, and peace. It is an open forum for all those who are interested in engaging in conversations, partnerships, and actions to improve the human condition (http://academics.utep.edu/comm4socialjustice). Civic education is all too often limited and far in between. Some preprofessional programs do a better job of civic education with internships and student affiliations with professional associations to which they might eventually affiliate.

At the January 2011 binational solidarity event in Anapra, through a chain-link border fence, Monsignor Bañuelas stated over and over, as did the crowds in response: "We will rise again." He referred to a binational border region beset, not with peace and justice, but with violence, militarization, and injustices. His words, and the words of the contributors to this volume, remind us that many official policies foster injustice, inhumane treatment, and impoverishment. The Department of Homeland Security's "Secure Communities" program, scheduled to spread throughout the entire United States by 2013 (Napolitano 2011), remains a far cry from the sort of human security and social justice that we analyze in this volume. While federal immigration enforcement is everywhere, public justice programs operate in few places. It is up to *us all*, through organized activism, advocacy, and reasoned policy analysis, to foster social justice in our North American border and bordering places.

References

Alba, R. (2006, July 28). *Looking beyond the moment: American immigration seen from historically and internationally comparative perspectives.* Retrieved June 9, 2011, from Border Battles. the U.S. Immigration Debates: http://borderbattles.ssrc.org/Alba/

Alvarez, S. (1998). Latin American feminisms 'go global': Trends of the 1900s and challenges for the new millennium. In S. E. Alvarez, E. Dagnino, & A. Escobar (Eds.), *Cultures of politics, politics of cultures: Re-visioning Latin American social movements* (pp. 293–324). Boulder: Westview Press.

Appalachian Regional Commission. (2009, May). *FY2010 performance budget justification.* As submitted by the federal co-chair to the Appropriations Committees of the House and Senate. Retrieved June 9, 2011, from http://www.arc.gov/images/newsroom/publications/fy10budget/FY2010PerformanceBudgetMay2009.pdf

Associated Press. (2010, May 13). *AP IMPACT: After 40 years, $1 trillion, US war on drugs has failed to meet any of its goals.* Retrieved June 20, 2011, from http://www.foxnews.com/world/2010/05/13/ap-impact-years-trillion-war-drugs-failed-meet-goals/

Associated Press. (2011, January 3). *Mexico plan to save violent border city is lacking.* Retrieved June 20, 2011, from http://www.azcentral.com/news/articles/2011/01/03/20110103mexico-plan-to-save-juarez-failing.html

Bajc, V., & de Lint, W. (Eds.). (2011). *Security and everyday life.* New York: Routledge.

Becker, A., & McDonnell, P. (2009, March 4). *Mexico's drug war creates new class of refugees.* Retrieved June 20, 2011, from *Los Angeles Times*: http://www.latimes.com/news/nationworld/world/latinamerica/la-na-asylum4-2009mar04,0,2188107.story

Bennett, B. (2010, October 22). *Costly virtual border fence in tatters.* Retrieved January 23, 2011, from *Los Angeles Times*: http://articles.latimes.com/2010/oct/22/nation/la-na-invisible-fence-20101022

Bernstein, N. (2010, August 29). *Border sweeps in north reach miles into U.S.* Retrieved June 9, 2011, from *New York Times*: http://www.nytimes.com/2010/08/30/nyregion/30border.html

Campbell, H. (2009). *Drug war zone: Frontline dispatches from the streets of El Paso and Juarez.* Austin: University of Texas Press.
Castañeda, J. (2007). *Ex-Mex: From migrants to immigrants.* New York: New Press.
Comisión Nacional para Prevenir y Erradicar la Violencia contra las Mujeres. (2009). *Diagnóstico sobre la realidad social, económica y cultural de los entornos locales para el diseño de intervenciones en materia de prevención y erradicación de la violencia en la región norte: El caso de Ciudad Juárez, Chihuahua.* Retrieved from http://www.conavim.gob.mx/work/models/CONAVIM/Resource/pdf/JUAREZ.pdf
Cornelius, W. (2006, September 26). *Impacts of border enforcement on unauthorized Mexican migration to the United States.* Retrieved June 9, 2011, from Border Battles. The U.S. Immigration Debates: http://borderbattles.ssrc.org/Cornelius/
Department of Homeland Security [DHS]. (2010, March). *The performance of 287(g) agreements.* Retrieved from Office of the Inspector General. OIG-10-63: http://www.dhs.gov/xoig/assets/mgmtrpts/OIG_10-63_Mar10.pdf
Department of Homeland Security [DHS]. (2011). *Individuals granted asylum affirmatively by region and country of nationality: Fiscal years 2000–2009. Table 17.* Retrieved April 21, 2010, from www.dhs.gov/xlibrary/assets/statistics/yearbook/2009/table17d.xls. 21 Apr 2010.
Department of Housing and Human Development. (2011). *Welcome to the community renewal initiative.* Retrieved from http://www.hud.gov/offices/cpd/economicdevelopment/programs/rc/
Department of Justice. (2010). *Looking at a decade of drug courts.* Retrieved from Drug Court Clearinghouse and Technical Assistance Project: Retrieved from: http://www.ncjrs.gov/html/bja/decade98.htm
Department of Labor. (2011). *Regulations and standards.* Retrieved from http://www.osha.gov/pls/oshaweb/owadisp.show_document?p_id=10601&p_table=STANDARDS
Drier, P. (2007). Community organizing for what? Progressive politics and movement building in America. In M. Orr (Ed.), *Transforming the city: Community organizing and the challenge of political change* (pp. 218–251). Lawrence: University Press of Kansas.
Drug Facts. (2011). *Prisons, jails and probation.* Retrieved from http://www.drugwarfacts.org/cms/Prisons_and_Jails
Dunn, T. (1996). *The militarization of the U.S.-Mexico border 1978–1992.* Austin: Center for Mexican American Studies, University of Texas.
Dunn, T. (2009). *Blockading the border and human rights: The El Paso operation that remade U.S. border enforcement.* Austin: University of Texas Press.
Ganster, P. & Lorey, D.E. (2005). Border and politics in a globalizing world. Lanham, MD: Rowman & Littlefield.
Greenwald, G. (2009, April 2). *Drug decriminalization in Portugal: Lessons for creating fair and successful policies. White paper.* Retrieved February 1, 2011, from CATO Institute: http://www.cato.org/pub_display.php?pub_id=10080
Grissom, B. (2010, October 22). *Hispanic Harris County sheriff on immigrants, jail.* Retrieved January 23, 2011, from The Texas Tribune: http://www.texastribune.org/immigration-in-texas/immigration/hispanic-harris-county-sheriff-on-immigrants-jail/?utm_source=texastribune.org&utm_medium=alerts&utm_campaign=News%20Alert:%20Subscriptions
Guild, E. (2003, May). The border abroad: Visas and border controls. In K. Groenendijk, E. Guild, & P. Minderhoud (Eds.), *In search of Europe's borders* (pp. 87–104). The Hague: Kluwer Law International.
Guild, E. (2005, June 10). *Danger: Borders under construction: Assessing the first five years of border policy in an area of freedom, security and justice.* Retrieved from Challenge. Liberty & Security: http://www.libertysecurity.org/article269.html
Hondagneu-Soto, P. (2008). *God's heart has no border: Religious activism for immigrant rights.* Berkeley: University of California Press.
Humane Borders. (n.d.). *1999–2009 recorded migrant deaths, USBP Rescue beacons, and HB water stations.* Retrieved June 21, 2011, from http://www.humaneborders.org/news/news4.html

JRL. (2010, September 20). *Abandonan Ciudad Juárez 230 mil personas en dos años [230 thousand people abandon Ciudad Juárez in two years]*. Retrieved June 16, 2011, from *Excelsior*: Excelsior: http://www.excelsior.com.mx/index.php?m=nota&id_nota=663668

Kim, Y. (2009, June 29). *Protecting the U.S. perimeter: Border searches under the Fourth Amendment* (CRS Report for Congress 7-5700). Washington, DC: Congressional Research Service.

Las Hormigas, (n.d.). *Las Hormigas. Comunidad en Desarrollo, A.C. [The ants. Community in development, Inc.]*. Retrieved June 10, 2011, from http://www.lashormigascomunidad.org/pages/whoweare.htm

Latin American Commission on Drugs and Democracy [LACDD]. (2009). *Drugs and democracy: A paradigm shift*. Retrieved September 21, 2009, from http://drugsanddemocracy.org/files/2009/02/declaracao_ingles_site.pdf

Martin, D. (2010, April). *Refugees and asylees: 2009. Annual flow report*. Retrieved from Homeland Security. Office of immigration Statistics: http://www.dhs.gov/xlibrary/assets/statistics/publications/ois_rfa_fr_2009.pdf

Mulock, B. (2002). *Empowerment zone/enterprise communities program: Overview of rounds I, II, and III*. Retrieved from Congressional Research Service: http://www.nationalaglawcenter.org/assets/crs/RS20381.pdf

Napolitano, J. (2011, January 31). The Department of Homeland Security. *Speech on the University of Texas at El Paso*. El Paso, TX.

Office of the National Drug Control Policy. (2010). *Drug courts*. Retrieved from http://www.whitehousedrugpolicy.gov/enforce/drugcourt.html

Orr, M. (Ed.). (2007). *Transforming the city: Community organizing and the challenges of political change*. Lawrence: University Press of Kansas.

Passel, J., & Cohn, D. (2009, April 14). *A portrait of unauthorized immigrants in the United States*. Retrieved January 23, 2011, from Pew Hispanic Center: http://pewresearch.org/pubs/1190/portrait-unauthorized-immigrants-states

Portes, A. (2006). *NAFTA and Mexican immigration*. Retrieved January 23, 2011, from Border Battles. Social Science Research Council: http://borderbattles.ssrc.org

Seelke, C. (2010, January 21). *Mérida initiative for Mexico and Central America: Funding and policy issues*. CRS Report for Congress. Washington, DC: Congressional Research Service.

Shirley, D. (1997). *Community organizing and urban school reform*. Austin: University of Texas Press.

Shome, R. (2006). Space matters: The power and practice of space. *Communication Theory, 13*(1), 39–56.

Smith, L. (2010, December 15). *U.S. Rep. Lamar Smith says border death toll is 28,000*. Retrieved from PolitiFact Texas: http://www.politifact.com/texas/statements/2010/dec/31/lamar-smith/us-rep-lamar-smith-says-border-death-toll-28000/

Staudt, K. (2008a). *Violence and activism at the border: Gender, fear and everyday life in Ciudad Juárez*. Austin: University of Texas Press.

Staudt, K. (2008b). Bordering the other in the U.S. southwest: El Pasoans confront the local sheriff. In D. Brotherton & P. Kretsedemas (Eds.), *Keeping out the other: A critical introduction to immigration enforcement today* (pp. 291–313). New York: Columbia University Press.

Staudt, K. (2011). Rethinking national security policy and practice in transnational contexts: Border resistance. In Bajc Vida & Lint De Willem (Eds.), *Security and everyday life* (pp. 101–121). New York: Routledge.

Staudt, K., & Coronado, I. (2002). *Fronteras no más: Toward social justice at the U.S.-Mexico border*. New York: Palgrave.

Staudt, K., & García, S. (2011). Economic policy matters: Incentives that drive Mexicans northward. In M. Baumann, A. Lorenz, & K. Rosenow (Eds.), *Crossing and controlling borders – Immigration policies and their impact on migrants' journeys*. Leverkusen-Opladen: Budrich UniPress.

Staudt, K., Payan, T., & Dunn, T. (2009b). Bordering human rights, social democratic feminism, and broad-based security. In *Human rights along the U.S.-Mexico border: Gendered violence and insecurity* (pp. 185–202). Tucson: University of Arizona Press.

Staudt, K., Payan, T., & Kruszewski, A. (Eds.). (2009c). *Human rights along the U.S.-Mexico border: Gendered violence and insecurity*. Tucson: University of Arizona Press.

Staudt, K., Fuentes, C., & Monárrez Fragoso, J. (Eds.). (2010). *Cities and citizenship at the U.S.-Mexico border: The Paso del Norte metropolitan region*. New York: Palgrave.

The Economist. (2010, July 22). *Too many laws, too many prisoners. Never in the civilised world have so many been locked up for so little*. Retrieved June 22, 2011, from http://www.economist.com/node/16636027

United Nations High Commissioner for Refugees. (2011). *The refugee convention, 1951*. Retrieved June 22, 2011, from: http://www.unhcr.org/cgi-bin/texis/vtx/home/opendocPDFViewer.html?docid=4ca34be29&query=1951 Convention Refugee Convention

U.S. Agency for International Development [USAID]. (2010a, May). *Mexico. Country profile*. Retrieved from http://www.usaid.gov/locations/latin_america_caribbean/country/mexico/Mexico_Country_Profile.pdf

U.S. Agency for International Development [USAID]. (2010b). *USAID budget: Mexico*. Retrieved from USAID: http://www.usaid.gov/policy/budget/cbj2006/lac/mx.html

U.S. Immigration and Customs Enforcement [ICE]. (n.d.). *Fact sheet: Delegation of Immigration Authority Section 287(g) Immigration and Nationality Act*. Retrieved June 20, 2011, from Fact Sheets: http://www.ice.gov/news/library/factsheets/287g.htm

Vaughan-Williams, N. (2008). Borderwork beyond inside/outside? Frontex, the citizen-detective and the war on terror. *Space and Polity, 12*(1), 63–79.

Woodward, C. (2011, January 9). Far from border, U.S. detains foreign students. *The Chronicle of Higher Education*. Retrieved from: http://chronicle.com/article/Far-From-Canada-Aggressive/125880/

Afterword: Peace and Justice Without Borders

Rally 29 January 2011, Anapra Fence El Paso Ciudad Juárez: Remarks by Monsignor Arturo Bañuelas

We are here today because we believe in justice and in the power of our united convictions to make a difference in our border area. We want a new Juarez and a new El Paso, cities that are the best places for our families to live in peace and harmony. Today, we demand no less than this.

We are here because we refuse to lay down in defeat before all the violence, killings, extortions, kidnappings, and beheadings that bloody our streets each day.

We are here because we are not afraid to stand up and speak up for what we believe. We will not be quiet any longer.

We are here to stand in solidarity with the victims of violence, with the families still crying for their lost loved ones, with the wounded, the scared, the disappeared, and the refugees.

We are here to denounce those in authority who pretend to protect us but instead lie, and participate in corruption, and in human rights violations.

We are here because we have a better non-violent solution to the problems that are destroying our lives along our border.

Right now we are living one of the worst crisis in our border history. Juarez and El Paso are two lungs of the same body that was once a thriving cultural, social, and economic community; but now both our communities' futures are at stake. Hundreds of thousands of our hurting brothers and sisters are fleeing Juarez with trauma and unbearable desperation to a nation unwilling to legally welcome them. America this is not worthy of our country.

Over 3,000 murders on our border is just too much blood running in our streets leaving unbearable scars of pain that will last a life time for fathers, mothers, brothers, sisters, and friends. We are disgusted and feel angry about our women so savagely tortured and our friends so viciously executed and mutilated. Fear and violence have become a way of life that for some has no end in sight. Recently, I had a funeral of a young man who was beheaded and his body was riddled with over 60 bullets. You can imagine the pain of his father who had to go identify the body of

M. Lusk et al. (eds.), *Social Justice in the U.S.-Mexico Border Region*,
DOI 10.1007/978-94-007-4150-8, © Springer Science+Business Media B.V. 2012

his dead son. At the funeral some of his friends pledged revenge for those who did this to their friend. I can understand their anger, but this is not the solution.

We know the causes of violence on our border: poverty, hunger, the growing gap between rich and poor, NAFTA policies that ignore the plight of the poor, racism, unjust immigration laws, bailing out Wall Street but not the poor who are losing their homes, illegal trafficking of guns going south, our US lethal addiction for drugs that fund the cartel's terrorism of our border community, the militarization of our border which has already shown its deathly face, and the profiteering of selling violence to children in the media. The list is long and dreadful. These failed policies and laws serve only to bring dark results: people die, violence flows in our streets. But we can say very clearly today, no law, policy, or profit of violence has ever succeeded. Also it is time to say it clearly: when we buy and use drugs, even recreationally, we are paying for bullets that kill others; and we bring unbearable suffering to families.

We have a solution. Today we bring an alternative to all of this violence and death in our midst. It comes from our solidarity for peace. There is nothing stronger in this world than our united convictions in solidarity for peace. There is always a greater power at work in our solidarity for peace even in the midst of the forces of darkness that surround us. God put in every human heart this desire for peace.

However, the most significant reason for violence comes from our disconnection with each other. This distance translates into bloodshed, hate, carnage, and brutal hostility. Peace is born from our efforts to connect with each other and to value each other as sacred. We are all linked as one human family. We stand together or we fall together. We are each other, and we need to help each other. If I diminish you I diminish myself. If I promote the good in you, I promote the goodness in me and also in everyone else at the same time. The road to peace is in our walking hand in hand with each other as one.

When we connect with one another, we live from our better side; and in us grows a profound desire to do good, not bad. We desire more life not death. We want to walk in our beauty not our blood.

Our creator God made us good not criminals, narcos, terrorists, or murderers. This is why I still believe that there are more good people in the world than bad, and there is really more good in the world than bad, that we have an unbelievable capacity for goodness; and today we are here to celebrate the coming victory of our oneness over the violence of our divisions.

As long as there is violence toward each other we all remain incomplete as human beings. At this time of such chaos and violence, when human life seems so dirt cheap, we much proclaimthat each person matters, that they matter enormously to us, for we are each other. When we do this we are renewed as a people, the world turns toward peace as a better solution, and peace reigns. Violence is not the way to solve violence. We can break this vicious cycle of violence with our solidarity for peace.

I have been with many families who have lost loved ones to the violence in Juarez. Yet in my heart I feel hopeful for a new Juarez and a new El Paso because I can see in you a desire to live in solidarity for peace. I see before me a giant that is waking up and ready to roar. Today we can believe that in the end of all our human struggles, we will see that it is our oneness that will prevail over all violence. Victory comes in our togetherness. United forpeace we win, not the narcos.

So today we have something important to say, and we want to say it loudly. It may look like Juarez is dying, that the narcos are taking over, and that there is no end in sight. But we are here in solidarity we believe that **we will rise again**.

- Today we can feel confident that violence will not win in our El Paso-Juarez border as long as we stand together because we believe that: **we will rise again**. If you believe it with me, say it out loud what you believe today: we believe that "we will rise again."
- You may fill our streets with blood, our bodies with bullets, our souls with fear, but you will never take away our hope because we believe that **we will rise again**.
- It may look like the dark forces of violence have the upper hand, that we are outgunned, ill-equipped, and unprepared. But we are not backing down, and we will not be silent anymore because we believe that: **we will rise again**.
- You can stomp on our work and try to break our lives with your murders, corruption, and terror, but we feel confident that your days are numbered because we have on our side a superior force that comes from our passion for peace. That's why we believe that **we will rise again**.
- We may feel wounded; our spirits may be down, our hearts disillusioned, our lives threatened, shaken in our beliefs in our capacity to overcome fear, but we are ready for the struggle and the victory because we believe that **we will rise again**.
- We are not afraid of the narcos, the threats, and your AK-47's, because from the sufferings of our brothers and sisters in Juarez and El Paso will emerge a stronger, more courageous border people because we believe that: "**We will rise again**."

Today is about our hope not our fears. We are ready, and we will not give up in our quest for peace. In our solidarity peace is coming. And we tell the narcos: the future does not belong to you. It belongs to the fearless, courageous peacemakers who live in solidarity for peace. The future belongs to us, and we are ready to anticipate its joy, excitement, and peace.

This is a historic moment for us on the border. Let us commit ourselves to one another today. Embrace each other and see our future exploding in our midst. Do not live in fear. Be ready to show your resolve. Justice will triumph over hate, love will conquer violence, and our compassion will overcome our divisions.

Today we reach out to all the youth. Join us not the narcos. Let us build together a new Juarez and El Paso. It is not too late.

I still believe in the dream of a better Juarez and El Paso. That is why we will not surrender to your bullets of fear. Hope runs through our veins and the cause of peace endures in our hearts. Justice is coming. Peace is at hand. We can feel confident today because God is on the side of peace. Let us become more passionately determined in our convictions for solidarity and its victory in our lives.

Ya Basta! Too many people have worked too hard, sacrificed too much; too much blood has been spilled for us to be bystanders in the emerging new border. Together we will prevail in the face of death. Amigos, Amigas, we will rise again!

Msgr, Arturo J. Bañuelas, STD

A girl at *Las Hormigas* (a community-based organization in Ciudad Juárez, Mexico) poses for the camera during a class. *Las Hormigas* offers specialist education to children who require alternative teaching methods. Their teaching helps students to move at their own pace and uses interactive activities that students can relate to (Photograph by Damien Schumann. Courtesy of Nuestra Casa Project (PCI, ABC))

A girl at *Las Hormigas* does a puzzle during a class (Photograph by Damien Schumann. Courtesy of Nuestra Casa Project (PCI, ABC))

The border between Cuidad Juárez, Chihuahua (Mexico), and El Paso, Texas (USA). Strict security monitors activity entering the United States to prevent illegal migration, drug trafficking, and importing of goods (Photograph by Damien Schumann. Courtesy of Nuestra Casa Project (PCI, ABC))

A billboard displays missing students from the Universidad Autónoma de Cuidad Juárez. Kidnapping and murder of women continue to escalate in the city (Photograph by Damien Schumann. Courtesy of Nuestra Casa Project (PCI, ABC))

(Linked to Chap. 9 – Border Health Disparities)
Nurses walk up stairs made out of tires to reach the home of a person affected by tuberculosis who lives on the outskirts of Cuidad Juárez, Mexico (Photograph by Damien Schumann. Courtesy of Nuestra Casa Project (PCI, ABC))

Pink crosses are found all over Ciudad Juárez (often on a black background) to represent the place where the body of a murdered woman was found. This form of activism is a painful reminder of the loss of girls and women and the close proximity to everyday life in which it happens (Photograph by Damien Schumann. Courtesy of Nuestra Casa Project Project (PCI, ABC))

A boy watches a border patrol helicopter as it flies over the fence uniting (or dividing) El Paso, Texas, from Cuidad Juárez. The drug war continues all over the US-Mexico border (and beyond), and its impacts are slowly starting to move across the border to the United States (Photograph by Damien Schumann. Courtesy of Nuestra Casa Project (PCI, ABC))

A family relaxes in their home made of scrap wood, on the border of Tijuana and San Diego. Communities made entirely of such materials are developing fast along the perimeters of Tijuana, Baja California (Photograph by Damien Schumann. Courtesy of Nuestra Casa Project (PCI, ABC))

Traffic and advertising on entering Tijuana, Mexico (Photograph by Damien Schumann. Courtesy of Nuestra Casa Project (PCI, ABC))

A family sits outside their home on the outskirts of Cuidad Juárez, Mexico. Resources in these areas are very scarce, with many homes being made out of scrap wood and other discarded materials. Many homes do not have running water and rely on long drop ablution facilities (Photograph by Damien Schumann. Courtesy of Nuestra Casa Project Project (PCI, ABC))

Remembering the faces of murdered girls and murder, as seen through the border fence in Anapra, New Mexico, at a binational solidarity rally for peace and justice, January 29, 2011 (Photograph by Kathleen Staudt)

(Linked to the environmental justice chapter):
ASARCO: A century of copper smelting and pollution at the El Paso, Texas, and Ciudad Juárez, Mexico, border (Photograph by Ana Matos)

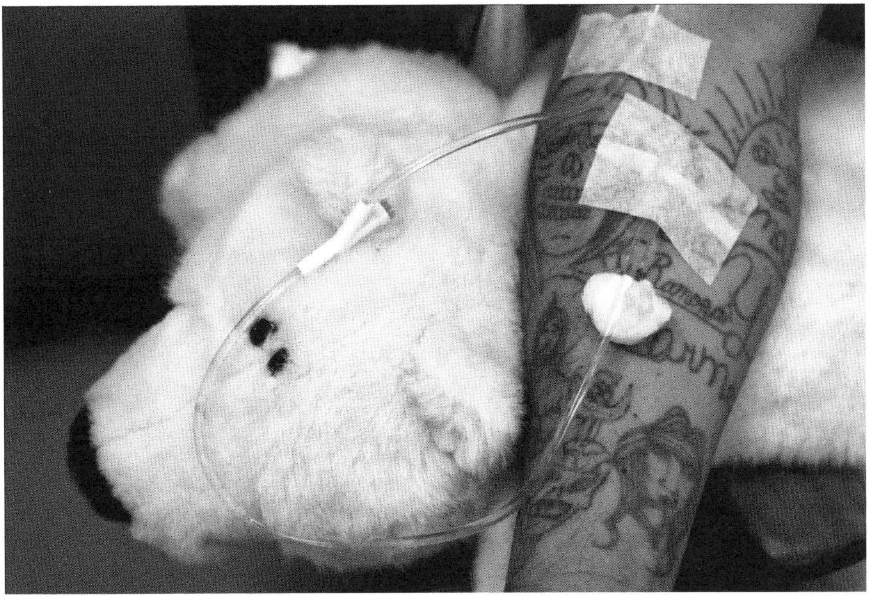

(Linked to Chap. 10 – Border Health Disparities)
A man receives his daily TB treatment, through an IV drip in a clinic in Reynosa, Tamaulipas. Lacking facilities, the man uses a teddy bear to rest his arm. The teddy bear was donated to the clinic (Photograph by Damien Schumann. Courtesy of Nuestra Casa Project (PCI, ABC))

Index

M. Lusk et al. (eds.), *Social Justice in the U.S.-Mexico Border Region*,
DOI 10.1007/978-94-007-4150-8, © Springer Science+Business Media Dordrecht 2012

Printed by Printforce, the Netherlands